# MY DEAR TIMOTHY

# MY DEAR TIMOTHY

*An Autobiographical Letter to his Grandson*

by

## VICTOR GOLLANCZ

★

LONDON
14 HENRIETTA STREET COVENT GARDEN
1952

O Lord, open thou my lips, and my mouth shall shew forth thy praise.

I have learnt that the place wherein Thou art found unveiled is girt round with the coincidence of contradictions, and this is the wall of Paradise wherein Thou dost abide.

NICHOLAS OF CUSA


For whether they looked upward they saw the Divine
    Vision,
Or whether they looked downward still they saw the Divine
    Vision,
Surrounding them on all sides beyond sin and death and
    hell.

BLAKE (from *Vala*)


Looking back on my own experiences [under the influence of nitrous oxide] they all converge towards a kind of insight to which I cannot help ascribing some metaphysical significance. The keynote of it is invariably a reconciliation. It is as if the opposites of the world, whose contradictoriness and conflict make all our difficulties and troubles, were melted into unity. Not only do they, as contrasted species, belong to one and the same genus, but *one of the species*, the nobler and better one, *is itself the genus, and so soaks up and absorbs its opposite into itself*.

WILLIAM JAMES

# CONTENTS

I AM WRITING THESE words, my dear Timothy, on the morning of January the twentieth 1951. I am writing them in the little library which we made only last summer out of our old bedroom, the little library where you pulled out the books and staggered over to me with them when you came here to see us two or three weeks ago. This room, which I had always wanted, has given me extraordinary happiness. As I sit writing here by the electric fire, I see breathing round me (for I have always felt life in everything) many of the things with which, during my fifty-two years of remembered existence, I have formed a sort of unity. On the mantelpiece is a bust of Milton by Ralph Wood, flanked by a couple of Leeds candlesticks which I knew to be bogus when they were offered me but pretended to think "right", because I couldn't resist them. Just above is Ruth's beautiful water-colour of Bedford Square in sunlight, with its sketchy nurses and hospital blue of the 1914–1918 war. Robert Atkinson, then her Principal at the Architectural Association, had originally bought it from her for sixpence; but I bought it back for £5 when we married—he had given it to a sale of work—though I had no money and no job, and a debt of seventy-two pounds to Blackwell's. On either side of Bedford Square is a little oil of Florence—the nearer one particularly exquisite, almost like a jewelled miniature, with the artist looking out over the Arno "the wrong way"—I mean, away from the Ponte Vecchio and towards the Cascine gardens. Ruth painted this, if I remember rightly, in the middle twenties, when I was still with Ernest Benn before starting on my own. She had got me to Florence with the utmost difficulty. I had then, as I had had since early childhood and have had ever since, a hideous conflict between an essential laziness, an almost ecstatically breathless delight in ease and comfort, and an obsessional drive not merely to work but, as I had been in the habit of calling it in my school-days at St. Paul's, "to work extra". If, for instance, we had a hundred lines of Vergil to prepare for homework, this job, being compulsory, possessed no reality for me at all; I did it as something meaningless, and then went on to the real thing— an "extra" hundred. The explanation is no doubt a guilt feeling, which has always been very strong in me, coupled with a hatred of external authority and a passion for self-direction. By the same token, I don't think I attended more than two or three lectures all the time I was at Oxford; and I refused to buy a gown—when I was summoned to the Warden I borrowed one.

On the occasion I'm recalling we had gone to Paris for a week-end, for it was years since I had had a holiday and I was very tired. Ruth suggested that we should go on to Florence for a fortnight or so. I wanted to, very badly; for I knew nothing of Italy except Rome, where we had spent a deferred honeymoon not too happily—we hadn't enough money, and hadn't learned how to live together—in 1921. But I fought against the temptation for several days, hanging about indecisively, standing by the hour at the entrance to Cook's near the Madeleine and then walking away again; for the obsession to be back in London, to be watching the orders, to be building up the list, had me in its grip. When at last I found myself in the wagon lit ("*sous le lavabo se trouve un vase*"), I was furious.

That was the first of innumerable visits that were to make our beloved Italy as familiar to us as England. We descended at the Grand Hotel, which, either then or a little later, had just got itself a new top wing. The rest of the hotel was at that time a bit dingily *de luxe* in a minor sort of way, though it seemed to become more attractive at each successive visit; but the new top floor, all white and agleam with its unpolished woodwork, was a thing to fall in love with. Best of all was the little balcony from which Ruth used to paint, early morning and later afternoon, in her dressing-gown. Usually she looked straight across the river, taking in the crowded left bank and San Miniato up above; but on this one occasion she looked away to the trees and the hills, and painted me my little jewel.

I had often been about for hours before breakfast. I would get up while it was still dark and go down to the Duomo. As the sun rose, the tower became lovelier even than Giotto had made it: all airy and transparent, it glowed like a piece of the rose-quartz that had given me so much pleasure when, as a boy of nine or ten, I had formed my little collection of minerals and rocks. The steps of the Cathedral itself had disappeared beneath the hillock of flowers, brought in by the market women, that rose against the marbled façade to the height of a man. The smell and the look of them in the morning air were as sweet to my senses as anything I had experienced before or have experienced since; not even sunrise in Venice, or flying into London on a summer night when all the lamps are lit, has seemed more beautiful.

And when I got back to our balcony, itself still grey with the earliness of the dawn, the houses on the opposite back would be a long unbroken stretch of flaming brown.

Almost invariably, in Florence, we spent the fine mornings in our own special way. We would take our newspapers and books to a cloister, and sit reading there till it was time for lunch. I always chose books that it was necessary to read very slowly, for to be at one, in peace, with the subtle beauty of words and phrases, and to turn the leaves with a quietness of remembrance and expectation, was to experience a suspension of the fever and fret that had characterised, and was again to characterise, my daily striving. Our favourite cloister was the *chiostro verde*, because there, sitting on the little parapet, we could dangle our legs towards the grass below. The first time we went there an old keeper picked a rose and gave it to Ruth, who must have been looking very beautiful and happy, with a movement of the most charming gentleness and courtesy. It was one of those roses that you see in the Botticelli Venus, and that Walter Pater calls "embrowned". Years later we still had it.

I wish this were a letter about Italy and not about the world of 1951, for the memories come crowding in on me. There were our days at Lucca—"little Lucca" as Max Beerbohm calls it— with the straightness of its Roman roads, just the two of them (or is this an illusion?), intersecting at right angles, and those encircling ramparts that seem as vast, when you walk on them, as the double boulevard at Aix, and the Fra Bartolommeo, the very gentle one, in the cathedral of the Holy Counten- ance, by the altar. There were the dark and narrow and rather sordid streets of Siena—and then our sudden catch of breath as we found ourselves, our eyes dazzled, in the enormous blazing square. There was the view over the plain from the Hotel Brufani at Perugia, and the little lights with great distances between them—monastery lights, I remember thinking—that came out for us by night as we watched from our window before getting into bed. There was the climb in Fedi's Fiat up the zigzagging road to the black-and-white cathedral at Orvieto, and the merchandise, rather rue de

Rivoli merchandise, laid out for tourists in the vestibule. There was Ostia—not the modern Ostia, but, a mile or so back from it, the quiet grass-grown ruin; we loved it more than Pompeii, more even than the Casa di Livia on the Palatine, and we loved specially, for some reason, the row of lavatory seats in fine marble, from which the Ostians had been in the habit of admiring the view as they gossiped and attended to their needs. There was the day at Paestum—*antiche colonne di Pesto!*—and the picnic of sherry and chicken sandwiches as we lay in the glare, "mad Englishmen," between the temples of Neptune and Ceres. There were the mosaics at Ravenna, and the egg in a cup of broth at the top of the Pordoi pass, and what started as *table d'hôte*, and a very scratch one, on the veranda at Gardone and ended as a banquet with both manager and *maître d'hôtel* in attendance. And two or three years later there was the halt at Meran on our way to Salzburg (they call it Merano now, so I can include it in Italy). We had intended to spend a couple of days at Verona; but it was high summer, there had been a drought for three months, and the heat was intolerable. Sitting at midnight in the amphitheatre at an open-air performance of *William Tell*, with a huge orchestra and a flock, equally huge, of bleating sheep, we sweated horribly; so we asked next morning whether a car might be available to take us to Meran, which we thought would be cooler. A racing motorist, who had broken the record in some contest or other the previous week, was glad to oblige us, and turned up with a very long and very low car that appeared to be made entirely of wood. Part of the structure flew off half-way to Meran, and the driver had to turn back and recover it; but in spite of this he told us, when we arrived at the Meranerhof, that he had now broken his own record, and I was not at all surprised.

It was the dead season at Meran, and we were alone in the gigantic hotel. But the town was adorable—more beautiful, I thought, than any small place I had ever been in, except perhaps Bibury or Winchelsea. The day we had intended to spend there lengthened into a week and then into a fortnight. In the early morning, before breakfast, I would walk barefooted on the hotel lawn, to feel the dew between my toes. For lunch we would sit alone at a little table on the veranda. In the afternoon we wandered in the cool shade of the pines down the long *Tapeiner-Weg*, or in the cobbled and arcaded streets; and at tea-time we paraded in the square for the town band, in the company of half Meran and (in patent-leather shoes) Sir Thomas Beecham. We would gladly have prolonged our stay there till winter, even at the cost of missing Salzburg.

But happiest of all, perhaps, was the first of many visits from Venice to Torcello. Apart from Santa Fosca and Santa Maria at the far end of it, there's really nothing "to" this little island; nothing but grass and a sort of canal and a very few uninteresting cottages. Then why did it delight me so when we chanced on it first in the twenties, and how did it happen that, as each subsequent visit to Venice loomed ahead, it was not the Piazza that I thought about most, or the tiny marble birds in the Miracoli, or Bellini's blue Madonna, or arriving by gondola at Verdi's Fenice, prettiest of opera-houses—but deserted Torcello? The reason must be, I think, that I cannot live without grass. Venice, which on a first visit, especially if the weather is grey, seems a trifle disappointing—such smells, such decay, such unseemly floating refuse in the world's fairyland!—draws you back to it more powerfully the better you know it, and ends by being irresistible. But after a few days you may see, as if with sudden rediscovery, a green plant or two on the roof of some building, or the shrubs in the courtyard of that one-storied, never-finished palazzo on the Grand Canal; and then you want grass, and you go to Torcello. We went, that first time, by vaporetto. In 1947, when we stayed for three weeks with our friend Giuliana Foscolo, the whole affair was more elaborate; we took a gondola with two gondoliers, and they sang their songs as the moon came up on the return journey and the lights of the Piazzetta appeared. I got to know one of these gondoliers well; he had once worked, if I understood him correctly, for Baron Corvo.

# CHAPTER II

# COVENT GARDEN

CLOSE BY MY Florentine jewel here in the library, on the little bit of wall behind the chimney-breast and to the right of the door, is the starry Blake engraving from the Book of Job —"And all the Sons of God shouted for joy"; and over it (near the cartoon David Low did in the thirties, to raise money for concentration-camp victims) Kapp's lithograph of Schnabel, brooding, with bowed head, above fingers poised for the decisive committal. The lithograph is dated, I see, 1932, and is autographed by Schnabel. It was in that year then, probably, that the greatest living interpreter of Beethoven, or the greatest at least that I have heard, played the whole series of sonatas for the first time at the old Queen's Hall, which night after night for so many years was as dear and familiar as home to us. As I sit here with half-closed eyes there hangs about my nostrils once again the peculiar smell of the hall and the refreshment room and above all the downstairs corridor: it never varied, from the day, long before the first world war, when I used my first season ticket for the opening night of my first proms, to the day, just before the second world war, when Toscanini conducted all nine Beethoven symphonies. Now the place has gone—gone for ever, even if they should have rebuilt it, which seems unlikely, before you read these pages.

Schnabel played Beethoven with an almost terrible gravity, and with an intellect that met the music in so absolute a unity that we seemed to be assisting, not at Schnabel's interpretation of Beethoven, but at some new and inevitable act of joint creation. In fifty years or more of joy in music, I can remember very few experiences that can compare with those performances of Schnabel, and with his attack, in particular, at the opening of the Hammerklavier Sonata. Casals, certainly, and sometimes the Casals-Cortot-Thibaud combination; Menuhin one night, playing the first subject of the Beethoven violin concerto, where it returns just after the cadenza, with a purity that was both

THE BLAKE ENGRAVING

THE LOW CARTOON

childish and divine; Gerhardt, when she was still at her best; Ysaye, fiddling with a tone that was fuller and graver than that of any other violinist of my time; Chaliapin's Boris and Lehmann's Marschallin; the Destinn night after night at Covent Garden, with that almost desperate urgency in her voice, a kind of spiritual urgency, when she sang at full strength, and the soft high notes that made one catch one's breath, not once but a hundred times in an evening (who could ever forget her miraculous change of register at the climax of *Vissi d'arte*?); Toscanini's *Meistersinger*, Act II—the senses became one, and the scent of the elder in the warm summer night was rapture to our hearing; and a particular performance of the Leonora Number III, played by the Vienna Philharmonic under Franz Schalk after the prison scene in *Fidelio*. This was one Saturday in Paris; the Vienna troupe were giving a fortnight's performances, and I had gone over on the Friday afternoon with the idea of returning, as at that time one could, on the Saturday at midnight. Lotte Lehmann was the Leonora and Richard Tauber, who was then still appearing in serious opera, the Florestan; but I remember, as nearly best, the glorious singing by Richard Mayer, with his mouth slightly askew, of that phrase in the last scene which one always waits for as at once climax and resolution—*es sucht der Bruder seiner Brüder, und kann er helfen hilft er gern*. But best of all was the playing of the Leonora Number III between the last two scenes.

The practice of playing it at this point, as Mahler had been the first to play it, unless I'm mistaken—in Vienna at the beginning of the century—has recently been condemned by some critics here as illegitimate, inartistic, mere repetition, an anticlimax. I do not blame them if they are judging by the present procedure at Covent Garden. When I saw *Fidelio* there a year or two ago the curtain was brought down after the Leonora and Florestan duet; there was much applause; the artists took several calls; and then Mr Rankl raised his stick, and the overture began. This is horrible; the spell is broken, and the overture, with applause at the end of it before the final scene, is nothing but an unwarrantable intrusion. But played as Mahler meant it to be played and as I have heard it played, that night in Paris and often at Salzburg and even, under Bruno Walter, at Covent Garden itself, the overture is not only a piece of great

music but a piece of great opera as well, for all that the invention
was Mahler's and not Beethoven's. You have been watching and
listening as the scene in the dungeon has run its course. Doomed
Florestan has sung his hymn to the wife, the *Engel Leonore*, whom
he sees with the faithful clarity of imagination while his body
thirsts and hungers; the real Leonora, disguised as Fidelio, has
come down into the deep and the cold—*das ist natürlich! Es ist
ja so tief*—and has dug with Rocco her husband's grave; Pizarro
has joined them, has reviled Florestan, has raised his dagger
to strike; and then Leonora, flinging herself between and revealing who she is, has opposed her protecting pistol at the very
second—inevitably at the very second—at which the trumpet
rings out in the distance to announce that Don Fernando, the
Governor, has come to bring salvation. Divine grace and
human freewill have co-operated; man has worked in fellowship
with God. And now the saved Florestan has asked, in speech
not song: "*Treues Weib! was hast du meinetwegen erduldet?*", and his
saviour Leonora has answered, in speech not song: "*Nichts,
nichts, mein Florestan!*"; and they have burst out into, and ended,
their duet of love and rapture. But the curtain does not fall
immediately. As the lovers go slowly up the dungeon steps, with
the torchlight of freedom now shining from above, we hear the
opening chord of the Leonora Number III; and only when a
few more bars have been played, and the lovers are nearer the
sky, is the curtain very slowly brought down and the music
left, wholly self-sufficient, to continue to its end. Played in
this way the overture, summing up everything we have been
living through, and proceeding from Florestan's song and by
way of the trumpet calls—*ja, ja, es ist eine Vorsicht*—to a paean
of thanksgiving which again and again you think can never
mount higher and yet again and again, with that incessant
enriching of the strings, it does—played in this way the overture provides a climax far more moving even than the lovers'
duet, though that had seemed at the time to reach the very
limit of musical expression. Beethoven, in the last movement
of his last symphony, broke into human speech, and no one
understands Beethoven who doesn't understand why; but
when I hear the Leonora Number III greatly played, not as an
interlude between two rounds of applause but as an integral
conclusion to the whole long scene of fidelity and salvation,
I have the feeling not merely that the human drama is being

superbly summed up, but that by the silencing of speech and
song what was before experienced as greatly human is now
experienced as an immediate and final reality which includes
and rests in the human, but transcends it.


   The first music I vividly remember hearing, other than my
sister's piano-playing and my father's uncertain humming of
operatic tunes, was *Traviata* at Covent Garden in my boyhood,
with Melba as Violetta. There was a great tradition of opera-
going in our family; like many synagogue cantors my grandfather loved singing the great tenor arias, and his conversation,
passed on to me by my father, was full of Mario, Alboni, Patti,
Jenny Lind, Christine Nilsson, Trebelli, Tamagno and the de
Reszkes. (But three singers only, he wrote in his modest little
autobiography, ever moved him to astonishment, namely Jenny
Lind, Adelina Patti and a cantor called delightfully Herr
Nachtigall: "these three alone seemed to me to be able to play
with their voices untiringly and with ease, just as children play
with their toys.") Though I did not care for Melba—but what
pleasure I should get, with our standards so lowered, from
hearing her now!—that first *Traviata* committed me to a delight in music, in opera, in singing and in Covent Garden that
is as fresh and keen today as on that early summer evening forty
odd years ago.   Those were the days when the rage, operatic-
ally, was for Wagner, and Verdi was still widely dismissed as
a barrel-organ composer. But the *Libiamo* in *Traviata* was an
ecstasy to me, and as I went on to *Aïda*, with Destinn, Caruso
and Scotti, and to *Otello*, with Zenatello's great leaping
*Esultate* at the entry in the first act, I became convinced that
Verdi was one of the dozen greatest composers in the whole
range of Western music. I even talked—I must have been about
fourteen at the time—of founding a Verdi society. And my love
of him has never changed. I love him at his worst: even in his
earliest vulgarities the same truth can be heard struggling for
expression that was to reveal itself, pure gold, in the surpassing
grace and delicacy of the old man's *Falstaff*. He is the most
loving of composers, as Rossini is the most heartless; but one
can enjoy Rossini too, for something net and brandy-like in
his sparkling Mediterraneanism.
   Soon I was saving up not only my small pocket money but

my lunch money too for my summer season in the Covent
Garden gallery. School was over at ten to five (how often since
then have I looked at my watch for no particular reason in the
late afternoon, and it has happened to be just ten to five!); and
after another quarter of an hour or so, spent with Roman
Catholics, atheists and fellow-Jews in isolation from the Angli-
can service that was proceeding elsewhere, I would rush across
to Baron's Court station, take the tube to Covent Garden, run as
fast as I could round the corner into Floral Street, and take up
my stand for the happy waiting. There was always great excite-
ment, as one rounded the corner, in estimating the length of the
queue. If its tail stretched beyond the stage entrance, everything
depended on how much head it had. This you couldn't tell till
you'd continued your run to the gallery door; because the practice was to open this door, and let people up the long staircase to
a point a little short of the pay-box, some varying time before
the pay-box itself was unbarred. So if the queue stretched beyond the stage entrance, and one also found that "the people
had gone up", the position was painfully critical. It happened,
however, that I never failed to get in, though I must have gone
almost every night during my last summer term at St. Paul's;
but once I very nearly failed, and the uncertainty was agonising—I was the last to squeeze through at the première of
*Elektra.*

Occasionally, towards the end of my schooldays, I was accompanied by Cecil Botting, the Greek master of the Eighth. This
blond, roundish man—his moustaches had little waxed tips to
them—was a great Wagnerian, but rather inexperienced, and I
took great pleasure in helping him with his leitmotifs. He was
always torn during the intervals between a desire to absorb my
expositions and a sense of duty that kept nagging at him to mug
up next day's Homer. He usually chose the latter. On top of his
school work, he slaved away with an army of private pupils
whom he coached for university scholarships and so on, for
many of his relatives were needy and he felt bound to support
them; and he died in his fifties, worn out by overwork. But his
sense of enjoyment was keen, and he loved good living; and
once a year he gave all his pupils who were leaving, private or
otherwise, a wonderful many-coursed dinner with all the appropriate wines. I smoked a very strong cigar at the one I was
invited to, and was sick. I didn't quite realise his quality at the

time, but I look back upon him now as pretty nearly my ideal of a man.

It was not only a sense of expectation that made the waiting in Floral Street so happy, poignant beyond description though this was for one who was still very young, and only beginning to grow familiar with the masterpieces. To have heard a piece of music once or twice, to have it veiled in your consciousness and struggling to reveal itself, and to know that very soon, at a moment that inevitably must come, you will see it face to face—that is a felicity such as few other experiences can equal, and of the same nature, perhaps, as the quiet of expectation with which a saint awaits the beatific vision. But there were other elements in our happiness. We were a little community, for the "regulars" all knew one another, and we passed the time in keen and surprisingly expert discussion about the merits or demerits of recent performances: our sense of fellowship was almost conspiratorial. Yet for me something sacramental in Floral Street itself was perhaps the greatest felicity of all. In the narrow, rather sordid street, with opera house on one side and high blackened buildings (for they seemed immensely high) on the other, there would come, in the early evenings of that June or July weather, patches of sunlight from a sun itself unseen. And then, for all the bustle and noise in the world's greatest city, and for all, or perhaps because of, the distant traffic—distant, though in fact only just beyond our deep and narrow chasm—there would happen, in the interior castle of one's spirit, a lull, a suspension, a silence and a peace in which joy and sadness, both incomparably intense and yet of an utter tranquillity, were one. The late sun in cities has always had this effect on me. I suppose something of the kind was meant by Omar Khayyam, when he talked of "the brave music of a *distant* drum"; and many people experience it, I think, when faintly, in a sunlit street, they catch the tones of a penny whistle or barrel organ, or the singing of a human voice. There are days in Aix-en-Provence, its blazing streets empty as the sun goes down and then footsteps ringing out—footsteps, they might be, of the mailed soldiery in some long-dead Caesar's legions—when the sadness would be unbearable were it not happiness as well; and I remember standing one August, as a boy of six or seven,

on the little stone balcony of my home near Maida Vale, and
feeling myself caught up I knew not whither as hussars came
riding down from a neighbouring barracks, and the paving
stones echoed to their horses' hooves, and the street was afire
with the afternoon sun, and everything was silent. It must have
been a few years later that I was walking down Oxford Street,
which is surely one of the noisiest streets in the world, and tried,
as the feeling again came to me, to write a childish poem about
it. I remember only the first two lines, which were

> *In the first hot days of the May-time weather*
> *The wheels of the world are hushed and slow.*

I shall not attempt to explain the experience of which I have
been speaking, and which, I am certain, a great many people
share: I shall only say of it, as of many other experiences which
are bound up with sights and sounds, that any explanation in
purely physical or "materialistic" terms is ludicrously beside
the mark. So I shall content myself with repeating the word
"sacramental". All physical things are sacraments, and the
world is so beautiful because it is a sacrament of the Supreme
Beauty. To quote what Oscar Wilde himself quotes from
Théophile Gautier, "I am one of those *pour qui le monde visible
existe*": exists absolutely, but at the same time exists as an
intimation. I have always loved the world; it is because I love
it so much, and cannot bear that it should suffer torture and
disgrace and deformation, that I am writing this letter. I love
it particularly on this twenty-seventh day of January 1951.
Five hours ago the hoar-frost was as thick as a light fall of snow;
it lay in the sunshine with a touch of green or pink in its whiteness, and stretched to the horizon under a cloudless sky. Now,
just after lunch, the sun and the blue are still there, but clouds
have come over; and the whole landscape, out across the lawn
and the field—which is just striped with vegetables—to the
ploughed earth and the still-dead osiers and the downs in their
low polychrome (a single house showing red) far beyond, has
that greeny brown tone that you often see in mezzotints of
country-house domains, while the sky looks like the sky in a
gouache of Naples, or how the sky in a gouache of Naples
might have looked if the place and the artist had been English.
And in the air—I have been strolling for a moment—is that
peculiar smell that you sometimes get at this time of year, and

particularly in the country round Oxford (or am I generalising from an undergraduate impression?): the smell of burning wood, as if a gigantic log-fire were alight in the universe.

To me up in seat B 49 of the Covent Garden gallery—so many of us knew each other, as I have explained, that "my" seat was always left free for me until it became certain that I shouldn't be coming—the singing was everything: or rather, to put it more accurately, great singing was the *sine qua non* of an enjoyable performance. We could put up with wooden acting or a stereotyped production or even, in some operas, with poor orchestral playing; but if the singing fell below a certain standard (and our standard was very high) then the perform-ance was an obvious failure. And our reaction was right. Nowadays the general level of operatic singing is so low that it must be impossible for a young opera-goer to realise what the Nile scene in *Aïda*, for instance, was like when interpreted by Destinn, Caruso, Dinh Gilly and Kirkby Lunn. All the beauty and drama came to life for us in those incomparable voices: not as an occasional rarity, but in note after note and phrase after phrase, and throughout the whole long series of arias and duets and ensembles. Later, as standards began to decline, it became the practice to put up the prices when even one famous singer was appearing; but in those days before the war, before the 1914–1918 war, we thought nothing (though in another sense, of course, we thought a very great deal) of a *Huguenots* with Destinn, Tetrazzini, Caruso, Scotti and Journet all in the same cast. Recently, there has been a craze for "production" in opera—and for a type of production, it must be added, which in the Covent Garden of the last few years has often been of a surprising vulgarity. The motive behind this craze is partly a misunderstanding of what opera essentially is, and partly the need to compensate for the absence of good or even of efficient singing.

So I sat up there in the Covent Garden gallery; and when the final curtain had come down, and we had brought the Destinn back for a thirteenth or fourteenth recall, there was the walk to the corner of Wellington Street, and the long 'bus-ride back to Elgin Avenue, and a little cold supper, and homework for an hour, and the lightest of sleeps, and the waking at six, and then, with face dashed in cold water and eyes blinking to keep open, the obsessional "extra work" till breakfast time and school. It was all very foolish, and I had to pay for it when, forty years later, I faced a nervous crisis, and the insomnia I had induced as a boy, and had suffered from in the meantime spasmodically and without serious inconvenience, became total and hellish. But perhaps this agony was unavoidable; perhaps what drove me to "extra work" and what caused my crisis were one.

This crisis came in 1943. I am not going to tell you about that now, for there are many other things I must tell you about first: I shall come back to it after taking you on a long journey. But I must tell you at once about 1942, which you will later see not only as the prelude to what followed but as a focal point of my whole story.

# CHAPTER III

# 1942

1942 WAS MY year of wonder: a time of joy and inner peace
such as I had experienced with so unbroken a continuity, and
then not so deeply, at only one previous period of my life.
This had been at Repton, where I taught for about two years
during the first world war. On both occasions—1917 and 1942
—certain human relationships were no doubt the immediate
cause of the experience; and on both occasions it may have
had, again in an immediate sense, a physical and perhaps even
narrowly sexual basis. But it was essentially religious none the
less, by which I mean that it was an experience of greater
access to reality: an experience that foreshadowed what release
from division and reunion with reality—the ἀποκατάστασις
τῶν πάντων, "the restoration of all things"—might be like:
and an experience of the fact that this reality, which came to
meet a man and encompass him while he was himself yet
already included in it, could not be less of a Person than he knew
himself to be but on the contrary must be immeasurably more
of one. There can indeed be nothing more childish than to
imagine that you have "explained away" a religious experience
when you have discovered something physical as the occasion
for it. Compassion can be explained, for all I know, in physical
or psycho-physical terms; but that is by no means to explain
away the something new, the something more real, the something, if you like, emergent—the something that we call
spiritual—which anyone not wholly insensitive must immediately perceive in it. You do not despiritualise spirit when you
connect it with matter; you rather glorify matter as being, in a
unity that includes both, the potential of spirit.

How shall I find the words to describe to you, my dear
Timothy, what I felt in my year of wonder 1942? I had a
heightened perception of everything, and everything was
perceived as beautiful and good. But it was more than a
perception; it was a meeting, for which I had gone out to the
other and for which the other had gone out to me: a meeting
with everything's self which at the same time was my self, but

was nevertheless of a difference in selfhood which alone made the meeting a possibility. But the going out and the meeting were not different things but the same thing, not successive but simultaneous; which is to say that they were not in time but in eternity. And the meeting, I say again, was with everything. With the greenness, the freshness, the slenderness, the littleness, the gentleness, the strength, the taperingness, the sun-accept-ingness, the daisy-and-buttercup-enclosingness, of the benign and far-stretching grass. With the trees in their various species, and with every branch and every twig and every leaf of them. With stones and mould and air and sun and a deck-chair in the garden and a car down the lane and a spire on the downs and the wall of our house as I come in for lunch at one. And with people. Not specially with people—it would be easy but untrue to say that—but equally with people. I would sit, going up to London, in a crowded railway-compartment, and know myself as in every one of my fellow travellers, and know every one of them as in me.

I was in the Royal Automobile Club, of all places, on an afternoon that summer, and my eye happened to fall on a door. It was quite an ordinary door, in so far as any single thing in the universe is ordinary, with small panels and big panels and a knob. I know that what I am going to say will sound grotesque, but I tell you that this door, and the look and sound and the life of it, filled me with joy inexpressible: such joy as I had felt when, as a boy of fifteen or so in a classroom at St. Paul's, I had seen a bit of paper fluttering to the floor, and had written a paean in praise of its movement. And I remember that on the same afternoon, in the same club, I suddenly saw something green through the doors of the winter garden, and saluted it with delighted recognition.

But perhaps I do not sound grotesque to you; for being young when you read these pages you may be experiencing what Thomas Traherne experienced, and was able to express in language that no one could hope to equal:

"Will you see the infancy of this sublime and celestial great-ness? Those pure and virgin apprehensions I had in my infancy, and that divine light wherewith I was born, are the best unto this day wherein I can see the universe. By the gift of God they attended me into the world, and by His special favour I remember them till now. Verily they form the greatest gift His wisdom could bestow, for without them all other gifts had been dead and vain. They are unattainable by books, and therefore I will teach them by experience. Pray for them earnestly, for they will make you angelical and wholly celestial. Certainly Adam in Paradise had not more sweet and curious apprehensions of the world than I when I was a child.

"All appeared new and strange at first, inexpressibly rare and delightful and beautiful. I was a little stranger which at my entrance into the world was saluted and surrounded with innumerable joys. My knowledge was Divine; I knew by intuition those things which since my apostasy I collected again by the highest reason. My very ignorance was advantageous. I seemed as one brought into the estate of innocence. All things were spotless and pure and glorious; yea, and infinitely mine and joyful and precious . . . I was entertained like an angel with the works of God in their splendour and glory; I saw all in the peace of Eden; heaven and earth did sing my Creator's praises, and could not make more melody to Adam than to me. All Time was Eternity, and a perpetual Sabbath. Is it not strange that an infant should be heir of the whole world, and see those mysteries which the books of the learned never unfold?

"The corn was orient and immortal wheat which never should be reaped nor was ever sown. I thought it had stood from everlasting to everlasting. The dust and stones of the street were as precious as gold: the gates were at first the end of the world. The green trees when I saw them first through one of the gates transported and ravished me; their sweetness and unusual beauty made my heart to leap, and almost mad with ecstasy, they were such strange and wonderful things. The Men! O what venerable and reverend creatures did the aged seem! Immortal Cherubims! And young men glittering and sparkling angels, and maids strange seraphic pieces of life and beauty! Boys and girls tumbling in the streets were moving jewels: I knew not that they were born or should die. But all things abided eternally as they were in their proper places. Eternity was manifest in the Light of the Day, and something infinite behind everything appeared, which talked with my expectation and moved my desire. The City seemed to stand in Eden or to be built in Heaven. The streets were mine, the temple was mine, the people were mine, their clothes and gold and silver were mine, as much as their sparkling eyes, fair skins, and ruddy faces. The skies were mine, and so were the sun and moon and stars, and all the world was mine; and I the only spectator and enjoyer of it. I knew no churlish proprieties, nor bounds nor divisions; but all proprieties and divisions were mine, all treasures and the possessors of them."

*Heaven and earth did sing my Creator's praises*; and the whole passage, and everything Traherne wrote, is his own hymn of thanksgiving to the Creator of beauty. I, also, sang my Creator's praises; not occasionally, as I had always done, but many times a day every day, as the spring and the summer and the autumn of my wonderful year slipped by. I would sing them in the early morning, while the sun was coming up behind the great aged oak on the road; I would sing them in the morning and afternoon, and I would sing them, after waiting for darkness, under the stars of night. Sometimes the praise was wordless, and sometimes, facing in turn towards the four corners of the earth, I would intone the *Hallel*—"O give thanks unto the Lord, for he is good, for his mercy endureth for ever"—in the manner, midway between tune and chant, that had been customary forty odd years before in my parents' synagogue. Or I would remember Repton: the cricket-field, and the play-readings, and the eagerness of young minds, and my own urgent delight in a kind of spiritual midwifery; and then I would sing my *Hallel*, still with its Hebrew words, to the tune of a Christian hymn, one as banal and indeed as grotesque as you could imagine, but meaning for me, even in the first second's interval between the first two notes, all the evensongs I had loved in the dull-bricked Repton chapel and the whole eternal moment of my Repton happiness. For 1942 caught up 1917; 1917 pre-figured 1942; and so it is time that you should take a first look at my Repton experience.

# CHAPTER IV

## REPTON—I

THE MONTHS AT Repton were crucial for my life, since they made it inevitable that, a few years after leaving (or, to be more accurate, a few years after being sacked), I should become a publisher. Yet nothing could have been more accidental, or could have had less to do with any sense of vocation or any choice of a future profession, than the circumstances of my going there. Technically, I suppose, I was never a schoolmaster at all; I was simply, during the whole period, a second lieutenant in the Repton School Officers' Training Corps, to which I had been "seconded" for duty. But parades were infrequent; I was a dud at them anyhow; and my real work was to do "English" with the smallest boys, and Latin with the candidates for University scholarships. Or the real work, rather, with which I began; for by the end of my first term some gust had got hold of us all—the boys and certain other masters and me—and was hurling us into an intensity of life not at all characteristic of an English Public School.

The whole affair started with two discoveries I made about my boys—for they hit me as discoveries—in the lowest and the highest class alike. The first discovery was simply that they were good. This may sound silly and sentimental; but I mean it as a statement of fact, which can never be sentimental; I mean that what struck home to me as the most real thing about them, when I was getting to know their hearts and minds in class or on country walks or up at my lodgings for tea, was their original virtue and not their original sin. I do not imply that any of them were without faults, or even that some of them were without a smaller or greater degree of viciousness or brutality in inclination or behaviour. This was no specially picked gathering of exceptional human beings, and the moral climate of the place was little better than average. I was not blind to a good deal that was base and revolting. One of the older boys—an ugly little poet, unpopular for both reasons, who was afterwards killed in the war—was suspected, whether rightly or wrongly, of petty thefts from his housemates; and one night they got hold of him, and pulled out his moustache hair by hair; and then several of them beat him in turn, while others held him over a table. I knew about this because I saw what he looked like next morning when he came into class, and made enquiries. There was another boy, very beefy and athletic, who was passionately masochistic, and would pay up to half a crown a time for so many strokes with the cane; and volunteers were always available. Yes, there was plenty of public-school brutishness, active or passive, and plenty, too, of the more respectable disorders, such as absence of charity and the like. Nevertheless in boy after boy, whether he was good or bad or strong or weak or worthy or worthless or an example or a warning or whatever else it may have been in the simplified classification of my colleagues, I found a stirring, a striving, a reaching out—sometimes very deep down and sometimes near the surface and sometimes already manifest—towards contact and union with the beautiful and good; and I knew immediately, by an automatic act of sympathetic self-identification, that this stirring and striving and reaching out was something far more real in the boy, something far more truly both of his own and of everybody's essence, than whatever it might be that was unpleasant or base in him. I remember very well going for a walk in March 1917 with a boy who was generally regarded as a dirtyish and rather corrupting sort of person: "unwholesome" was what they usually called him. After some casual conversation we walked for a time in silence; and then, as we emerged into a patch of sunlight beyond Crewe's Pond, he said something like this to me: "I think the spring's almost here. It seems—rather wonderful. I wish I could write—I'd like to try to make you understand what's in my head." It was desire for union with the whole, coming out as a sense of beauty, that was real in him, and not "unwholesomeness", which was a mere by-product.

There was nothing new, of course, in this apprehension of the relative unreality of evil. The mystics and theologians of a school still unbroken in its continuity have always insisted on it; so have sundry metaphysicians and psychologists. "Nothingness," says Nicolas Berdyaev, "is immanent in evil." "Evil," says Samuel Alexander, "is not therefore wholly evil; it is misplaced good." "There is no not-holy," says Martin Buber; "there is only that which has not yet been hallowed, which has not yet been redeemed to its holiness." "Disorder," says Dostoevsky, "is often a secret desire for order and beauty." "Self-will," says F. H. Bradley, "is opposition attempted by a finite subject against its proper whole . . . *It is connexion with the central fire which produces in the element this burning sense of selfness*." "Hate and evil," says Ian Suttie, a great psychiatrist who died before his time, "have no independent existence but are merely the frustration-forms of love itself." "Destructiveness," says Erich Fromm, "is the outcome of unlived life." I could indeed quote enough, from the most varied sources, to fill a letter longer than this.

Why then do I describe what I felt during my first few weeks at Repton as a discovery? Because you can believe or assent to a thing, and still not discover it; because discovery when it comes, and whatever steps may have led to it, in itself is unmediated recognition; because a truth discovered is a truth that is more than self-evident, it is a truth become one with the knower; and because I knew in just such a way that, beyond all relativities of goodness or badness, what finally mattered about these boys was the fact that in essence they were good. I have felt the same, since that time, about everybody, whether in the world or anywhere else, whether actual or imaginable: about the Devil, about Antichrist, about Hitler. You'll have a sense of humour when you grow up, my dear Timothy, because even now there's a smile round the corner of you, or at the back of you, or somewhere or other where no one can see it (and yet we all know it's there); so you'll never be the solemn sort of ass who, noting what I've said about Hitler, might imagine that I'm indifferent to wickedness—to the unspeakable wickedness, for instance, with which he gassed and incinerated God knows how many millions of his fellow human beings. I shall have something to say about that, in any case, a little later on. Meanwhile I shall copy out for you a few passages from Diony-sius the Areopagite, for when I first came to read him, many years after Repton, I felt that shock of instantaneous assent with which one hears something said that one has so long been thinking oneself:

"The depraved sinner, though bereft of the Good by his brutish desires, is in this respect unreal and desires unrealities; but still he hath a share in the Good in so far as there is in him a distorted reflection of true Love and Communion. And anger hath a share in the Good, in so far as it is a movement which seeks to remedy apparent evils, converting them to that which appears to be fair. And even he that desires the basest life, yet in so far as he feels desire at all and feels desire for life, and intends what he thinks the best kind of life, so far participates in the Good . . .

"The Good must be the beginning and the end even of all evil things. For the Good is the final Purpose of all things, good and bad alike. For even when we act amiss we do so from a longing for the Good; for no one makes evil his definite object when performing any action. Hence evil hath no substantial being, but only a shadow thereof; since the Good, and not itself, is the ultimate object for which it comes into existence . . .

"And if no thing in the world is without a share in the Good, and evil is the deficiency of Good and no thing in the world is utterly destitute of Good, then the Divine Providence is in all things, and nothing that exists can be without It."

My first discovery at Repton, then, was that the boys were good. My second discovery was that (with exceptions) they were intolerant, class-ridden, narrow, self-righteous, smug, superior, ignorant; grotesquely ignorant, in particular, of conditions on their own doorstep and in the world outside. Now these two discoveries, in combination, made it inevitable that the person who discovered them should do the things he proceeded to do—as you will presently hear—both immediately at Repton and later elsewhere. They made it inevitable, because the person who discovered them was the sort of person he was. So you must know what sort of person he was, and I must take you a stage further back with me.

# CHAPTER V

## WAR AND POVERTY

I HAD LIVED, SINCE the age of six in the one case and eleven or twelve in the other, with a horror, the sort of horror that goes about with a man and never leaves him, of two abominations—which I constantly visualised as happening here and now, and happening to me: poverty and war. I don't mean by this that I was *afraid* of them happening to me, though some fear of the kind, for all I know, may have been the real explanation: I mean that when I came up against them I immediately thought myself into them, imagined what I should be feeling if I were suffering them, and then imagined the other man in my own imagined shoes. It was war, and not poverty, that was my first horror. On a table in our drawing-room, by the piano, was a very large and very thick volume, bound in elaborately gilt buckram with broad bevelled edges, called "Sixty Years a Queen": it had been issued in commemoration of the Diamond Jubilee, and was chock-full of pictures, on heavily coated "art paper", illustrating events of the reign. I was looking through this book one day, round about my sixth birthday, when I came across a couple of pictures that faced one another: on the right-hand page was the Charge of the Light Brigade (at Balaclava) and on the left-hand page was the Charge of the Heavy Brigade. In one or other of them, I don't remember which, a man on horseback was slashing down with a sabre at another man's head, and the other man's head was—half off. I'm back again now, from half a century later, in the Elgin Avenue drawing-room; or not in the Elgin Avenue drawing-room, because as I looked *I* was the man with his head off, and the whole of me was an agony of pain and an obscene degradation. It was at this moment that my horror of war was consciously born; a horror that was then, as it has been ever since, a horror as of something that was in the same room with me, that was on the very table in front of me, that was outraging *me*, even though it might really be happening in China or Spain. And a horror not only of war; a horror also of violence, and of flogging, and of capital punishment, and of all the other unspeakable outrages that never fail to produce in me a feeling of personal contamination.

It must have been only a month or so after the Balaclava episode that I learned, I don't remember how, about guns. What appalled me immediately was that a man could be killed in a *second*. I said in my mind—my recollection is so clear that my mind might be saying it now—"But how . . . how . . . *nothing*" (that is the way my childish thought formulated it: nothing, unreality, no purpose or meaning) "how *nothing* that a man it's taken twenty years to make, with all the meals and the lessons and the getting up and the going to bed and the dressing and the walks and the being 'brought up', can completely *stop* from a bullet *immediately*. What was the *point* of all the things *before* the bullet?" If I am not mistaken, Talleyrand, at a riper age, said very much the same.

My other horror, my horror of poverty, came later, when I was eleven or twelve. This was during my first term at St. Paul's. I used to get there by walking up Elgin Avenue to Westbourne Park station, and then taking the Metropolitan to Hammersmith. Just outside Westbourne Park, flanking the line on the left as you went westward, was a long row of houses, so miserable and squalid, so black and beastly and corrupt, that the idea of people actually living in them, actually getting up every day in them and having meals every day in them and going to bed every day in them, filled me with a sensation of loathing and despair. For at once I thought "people like *me*"; at once I contrasted my own comfortable bed, and the curios my Aunt Minna had given me from the Sahara desert, and fires, and our little narrow garden, and lying on the sofa in the downstairs parlour on Saturday afternoons with a book and raspberry-jam sandwiches for tea—I contrasted all this with the dirt and the smell and the decaying fish-bones to which these other people, these people like me, these people who suddenly *were* me, were condemned. And just as it was the instantaneity, the all-over-in-a-secondness, that had appalled me in the case of the bullet, so it was the interminability, the never-to-be-over-at-allness, that appalled me in the case of my Westbourne Park houses. It is this aspect of the direst poverty—the utter lack of hope that it can ever end—that still seems to me the most awful thing about it.

You may think, my dear Timothy, that I was exaggerating, and that it was only by contrast with the palace in which I lived that these other houses struck me as so disgusting. No, I wasn't exaggerating. I didn't live in a palace: houses in Elgin Avenue weren't palaces, and my father was a small business man, midway between a jeweller with a shop and a petty whole-saler, whose income from a twelve-hour day varied from five or six hundred a year to an occasional thousand. And I was right about the Westbourne Park houses, I feel certain; for I "looked into" similar ones when I was old enough to know how to go about such things, and confirmed my childish impressions.

Within a very few weeks I was to see the most disgusting poverty at even closer quarters. My parents were orthodox Jews, and it is "forbidden" among such to ride, drive, or be driven anywhere from sunset on Friday evening, when the Sabbath begins, to sunset on Saturday evening, when it ends. You mustn't pedal a bicycle, or be driven by a horse, or go in any sort of car or train; if you want to get anywhere, you must walk.

This ban (to anticipate by a few minutes what I shall presently be saying in much greater detail) was one of those irrationalities that made me detest orthodox Judaism almost as soon as I was born. The thing, of course, had long since been nothing but a tabu, even at the time of which I am writing, and I imagine that the number of Jews who observe it today is comparatively negligible; but there's an explanation of sorts, if you go back far enough. God rested on the seventh day: men must do no work on it: but to manipulate a vehicle means work—your own, if you do the manipulating, or other people's, if they do. Therefore you may neither drive nor be driven. Now back in Biblical Palestine, or even in the ghetto, this had logic of a sort, granted the premises; for the entire community, more or less, being Jewish—the potential drivers as well as the potentially driven—no vehicle could proceed without somebody breaking the Sabbath. But the entire community was by no means Jewish in the England of the nineteen hundreds. The trains ran anyhow, on Saturday if not on Sunday, so if a Jew took a ride in one how possibly could he be committing an *avārah*?*

* Sin. I have transliterated Hebrew words, etc., not in the correct manner (except in the case of some very familiar ones), but so as to give as close an idea as possible of the sound.

Puzzling all this out, I thought at first that maybe a rigid observance of the Jewish Sabbath was incumbent on everyone, Jewish and Gentile alike; but then I reflected that this could hardly be the case, since (a) we were strictly forbidden to touch the fire once Sabbath had come in, touching the fire being "work"; and (b) not only was our Gentile maid regularly summoned to put the coal on for us, but that was precisely, among other things, what she appeared to be there for. I heard rumours, indeed, that among Jews even more orthodox than ourselves, and too poor to have ordinary servants, there was a mysterious individual known as the *Shabbas goy*—"the Saturday Gentile"—whose whole *raison d'être* was to do things on *Shabbas* that her employers couldn't do for themselves. But sometimes, I gathered, there was a reservation; once *Shabbas* had actually "come in" you mustn't ask your *Shabbas goy* to put the coal on, but must have given her your instructions in advance. This struck me as being what I should now call, in the popular sense of the word, casuistical. I soon came to the conclusion, anyhow, that in this matter of not riding on Saturday all questions about who did the work and who didn't were quite irrelevant: that there was simply some iron compulsiveness which made "riding" on the Sabbath impossible for a Jew: that the impossibility would remain (and here I was perfectly right) even if the vehicle were miraculously propelled without the remotest human agency: and that though a three hours' walk was obviously "work" of the most fatiguing nature, it nevertheless wasn't work, as taking a train was, within the meaning of the act.

Now sunset gets earlier and earlier as the winter gets nearer and nearer; and I was in my first year at St. Paul's; and a Friday arrived; and school wasn't over till five; and Sabbath "came in" at 4.50, or maybe 4.59; and riding was tabu; and from Hammersmith Broadway to Maida Vale is a distance of —heaven knows how many miles. These miles had to be walked, that Friday night and every Friday night till the days drew out, that year and every year until the year of my revolt. I was chaperoned by two much older boys, who of course were also Jews—otherwise they wouldn't have been walking—and who lived in my part of the world and knew the way. They were

"nibs" of eighteen or so, and one of them had already got a
scholarship at Trinity, as you could tell from the mortar-board
and gown in which he strode like a master down the corridor
that led to the Eighth; and they were very stand-offish as they
guided me those many Friday nights from Hammersmith to
Elgin Avenue, forbidding me to speak unless spoken to, and
keeping me ashuffle in their rear from the moment we set out
till the moment, hours later, we arrived. Our way took us
through a number of indifferent localities; but through a
couple (the routes being alternative) which might almost have
deliberately been put there to typify the "two nations" into
which the England of that day was as surely divided as it had
been in Disraeli's. One of these localities was Kensington
Palace Gardens, already known, I think, as "Millionaires'
Row": it stretched, a great noiseless carriage-way, with its own
private gates and its line of what I had once heard described as
domestic palaces, from Kensington High Street to the Bayswater
Road. Flunkeys were at the entrance to guard it, in greatcoats
of blue and chimney-pots braided with gold. The other locality
was the neighbourhood of Latimer Road. I am not sure whether
this was actually identical with the district nicknamed "the Piggeries" or merely adjacent to it, nor whether "Piggeries" was
a term to be understood literally, with reference to some occupational tradition, or was just pejorative; but what I do know
is that though I have been through many slums in the meantime that have made the sick saliva come dribbling into my
mouth, I can think of none more hellish than the Latimer
ones of nineteen hundred and five. Their beastliness was intensified for me, no doubt, by the drizzly coldness of the weather
in which I traversed those November streets, and by the
wretched dimness of the lighting that made of the darkness
and night not the lovely things they are, but images of an evil
half exposed. Hot sun can redeem anything. There are slums
in Naples even viler, perhaps, than the vilest in the England of
some fifty years ago; but the radiance of noonday somehow
encloses and absorbs them, and half purges them of their
misery.

Even worse than the walls and the windows of my Latimer
houses, and the general aspect of the streets, was what I saw or
half saw every now and again through an open doorway, spotty
with sprawling children; and even worse than what I saw was

what I imagined. I imagined the lavatories. Dirty and sordid lavatories have always obsessed me, and I still occasionally have nightmares about them. There are Freudian explanations for this obsession which seem reasonable to me; but I derive it in my own case from a visit to the lavatory on my very first day at St. Paul's, and the shock it gave my instincts for cleanliness and beauty. Through one of many doors in a row, with the paint flaking off them, you entered a cubicle of rather grimy roughcast, and sat down on a depolished seat. Below the hole in the seat was a trough of stale water, which ran undivided from the beginning of the row to its end. Lying in the water, or floating sluggishly down from higher up the stream, were lumps of ugly faeces, which emitted a mouldering smell. I didn't like it; I liked it so little that I preferred, during my whole time at St. Paul's, to endure agonies of restraint right up to the last possible minute, rather than visit the horrible *cabinetto*. (I must hasten to add that all this has long been changed, and that the lavatories at St. Paul's are now of quite exceptional beauty.) And I asked myself now, as I walked down Latimer Road on my Sabbath pilgrimage: if even at St. Paul's there are lavatories like that, what on earth must they be like in the Latimer Road? I was to find later on, when I was visiting a slum area in the North of England, that my imagination had been feebly inadequate.

So the horror of poverty and the horror of war, which together would be shaping my future, were already an inextricable part of me, the one when I was six and the other when I was twelve. But the two were accompanied by, or enclosed in, or perhaps took their life from, a less particularised, a more integral passion: a passion for liberty in every possible meaning of the word (so far as I then understood it), liberty for myself every bit as much as for every other living thing and for every other living thing every bit as much as for myself. This passion, clearly always latent in me, came blazing up, I think, as a reaction to two particular manifestations of the mental climate characteristic of our home: namely, my father's attitude to my sisters, and his religious orthodoxy.

I shall try a little later on, my dear Timothy, to sketch out for you your great-grandfather's character, for his attitude to

my sisters and religion was part and parcel of his whole attitude
to life, and unless you understand that attitude you cannot
possibly understand my reaction to it. But because I would not
wish you to be unfair to him even for a minute, as I, to my grief
now, was unfair to him during almost the whole of my childhood, I want immediately to say at least this: if to be good is
"to do what's right" (this was a favourite phrase of his)
according to your understanding of "right" and to the best of
your ability, then my father was a good man to a degree very
much above the average. I cannot tell you how painfully I now
wish that somehow I could make up to him for my harshness as
a boy; but what happened between us is irreparable, by the
nature of time past and the fact of his death; and the only thing
left for me is to write what I have to write with a sympathy and,
as I can now feel, with a love which, while leaving candour
intact, will rule out the self-righteousness that, unconscious
though I was of it, matched and perhaps even more than
matched his own.

# CHAPTER VI

# MY FATHER AND MY SISTERS

To use a term that I soon picked up from the surrounding atmosphere, my father's attitude to my sisters was one of the most uncompromising antifeminism. I can't quite remember when I first came to feel this: at nine or ten, perhaps, or half-way between my Balaclava episode and my first term at St. Paul's. By the time I was in my early teens I was in a constant mood of protest and indignation. Here was I (so I thought and shouted) with all life's glorious possibilities opening out before me. I could do what I wanted; I could express myself in any way I chose; I could be independent, I could be free, I could be *me*. What happiness! What vistas! What a fullness to look forward to of wonder and delight! But my poor wretched sisters (who were two and four years older, respectively, than me)—what about *them*? They were being trained for nothing; there was never any suggestion that one day they were going to *work*, that they were going to do a *job*, that they would be living the gloriously free, independent, self-expressing existence that I envisaged for myself. Quite the contrary. There was only one goal for them, one general woman's goal that was despotic-ally imposed by the whole wretched negative procedure: they were to get married. I had nothing against marriage; indeed I was passionately in favour of it; for my heart was romantic and tender, and often I would dream of a good and lovely bride (who duly materialised) and of all the happiness that should follow (as it duly did). But marriage wasn't a *job*; marriage was two people *both* with a job, who lived with one another and loved one another for ever and ever. Marriage was *equality*.

But my father would have none of it. "Girls don't *work* in our walk of life," he would say. "That's not at all the correct thing. The correct thing is for girls to get married. Do you think I can't afford to keep my daughters till they get married? I hope I know what's right."

This differentiation between boys and girls, men and women, me and my sisters, infuriated me. I saw it as a gross affront to the ideal of human equality; I saw it as infringing a most obvious natural right, the right of every soul to realise, in complete freedom, all the potentialities inherent in it. I saw it, in a word, as an outrage against personality. What the devil did it matter, I cried, if some people happened to be men and others women? Weren't they all persons?

Sometimes, I am afraid, I completely lost my head. Leading down from the hall of our house to the basement was a flight of stairs, enclosed, in some curious fashion I can no longer visualise, by a sheet of coloured glass. One day in the middle of a furious argument I smashed my fist through this smokily yellowish screen, and the resulting wound spread down to my finger tips and up beyond the shoulder. The remains of it are still visible: a tiny bleached scar just above my right wrist.

My father's antifeminism rapidly became symbolic for me of all inequalities, all oppressions, all unwarrantable attempts to interfere in any way, positively or negatively, with a free, spontaneous, self-directing development of the life and spirit in every human person. Rich and poor, masters and servants, parents and children, ushers and schoolboys, Englishmen and foreigners, black men and white men, Jews and Gentiles—especially Jews and Gentiles: I grew to detest all such categor-isations, and any exclusiveness, superiority, inferiority, excess of respect, deficiency of respect, and above all inequality of rights that might issue from them. My reaction was direct and naïf, and I didn't, at that early age, go seeking for categories to add to my list: I was merely concerned with what "hit me in the eye": but a little later on I was to detest even more yet another division of humanity, namely into "the good" and "the bad", "the law-abiding" and "criminals". Even at the time of which I am writing, even before I went to St. Paul's, I was rapidly approaching this position; for, owing to a par-ticular trait in my father's character which will shortly appear, I was constantly brought up against the idea of "respectability" —and concluded that to classify people as respectable or dis-reputable was poppycock. I didn't mean, of course, that at any level all such classifications were meaningless. I realised that a given classification could be understood in a number of ways, and that it might correspond to a reality when understood in one way but not when understood in another. What I was get-ting at was simply this: that while a black man is undoubtedly black and a white man white, the fact of such a distinction couldn't modify the fact, the immensely more important fact, that both, in utter equality, were human.

Let me assure you, my dear Timothy, that in seeing my father's antifeminism as typical of all the various disrespects, whatever their character, to human personality, my instinct was sound; for apart from the direct idea, which often emerged in him though never discourteously, that women were somehow inferior—an idea always present in antifeminists, however consciously or unconsciously disguised—his attitude to marriage implied a fixed status for women as such, in contrast to the freedom of choice that was the birthright of men; and to impose a fixed status on any group of people, whether what imposes it be tradition or custom or economic circumstances or one or more individuals or "public opinion" or the State, is to depersonalise them. This is not to deny that motherhood may be for many women—perhaps, I don't know, for the majority of them—an all-absorbing "job" and a means for complete self-expression, though only, at best, during part of their lives; nor is it to deny that a certain and much rarer type of woman may genuinely find in the home-keeping of marriage—of marriage as such, marriage perhaps without children—the opportunity for realising all her most precious potentialities; but then the thing must just come of itself, must just happen, like Blake's joy, and may never, without the gravest outrage to the sacredness of human spontaneity, be imposed as a species of status or universal destiny. I lived, of course, in a middle-class environment, and was without direct access to working-class conditions; but I should have realised, I think, had I known more about them, that though the problem was far more complicated there, owing partly to the character of such work as could alone be in question—soul-destroying work, for the most part, rather than soul-expressing—and partly to the pressure of economic circumstances, it was in essentials the same.

# CHAPTER VII

# JEWISH ORTHODOXY

THERE WAS NOTHING peculiar, as I need hardly tell you, in my father's antifeminism. It was typical of the circles in which we lived, and of circles far wider than those; and though it has long been dying out, even today, even in 1951, it is still quite prevalent. Equally typical, this time of orthodox Jewry, is what I will call, with a considerable misuse of the adjective, the religious atmosphere of our home. I ought to explain, before attempting to describe it, that we were orthodox Jews but not *Shulhan A'rukh* Jews. How on earth am I to convey to you, forward in 1960 or thereabouts, the flavour of this distinction? Well, the *Shulhan A'rukh* was a codification made by Joseph Caro of Safed (which is in Palestine), and published in 1565, of the legalities and illegalities, the things prescribed and the things forbidden, which positively or negatively must be considered binding on a Jew. I don't remember just how many of them there are in Joseph Caro's book, and I don't propose to look it up; but somewhere at the back of my mind is the number six hundred and thirty. You must not imagine, however, that this was the grand total of ordinances which, up till 1565, Jews had held sacred; on the contrary, many thousands of them had accumulated down the Rabbinical centuries, as a stream of clarification had poured in about the precise implication of various Biblical injunctions. What exactly, for instance, did it mean to do no work on the Sabbath? Was it work to blow your nose? The answer (whatever this may have been) was duly given; and so a list was arrived at of the things, many hundreds, that were authoritatively work, and the things, many hundreds, that weren't. Mixed up with all this was the process known as "putting a hedge round the Law". We are commanded, for example, in the Bible to "keep the New Year" on such or such a day of such or such a Hebrew month. Converted, this might mean, say, the twenty-third of September in the year fourteen hundred, or the second of October in the year fourteen hundred and five. But what if there had been an error in calculation? What if the correspondence wasn't exact? In that case you would be breaking the commandment. It followed that you must "keep two days": you must observe the New Year on the twenty-second (or twenty-fourth, I'm not sure which) of September in the year fourteen hundred as well as on the twenty-third, and on the first (or the third) of October in the year fourteen hundred and five as well as on the second.

Now what Joseph Caro did was to cut the thousands and thousands of obligatorinesses down to hundreds and hundreds. These were to be considered the absolute minimum, if you were to call yourself a Jew at all. You will see, therefore, that the *Shulhan A'rukh* was, at the time of its issue, a work of radicalisation; I should imagine, though I really know nothing about it, that among certain sections of sixteenth century opinion it may even have been regarded as a little *link*—a word implying, in Jewish patois, not politically "left", but something a bit off colour, rather lax, not quite *kosher*. It was accepted, however, as authoritative, and has in fact never been superseded; and today it still stands, unless I am mistaken, as the touchstone of Jewish orthodoxy.

But nineteen hundred was a long time away from fifteen hundred and sixty-five, and Elgin Avenue was neither Palestine nor the Polish ghetto. The edge wears off everything; and though we were "strictly orthodox", as my father was at pains to make clear, our orthodoxy was that of English Jews at the turn of the century, and not of the *Shulhan A'rukh*. The latter, for example, forbids you to carry a handkerchief on the Sabbath, unless it's actually sewn to your coat: the theory being that if you carry it loose you are manipulating an external burden, and so "working", whereas if it's sewn to your coat then you and the handkerchief are one. My father carried a handkerchief in the ordinary manner. He went even further after the death of my grandfather, for after a decent interval he gave up "keeping two days". The rot had already set in.

My grandfather, by the way, the Reverend Samuel Marcus Gollancz, was an adorable old gentleman, who had been the *chazan*, or cantor, at the Hambro Synagogue in the East End of London, and had the charming hobby, in addition to his operatic "vocalisation", of carving *objets d'art* out of pebbles and fruit-stones, and of engraving psalms, through a magnifying glass, on the smoothed-away surface of sixpenny bits.

Another of the things he went in for, I believe with beautiful expertise, was the inscribing of *Sifrei Torah*, or Scrolls of the Law; and he managed somehow, diminutive by modern standards though his salary was, not only to bring up a large family in modest comfort but even to send my Aunt Emma, as well as my Uncle Israel, to the University of Cambridge. He died up in semi-rural Cricklewood, whither Jews were then migrating from the East End, at the age of over ninety. What I like most of all to remember about him is that at Bremen, where he was *chazan* for a few years, he was presented, as a tribute to his workmanship in ivory and amber and mother-of-pearl, with a free pass for the opera on Jenny Lind nights.

But though we were not *Shulhan A'rukh* Jews we were orthodox enough. I have mentioned already the ban on Sabbath riding, and the treks on Friday evenings in winter from the Hammersmith Broadway to Maida Vale. But this was only half the story; for winter or summer, wet or dry, there was the forty-minute walk after Saturday breakfast to the Bayswater Synagogue in Chichester Place, and winter or summer, wet or dry, there was the forty-minute walk, after a service of an hour and three quarters, back to Saturday lunch. But wet or dry is an exaggeration. If I thought that there was the slightest hope of sensationally bad weather, I would get up as soon as it was light and anxiously examine the sky; for there was quite a good chance that if it was really pouring cats and dogs, or was obviously very soon going to pour them, my father would announce, to my—I was going to say "to my relief", but that is a feeble expression, for often I would hop from foot to foot in an ecstasy of delight—my father would announce "No Synagogue today". (Not to go would be a pity: to go in a vehicle would be unthinkable.) The anxious question, before promulgation of the decree, was always "Is this *really* cats and dogs?" About the effect on my father, however, of certain more specialised climatic phenomena there could be no possible doubt whatever, and these were therefore more satisfactory: for example fog, ice, and, best of all, an adequate depth of snow.

But what was so terrible, you may ask, about a couple of walks of forty minutes each, particularly in fine weather? Nothing terrible at all. As a matter of fact I have always loved walking, and in almost any weather, fog included; once, during an Oxford vac, I walked in a single day with my friend Paul Hobhouse from Trefriw in North Wales to Llandudno and back again. What was terrible about these walks (apart from the boredom of Synagogue itself) was that willy nilly I *had* to walk them. It was the dead, sterile *compulsion* that was terrible.

It was not only on Saturdays that we had to walk if we wanted to get anywhere. What applied to *Shabbas* applied equally to the first and seventh days of Passover, to the first and seventh days of *Succoth* or the Feast of Tabernacles, to *Shevúoth* or the Feast of Weeks, to the (Jewish) New Year, and to *Kippúr* or the Day of Atonement. Also, during my grandfather's lifetime, to the "second days" of all these various days, except the Day of Atonement. There is no "second day", even, I believe, in the *Shulhan A'rukh*, for the Day of Atonement. And yet the possibility of an error in calculation is as great as in all other cases, and the consequences of it, should it occur, even graver (though the comparative, as you'll see, is quite meaningless); for the tabus of *Kippúr* would be far more tabuish than every other tabu put together, if degrees in tabuishness were admissible. The explanation, which I give as subject to correction from the more learned, is simple. From the "coming in" of the Day of Atonement to its "going out" twenty-four hours later no morsel of food nor drop of drink may pass your lips. A day and night of such abstinence is difficult and sometimes painful for the mean sensual man, however genuinely devout he may be: two of them on end may have been considered impossible.

It was not only riding that was forbidden us on the Sabbath and holydays; there was a wide range of other tabus. One of these, as you know, prohibited any sort of contact (except through Gentile servants or *Shabbas goyim*) with the various forms of "fire", primary or, by a fiction, derivative. To stoke up the fire, or strike a match, or, worst of all, to smoke, would have been to "touch fire" in one or other of its primary forms; to switch on the electric light or ring someone up on the telephone (but not, I think, to answer the telephone if someone else rang you up) would have been to "touch fire" derivatively. Not that we had a telephone at Elgin Avenue; but there were friends of my parents who had, and the religious technique of it was occasionally discussed. But I remember very well when

the electric light was installed—how grand I thought this was!
—in place of incandescent mantles; and I remember very well,
also, sitting one cold winter night on the lavatory seat in pitch
darkness, because I "wasn't allowed" to switch on the electric
light. No one, of course, would have known if I *had* switched it
on; but that was irrelevant; for a reason that will be clear to
you in a very few minutes, one just couldn't do it.

I hope I am right, by the way, in explaining that I couldn't
switch it on because anything electrical was derivatively "fire".
The reason may have been, rather, that electricity was a
*substitute* for "fire", and therefore, partly by extension and partly
by way of "putting a hedge round the Law", automatically
came under the ban. But I don't think so, because the prohibited telephone was a substitute not for "fire" but for human
speech, and this was as freely permitted on *Shabbas* as on weekdays. And now there suddenly occurs to me, apropos of substitu-
tions and derivativenesses, a very probable explanation for the
ban on *Shabbas* riding: namely that (*a*) a horse is a horse, and
neither Jewish nor Gentile (or perhaps always Jewish); (*b*) a
horse, like all other animals, must rest (very properly) on the
Sabbath; (*c*) trains are substitutes for horses.

Another of the things you couldn't do on the Sabbath or
holydays was to write (whether in pencil or in ink) or paint or
play the piano (or any other musical instrument) or saw (I was
at one time rather fond of fretwork) or hit a nail on the head
or use either your right hand or your left in a variety of other
ways too numerous to mention. The reason, doubtless, was that
all such operations were "work". On the other hand you could
open a door or put on your clothes; the reason, doubtless, was
that these operations were necessary. For a short period, when
I was about eight or nine, I imagined, quite erroneously, that
I could paint. I got almost painfully eager about it, as I have
got almost painfully eager about so many other things during
the course of my life. I can see a picture of myself now, as I
write half a century later, up in our old day nursery, with its
bogus mahogany table, one afternoon in December. On the
mantelpiece, above a roaring fire, were my colours and a brush
and a cupful of water; and I was standing with a watch in my
hand, waiting for the exact second at which, on the authority of
the "Jewish Chronicle", Sabbath would that day "go out"
and at last I could paint. The exact second was everything;

the previous second you *couldn't*, the following second you *could*.

I want you to understand if you can, for otherwise you won't get the atmosphere at all, what I may call the hundred per cent character of these prohibitions. I mentioned a minute or two ago that we were forbidden to write. I don't mean by this that we were forbidden to write a book, or an essay, or a long letter, or a short letter, or a sentence, or a word; I mean that we were forbidden to *write*. A minute stroke with a pencil on a piece of paper was as bad as an hour's composition. Nor should I be giving quite the right flavour if I were to say that the whole thing was a "question of principle", and that we were forbidden to make a mark with a pencil because once we did that we might do anything; though some calculation of the kind was also perhaps, though unconsciously, involved. The essence of the matter was that writing as such, the combined operation as such of hand, pencil and paper, was absolutely and irrevocably, not so much wrong or wicked (though it was these too), as impossible. There was however one reservation, and suddenly, as I recall it, all the darkness I have been describing and must describe still further is lit up as with a flash of moral radiance, and I grow ashamed of my criticism, and proud (but why proud? What have I do to with it, though born of the race? But proud, irrationally, none the less)—I grow proud of that essential glory at the heart of Judaism which, for all its fossilisations and obscurations and killings of the spirit by the letter, was nevertheless destined, through Christianity, to sow good seeds in a stony world: and one day those seeds, though as yet hardly stirring, will grow high above the ground and make a tabernacle; and in the shadow of it, please God, Timothy, some generation of your descendants shall establish, or help others to establish, the divine Kingdom foreshadowed in our history, and guaranteed by the example, thereafter always present, of Jesus Christ. The reservation was this. You could drive, write, or telephone on the Sabbath; you could break every injunction in the *Shulhan A'rukh*; you could even eat pig on the Day of Atonement: if by so doing you could save, or might conceivably be able to save, a single human life.

Does this reservation seem quite natural and obvious, and nothing to be making such a bother about? But if you think that, it's because you don't understand the really awful compulsiveness of these various tabus. There hung about them a sense of quite inescapable finality. If you ate, for instance, on the Day of Atonement you "cut yourself off from among your people"; you were finished, God had cast you out, you were no longer a Jew. And what the reservation was saying was this: that beyond all these many finalities there was nevertheless one, but only one, still more final finality, namely the sacredness of human life. All this came back to me one Saturday early in 1943, when I was rung up on the telephone by a Rabbi well known for his ultra-orthodoxy, in connection with some detail of the campaign, with which I was then helping, of the National Committee for Rescue from Nazi Terror. When we had finished our conversation I asked him, having forgotten the reservation, how he came to telephone on *Shabbas*. "It's a question of saving life," he replied, clearly as astonished by the stupidity of my question as I was delighted by the unstuffiness of his reply.

All the year round, on weekdays as well as on Sabbaths and holydays, we had with us, as a kind of ubiquitous background wherever we might be, the dietary laws. It was not only a question of the many things we couldn't eat: pork, ham and bacon; crabs, lobsters and shell-fish of every kind; eels (because they hadn't got fins—but why on earth should anybody want to eat the slithery things anyhow?) and game (because it was shot). It was a question of *kashrus* in a far wider sense than that, *kashrus* being a noun derived from the adjective *kosher*, which literally means clean in the ritual sense, but is applicable by extension to anything decent, proper, *comme il faut*, or in a word "Jewish". There are many divisions and subdivisions of *kashrus*. One of the most important is derivable from a passage in the Pentateuch which lays it down that, while the flesh of certain animals may be eaten, given an absence of "blemishes" and with a number of other provisos, nevertheless "thou shalt not eat the blood, for the blood is the life". This is a magnificent prohibition. There's nothing specially Jewish about it, for a similar or identical tabu has been found among Estonians, various Indian tribes, the Malepa in South Africa, and many others; and it is allied to a more general blood tabu very common among primitive peoples. At the back of it is the idea that

the soul, which is in the blood, is somehow awful: and what is
that but a groping realisation that all life is sacred? To act in
the spirit of Leviticus, for a modern man, is to be a vegetarian;
and at this point I shall break in on my description of *kashrus*,
and say something I've wanted to say for ages about
vegetarianism.

# CHAPTER VIII

# AN INTERLUDE ABOUT VEGETARIANISM, WITH A REMARK OR TWO ABOUT PSYCHOANALYSIS

THERE IS A GOOD deal of misunderstanding about vegetarianism: I do not mean the vegetarianism of health faddists, but what is called "religious" or "conscientious" vegetarianism. The cruelty behind meat-eating and fish-eating is only half the story. It may even be that sometimes there is no cruelty at all. I happened to be at a party here in Brimpton last night at which the matter was discussed, and I was informed that cold-blooded animals (namely fish) feel no pain when their mouths are impaled on a hook and they are dragged panting from the river. I know nothing of biology or neurology or whichever other of the sciences may be involved, and so I must say humbly that my informant may have been right; but I shall also say arrogantly that I feel pretty certain he was wrong. I was further informed that lobsters (which, I gathered, have for some reason to be cooked alive) feel no pain if gradually boiled, but only if they are plunged suddenly into scalding water, which is a thing, therefore, that you shouldn't do. When I asked how anybody could know what the lobster felt, I was told that in the one case (that of sudden immersion) there were twitchings or other physiological reactions, whereas in the other (that of gradual boiling) there were none. Maybe. But apart from the question of cruelty, which is vital—and I think it humbug to assert that a lamb feels no fear when being led to the slaughter, and no pain at the moment of it—the point is that, cruelty or no cruelty, fear or no fear, pain or no pain, by killing an animal for the pleasure of eating it you are stopping something precious and happy, and diminishing the hymn of thanksgiving to the Creator. A life that hopped or sang or gambolled or browsed is suddenly, by your action, no more. Nature is red in tooth and claw, undoubtedly, and hawks will kill sparrows anyhow; but men are spiritual and thus superior to nature, and they dehumanise themselves when they imitate it. Let us at least go so far as to realise that when we kill any creature, even necessarily as we may honestly think, we do it a wrong. Everybody feels this, surely, about an animal they *know*. A week or so ago we "put to sleep", Ruth and I, our old dog Spottle, who had been our companion for more than sixteen years. He was still enjoying life for a greater part of the time, but suddenly, at that great age for a terrier, had grown quarrelsome and almost savage, and, courteous gentleman as till then he had invariably been, was endangering the life of our gentle cocker Sambo. As he lay dead on the kitchen table after a quick injection, we both knew that, necessary though our action might have been, we must beg for his forgiveness.

I would ask opponents of vegetarianism to reflect for a moment about a slaughterhouse in England or a stockyard in Chicago, and then to read this passage from *The Life of Blessed Henry Suso by Himself*:

"I place before my inward eyes myself with all that I am— my body, soul, and all my powers—and I gather round me all the creatures which God ever created in heaven, on earth, and in all the elements, each one severally with its name, whether birds of the air, beasts of the forests, fishes of the water, leaves and grass of the earth, or the innumerable sand of the sea, and to these I add all the little specks of dust which glance in the sunbeams, with all the little drops of water which ever fell or are falling from dew, snow, or rain, and I wish that each of these had a sweetly sounding stringed instrument, fashioned from my heart's inmost blood, striking on which they might each send up to our dear and gentle God a new and lofty strain of praise for ever and ever. And then the loving arms of my soul stretch out and extend themselves towards the innumerable multitude of all creatures, and my intention is, just as a free and blithesome leader of a choir stirs up the singers of his company, even so to turn them all to good account by inviting them to sing joyously, and to offer up their hearts to God. 'Sursum corda.' "

You will assume from what you have just been reading that I am myself a vegetarian. I am, of course, in theory—I am utterly convinced that it is wrong to kill animals for food, or to acquiesce in the killing of them by eating their corpses—but not, I am very much ashamed to confess, in practice. I was a strict vegetarian, in practice as well as in theory, for the two or three years up to a year or so before I went to Oxford. But gradually I began to compromise, and within a few months I had become the flesh-eater which, with continuous stirrings of a normally faint but sometimes obtrusive uneasiness, I have been ever since. I cannot remember the reasons for my apostasy. It certainly didn't spring from any desire to conform, for this was never a temptation to me; nor from a dislike of making a nuisance of myself and demanding special arrangements and generally upsetting things, for consideration of that kind was no part, I fear, of my attitude to my parents. Nor again, I think, was it then, as it surely is now, the result of moral weakness—of my pleasure in attractive meals proving stronger than my sense of what was decent. There was no question, during my vegetarian period, of my *wanting* to eat flesh, and of fighting this desire with eventual defeat; it was a question, rather, of fighting, towards the end of that period, a hatred of flesh-eating that had become all but compulsive. Even when I was able to eat meat again I could not cut it at first with an ordinary steel knife, for this I thought cannibalistic; I divided it painfully with the sharpest silver fish-knife I could find.

Psychologists will probably see in this latter curiosity a proof that the whole episode of my vegetarianism was nothing but a manifestation of suppressed sadism. Now let us be clear about all this.

First, some vegetarians, undoubtedly, *are* suppressed sadists; others, just as undoubtedly, are not. Take the analogous case of pacifism. There is a certain type of pacifist, whom we will call pacifist number one. He may be a man in whose make-up, deep down to the roots, there is more than the usual quota of gentleness and compassion; or he may be a man who is responsive beyond the average to spiritual realities; or he may be a man who has observed on his daily occasions that violence breeds violence while a soft answer turneth away wrath; or he may be a man who has concluded from his study of history that "war settles nothing"; and so on. A man of this or that type is a man of this or that type, and not of some suppressed other type: when Christ, for instance, told us to love our enemies "that we might be the children of our Father which is in heaven", he said it because he was divine, not because deep down in his subconscious he hated his enemies and felt a sexual craving to torture them. But there is another type of pacifist, whom we will call pacifist number two. He is indeed a specially neurotic person (we are all, fortunately, neurotic to a certain degree) who is "compensating" by his pacifism for aggressive or sadistic drives of an unusually powerful kind. And the two types must not be confused (though there are mixed types) and it must not be imagined that because some pacifists are neurotic, all are. And as with pacifists, so with vegetarians.

Secondly, my silver fish-knife proves nothing about the roots of my own vegetarianism. It may have been a sign that to cut and tear was what I secretly longed for: but it may have been a sign, equally, that I was a respecter of life *pur sang*, who was attempting to hide from his conscience. And it may have been a sign that the elements were mixed in me.

But suppose, thirdly, that my silver fish-knife proved the utmost anybody could want it to prove; and suppose that all vegetarianism, and all pacifism, and all humanitarianism, were sadistic in origin: this would not discredit my vegetarianism etcetera, or vegetarianism etcetera in general. Because it is from something "lower" that, by a process of compensation, something "higher" emerges, this doesn't discredit the something higher or make it less valuable: but shows that in the graciousness of a divine economy something higher may be occasioned by something lower. If, deep down, you have a rather unusual amount of destructiveness in you, and for that very reason behave with a rather unusual amount of gentleness, the gentleness is not any the less good because the destructiveness is bad: the gentleness is not robbed of its good, the destructiveness is robbed of its evil. The specially gentle man who is specially gentle because in his basic drives he is specially aggressive is not so valuable a creature, admittedly, as the specially gentle man who is specially gentle simply because he is specially gentle, for the latter is purer in heart; but a person who is specially gentle for any reason whatever is more valuable a person than the person who isn't. If, nonsensically, all humanitarians were in fact suppressed sadists —including people who don't shoot birds on the wing, or hunt terrified animals for enjoyment—then the more suppressed sadists the better.

(Apropos of hunting and shooting, I was spending a weekend last winter with some friends in a neighbouring county who

were all Christians: not nominal Christians, but deeply concerned with their religion, and rather given to discussing it: and,
apart from that, exceptionally decent and kind. Well, on the
Saturday afternoon a party of them went off shooting, and
I couldn't help referring to the matter when they came home
to tea. All but one of them were obviously thinking that
this was just another of Victor's eccentricities, but that one
seemed a trifle troubled: so to save him from embarrassment
I said "Anyhow, it's not like hunting: it's all over in a
second." "Oh no," said another, "you should see a bird lying
on the ground with its wing broken." And this was a good man,
a gentle man, not at all a callous man. I give it up.)

Don't imagine that I've just been attacking psychoanalysis,
or modern psychology in general. On the contrary, I regard
Freud as one of the supreme benefactors of the human race,
though I disagree as completely as possible with some of his
fundamental positions. What I am attacking is the attitude of
people who imagine they've explained away something "good"
when they've discovered something "bad" at the back of it,
whereas they've really, in a sense, explained away something
bad by discovering something good as the end of it. How, then,
could I attack psychoanalysis, which is always trying to help
people "sublimate"?

Having hit on this subject accidentally, however, I shall take
the opportunity—for one of my pleasures in writing this letter
is that I can say anything I like on any topic I like in any order I
like—I shall take the opportunity of attacking, not psychoanalysis in suitable cases, but the attitude of mind that regards
all inner conflicts as undesirable, and to be done away with as
completely as possible by whatever kind of "treatment" may
prove most effective. This attitude is quite common in England
among intellectuals of a certain type, or was when they had
enough money for the purpose; and in America the thing is
a perfect craze—in moneyed circles with a tinge of culture
people talk of "my analyst" as glibly as our grandmothers
used to talk of "my grocer", or as business men talk of "my
chauffeur". You sometimes get an impression in the States that
"my analyst" is a glorified version of the little black boy who
pirouettes on with the Marschallin's chocolate in the first act
of *Rosenkavalier* and pirouettes off with her handkerchief in the
last.

The motive of such people, when it's something more than merely to be in the fashion, may be a frankly commercial one: once you've been psychoanalysed, they may imagine, your social life will be smoother, you'll "make friends and influence people" more easily, you'll buy better, you'll sell better, and, in a word, whether as hostess or salesman or whatever else it may be you'll "get on". The motive, on the other hand—and this alone need concern us—may be to save themselves from inner turmoil: to get rid of fears, hatreds, irrationalities, compulsions and the rest: in a word, to live at peace with themselves and their neighbours.

Now a man may be such, or may have become such, that he cannot win through to any sort of fruitful living solely by his own effort and the unmediated grace of God. In that event there is need of aid from without. The helper may be, in the broadest sense, a priest: and by a priest I mean anybody, from a priest in the dictionary sense to a friend or just someone now living or long since dead, who by finding the right words, or by putting himself in the right relation, or (perhaps best of all) simply by example, becomes the mediator of God's grace. But the helper may also be an analyst: and an analyst will make the man far more of a man if he frees him for fruitful inner struggles by freeing him from the compulsion of sterile ones. But to free a man not for the right kind of conflict but from conflict as such, that is another matter; and to be freed in this way is sometimes a man's aim in seeking treatment, and sometimes, anyhow, what results from it. There are people who desire, morally as well as otherwise, too quiet a life.

For the struggle in our own hearts between the better and the worse in us, the higher and the lower: between generosity and meanness, mercy and ruthlessness, well-wishing and ill-wishing, gentleness and aggression, respect and contempt, tolerance and intolerance, humility and pride; this struggle is not something undesirable, something to be magicked away for the speedier calming of the turmoil within, but the very stuff and meaning of us as living human souls. The plain fact is that, whatever may be the explanation in terms of psychology or physiology or metaphysics or religion, we *are*, to a greater or lesser degree, mean and proud and revengeful and aggressive and egoistical; and we know quite as plainly, by a direct and immediate knowledge, that we ought not to be. So we struggle

against our meanness and pride and aggressiveness and egoism
because, compelled by some responsibility that seems put upon
us in the nature of things, we feel we must. Somehow, we
apprehend, these impulses within us are of a nature that spoils;
they darken the universe; and since we alone can subdue them,
if we make no effort to do so we are like a Moses who would
have refused to speak for God because he stammered, or like
an Isaiah who, after his mouth had been touched by the live
coal, would have failed to answer "Send me." There is a
passage in *The Will to Believe*, by William James, which expresses
what I have been trying to say with superb clarity:

"I confess that I do not see why the very existence of an
invisible world may not in part depend on the personal
response which any one of us may make to the religious appeal.
God himself, in short, may draw vital strength and increase of
very being from our fidelity. For my own part, I do not know
what the sweat and blood and tragedy of this life mean, if they
mean anything short of this. If this life be not a real fight, in
which something is eternally gained for the universe by success,
it is no better than a game of private theatricals from which one
may withdraw at will. But it *feels* like a real fight,—as if there
were something really wild in the universe which we, with all
our idealities and faithfulnesses, are needed to redeem; and
first of all to redeem our own hearts from atheisms and fears.
For such a half-wild half-saved universe our nature is adapted.
The deepest thing in our nature is this dumb region of the
heart in which we dwell alone with our willingnesses and our
unwillingnesses, our faiths and our fears. As through the cracks
and crannies of caverns those waters exude from the earth's
bosom which then form the fountain-heads of springs, so in
these crepuscular depths of personality the sources of all our
outer deeds and decisions take their rise. Here is our deepest
organ of communication with the nature of things; and compared with these concrete movements of our soul all abstract
statements and scientific arguments—the veto, for example,
which the strict positivist pronounces upon our faith—sound
to us like mere chatterings of the teeth . . .

"These then are my last words to you: Be not afraid of life.
Believe that life *is* worth living, and your belief will help
create the fact. The 'scientific' proof that you are right may

not be clear before the day of judgment (or some stage of being which that expression may serve to symbolise) is reached. But the faithful fighters of this hour, or the beings that then and there will represent them, may turn to the faint-hearted, who here decline to go on, with words like those with which Henry IV greeted the tardy Crillon after a great battle had been gained: 'Hang yourself, brave Crillon! We fought at Arques, and you were not there!' "

"The sweat and blood and tragedy of this life." This is a reality and has meaning, just as the joy of this life is a reality and has meaning; and if we attempt to escape it, if we attempt to end the conflict within us, and the agony that this conflict involves, by being *acted upon*, we are giving up reality and becoming less than fully human. It is the tension of this struggle that gives us our glory: it makes us rich and meaningful, allies of and fellow workers with the divine. Or, to put it in another way, it is the combination of the evil within us and our struggle against it—precisely this—that produces, in every one of us save those rare souls that are born almost without sin, the very best of which we are capable: that produces a value greater than could ever have been there if neither evil nor struggle had existed. So evil, though a terrible reality for *us* and to be struggled against without respite, is, as I have already said, in ultimate reality non-existent: the evil and the conflict are instruments, both, of a final "rightness" beyond good and evil. The world, as Keats said in a famous letter, is the vale of soul-making: "Do you not see how necessary a World of Pains and troubles is to school an Intelligence and make it a Soul?"

Saul was cruel, intolerant, a persecutor: when cruel, intolerant, and a persecutor he was struggling already with the struggle that reached its climax on the road to Damascus: and Saul became Paul. Paul preached the gospel of love: and Paul would not have loved with Paul's love if Saul had not hated with Saul's hatred: and Paul and Saul were one: and when hating and persecuting, indeed by hating and persecuting, he was reaching out to the same reality and truth—to what, as creatures, we must call the same goodness—as he was reaching out to when he wrote the thirteenth chapter of the first epistle to the Corinthians. Would we have had this man *acted upon*—by anyone except the God in his heart and in the universe?

There is a sense, I must hasten to add, in which to be at peace with oneself and to be freed from the conflict is to have achieved a saving wisdom. Peace so comes when we have learned to accept, not so much with resignation as with a dutiful response to reality, the evil we confront as a part of our nature. We no longer hate ourselves for being what we are; we no longer blaspheme because we have been created just so and not otherwise; we are no longer in revolt, with an insolent egoism, against our own imperfection. We are content, in a word, to be men and not God. The struggle continues, for to accept ourselves for what we are is by no means to abandon the effort to change; the struggle, indeed, is more intense than before; but we struggle now with greater calm (and therefore with more depth), with a sort of detachment from any personal interestedness—we no longer desire to be good because of the *we*, but because of the *good*—and with a love of ourselves as well as with a love of our neighbours. And we struggle now with a greater steadiness. Before, we felt at every defeat as if we had failed in the final examination; now, the past is always irrelevant and the next attempt is all that matters.

There is nothing more precious in life than the gaining of this inner tranquillity. But it comes to very few (if, when it does come, it is really to be of the kind I have been attempting to describe) except after a long period of agony. For the agony is a preparation for the peace, which is something not to be induced, mechanically, from without, but to be won, in freedom and responsibility, from within.


Well, to get back to vegetarianism, my own, whatever its origin, was over in practice before I went to Oxford. My motive for never resuming it during the thirty-nine years that have since gone by is as obvious to me as my motive for once abandoning it is obscure. Moral weakness, as I have already said, is the explanation. Vegetarianism involves discomforts and inconveniences of various kinds, and these I have always disliked. What is more important, I greatly enjoy good food and good cooking (though I'm nothing of an expert in either): and having tried quite a number of vegetarian restaurants, I must say plainly, at the risk of a collective libel action, that the food-and-cooking combination provided is so monotonous, unappetising, sawdusty, and sometimes even, in the root sense of the word, nauseating, that my one idea has been, after a first bite at the nut cutlet or mock chicken, to get away from the place just as quickly as possible.

I should abandon with regret, too, what is always a great pleasure to me: the occasional feast at a restaurant of the first order, with its ritual of dishes and wines—can you imagine wanting to drink a fine claret with mock chicken or nut cutlets?—and its atmosphere of gaiety and good-fellowship. Such feasts can be best when they are feasts for two. Ruth and I have shared many of them all over Europe. There was the little inn a few miles' drive from Montpellier, on our way down to Beauvallon for the sun and the sea. It was a quite unpretentious sort of place, and no one seemed about; but we were told after a few minutes that if we sat on the balcony above a stream and waited a bit they would cook us something. They first brought us bread, and we amused ourselves by throwing little pellets of it into the water, and watching the fish play polo with them. Then the feast began to arrive: an omelette first: fish, chicken and cheese: and we were very happy. (Opposite were some Utrilloish houses.) Walterspiel's in Munich, on the other hand, was not at all unpretentious. It was attached to the Vier Jahreszeiten Hotel, which afterwards, to our distress, became a Nazi Headquarters: and there one evening we had, among other things, their special contrivance of turkey or goose, I don't remember which, cut up into pieces and cooked inside a series of trépanned melons; and Richard Strauss was sitting at the next table.

What a catalogue I could make of the meals that I specially remember! There were the open-air lunches at Ledoyen, with the chestnut-trees in blossom, and petrol smelling faintly, and the cars, smooth and muted, on their way to the Etoile or the Place de la Concorde; and a special sort of cheese, capped with cinnamon, that we eat one July afternoon by a window on the courtyard at Avallon; and *médaillons de veau Orly* at Lapérouse. And there was our lunch this Christmas at the Vert Galant. We had ordered, to end with, *crêpes Suzette*; and the tall head waiter, who had an immensely broad stripe down the leg of each trouser, did a strange sort of ritual dance as he attended to his incipient *crêpes*, tossing them with a flick of his wrist out of one pan and catching them in another, and so *vice versa* and *ad infinitum*: a statuesque dance, but springy too: rather like Sir Thomas Beecham's, when, chin up and foot pointing downwards, he encourages now the fiddles to left and now the fiddles to right in a symphony by Haydn or Mozart.

There is a mingling of pleasure and joy on such occasions: pleasure in satisfying so exquisitely the sense of taste, and joy in sharing this pleasure with a person or persons you love. Added are all sorts of other elements, such as agreeable conversation (or sometimes silence), and the sight of beauty as you sit in the open or look out from a window, and the atmosphere of gregariousness: a gregariousness in which you and your party are nevertheless not completely involved, for you are making the best of both worlds, the world of the herd and the world of intimates. But apart from the unseemliness of luxury in a civilisation where millions are starving there is a shadow at the back of all this, for the price of it is the murder of living and rejoicing things. This shadow becomes dark and menacing to me whenever the reality obtrudes, in the shape of fishmongers' and butchers' shops, and underdone steaks, and the loathsome query *saignant?*, and scales on sardines, and the word "brains" on a menu, and *poussins* complete, and a sole from which an ass of a waiter (or should it be the chef?) has forgotten to remove the head. One day I shall give up flesh-eating, and live decently. But time is getting short, for I am approaching sixty.

# CHAPTER IX

# JEWISH ORTHODOXY (RESUMED)

MY FATHER WOULD have been exceedingly astonished at the idea of this excursus on vegetarianism (with some remarks on psychoanalysis thrown in) resulting from a reference to the Biblical injunction "But the blood thou shalt not eat, for the blood is the life", and perhaps equally astonished by my having made such a reference at all in connection with practices I am about to describe; for though he knew the connection— even the most ignorant Jew did that, and my father was by no means ignorant but, on the contrary, a bit of a *melammed* or learned man—it had long since ceased to have the slightest living relevance: you did certain things simply because there were certain things that you did. Among the things you did under this particular heading of "thou shalt not eat the blood" were the following. First of all you killed the animal (a chicken as well as a sheep or bullock or calf) in a special way, described, accurately but disagreeably, as "ritual slaughter". This consists in cutting the windpipe so as to drain off the blood, though I understand it drains off very little. You will probably be anticipating a short digression here on the pros and cons of ritual slaughter; and on whether, as is alleged in little pamphlets that are occasionally sent me, it ought to be prohibited as unnecessarily cruel. The answer is that I don't know, and I shall therefore refrain from discussing the matter. I am inclined to believe, on the whole, that there's very little to choose, from the animal's point of view, between "ritual slaughter" and what is officially described as the "humane killer"; and that some of the pamphlets in question emanate (I judge this by their tone) from more or less professional antisemites. But this is a mere impression. There is something else, however, about which I can be very definite indeed. If you had been able to demonstrate that "ritual slaughter" involved the most atrocious cruelty, and with such evidence as would immediately have convinced any ordinary human being who was capable of uninhibited reasoning, this would not have made the slightest difference to the overwhelming majority of orthodox

Jews: not because Jews as such are unusually indifferent to cruelty, which is nonsense, but because something deeper and more compulsive than reasoning would so automatically have determined their reaction to your evidence that immediately, and quite honestly at the ordinary level of honesty, it would have impinged on them either as faulty or as faked, or even as evidence to the contrary. They *had* to have their ritual slaughter; it was something that as a Jew you imperatively *did*, something you couldn't possibly *not* do without becoming the sort of person you couldn't possibly *be*: but cruelty was repugnant to them; so ritual slaughter just wasn't cruel, whatever arguments the ill-disposed—for how could a man be other than ill-disposed if he attacked something Jewish and therefore self-evidently proper?—might dishonestly bring forward. You will understand very imperfectly what I am trying to explain to you if you fail to realise that the *rationale* of this method of killing had become almost entirely irrelevant.

Ritual slaughter was only the first stage in the process of draining the blood. When you got the meat home you soaked it in a bowl, and then laid it out on a contrivance of wooden slats in the sink, and left it there with a covering of salt on it for a certain length of time. I don't remember how long this was; I think two hours, but Ruth tells me that I am exaggerating, and that half an hour is nearer the mark. Perhaps the time varied as between one household and another, for Ruth's parents were "reform"; and it is possible that *Shulhan A'rukh* Jews were more *froom*—more strict—in this matter even than such ordinarily orthodox Jews as my parents, and let the meat soak longer. The purpose of the soaking and salting was to get rid of any blood that, in spite of the ritual slaughtering, might still remain in the animal's carcase. I don't know whether the process was scientifically sound, but it certainly wasn't a hundred per cent effective. Sometimes, before my vegetarian days, I would cut some little vein in a slice of mutton, and a gout of blood would ooze out and mingle with the red currant jelly. I was always horrified, but such an occurrence did not worry my parents in the least. The meat had been properly killed, properly soaked, and properly salted, so officially the blood didn't exist.

A minor matter, if one can talk of minor and major in connection with a ritual that was uniformly sacrosanct, was the process called "porging". I don't know the origin of the word, nor even if it was spelled in this way, and I have been unable to find it in the two-volume Oxford Dictionary; but this is certainly how it was pronounced. Will you read the Bible, Timothy, when you grow up? I suppose not, for few of the young people seem to do so nowadays. This is a pity, for the New Testament is the greatest book in the world, and the Old is only second to it for beauty and wisdom, and the two of them, read selectively, can teach you how to live as few other books can. In any case, I shall give myself the pleasure of writing down for you (being unable to recite it, as I should prefer) the magnificent and mysterious story of Jacob and the angel in the thirty-second chapter of Genesis, beginning with verse twenty-four:

"And Jacob was left alone; and there wrestled a man with him until the breaking of the day.

"And when he saw that he prevailed not against him, he touched the hollow of his thigh; and the hollow of Jacob's thigh was out of joint as he wrestled with him.

"And he said, Let me go, for the day breaketh. And he said, I will not let thee go, except thou bless me.

"And he said unto him, What is thy name? And he said, Jacob.

"And he said, Thy name shall be called no more Jacob, but Israel: for as a prince thou hast power with God and with men, and hast prevailed.

"And Jacob asked him and said, Tell me, I pray thee, thy name. And he said, Wherefore is it that thou dost ask after my name? And he blessed him there.

"And Jacob called the name of the place Peniel: for I have seen God face to face, and my life is preserved.

"And as he passed over Penuel the sun rose upon him, and he halted upon his thigh.

"Therefore the children of Israel eat not of the sinew which shrank, which is upon the hollow of the thigh, unto this day: because he touched the hollow of Jacob's thigh in the sinew that shrank."

The last verse of this great passage, which seems to bring one, naïvely and primitively, into contact with something ineffable at the very heart of reality, does not mean that the children of Israel eat not of the sinew upon the hollow of Jacob's thigh unto this day, a thing anyhow impossible: it means that they eat not of what is held to be the corresponding sinew in a leg of mutton, and indeed in hindquarters generally. Why they don't isn't clear to me, nor is the connection between these animals and Jacob: but they don't: and the excision of the sinew, together with that of certain specified fats and blood-vessels, is called porging. I mention leg of mutton in particular, because it was always leg of mutton I heard about: perhaps because the porging of leg of mutton is specially hazardous, so that the housewife must satisfy herself that it has been properly done before the meat is delivered at the area door. Many years after the time of which I am writing, when I was already married and the father of my first baby, I heard a rumour to the effect that the *Beth Din* (which means "House of the Law", and makes authoritative pronouncements on ritual questions) had taken drastic action in this matter. Discovering, perhaps, that butchers had been growing slack, it prohibited leg of mutton altogether.

Porging, however, was a detail that had begun and ended long before the dining-room stage (or in the case of Elgin Avenue the downstairs breakfast-room stage) had been reached. Very obtrusive at this stage, on the other hand, was the whole series of minutiae that spread out from the centre of "milk and meat". There is a passage in the Pentateuch that runs thus: "Thou shalt not seethe a kid in his mother's milk." Whatever may be the origin of this prohibition if you dig deep enough, of itself it is gracious and humane. It expresses that "reverence for life" which Albert Schweitzer has been trying so long, and so vainly, to teach the world; and to observe it, for a modern man, is to let the kid gambol and not seethe it at all. But the vast superstructure that has been built on the basis of the injunction—how incredible this is, and yet, in a sense, how intellectually delightful! It wasn't a question with my parents, or with orthodox Jews generally, of not cooking a kid in its mother's milk, or of not cooking any other sort of animal in its mother's milk, or of not cooking any sort of animal in any sort of milk whatsoever; it was a question of ensuring, by a long series of devices that provided for all conceivable possibilities, that nothing derived from meat and nothing derived from milk should ever come into any sort of relation with one another. My parents, naturally, didn't invent these devices; they were fixed and static, things you learned from your parents, things you *did*. You neither added to them nor subtracted from them ("a jot or tittle of the Law"): they were there: you observed them.

*Imprimis*—not that the primary applications of the prohibition were any more binding than the secondary or most remote— you didn't cook any kind of meat with milk or with any of its products. As an extension of this, you had a rigidly separate set of utensils for cooking or in any way dealing with meat things and milk things respectively. There were two sets of pots and pans, two sets of plates, two sets of knives and forks, two sets of spoons. If some accident occurred, and owing perhaps to the stupidity of a *goyische* maid a meat thing was contaminated with milk or a milk thing with meat, there were various ways of dealing with the catastrophe—and I assure you that in using the word catastrophe I am by no means exaggerating the local reaction. If a plate was involved, you smashed it and threw it in the dustbin. If a pan had been misused, there was some special method of scouring it. If a meat knife had come into contact with butter or cheese, or *vice versa* and *mutatis mutandis*, you buried it in the earth and then used it again for its legitimate purpose: the idea being, I like to think (but possibly I'm inventing), that Mother Earth cleanses as nothing else can. This, at any rate, was the method adopted by my parents: "with my own eyes" I saw my mother doing it in an English garden at the beginning of the twentieth century: and I would have you know that my mother was a cultivated lady, who had once had a piano lesson from Vladimir Pachmann, and "read" at the Reading Room of the British Museum, and wrote plays. But though this was my parents' practice, and therefore good orthodox practice, I'm not sure that it was *Shulhan A'rukh* practice; a *Shulhan A'rukh* Jew, I rather think, threw the knife away.

What applied in this matter of "milk and meat" to externalities, such as knives and forks and pots and pans, applied even more (or would have if that had been possible, which it wasn't) to internalities, namely the human body. To eat bread and butter with a slice of meat would have been unthinkable; and as to eating butter *on* meat, this would have been the final abomination (but see the bracket above). Many years after leaving Oxford I was giving lunch at the Ivy to a very fat man who had been Rabbi, in America, to a "reform" congregation: it follows that he was exceedingly *link*. He first called for a

porter-house steak, which is something you will never have
heard of: so multiply an ordinary large steak, the largest you
can think of, by three or four (if you don't know what an
ordinary steak looks like either, ask your mother to explain) and
you'll get the idea. I was rather distressed, because I was poor,
and even in those days a porter-house steak cost nine shillings.
He next asked that his steak should be "rare", and this distressed me still more, for a reason with which you are already
familiar: "rare" being on the very verge of, if not equivalent to,
*saignant*, which means "bleeding". Finally, he called for a large
pat of butter, put it on the purplish mass, and kneaded it home
with his meat knife. I was no longer merely distressed: I was
faint and sick with an atavistic horror.

But lack of simultaneity in the eating of "milk" and "meat"
was by no means sufficient; a certain interval must elapse
between the two processes, to prevent the forbidden mixture
from occurring inside. Thus not only were you strictly limited
in the choice of what you might have for the sweet course if the
main course had been meat, anything involving milk or cream
or cheese being impossible, but you had to wait quite a time
—interminably, as it seemed to my impatience—before eating a penn'orth of milk chocolate after lunching on beef. I
don't remember just how long; the practice probably varied.
Theoretically, you had no doubt to have digested (though not
presumably to have evacuated) the one element before super-
imposing the other.

There were special dietary regulations, on top of the ones
just described, for Passover. During the seven days of this
festival, as everyone knows, Jews eat motzas, or unleavened
cakes, instead of bread, in commemoration of the flight from
Egypt. "And they baked unleavened cakes of the dough which
they brought forth out of Egypt, for it was not leavened;
because they were thrust out of Egypt, and could not tarry,
neither had they prepared for themselves any victual." The
motzas—large, round, thin and brittle biscuits, with tiny
hillocks and valleys all over them in brown and white—are
extremely palatable, and when I was a boy people who were
neither *Shulhan A'rukh* Jews, nor ordinary orthodox Jews, nor
even perhaps reform Jews or liberal Jews, but still "Jews at
heart", used to make the best of both worlds and eat bread
and motzas simultaneously. And here I would mention a very

curious trait in my father's character, which is relevant for the
effect, positive and negative, that he had on me and that
presently I am going to describe. Being "strictly orthodox"
himself, he would sooner have died, almost and perhaps quite
literally, than eat anything remotely connected with bread on
the Passover. Nor was he, other things being equal, at all a
tolerant man: it was no part of his general philosophy of life
that what he did was his affair and that what other people did
was theirs: on the contrary "he hoped he knew what was
correct", and what was correct for him was correct, other
things again being equal, for the next man. But the "other
things being equal" was curiously applied, though without the
smallest element, I am convinced, of conscious hypocrisy. If,
for instance, he had heard that Sir Moses X or Baron Y—
famous and distinguished Jews, playing quite a prominent part
in English public life, and perhaps even accepted, or almost
accepted, in English "society": men, let us say, of the kind
once described by the French *restaurateur* Henri as "those rich
and great ones"—if he had heard that Sir Moses X or Baron Y
was in the habit of providing both bread and motzas at the
Passover table, he would probably have murmured, with a
rather charming smile, "Very nice", as he often used to murmur
it in other but very similar religious connections: the "very
nice" applying, you will understand, to the eating by such
people of motzas, not to their eating of bread. What he liked
about it, and this was to his honour, was that they were not
ashamed of showing their "Jewishness". But if he had heard
the same thing about any "ordinary" Jew his concentration
would have been on the bread and not on the motzas, and
there wouldn't have been anything nice about it at all.

I used the words just now "anything remotely connected
with bread". The degree of remoteness which was held nevertheless to involve a connection will seem incredible to you.
Before Passover "came in" every corner of the house was
spring-cleaned, to remove any remnant of 'hōmetz or leaven;
and as each room in turn was made ready it was metaphorically
sealed up, the greatest care being taken to keep 'hōmetz away
from it. Then, on the eve of the festival, a symbolic ceremony
was enacted. A tiny piece of bread had been carefully placed
on the corner of a mantelpiece. This was "discovered", swept
off by my father (as head of the household) with a feather, and

thrown away. The house was now *pāsachdich*, or clean for the
Passover.

You will probably have anticipated what I am now going to
tell you; namely that no cooking or eating utensil of any kind
that had ever come into contact with '*hōmetz* could be used
until *Pāsach* had ended. There was a separate set of Passover
knives and forks, a separate set of Passover plates, a separate
set of Passover pots and pans, a separate set of Passover spoons;
or rather separate sets; for since "meat and milk" applied quite
as strictly to Passover as to the rest of the year there had to be
two sets for Passover on top of the two normal sets for the other
fifty-one weeks. As to the food itself, everything, including
anything that would normally have come from a *goyische* shop,
had now to be got either from a Jewish shop or from a *goyische*
shop which, like the then newly established Selfridge's, had a
special *Pāsach* department supervised and certified by the
Ecclesiastical Authorities: the point being that by this pre-
caution the possibility of any previous contamination by
'*hōmetz* was held to be satisfactorily ruled out. This ritual
punctilio had certain advantages from the sensual point of
view. Instead of ordinary biscuits or cakes there were delightful
confections of a rich brown, riven by little chasms on the
surface and coated with powdery white; they were called
cinnamon balls, and were exclusively of Jewish (which may
have meant of East European) manufacture. But best of all was
the cheese. Only one kind of cheese could be eaten at Passover;
it was of Dutch type, very soft but without either flabbiness or
liquidity, very full in flavour but also very mild. I never quite
understood how it had come about that Passover cheese, and
Passover cheese exclusively, *was* Passover cheese. Possibly one
particular Dutch-Jewish product had traditionally established
itself as the best and purest obtainable: purity being of particular importance at Passover. Or were there special cows,
uncontaminated by '*hōmetz*? Anyhow, I should be inclined to
say that I have never eaten such wonderful cheeses since, did
I not realise that childhood casts a glamour over everything.

I have been speaking a great deal about food in this description of Jewish orthodoxy, and the fact of my having done so,
without any previous planning and just as the memories have
come flooding into my mind, is a sufficient indication that the
dietary laws, together with the rules about "work" on the

Sabbath and holydays, obtruded in our lives far more forcibly, because with a much more regular incidence, than any of the other things, the things prescribed or the things forbidden, which were recognised as automatically binding on us. There was a very large number of these, and I shall not describe them. But I must say a word about the Day of Atonement, which in its rigidity and inevitability seemed to sum up, in a pitilessly concentrated form, all the various compulsivenesses that hemmed us in.

# CHAPTER X

# THE DAY OF ATONEMENT

Every year, as *Kippúr* approached, I began to feel something I find it very difficult to express: something midway between apprehension and *malaise*: something concerned with the body, but spiritual, in a groping sort of way, as well: something stemming, at the same time, from the reasoning faculty and power of judgement. The more inescapable it became, as the days passed by, that *Kippúr* would eventually arrive, the more eagerly I looked forward to the moment when it would at last have gone by and be behind me; and the relief I envisaged as awaiting me at the end of it was the relief of not stifling, the relief of drawing breath again, the relief of no longer having steel bands on me, the relief of being free. I could not have said, at the time, what I meant by this freedom, but I think I understand it now.

We had a fairly heavy meal on the eve of *Kippúr*; this was known as "taking the Fast". For the next twenty-four hours we could eat or drink nothing, unless damage to health might result. But "could eat or drink nothing" seems to me, as I write down the words, to be almost meaningless; they fail to convey anything at all of the atmosphere, anything at all of the situation, the reality, that impinged on our consciousness as involving us. Or perhaps I ought to say "on my consciousness", for I may be generalising too broadly; but I am certain, at least, that what was true of me was also true of my parents, and of everyone else in our circle. Possibly I can best convey my meaning by saying something like this: we knew instinctively that to eat or drink on the Day of Atonement would be to do something monstrous and unnatural, something impossibly opposed to the order of things. And not to eat or drink meant not to eat or drink; we were forbidden by our parents to clean our teeth, lest a drop of water might be swallowed.

After "taking the Fast" we drove to the Bayswater Synagogue; we were able to drive because the meal had been so timed that we could arrive at the service before the Fast had begun. In the crowded lobby people, before they went in, wished one another "well over the Fast", meaning by it "I hope the fasting won't make you ill". I am writing all this with distress, and with that feeling of being a traitor which no Jew who criticises anything Jewish, particularly after what happened at Dachau and Buchenwald, can ever escape; but I must surely speak the truth as I see it, for I am trying, in this letter, to unfold a *Weltanschauung* that has gradually been won during a fifty years' pilgrimage, and of use, I dare to think, for your guidance. I shall therefore go on; but only after giving notice that there will be a good deal to be said on the other side of the question, and only after making it clear, also, that the failure of institutional Christianity is in my opinion far more reprehensible, if only because its opportunities have been far greater, than the failure of that orthodox Judaism in which I was reared.

I was saying that people in the lobby wished one another "well over the Fast". And not only in the lobby on the eve of *Kippúr*. Ten days before, on the Jewish New Year, the customary greeting had been "A happy New Year and well over the Fast"; and this was repeated whenever you met anyone fresh during the intervening period. I used to get sick of hearing it, for it reminded me that very soon now the Day would *have* to come. But it impinged on me in another way too, and a dual one. It made me think about my own body, and wonder whether I should get agonisingly hungry, as I frequently did; and it simultaneously made me disgusted with this concentration on the body, my own concentration and other people's but particularly other people's. Here, I used to think (and later on very violently to say), is what is supposed to be the most sacred day in the whole Jewish year: people are supposed to devote it to communing with God and repenting of their sins: and what they actually do is to think about nothing but their own miserable stomachs. Physical apprehension, a spiritual stirring, and intellectual contempt for what I felt to be the humbug of the whole thing were all mixed up in my reaction. My feelings were intensified by my mother's attitude. A sort of gravity would develop in her as *Kippúr* grew nearer. "It's a very *big* day," she would explain to our Gentile maids or a Gentile friend, in a tone of voice in which awe, a sense of being in the secret and a suggestion of apology were all represented;

but I felt that there was something sentimental, lacking in depth, a little phoney and "put on" in her whole demeanour. Looking back, I should now say that consciously she was as sincere as anybody could be, but that there was a great deal of insincerity under the surface, as there is, of course, with very nearly all of us.

*I wrote the last few paragraphs in the train, coming up on Monday morning from Brimpton to Henrietta Street. When I got to the office I found the following letter among the others on my desk. Bear it in mind while you read what I am writing hereabouts, for the spirit of it illustrates "the other side of the question" which I shall be touching on presently. The cheque, from an undergraduate, was for £100:*

—— *College, Oxford.*
*February 16th 1951*

*"Dear Sir,*

*"I made out the enclosed cheque to you because I remember that you were a firm supporter of a fund to help Arab refugees. I should be very grateful if you would put it towards that cause, provided that you are certain that it will be used to aid the destitute.*

*"I am both an orthodox Jew (in my rather broad definition) and a Zionist who, like you I imagine, deplores the maintenance of Talmudic observances without an appreciation of the ethical standards basic to Judaism and other faiths. No doubt you will understand why I, as a Jew, am particularly eager that this money should be used for Arab refugees—I only wish I had more to give.*

*"Yours sincerely,*

*"——"*

The service on the eve of *Kippúr* began with a chant called *Kol Nidrei*, which means "All vows". I cannot imagine that you will ever hear it in a synagogue, but you may run across the concert version, a very stuffy affair, by Max Bruch. It was chanted three times running, gradually getting louder and louder: the first few words at the first recitation being whispered *pianissimo*, and the last few words at the last recitation being— I won't say bellowed *fortissimo*, though that would be an excusable exaggeration. This chant doesn't mean what it appears to mean. It appears to mean that you are forgiven in advance for any vow, oath or promise that you may break between this Day of Atonement and the next; and it used to be, and perhaps still is, one of the favourite weapons of antisemites whose own type of morality can be gauged by the propaganda they base on "The Protocols of the Elders of Zion". What *Kol Nidrei* really does mean I don't know, though I think I was given an elaborate explanation. The real answer is that by eighteen hundred and ninety-eight, when or whenabouts I first heard it, it had become so completely meaningless that anyone of an inquiring mind, who preferred not to take things for granted, had to burrow very deep if he wanted to uncover the secret. Yet it was considered quite exceptionally holy and awful, because the Day of Atonement had always begun with it. For some years I was moved by it myself, but in a sentimentally ancestral sort of way which as time went on made me more and more uncomfortable.

When the service was over we went back to bed, this time on foot. Or most of us did. A very few of the ultra-orthodox stayed in synagogue all night, covered with the shrouds in which they would one day be buried.

Next morning at half past eight or so came another walk to synagogue, where we remained, more or less, till the whole thing was over in the evening. With me it was as much less as I dared, for the endless service, with everything sung or recited or mumbled over and over again, oppressed me with an intolerable boredom. I developed an unusual incontinence of urine which made it necessary for me to visit, every now and again, the *pissoirs* in the lobby; and on my way to and fro I would pass a few people standing about in little groups, and asking one another how they were fasting. Sometimes I would go for a short walk outside. This was both a relief and an agony. It was an agony, because everything in the streets was *normal*; people were doing what they liked, the shops were open, the traffic was moving, nothing was in any way different from what it was at any ordinary time; but I was cut off from it all, I was abnormal, I was bound. I *had* to go back to synagogue and fast and "say prayers". And why? Wasn't the day, the sky, the weather, everything, exactly the same day, the same sky, the same weather, the same everything for me as for all the other men and women in the London

streets and in the whole world? And if I must be different
on a particular day, why just on this day? Why not yesterday
or tomorrow or some day I might choose to be different on?
What *meaning* could there be in this compulsion to be automatically different on an arbitrary date automatically descend-
ing on me?

These respites in the *pissoirs* and streets were very brief, only
the tiniest fraction of the eight or nine hours' prayer-saying.
There was one element in the latter that affected me as
peculiarly distasteful, and this was the *Al 'Hīt* ("For the sin")
or General Confession, which consisted of forty-four versicles
(with intermediate petitions and a coda) each beginning with
the words *Al 'Hīt* and each confessing its own special sin; the sins
being arranged alphabetically, two sins to each letter. The *Al
'Hīt* was repeated several times during the day, with other
prayers, and various readings and psalms, in between. This
mechanical collection of meaningless formulae was recited by
the congregation in unison, the cantor leading, and in a per-
fervid sing-song that lingered with heavy emphasis on the word
*'hīt* or sin, and was accompanied by forty-four beatings of the
breast, where the heart is, with clenched fist. The breast-beating
was carried out with varying degrees of intensity; my father did
it quietly, but an ultra-orthodox old man at the corner of the
very top row, who had a special little reading-stand of the
swivelling kind for his prayer books and commentaries in addition to the ordinary ledge, made a tremendous to-do with his beatings and groanings. Some people on the other hand—they must
have been rather *link*—didn't beat at all. There was nothing
hypocritical, in the ordinary sense of the word, about this breast-
beating or about the actual confession, and when I used the
words "meaningless formulae" I didn't intend to imply anything of the kind; what I meant was that the words and the ges-
tures accompanying them, and the emotion involved, had no
living relation with any individual, as an individual, at the Bayswater Synagogue in Chichester Place in the year nineteen hundred and so and so, nor was remotely intended to have, but was
a kind of traditional performance, and at that level sincere: for
by taking part in this performance Jews were simply manifesting
as Jews, and nothing could have been sincerer than that. When
I complained to my parents that I had never "committed a sin
before thee" by "the taking of bribes", or "in business", or

"by usury or interest", or by "wanton looks", I was told that this had nothing to do with the matter: the reference was not to me or my parents or Mr Isaacs or Mr Cohen, but to the whole House of Israel collectively. This maddened me; House of Israel or no House of Israel, how could I, Victor Gollancz, of two hundred and fifty-six Elgin Avenue, Maida Vale, include myself in the "we" who had been wicked in business when I wasn't in business at all? Ah, I was told, but as a Jew I must identify myself, or rather was automatically identified whether I liked it or not, with "the Jews", and "the Jews" had been guilty of wickedness in business, as well as of all the other wickednesses confessed, including those for which "we are liable to the penalty of chastisement", "to the penalty of forty stripes", "to the penalty of death by the hand of heaven", and "to the penalty of excision and childlessness". The sins punishable by these latter unpleasantnesses were not specified, nor were those "for which we are liable to any of the four death penalties inflicted by the court—stoning, burning, beheading, and strangling"; there was a footnote in the prayer book, however, explaining what was meant by "the violation of positive and the violation of negative precepts, whether these latter do or do not admit of a remedy by the subsequent fulfilment of a positive command". "There are prohibitions," ran this gloss, "the transgression of which cannot be rectified by any subsequent act of the offender. Such, for example, are the laws forbidding work to be done on the Sabbath, and leavened bread to be eaten on Passover; to each of these the statement applies."

So, as "the Jews" had committed all these sins and rendered themselves liable to all these penalties, I, as a Jew, had *ipso facto* so sinned and was so liable. The idea of such a metaphysical monstrosity produced in me, at every recital of the Confession and on every Day of Atonement for so long as I continued to attend synagogue, an intellectual brainstorm which had something in it that was spiritual as well. How could I, a unique individual (I am not rationalising after the event, this was what I passionately asked myself long before I became *Barmitzvah*, that is to say was confirmed, at the age of thirteen)—how could I be responsible for what other people did, and how could I not be dreadfully responsible for what I did myself? The emotion I then felt at the *Al 'Hīt*, nearly fifty years ago, was one among the sources, but deepest perhaps of all, for the horror I have felt ever since at the doctrine of collective guilt or responsibility in any of its forms, whether it be the idea that all mankind is guilty for the sin of Adam, or the idea that because the Nazis did evil and the Nazis were Germans, then a German anti-Nazi who was tortured for *being* an anti-Nazi was nevertheless as guilty as the rest of them—being also a German. You will think this last illustration far-fetched, but that is because you were not alive in nineteen hundred and forty or for that matter in nineteen hundred and forty-six.

I find, on looking through the prayer-book to refresh my memory, that I was in fact personally guilty, as no doubt was almost everybody else in greater or lesser degree, of many of the sins for which we made confession in the *Al 'Ḥīt*. Hardening of the heart; wronging our neighbour; sinful meditation; unclean lips; denying and lying; "the stretched forth neck of pride"; effrontery; envy; levity; stiff-neckedness; "confusion of mind" (certainly, but how could I help it?); even perhaps, on second thoughts, "wanton looks"—not only do I now know that most if not all of these things were ingredients in my character, as many of them still are, but I was painfully aware of it then. But you will utterly fail to understand what I have been getting at unless you realise that, just as confessing a thing didn't and in some cases quite obviously couldn't imply that you'd done it, so confessing what in fact you *had* done didn't necessarily imply that you were aware of having done it; nor again did confessing what you couldn't help knowing you'd done necessarily imply that you sincerely repented of it and would try not to do it again. Though there might accidentally be a coincidence at certain points, the real personal life of a man and what he automatically proclaimed on this occasion were in almost totally separate dimensions. This is a phenomenon not, of course, peculiar to orthodox Judaism. What indeed most distressed me, when later on I began to examine the matter more closely, was that the split in question was not merely an aberration from the essential genius of Judaism, but was an aberration actually arising, by a process of fossilisation, out of the very insistence that there should be no split at all, but that life in all its aspects (on the one hand) and "religion" (on the other) should be unquestioningly and indissolubly one.

I shall return to this topic later. Meanwhile, let me give two examples of the split.

First, my father was meticulous in his recitation of the *Al 'Hīt*: one of his favourite phrases, on the other hand, was "I've never done anything wrong in my life." Now a man cannot one day beat his breast and accuse himself of every vice under the sun, and next day proclaim himself spotless, if he imagines that the self-accusation is really an accusation of himself. The fact of the matter is that my father had done many of the things he confessed, wasn't aware that he had done them, and therefore couldn't be indicating any awareness of having done them by confessing. Secondly, there were some well known money-lenders, which is to say usurers and interest-mongers, in the congregation of the Bayswater Synagogue. They chanted, with the rest of us, "For the sin which we have committed before thee by usury and interest". Now by no process of suppression of which I am aware could they have been ignorant, on the Day of Atonement as on any other day, of how they earned their living: and the concept of sin, though a troublesome one for theologians and for anyone else who thinks deeply about it, presents no great difficulty to the man in the street. These people were money-lenders; they knew they were money-lenders; they publicly proclaimed that it was wicked to be a money-lender; yet they did nothing about it, or so one must suppose, for if a Mr. Macpherson had suddenly changed his profession the rumour of it would presumably have got around. And all this was quite natural, and has nothing to do with weakness of the flesh; the explanation is simply that a man's personal life was one thing and the *Al 'Hīt* quite another. Indeed, if you had met a gentleman of this profession in the lobby or at the *pissoir*, and had been so insolent as to inquire of him what method of livelihood he was proposing to substitute for the one he had just been describing as sinful, he would, I really believe, have been gravely offended by so unheard-of an imputation of sinfulness.

Do not, I beg of you, misunderstand me. I am not suggesting, God forbid, that repentance was impossible, or never occurred, on the Day of Atonement: knowledge of such matters is with the Almighty and the person concerned. I am suggesting this: It was a desire, deep in the Jewish consciousness, to heal the breach with God that led to the establishment of *Kippúr*. But out of the very intensity of this desire, out of an anxiety to make the effort complete and leave nothing unprovided for, there developed a machinery of observances, uniform for everyone; and this machinery had ended by so occupying the field as almost to preclude that free intercourse between the individual and God without which restoration, reconciliation, at-one-ment is forever impossible. The qualification "almost" is important; first because there is a last remnant of spiritual spontaneity in almost everyone, and secondly because there are some rare types so spiritually strong that they can turn the most unpromising material to good account. There must have been people in my parents' circle, however few, who found the Day of Atonement just the occasion that they spiritually needed.

I don't know whether my mother was one of these, nor whether, if she was, it was spiritual strain rather than physical constitution that affected her body so lamentably. For she always fasted "badly", and sometimes very badly indeed. As what should have been lunch-time approached and then dragged itself away—one of the abnormalities about *Kippúr* that most worried me was the absence of this familiar watershed of everyday existence, quite apart from any question of food—anxiety would develop in my father, and communicate itself to me, about how my mother "was". To find out necessitated quite an elaborate manœuvre. The sexes were strictly segregated in an orthodox synagogue, males being on the ground floor and females in a gallery—which might even be shut off by a grille for the better concealment of its occupants, as you may see any day for yourself if you visit the little upstairs synagogue, the loveliest imaginable, in the old Venetian ghetto. This segregation, an additional spur to my feminism, typified the whole attitude to women in orthodox Judaism—an attitude that was highly ambivalent. There was in one sense great respect for them, and the wife and mother, as she lit her candles at the Friday evening table, became the central figure as of right in the beautiful atmosphere that enveloped the inauguration of the Sabbath. But women were *ipso facto* debarred from, or as it was explained to me "relieved of", nearly all religious duties of the more public sort: from being "called up", for instance, in synagogue to assist at the reading of the *Torah*, or from opening the Ark of the Covenant and bringing out the Scrolls: and from some private ones too, such as binding the phylacteries on

forehead and arm every morning in the home before breakfast.
By the same token, women wore no *tallīsim,* or praying-shawls, for
synagogue, as men were bound to do. The fact is that ceremoni-
ally they were lay figures, for all their importance in ensuring
that everything about the house, such as the preparation of
meat for cooking or the cleaning of rooms for Passover, was
properly Jewish: their status in general being one of mingled
superiority and inferiority, with the inferiority predominating.
At early morning service, in between some very appropriate
Blessings, such as "Blessed art thou, O Lord our God, King of
the Universe, who hast given to the cock intelligence to distinguish between day and night", and some others of great
charity, such as "Blessed art thou, O Lord our God, King of the
Universe, who openest the eyes of the blind", "who clothest the
naked", and "who loosest them that are bound" (the last one
often comes to my lips when I visit the prisoners at Wormwood
Scrubs)—in between these Blessings the men say "Blessed art
thou, O Lord our God, King of the Universe, who hast not
made me a woman", and the women say "Blessed art thou,
O Lord our God, King of the Universe, who hast made me
according to thy will". I was infuriated, naturally, by so monstrous a piece of sexual discrimination; but my father explained
that I didn't understand the real meaning of these *B'rōchas,*
though his own interpretation of them, when it came, was very
puzzling and confused. What he must have been trying to say
was that they referred to menstruation, and expressed gratitude
(for being spared it) in the one case and a dutiful resignation in
the other. My father could not have hoped to make himself clear
on this point, owing to a native and decent-minded reticence
in sexual matters which makes him very lovable to me in
retrospect but wasn't at all helpful in my adolescence. The
explanation, in any case, is unconvincing. I notice that in the
Authorised Daily Prayer Book the blessing for women is printed
in a smaller type than the blessing for men.

Anyhow, whether as a sign of inferiority or not the women
were segregated in synagogue, on the Day of Atonement as on
all other days: so if a male on the ground floor was feeling
anxious about a woman in the gallery he would summon the
beadle and ask him to go up and inquire; and the beadle would

beckon to the woman-beadle from the gallery door, because
he wasn't allowed to enter; and they would meet in no man's
land outside; and the beadle would come down and report. In
my mother's case the report was almost always distressing.
Meanwhile two things were happening: I was getting hungrier
and hungrier, and so more and more incapable of concentrating
on the prayer-book; and my father, like many others, was growing increasingly concerned about the time. He would pull out
his watch every now and again, and either nod or do the opposite, in a sagely conspiratorial sort of way, after examining what
it said. This was not a sign of impatience. My father was not
counting the minutes, as I was, because he longed for the ordeal
to be over; after his own fashion he was too religious a man for
that. What he was interested in, as an expert, was technique.
Was the *chazan*, or cantor, proving up to his job? Had the passing
of a particular landmark, or had it not, been in so nice a conformity with the schedule that the whole service would be
finished, without either dragging or scurry, at the exact moment
prescribed? The exact moment, as you already know, played a
very important part in orthodox Judaism.

When this moment arrived, after the affirmation, seven times
repeated, "The Lord he is God" and a blast on the *shofar* or
ram's horn, the clatter of departure ensued. From all over the
synagogue you could hear a dry rattle of woodeny crashes and
bangs, as *tallīsim* and prayer-books were stowed away in the deep
receptacles of which the seats we had been sitting on formed lids.
Then most of us hurried home. A tiny minority, the very pious
—including the old gentleman in the high place whose groanings and beatings had so greatly intrigued me—stayed on to
recite the *maariv* or ordinary service prescribed for every day of
the week after sunset. For us, the first thing to do was to find the
brougham, for we could now ride. This was a closed carriage,
smelling darkly but delightfully of "stuff" and drawn by a nice
old white mare that I used to like patting; my father kept it in
the city for business, but occasionally had it brought up west,
and always on *Kippúr* to take us home for the breaking of the
fast.

Finding the brougham wasn't easy: there was usually a considerable to-do about it, and sometimes a downright row
between my father and Henry, the coachman. It was dark,
naturally, the sun having set, and even, God forbid, might be

raining; and most of the carriages and four-wheelers had little distinctive about them, though as motor-cars became increasingly
common (and also less awe-inspiring) the area of possibilities
grew narrower. And nerves were strained. The search would
have been simplified if only we had known where to look;
but we didn't, because my father and Henry had opposite
theories about the best position in the huddle for Henry to aim
at, and though they always imagined that they had reached a
satisfactory compromise in advance, they were both so unusually obstinate that this was mere self-deception. Henry was
certain that much the best place, particularly as it might be
raining, was the nearest he could get to the front or back door
of the synagogue; my father was equally certain that this was
impossibly speculative, and that some more or less remote side-
street, where the number of carriages would be fewer, should
obviously be chosen. We always looked first in my father's street,
and always without success. Meanwhile mother would be col-
lapsing, and smelling salts could do little to restore her. Eventually Henry would be spotted somewhere as far from the synagogue as my father had suggested but differently far, and we
would get mother in and drive off. My father would mutter
furiously, year after year, "that damn fool of a Henry", though
in ordinary circumstances he was on excellent terms with him.
I felt very censorious about such behaviour, and used to think,
and perhaps even to say, that it came ill from a man who had
just been begging forgiveness in the *Al 'Hīt* "for the sin which
we have committed against thee by contentiousness". It never
occurred to me that I was being contentious myself.

And now, since I've practically finished with *Kippúr* and have
only a few words to add about the rest of the evening after our
return to Elgin Avenue, I shall talk a little, as a sort of interlude
on our way back there, about something that mention of the
brougham has brought into my mind. For the brougham was
only one of the two kinds of carriage I knew; the other being an
open victoria which we hired once a year for a drive "in the
country". The "country" was a semi-rural suburb called Dollis
Hill. These drives were a great delight, for country, real
country, was almost unknown to me. My father, you must
understand, worked harder than anyone I have ever known.
He took not a single day's holiday, other than Sabbaths and
Festivals, from the day I first remember him to the day of his

retirement from business. So holidays away from London were rare for me too. Exceptionally, at long intervals, we children went with an aunt to the sea, but in general I disliked these occasions and was anxious to get back again as quickly as possible; for the "resorts" we were dumped down in struck me as nothing but inferior Londons, with the addition of monotonous water. (I was to fall in love with the sea very much later, when I returned from Singapore on a cargo boat at the end of world war one, up the Straits of Malacca to Suez across the Indian Ocean.) Margate, however, was an exception. The place itself I thought little of; but every now and again we took a tram into the open country, one of those trams that went swishing or humming with a tone that continually changed as the arm sticking up from the top of it glided section by section along the wire overhead. The long flat fields of corn, blazing with poppies in the August heat, were an ecstasy to me. Our occasional visits to Hastings were also exceptions. We stayed there with my great-aunt Rosetta, who had some wonderful old silver and Dresden inherited from her mother, though she was now very poor. She loved me a lot and I liked being with her; and I also took immense pleasure in going on excursions to the nearby Fairlight Glen with my geological hammer, in the hope of discovering one of the fossilised leaves or plants that were occasionally to be found in the strata there. I was never successful. Other things I enjoyed about these visits were the coconut shies and occasional ginger-beer dumps on the further cliffs, and "scenes from the operas" ("I drea-eamed I dwe-elt in mar-a'arble halls" and "Yes, let me like a sōl-ja fall, upón some ópén plain") every night on the pier.

The nearest approach to country that I knew with any familiarity as a boy was our own Elgin Avenue. Although not nearly as "countryfied", to use my expression of those days, as Dollis Hill, it might itself have been called semi-rural in the last years of the old century and the first of the new. Just beyond our number 256 began the "ups and downs", little hillocks of earth, with occasional patches of grass, that took the place of a regular pavement on either side of the thoroughfare. But the most rural thing about Elgin Avenue was the unkempt and tussocky field that stretched, for some seven or eight acres, beyond our garden wall. We were not supposed, for a reason I forget, to go into it, but I used to jump down—this I thought very "venturesome"—to play a crude sort of football or pick clover. There were small market gardens to the left of the field, which the owners attended to on Sundays; and in the autumn, just before lunch, I would see them coming away with a bunch or two of multicoloured dahlias, still glistening with dew from the mist. I have loved dahlias ever since, and one of the first things I did when I bought Brimpton in 1933 was to plant a bed of them. I like them as vulgarly large as they can be. I was proud of my dahlias in the late nineteen thirties, and delighted when Robert Lynd made a reference to them in one of his Y.Y. middles for *The New Statesman*. He was referring to the sense of proprietorship that at times seems to clash with a man's views on property, and added in parenthesis "Did you ever see the dahlias at Brimpton?"

When the brougham had at last got us home to Elgin Avenue for our fast-breaking meal, my mother usually went straight to bed. I did not. After impatiently cleaning my teeth I would rush down to the parlour. The table would be covered with cold fish and sweets, and, best of all, with great platefuls of heavenly bread and butter. This I would begin eating with incontinent rapidity, and soon the acid flavour that hangs about the stomach and mouth after a twenty-four hours' unaccustomed fast, and makes cold water taste so peculiar, would gradually vanish. The family meal would follow, and the rest of the evening would be spent with books or paints or friends or opera programmes or homework or any other manifestation of blessed normality; except that Henry, in the absence of a telephone, would take the brougham round to my Uncle Hermann and other neighbouring relatives, and find out for my father how they "were". The nightmare was over; and though I was constantly reflecting on it as the days went by and formulating my conclusions, it was not till eight or nine months later that the inevitability of its recurrence would begin to impinge on me. Just so most young people in their teens, who are quite well aware that death awaits everyone, never worry about something so fantastically remote or regard it as applying to themselves; or never did, until, with all their life before them and with endless opportunities for usefulness and joy, they have been compelled these last few years to face the sudden ending of it, not as a possibility after three score years and ten but as a probability for tomorrow.

I may have given you the impression that a total fast for twenty-four hours must, as such, be almost unendurable. This of course is nonsense. For most normal persons, and particularly for growing boys, it is likely in itself to be uncomfortable and even painful at times; but postulate an absorbing motive that really demands it and the absence above all of any meaningless compulsion, and the physical discomfort can be negligible. I have fasted on occasion since then for as many hours and almost as totally but of my own free will, and have been hungry yet quite untroubled. But I wonder whether my experience of fasting in boyhood, petty though in retrospect it seems, has anything to do with the horror I have subsequently felt, and felt as if the thing were happening there and then to me, at the starvation or near-starvation, not for twenty-four hours but for weeks and months, that I have occasionally come up against: as in the cellars of Hamburg or shanties near Düsseldorf during the autumn of 1946 and the summer of 1947.

*February 23rd*

*The beauty of great cities in the early morning! At noon today, which is a Friday, my partner Sheila Hodges is sailing on the Elizabeth for a book-hunting visit to the United States, and I am writing this on my way back to London after putting her on the boat at Southampton. I drove down from Ladbroke Grove to Waterloo at half past seven. I wish Wordsworth had not written "Earth has not anything to show more fair"; I should have liked to give praise and thanks for "a sight so touching in its majesty" with words that were something more than a mere echo of his. We have had, according to the newspapers, the wettest February since records were started; but last night the moon was almost piercing, and this morning the sky, a little gusty still and with a look about it as of something just washed, was shining like a sky in May over the quiet streets. It seems as if the spring will be very early this year, en revanche for so much rain.*

*But Wordsworth's "majesty" needs qualifying. A city in the early morning, before the people are about, is a living thing in its own right, and seems to be stretching up its arms, breathless with adoration, to the Power that made it—and made it with a beauty at once so delicate and so strong—by the hands and hearts of men. It is like someone who worships freely in his own room, unencumbered as yet by the coming day; its vastness has grown humble as it silently communes with a vastness so immeasurably greater than its own; and if it is majestic, its majesty is the majesty of praying hands.*

*As we came into Parliament Square from Birdcage Walk, the sun was just above the roof of the House of Commons; and in that light and silence the place moved me as if I were seeing it for the first time, though my busybodying on the margin of politics has in fact made me far more familiar with it than are many of its more absentee members. I suddenly remembered, so strong had the habit of remembering become in me, a dream of early childhood: that one day, as Home Secretary, I would move for the abolition of the death penalty in a great speech, and a very beautiful lady, my wife, would be listening with moist eyes from the Strangers' Gallery. I also remembered a very small episode that had impressed me more than any speech I had ever heard in praise of democracy. I was standing one day in the lobby, just before question time, with Eleanor Rathbone, who was the greatest Englishwoman of her day. The Speaker's procession came along, and we all fell back in respectful silence, making a lane for it. When the procession had passed on the old lady said to me "I couldn't live without this place".*

*As I drove over Westminster Bridge I glanced back to the left. The Shell-Mex building had, absurdly, become one of Wordsworth's "temples": not "all bright and glittering in the smokeless air", but beautiful with a radiance more subdued.*

*February 24th*

*And now, back in my Brimpton library at nine o'clock on Saturday morning to start writing again, I can hardly bear to settle down and stop looking out of the windows at so much loveliness. It is said that the garden here was at one time a bird sanctuary, and there is always a great deal of singing; but this morning the trills, the shakes, and all the rarer things that you never hear in human coloratura seem more richly interwoven and more tirelessly persistent than ever. Some motor thing, perhaps a tractor, is chugging up the lane, and seems, though you'd expect the opposite, to be musically co-operating with the birds. The sun, to the right of the great oak, looks enormous and very liquid, and its rays are just touching a ladder, stripped of paint to matt whiteness, that leans against the conical roof of the cottage across the way, and then rises against the green of the dense yews beyond. Out of the other window the downs look like September rather than February, with a softening haze quite thick on them; and a long white line of smoke almost blends with it, as a train passes by on the level in front. I was right in saying that spring would be early this year. If this is not spring, it is nuntia veris.*

# CHAPTER XI

## JEWISH ORTHODOXY—HOW IT IMPINGED ON ME

I NOW HAVE TO explain just how orthodox Judaism impinged on me. I have already given some indications; I want at this point to bring them together, add to them, and paint for you as vivid a picture as I can. How it impinged on me, not what it made of me by my reaction to it; I shall come to that later, for to describe what elements in my make-up I owed, when I was teaching at Repton, to my father's orthodoxy, on top of what I owed to his antifeminism, has been one of the two main purposes of the last fifty pages. But before I can explain my reaction, I must first explain, if the reaction is to be understandable, what the thing I was reacting to seemed like to me; how it struck me, how it "hit me in the eye". And here I must give a couple of warnings. First, I am clearly speaking of my parents' orthodoxy, of the orthodoxy I experienced in my own home. To generalise too widely from it, to imagine that all Jewish orthodoxy, without exception, was entirely of a piece with this particular orthodoxy, would be an error; one of the things, for example, that I am going to ascribe to the environment in which I was brought up is absence of spirituality, and there are certainly Jews whose orthodoxy is not only compatible with a deeply spiritual life but the ally and servant of it. Nevertheless, I must also make it clear that, in my opinion, my parents' orthodoxy was broadly typical of all Jewish orthodoxy as it then was, as it had been for centuries, and as it now is, and not only in England but throughout the world. (I must except, however, the Chassidic movement, which has claimed so many millions of adherents since its rise in Poland during the eighteenth century, and which, though in a sense orthodox, was almost Pauline in its impulse to renew, and as spiritual a religion, until a rapid degeneration set in, as the world has ever seen.)

And my second warning is this: How Judaism impinged on *me* is alone in question. Whether my reaction may have been untypical is a thing you must decide for yourself.

I can have little hope of expressing satisfactorily that main element in my—discomfort? distaste? horror?—at which so many times I have hinted. But I must try. The compulsiveness of it all, then, was really and utterly compulsive; the "must" of doing a thing or not doing a thing was a "must" in its own right, over and above any question of the doing or not doing of it being what everybody else did or didn't do, or wise or stupid, or righteous or wicked, or commanded or prohibited by one's parents or even by God. And this is not yet the whole story. Not only *must* you do a thing or not do a thing; you *couldn't not* do it (in the one case) and *couldn't do* it (in the other). I mean, quite literally, that at first, struggle as you might, you could no more eat pork, or take a 'bus on the Sabbath, than a man riveted to a wall in a dungeon could walk out into the air. If you struggled very hard you might gradually break your bonds—the bonds inside you, not the comparatively unimportant bonds put upon you by your parents or public opinion; but the process was horribly painful. I struggled myself with some success. By the time I went to Oxford I was "observing" nothing compulsively, nothing that I didn't want to observe, with one big exception. There were a few things that I still observed (and still observe) because, in complete spiritual freedom, I saw fit to observe them; but although they were the same things that I had formerly observed compulsively, the fact that I now observed them of my own free choice, spontaneously, almost as if I had myself just invented them, meant a radical transformation of their character. My observance of them had nothing in common with my observance of the exception.

The latter, significantly, was the whole fantastic complex of the dietary laws. From some of these, I am ashamed to say, I have never, even yet, got free. I was able to manage bacon quite early, provided it was lean and crisp and not too greasy; but even today, if I realise from the smell as I go down to breakfast that my children are eating the forbidden thing, I sometimes mutter, only half by way of joke, a depreciatory *Goyim!* Pork and ham, and other forms of pig, if there are any, I have never tasted; and though game, which is forbidden as being shot but looks quite ordinary, doesn't worry me in the least, the very sight of an oyster, even if someone else is eating it, makes me feel queasy. I am afraid I go a little bit too far sometimes in this matter of other people eating things; for if I have asked a man out to lunch and know him well enough, I sometimes give him a list of the more obvious items I'd sooner he didn't order. As to sandwiches, if they are chicken I prefer them made with mustard instead of butter; if they are beef, I insist on it; and if I happened to know that my instructions had been disregarded, and that the meat in addition was underdone (blood and milk!), nothing would induce me to eat them. Or almost nothing; for from time to time I am not a host but a guest, and then the question of courtesy is involved. I am invariably apprehensive before dining out at a private house; I wonder how much forbidden food there will be and whether I shall have to make myself conspicuous by refusing too much of it. Once, at the house of a parson who is a good friend of mine, I had to refuse everything; but he understood, and gave me an egg. Ruth and I were not so fortunate when we visited Edmond and Madeleine Fleg in Paris for the first time since the beginning of the war. We love them very much; we had not seen them for nearly ten years; and they had clearly made special arrangements for our reception, at a time when the food situation in France was exceedingly difficult. On our plates as we sat down for lunch were those things like champagne glasses—perhaps they are champagne glasses—that I had learned to associate with prawn cocktails and similar abominations. I caught my wife's eye. We couldn't just do nothing about it and let the Flegs eat by themselves. We must either eat with them, or explain; but by explaining we should greatly embarrass them, and perhaps the more so because, though in a still further stage of "emancipation", they were not the tiniest bit less Jewish than we were. So I nodded to my wife, and she nodded back, and somehow or other we got the horrid little lumpy things down. As one by one I forced them home I prayed for the moment when the glass would be empty. We learned some years later, when we told the whole story, that our sacrifice had been in vain; for the Flegs, it turned out, would not have minded in the least if we had been sensible enough to make a clean breast of it. I don't know whether an American I once entertained at lunch would have shown a similar kindliness if I had followed my instincts; perhaps so, for the Americans are a kindly people. He had ordered a steak as the main item, and I asked him, fiddling about with the wine-list, what he would like to drink with it. He guessed he'd have a glass of milk. I was on the point of peremptorily forbidding it, when I remembered my responsibilities.

All this may sound trivial or even comic, but I assure you that the underlying reality isn't trivial or comic at all. Here am I, a man of fifty-eight who has travelled widely, read a lot, and played some sort of part, however minor, in the life of a western community; and it is only after a serious struggle, and then with a feeling of disgust, that I can break a tabu not only long since quite meaningless to me, but one I passionately disapproved of half a century before you were born. Does this enable you to understand the terrible compulsiveness I have been trying to describe? Not the modified compulsiveness that in my own case still freakishly applies to those few of the prohibitions that I have never or rarely succeeded in breaking—freakishly, for my own case must be exceedingly uncommon among contemporary Jews of the "emancipated" sort—but the naïf compulsiveness that was characteristic in my boyhood of people who had never broken a single one of them or could conceivably have imagined themselves as doing so?

I am not suggesting that this compulsiveness has applied to every Jew in every country and at every time: far from it: for if so, how explain the existence of reform Jews, liberal Jews, *link* Jews, *Yom Kippúr* Jews, intermarrying Jews, even Jews who, like my father, were orthodox Jews without being *Shulhan A'rukh* Jews? But this compulsiveness, this involuntary submission to "the yoke of the Law", is characteristic of the main stream, the hard core, of traditional or orthodox Judaism; and though it can obviously be overcome, from whatever motive and with whatever difficulty, in respect of this or that observance (which will then be abandoned), it is nevertheless experienced as identically compulsive in respect of every single one of such observances as the particular Jew in question may not yet, at the particular time in question, have "given up". Now my father was in the main stream, and I am accurately describing my home. I would add that involuntary submission is something quite different from voluntary submission, such as you may find from time to time in very intelligent and even very saintly Jews; their motives are various, but among them is a genuine belief that Jewish particularism is of permanent value to the world as a whole.

And still I have told only half the story of how the ritual

"musts" of my environment impinged on me. For the idea of
sin was bound up with them in a very peculiar way. I am not
referring to the fact that it would have seemed sinful to do
something forbidden or to refrain from doing something prescribed: this is obvious, although, as I have already tried to
explain, it was the *impossibility* of doing a thing rather than the
sinfulness involved in the doing of it that was the main element
in the tabu. What I am referring to is my idea, or realisation, that the thing forbidden or the thing prescribed was
not merely the objective occasion for sin but was subjec-
tively sinning itself: or rather not the thing forbidden or the
thing prescribed, but the thing-as-forbidden or the thing-as-
prescribed. I mean that not-to-eat-pork or to-rest-on-the-
Sabbath seemed actively wicked because it was a-not-to-eat
pork-that-compelled or a-to-rest-on-the-Sabbath-that-com-
pelled. I can best explain myself, perhaps, by saying that if I
had personified all the various prescriptions and prohibitions
into a single living person and called it the Law, as possibly I
came near to doing, I should have described it as a sinning person. "What shall we say then?" asks St. Paul. "Is the law sin?",
and replies "God forbid." I should have replied "Yes." I am
not sure that St. Paul does not himself imply something of the
sort in other passages of the Epistle to the Romans. I have read
this Epistle many times, and brooded on it, and consulted
numerous commentaries; but I am still far from understanding
the precise meaning of many of its phrases, which is perhaps not
surprising, as the subject is a very puzzling one. But I sometimes feel that if I understood St. Paul better I should understand myself better too.

The Law seemed a sinning person because somehow, by
compelling, it made everything dirty. There was something
dark and nasty about it, which, as I might have put it at the
time, messed everything up. This applied to its moral quite as
much as to its ceremonial aspect, and the fact that what it prohibited might clearly be bad had nothing to do with the matter.
There didn't seem much point in not doing a thing, however
bad, when there was no possibility of your doing it anyhow; the
not doing of it had been spoiled. Even when the Law, positive
this time, compelled you to do something that ought obviously
to have seemed good, it no longer seemed good, because the
Law compelled you to do it: it had become at best neutral and

uninteresting, if not, perversely, actually bad. Whenever the
Law was there, and it was there the whole time, it brought the
idea of sin with it; and the idea of sin and sin were really the
same, or at any rate were equally dirty. ("Hath already committed adultery in his heart.") So the Law was sinful. I don't
know how much of this I consciously thought out at the beginning of my revolt against Jewish orthodoxy, but I'm sure it's
what I felt, however obscurely. I was getting, of course, at the
ideas of freedom, intention and spontaneity. How I should put
it now is that the Law was sinful because it interfered with the
glorious liberty of the children of God, in which true blessedness consists.

But you would be wrong to assume, as you probably will,
that the sinful compulsiveness of all the things I had to do or
had not to do made me personally unhappy, or, to put it better,
unhappy with and about myself. I don't mean that the whole
business wasn't hateful to me: it was. I don't mean that I didn't
feel personally bound and compelled, bound and compelled
from within as well as from without, until gradually, with
painful struggles, I began to break away: I did. I don't mean
that being bound and compelled wasn't a horror to me: it was.
But while in one very real sense I felt personally involved, simultaneously, in another and even realer one, I didn't feel involved
at all. The thing touched me and didn't touch me at the same
time. The reality of my involvement was an accidental reality,
not an essential reality. It was the real me that was affected, but
not (I knew by every instinct and lived with the knowledge) the
realest me. It was as if the realest me, which was the free me, was
waiting quiet the whole time under the real me that was bound;
and so not only was it obvious that I should one day be free—
when didn't seem to matter much—but it was equally obvious
that I was free now, or rather just free, without any question of
now or then. So I wasn't unhappy—or not, in this matter, about
myself. The routine of orthodoxy, and the remarks my parents
made about it, frequently irritated me, and from time to time I
was angry or even furious; but what I was feeling on such occasions was primarily an intellectual passion at the idea that anything could be so wrong—primarily an emotion more disin-
terested than not, though there was also, undoubtedly, a great
deal of egoism in it. When I had been more insufferably contentious than usual I was capable of feeling ashamed of having

made such a beast of myself, and to that extent unhappy; but the joy of living that was the general background of my boyhood except for a few months, and can be truly so described in spite of quite awful agonies of mind that sometimes stood out against it, was unaffected. This background has remained with me ever since, again with the exception, during the recent war, of a year or so; and my gratitude for it is, to use the word exactly, inexpressible. "Ah, to whom?", asks Shelley about a similar feeling, when he describes how he picked the wild flowers by the stream and brought them—but to whom?—as an offering; and Coventry Patmore answers "But what is gratitude without a God?"

Sinful compulsiveness, then, was what mainly "struck" me about our domestic orthodoxy. But something else, which was really the same thing in another aspect, struck me almost as forcibly. You will understand that what I am about to describe is not the objective truth about other people's hearts and minds, but my own judgment, at the time, of what I saw around me; and the fact that I was being horribly self-righteous—while detesting self-righteousness even then more than most other vices—is irrelevant. I try nowadays, though with very limited success, not to judge other people at all; but then I judged; and if I am to be honest I must reproduce my judgment as accurately as possible, and not shrink from saying things that sound beastly because they sound beastly to say. And I must add, again if I am to be honest, that though my judgment was too harsh and uncompromising, and though I shall qualify it presently, I still think it essentially valid.

I felt, then, that all this orthodox paraphernalia had nothing whatever to do with religion. Did a single money-lender, I asked myself—I return to this example, for it was constantly in my mind—did a single money-lender stop being a money-lender after fasting and praying and confessing his sins? Was a single person better, or "gooder", for walking on Saturday or not eating bacon? I don't remember whether I actually used the word "gooder" to myself, but it suggests my childish thinking more accurately than the usual comparative; for I brooded a great deal on the notion of "goodness", and though I wasn't at all good myself I had a rudimentary inkling of what goodness implied. And things were constantly happening which confirmed my impression that religion and "religion" were quite unconnected. After the Sabbath lunch, for instance, it was customary to "say" a very long grace. My father intoned it in Hebrew, and every now and again all the rest of us came in with a peculiar sort of sing song chorus; and there was a longer bit of ensemble, a sort of miniature grand finale, at the end. My father understood Hebrew perfectly, and my sisters and I knew enough of it to follow the drift; but I was perfectly certain, Saturday after Saturday, that our minds were quite blank both to words and to sense, and that everything would have been precisely the same if we had sung not in Hebrew but in African clicks. We were not thanking God for the blessing of food: we were intoning a particular rigmarole in a particular way, because the rigmarole and the way were traditionally Jewish. My father had a trick that convinced me of this, so far as he was concerned. Towards the end of the finale he would perform a very marked *accelerando*, as if something was on his mind that he wanted to get off it the moment he'd finished. And this was the case; for as he got to the last Hebrew word he would turn to my mother and, literally in the same breath, would say in English, "Nellie, I remember now where I put that . . ." or "Nellie, I'm perfectly certain . . ." What he had been thinking of during grace, or at any rate during the last stages of it, was clear. It was wicked of me to feel so censorious about this, but I couldn't help noticing it; and I am describing my feelings as they actually were, and not as they ought to have been.

I felt much the same about prayers before breakfast, when we "laid *tephillin*". This was an exclusively male affair, and at first, when I was still a very young boy, my father and I did the "laying" together; but I soon gave it up without much protest from him, for though extremely meticulous himself in the performance of all religious duties he attached more importance, so far as others and anything public were concerned, to the negative rather than to the positive: so that I offended him less by not "laying *tephillin*" than I or anybody else would have done by publicly striking a match, if that had been thinkable, on the Sabbath. These *tephillin*, or phylacteries, are little square boxes, and are of two kinds, one for the forehead and one for the arm. They are "laid" in accordance with the Biblical injunction "And these my words, which I command thee this day, shall be upon thy heart; and thou shalt teach them diligently unto thy children, and shall talk of them when thou sittest in thy house, and when thou walkest by the way, and when thou liest down, and when thou risest up. And thou shalt bind them for a sign upon thy hands, and they shall be for frontlets between thine eyes." This passage, together with the immediately preceding *Shemá* ("Hear O Israel, the Lord our God, the Lord is one") is what the little square boxes contain. Both have leather attachments—one a circlet, like a snood, for fixing it to the forehead, and the other a quantity of strapping which, at the appropriate moment, is first bound round the forearm and then arranged on the fingers so as to form the letter ש, this being the first letter of *Shaddai*, God. The ש is not shaped haphazardly, but in an unvarying pattern of twists and turns; and the process, which has to be learned, requires, at first, some little expertise.

Early morning prayers, with this special ritual accompaniment, ought to have been impressive, but I found them the reverse. The intoning was done by rote, some passages being mumbled *prestissimo* in an undertone and others proclaimed loudly in a slow *coloratura*: particular words would be emphasised and others would be long drawn out. There was much more mumbling than anything else (rather like the humming of bees, but not so beautiful), and the words would trip over one another at so breakneck a speed that if the language had been English, and the meaning had compelled one's attention, the effect would have been impossibly irreverent (which was not the intention). Morning after morning the performance was identical: precisely the same mumbling for some passages, precisely the same *coloratura* for others, precisely the same stressings and long drawings out; and I was utterly convinced that though you might properly describe it all as "saying your prayers" you certainly couldn't describe it as praying. The words, it seemed to me, were irrelevant, even the ones you lingered over: you didn't say them as having a meaning: any other words would have done as well: even the general sense was beside the point: what really mattered, and it mattered vitally, was the performing of a *mitzvah** as such. The whole thing, *tephillin* included, was Mumbo Jumbo-worship.

Quite apart from this particular instance, I was convinced that both at home and in synagogue, where there was so much prayer-saying, there was never any praying at all. I am trying to recall, as I write this, what I meant by praying. My idea

* Religious duty.

of it no doubt changed and developed as I passed out of child-hood into my early teens; but in general I think I meant a process in which getting outside oneself, getting inside oneself, communing with God (very vaguely felt as something all-pervading and good), communing with the leaves and the sky and London and the dahlias in the market gardens, flinging up one's arms and expressing gratitude for the joy of living as one sniffed the air, and making up one's mind to be a better boy so that one shouldn't feel shut out from all these cleannesses and beauties—I think I meant a process in which things of this kind and others like them were somehow all mixed up. Now to accuse my father and mother and the Bayswater Synagogue people of never praying at all was a piece of impertinent self-righteousness, of irreligiousness in the name of religion, that I look back to with amazed disgust, wondering how I could have been so detestable. I could not possibly know whether these people prayed or not, and it was none of my business anyhow. Nevertheless, I think it probable, even today, that there was extremely little praying during the saying of prayers, what-ever may have been the case about entering into closets, and shutting doors, and praying "to thy Father which is in secret".

*Dávaning*—the recitation of correct prayers at prescribed times, whether at home or in synagogue—was a very peculiar affair. The manner and what might be called the discretion of it varied a good deal as between individual and individual, and so did the number of prayers indulged in; for the real *Shulhan A'rukh* Jew—a man who, as the saying was, "fasted Mondays and Thursdays"—must have *dávaned* a good half of some days and almost the whole of others. But, in spite of the variations, there was a certain flavour which, in greater or lesser degree, seemed common to *dávaning* as such. I will give you an extreme example, that of a well-to-do solicitor, known as "a pillar of the community" (the Jewish community), quite "English" in his general demeanour, and, as it subsequently turned out, a relative of my future wife. What grated on my so prematurely critical and censorious mind when I came across him *dávaning*? Something that looked like showing off, or, as we should now say, exhibitionism? There was an element of this about it, but the flavour isn't yet quite right. A certain blandness or self-satisfaction? Again yes, and again inexact. Rather, perhaps, I imagined him as thinking "What fun all this is! What fun

D

to be saying these prayers! What fun to know the correct prayers to say, and to know how to say them correctly! What fun to be a Jew, and above all a correct Jew!" The "fun" was irrespective of what the prayers might happen to be about, and would apply quite as much to the *Al 'Hīt* as to the *Hallel* or Hymn of Praise. And mixed up with this sense of it all being such fun was the idea, perhaps conscious and perhaps not, that some merit attached to the *dávaner* himself for knowing the prayers and for knowing how to say them and for being so pious and above all for being a Jew. There was something about the performance which I was to find later on in the "hearty" Christianity that made a certain type of boy-clubbist and conversionist, though by no means all of them, so embarrassing; but there was something more about it as well.

I have said that the paraphernalia of orthodoxy, whether eating motzas on Passover or not riding on Saturday or fasting on *Yom Kippúr* or *dávaning* at any time, struck me as having nothing to do with religion, by which I meant very much what I meant by praying. But I have understated. It struck me, not merely as having nothing to do with religion, but as being definitely irreligious or anti-religious. I was persuaded that people would pray more if there was not so much saying of prayers; that they would repent more if there was no Day of Atonement; that they would thank God more if there was no *Hallel* to sing at stated times on stated occasions; that they would rest more, in the sense that they would have more peace of the spiritual kind that blesses a man when he detaches himself from personal cares, if most things about the Sabbath were wiped out; and so for every other observance. All this "religion" was a substitute for religion in the true sense. A man didn't repent from his heart, because the repentance was automatically done for him, as it were, by his observance of the Day of Atonement. Similarly, a man didn't pray, because the prayer-saying was already there, waiting ready-made for him when otherwise the intention to pray might have risen spontaneously. And a man didn't praise God in an act of free communion, because the praise was prescribed in a formula.

This is not the end of the things that struck me about Jewish orthodoxy as I daily experienced it. What offended my intellect most—my intellect, as distinct from my obscure spiritual strivings—was something irrational at the heart of our manner of living: the irrationality that we, Victor Gollancz and his parents and his sisters and their friends and the people at the Bayswater Synagogue, should be doing a whole host of things and not doing a whole host of things, and doing them or not doing them as a matter of ultimate importance, simply because, by a mere accident of birth with which none of us had anything to do, we just happened to be Jews. The agony I've described myself as feeling in the streets on *Kippúr* stabbed at me every Friday evening as autumn and winter came round; and with the greater insistence, because the details of my essential similarity with people I must deliberately differ from were more obtrusive and more sharply defined. What possible meaning could there be in my walking home when the sun had set early, if Tommy Jones, in the same class at St. Paul's and doing the same Latin prose, took a train in the ordinary way from Hammersmith Broadway? Wasn't it the same Friday, the same sun, the same train, and the same Hammersmith Broadway, and if Victor Gollancz was the same sort of person as Emanuel Cohen, wasn't he, every bit as much, the same sort of person as Jones? Wasn't he, as I was often to find, even more the same sort of person as Jones, since it was with Jones and not Cohen that he shared the greater number of instincts and tastes? Worst of all, in this context, was the ban on intermarriage. A man and a woman, each of them unique, spontaneously loved one another: God had created them expressly to love one another: but their love must be frustrate and sterile—I felt a kind of despair, as for the hopelessly trapped, when I thought of it—because one was a Jew and the other a Gentile.

This was not the only irrationality that oppressed me. It seemed quite idiotic that because we were Jews we must do things (or, as the case might be, not do things) which had to be elaborately and sometimes most unconvincingly *explained*, or even explained away. There was the case of "Blessed art thou, O Lord our God, King of the Universe, who hast not made me a woman." There was the case of the electric light being a species of or substitute for fire, when the only solid reality involved was that Stygian lavatory after Sabbath had come in. Later, there was the case, even more remote and therefore fantastic, of the telephone. The nadir of folly seemed

reached when I could get *no* explanation at home of something
very strictly observed—these occasions were rare—and was referred to my Uncle Hermann, who, being a Rabbi, was an
even greater *melammed* than my father.

It was about synagogue that my various discomforts, intellectual and spiritual, reached their greatest intensity. The
atmosphere had no tang of spring about it; the services were
boring, stereotyped, repetitious (in respect of each other as
well as of themselves) and often ludicrously or even offen-
sively inapplicable to *me*, or, so far as I could judge, to any
single person present. All these readings from the *Torah* about
blemishes and leprosy and red spots and white spots and
women with issues of blood! Nauseating! And why on earth
should I listen to them, as the only result was to make me
stick pins into my body whenever, with a sharp stab of terror,
I suddenly detected a little whiteness here or redness there,
and wondered (nevertheless feeling quite certain about it)
whether *here*, on *me*, *this* might be the hideous "blemish"? And
the animal sacrifices! Hadn't they been put an end to, thank
Heaven, centuries before, and could anybody be so foul as even
to contemplate reviving them? Equally distressing, or more so,
were some of the things I had to listen to about God. We had
furious arguments about the slaughter of the Amalekites, and
one of my earliest recollections is of shouting myself hoarse,
when we had got home from synagogue one Saturday, about the
wickedness of a God who could be responsible for such abominations. Then there was "for I the Lord thy God am a jealous
God, visiting the iniquity of the fathers upon the children unto
the third and fourth generation of them that hate me." This
was another of the things that angered me as a very small boy,
for we had learned the ten commandments, as perhaps was
proper, almost in our cradles. God, I understood, was supremely
good: then how could he also be jealous, when to be jealous,
as I was taught but knew anyhow, was something we should
strive to avoid? As for "visiting the iniquity", what could be
more unfair than to punish a person for something he could
have had nothing to do with? My mother, who was well up in
what was then modern science, explained that there was a
reference in this passage to the unalterable laws of heredity.
I'm sure I didn't understand what she meant, but I do remember answering back (with a conceited know-allness which was

very characteristic of me but doesn't affect the aptness of my retort) that it was God, one must presume, who had created heredity, and that therefore she hadn't improved matters at all. She then pointed out, being anxious, no doubt, to save me for religion, that the "visiting" only applied if the descendants of the iniquitous one themselves hated God, and then only to the third and fourth generation; and that God, being good, shewed mercy to thousands and thousands of generations of men who loved him, and was prepared, in such cases, to overlook the iniquity of their ancestor. This seemed to me a very poor sort of argument, for God was still rewarding or punishing people for their attitude to himself, and this was surely the essence of immorality. I hadn't tumbled to the fact, and could hardly have been expected to do so, that Exodus chapter twenty, verses five and six, is one of the great landmarks in the history of religion; for the Jewish consciousness is here advancing on the road, to be explored far more thoroughly by the prophets, which will end with an understanding, when the earth shall be full of the knowledge of the Lord, that the swallowing up of justice in love is divinity and divine humanity. (I would add that institutional Christianity is still nowhere near the end of that road: when it has any real morality at all, it is just about arriving, with saintly exceptions, at the pre-prophetic Old Testament morality of righteous justice.) The *lex talionis*, again, was an abomination to me. It was unquestioningly accepted by orthodox Judaism, as embodying the common-sensible morality of all decent people to whom justice is precious; and official Christianity still tacitly obeys it. I was not told, as is the fact, that "an eye for an eye and a tooth for a tooth" registered an immense advance on the indiscriminate vengeance that had preceded it, and so points forward to the law of love.

In this account of how our orthodoxy impinged on me you will find quite a number of paradoxes. It is clear that I was deeply concerned about religion and morality; and the concern was not only intellectual, a pygmy thinker's interest in the nature of things, but self-regarding also in the better sense: in the sense that whenever I had the grace to think about the matter I earnestly desired to be good. Yet this very concern— this intellectual passion about religion and morality, which was wholly good, and this preoccupation with my own religion and morality, which was partly good—constantly betrayed me into attitudes that were grossly irreligious and immoral: into the judging and condemning of people around me, and into the disrespect, anger, contention and, worst of all, unkindness which, by very reason of my religious and moral concern, I was constantly attacking in others. This is the first paradox, and a very familiar one it is in the history of religion. It means that some seed of goodness, mercifully implanted in me as in every other human being, was pushing towards the light through a huge dead tonnage of carnality and unsaintliness: a seed that after another fifty years of struggle and experience is still only an inch or so nearer the goal. Some people are born with a purity of heart that is greater than the average, and they bless the world. I was not: perhaps I was born, indeed I think I was born (though I'm bound to say that when I look around me I begin to feel doubtful), with even less of it than usual: but I can still thank God that I was born with any of it at all and with a desire, which made a lot of false starts till it found some direction, to improve.

The second paradox, this time a hypothetical one, is perhaps more unusual; and it may seem to contradict, and possibly does contradict, a great deal of what I have previously been saying. You must bear it in mind, in any case, when you read what I shall have to write presently about "the other side" of orthodox Judaism. The paradox is this. Isn't it possible that the very ubiquity of "religion" in my boyhood's environment, the very crowding in on me of customs, observances, prescriptions and prohibitions that I felt, and think rightly felt, to be positively inimical to the religious life—isn't it possible that this irreligious (as I thought it) "religion" may not only have strengthened my own religious impulses but may even have been to some extent the source of them? And I do not mean merely in a negative way: I do not mean merely, what is obvious, that seeing so much letter about I instinctively turned to the spirit. I am wondering, additionally, whether the ubiquity of "religion" (with quotation marks) may not at any rate have helped me, positively and in its own right, to think about religion, to have a desire for and impulse towards religion (without the quotation marks). I am a religious man (you will not misunderstand me, or take me to imply that I think myself even a reasonably good man): is it certain that I should be so if my parents had been devoid, not only of religion in my sense, but also of "religion" in theirs? I am putting this in the form of a question, and I leave it as such; for I do not know the answer.

*Brimpton, Saturday, March 3rd*

*I had no intention, when I started this letter, of interposing little bits about things that might be happening around me during the actual writing of it. But I find, for the second time, that I cannot resist doing so. I am not referring to events in the world, such as "the Great Bevin Mystery" which is the headline in today's newspapers: or even to the meeting next Monday of the Foreign Ministers' Deputies in Paris, which may very well decide whether I shall live long enough to finish this letter or you will live long enough to read it. Politics are in my blood, and not to be concerned about them, and concerned about them passionately, is the mark, for me, of civic idiocy; but I am thinking, for all that, of events in a world still bigger than theirs, events beside which they seem fretfulness, events that are cosmic and, in all but the most obvious sense, eternal. I mean that I want to praise the weather.*

*I felt such happiness, perhaps, when describing my feelings on Westminster Bridge that I have the urge to feel a similar happiness in a different setting. Or is it that I have grown so accustomed to expressing myself that I must express myself now about everything? Or is it that I had a particularly refreshing sleep after lunch, and woke up about twenty minutes ago very peaceful and stupidly smiling? Or is it that my heart sings so often, and I can rarely do anything about it? However this may be, there was a ground frost this morning; but the sun soon came up, and now the sky is quite cloudless, and a shadow from the elms almost covers the lawn; and the ploughed earth beyond, where there aren't any elms, lies open and rosily brown; so I shall copy out a verse or two from "Love in the Valley", for they suddenly came into my head as I stood at the window a few minutes ago before settling myself down to resume:*

*"Soon will she lie like a white frost sunrise.*
  *Yellow oats and brown wheat, barley pale as rye,*
  *Long since your sheaves have yielded to the threasher,*
  *Felt the girdle loosened, seen the tresses fly.*

*Soon will she lie like a blood-red sunset.*
*Swift with the to-morrow, green-winged Spring!*
*Sing from the South-West, bring her back the truants,*
*Nightingale and swallow, song and dipping wing.*

*"Soft new beech-leaves, up to beamy April*
*Spreading bough on bough a primrose mountain, you,*
*Lucid in the moon, raise lilies to the skyfields,*
*Youngest green transfused in silver shining through:*
*Fairer than the lily, than the wild white cherry:*
*Fair as in image my seraph love appears*
*Borne to me by dreams when dawn is at my eyelids:*
*Fair as in the flesh she swims to me on tears."*

CHAPTER XII

# JEWISH ORTHODOXY:
## MY REACTION TO IT

IT SHOULD NOW hardly be necessary to describe to you how
I reacted to this conception of mine, true or false, of my father's
orthodoxy: what it made of me, on top of what his antifeminism
was making of me. To say "made of me" is no doubt to speak
too positively and too exclusively, for it seems pretty certain
that I was naturally the sort of person who in any case would
have turned out to some degree as I have, and that, in so far
as the particular development in me of which I am speaking
was the result of environment, my father's orthodoxy was not
the only element in this environment that conditioned it. But
I have no doubt whatever that it was the main element: that
it gave a depth and a passion which might otherwise have been
lacking to certain characteristics of thought and emotion that
have ruled my life for nearly fifty years and now rule it more
strongly than ever. And because I think these characteristics
are valuable characteristics I am grateful to the old man for
giving me them, and salute him. Then, when in earthly life,
he would have considered it an odd sort of gratitude that I
should thank him for making me what he would have thought
so improper: a person in so many respects so completely the
opposite of himself. But he is now in eternity, and so understands far better than I do that it is by the clashing of contraries
that the world proceeds, and that these goodnesses and bad-
nesses, as we see them, are but elements, each with its own
purpose, in the divine economy. I have the feeling, as I write
this, that I am communing with him now far more freely and
far more lovingly than I was ever able to do in his lifetime;
and I know that he has long since forgiven me (though "long
since" is inapplicable to eternity) for the crudity and harshness
of my so frequent behaviour.

I hope, by the way, that my reference to certain valuable
characteristics in me has not shocked you. Nothing could be
sillier than a refusal to judge oneself as objectively as one judges,
or ought to judge, one's neighbour, and to recognise what seems

valuable as clearheadedly as one recognises the reverse: provided that, in one's own case at least, one disclaims any personal
merit for what appears to be better, and that, in the case at least
of one's neighbour, one abjures the other kind of judgment, the
kind Christ warned us against, when observing what appears to
be worse. We should be in charity with ourselves, says the wise
Fénelon, as with our neighbours. We are all persons, and so of
equal value in God's sight, myself no less than you or the next
man; and we should thank him for anything useful in us, if we
honestly think it such, quite as much as we should thank him
for anything useful in others.

My father's orthodoxy, then, gave me an utter detestation of
anything that might fetter the human spirit. Compulsion in all
its forms became anathema to me: spiritual compulsion, intellectual compulsion, physical compulsion. (1) Spiritual compulsion: any interference, by custom or tradition or public opinion
or commandments or prohibitions or routine or tabus or (this
came later) the accumulated rubbish in one's own unconscious
—any interference by them with a free intercourse, a meeting,
between the individual human person and God or the divine
or the Whole. And if you object that nothing whatever, in the
last resort, can interfere with this free intercourse, provided the
impulse to it is strong enough, I will amend the statement, and
say, instead of "any interference with free intercourse", anything, whether it be custom or tradition etcetera, that weakens,
discourages or atrophies the impulse to this free intercourse.
(2) Intellectual compulsion: any conditioning of a person's mind,
or any attempted conditioning of it, to believe certain things (if
so disgraceful a perversion of the word "believe" may be over-
looked), because one's father believes it, or one's ancestors believed it, or every one of all the billions of human beings in the
world, save only oneself, believes it. And if your objection now
takes a different form, and you complain that the very existence of
your father's belief or your ancestors' belief (to say nothing of the
billions) must tend automatically to condition people of a certain
temperament to believe likewise, I will again amend my statement, and say, instead of "any conditioning of a person's mind",
any indifference to such conditioning, or any failure to counteract
such conditioning by every device in one's power. (3) Physical
compulsion: any restraint of a man's body or movements or way
of life, whether agreed upon or not by democratic process or

public opinion, and unless the individual in question has genuinely consented to it in his own case of his own uninhibited will.

My opposition to the first two compulsions—the spiritual and the intellectual—has always been absolute. My opposition to the third, the physical, has been qualified in practice by counterbalancing considerations. Nothing could be more tempting than political anarchism; but thorough-going anarchists must be politically stupid if they've reflected with any depth on the difficulties involved, and irresponsibly slap-dash if they haven't. For a responsible libertarian, however passionate his convictions, political anarchism is far too easy—"very convenient", as my father was given to saying in another and less appropriate connection. ("So you see nothing wrong in riding on *Shabbas*? Very convenient!") All libertarians, myself included, would be political anarchists tomorrow if our rudiments of intellectual honesty permitted it. I am referring, you will understand, to political anarchism as a theory of how society can here and now be organised—or rather non-organised—and not to a conviction of what the ultimate goal, which we must try to achieve with the maximum speed, should be. But *emotionally* my opposition to physical compulsion of any kind, from concentration camps at one end of the scale to passports and direction of labour at the other, has always been quite undiscriminating. I detest prisons and punishments and lawcourts and barracks and conscription (especially conscription) and party whips and drilling and saluting and ticket-collecting and barriers at railway stations and a hundred and one other things that you can supply for yourself: and I react to policemen, not as to the necessary custodians, and in the main very kindly ones, of a peaceful way of life, which is what my reason rightly tells me they are, but as to the impudent symbols of an alien authority; and I am sometimes uncomfortable when I see one. For authority, and *a fortiori* authoritarianism, are extremely repulsive to me. I even dislike talk, or specially dislike talk, about obeying God, as if he were some Stalin or Hitler: I cannot think that he wants me to obey him: what he wants, I think, is that I should learn to co-operate, quietly and in complete freedom, with his blessed and blessing will, that will of his which I discover deep in my own heart as my own will also—as the best, essential me—and which, discovering it also deep in the heart of everything else, I find to be not only vaster, but also saner and more fruitful of life and peace and joy, than the self-regarding wilfulness that would deceive me with its appearance of leading me to my goal, but would in fact cut me off, if it had its way, from my birthright of unity with all things.

By the same token, my father's orthodoxy made me dislike and distrust all orthodoxies as such, and in particular religious orthodoxies: it made me what is called a liberal in religion. I am still a liberal in religion. The impulse I received, by reaction, from my early environment was so powerful that I am now in many ways, and contrary to the general belief, an exceedingly old-fashioned person; and I cannot pretend to be regretful about it. The case for liberalism in religion seems to me every bit as strong today—I would not say stronger, for this would be impossible—as it did when I first went one Saturday afternoon (still walking) to what was then a makeshift Liberal Jewish Synagogue in some strange part of London. I dislike neo-orthodoxy in the religious sense, as I dislike neo most other things: neo-patriotism, for instance, which has so largely replaced in the Labour Party the splendid old internationalism of men like Keir Hardie, and neo-anti-progressivism and neo-anti-humanism and the rest. I still believe quite passionately in humanism and even, odd though this may seem with the world as it is, in the idea of progress: provided, naturally, that both humanism and progress are what I should regard as sanely defined. So I might, I suppose, be described as a reactionary: wrongly, I think, because it is the neoists who in my view are the real reactionaries, the difference between us being that their *terminus a quo*, the point to which they react, is a lot more remote than mine. The Bishop of Birmingham takes certain theological positions with some of which, it happens, I am not in agreement; but when his whole point of view and the general manner of his thinking are contemptuously brushed aside, by people who are neither cleverer nor more Christian than himself, as "a throw-back to the outmoded ideas of the nineteenth century", the old familiar anger begins rising in my Adam. I am not denying that there are men of great spiritual depth and the acutest brains who hold antiliberal views, in religion or anything else, because their conception of reality differs from, as it may be truer than, mine; but this is something quite different from the new intellectual snobbishness, as I occasionally detect it, of being antiliberal, in religion or in anything else, because to be antiliberal is to be in the swim. This is even more disagreeable than the old intellectual snobbishness that required one, in certain circles, to be radical about everything.

There is a passage in the preface to Mr C. S. Lewis' *The Problem of Pain* that runs as follows:

"If any real theologian reads these pages he will very easily see that they are the work of a layman and an amateur. Except in the last two chapters, parts of which are admittedly speculative, I have believed myself to be restating ancient and orthodox doctrines. *If any parts of the book are 'original', in the sense of being novel or unorthodox, they are so against my will* and as a result of my ignorance. I write, of course, as a layman of the Church of England: but I have tried to assume nothing that is not professed by all baptised and communicating Christians."*

It is not suggested—even the disclaimer is impertinent—that Mr Lewis is other than a good and sincere man whose quest is for truth, as he is certainly of brilliant intelligence; nor is it denied that there is a case, an intellectual and spiritual case, for "belief" in accepted dogmas as such, even though I may think it a very bad case and feel bound to beg the question by putting the word belief between quotation marks. The paragraph is reproduced solely because, with its flavour of spiritual and intellectual masochism, it expresses with great candour an attitude, or quite a series of attitudes, that my early environment makes detestable to me. Implicitly denying that God relies on every one of us to be his prophet, stammer a thousand times worse than Moses though we may ("Now therefore go, and I will be with thy mouth, and teach thee what thou shalt say"), the passage italicised seems to me far less religious in feeling than the atheism of a Bradlaugh or the antichristianity of a Nietzsche, both of whom—those passionate, conscience-driven and mistaken missionaries—God must rather specially have loved. For they listened to the Him within them, and refused to be put off with anything second-hand: and so were excused, surely, for hearing Him wrong.

There was an argument once in the breakfast-room at Elgin Avenue about the resurrection of the dead. Now in Biblical times there had been a difference of opinion on this point, as you can learn from the New Testament: the Pharisees were for,

* The italics are mine.

and the Sadducees against. But a creed was compiled by Moses Maimonides in the twelfth century, which affirms, among other things, "I believe in the resurrection of the dead"; so the question was settled. I don't remember how I came to raise the matter; I may have overheard the Christian creed at my prep school, and when I got home expressed scepticism. Anyhow, my father said "Jews believe in the resurrection of the dead." I was furious. "How can you talk about what *Jews* believe?" I asked him indignantly; "how can *people* believe a thing? It's only *a person* who can believe a thing, not *people*." I can remember with the utmost vividness the intellectual agony I suffered at the idea of being calmly told that believing was something that automatically happened to you, something ready-made for you whether you liked it or not, just because you were a Jew: at the irrationality, the wickedness of it. My father probably murmured to my mother, as he frequently did on such occasions, "The boy's *meshuggah* [which means cracked]." Cracked or not, I am sure I was insufferably rude. But formulae and creeds, as a result of such episodes, went the way of a great many other things; and so did organised or institutional Judaism, and organised or institutional religion in general. I quickly came, also, to feel a deep intellectual horror for anything that struck me as an irrationality, quite apart from the irrationality of "believing" in the manner just described: any doing of a thing or not doing of a thing for no reason, or for a fictitious reason, or for someone else's reason, or for everybody else's reason, or for any reason whatever except a reason that honestly seemed sufficient to oneself; and all special pleadings, all self-deceiving explanations. I was acquiring, in fact, the Socratic urge, but not the Socratic patience.

Finally, my father's orthodoxy made me, in my reaction to Jewish particularism, an utterly whole-hearted universalist. By a universalist (a theological expression that can be conveniently adapted) I mean something much "more" than an internationalist. An internationalist is a man who dislikes any barrier between nations, and does everything in his power to break them down: a universalist is a person for whom nations don't exist, only persons.

Apart from a chapter or two of important qualifications, I have now finished what I have to say about orthodox Judaism;

and you may wonder why I have talked at such length about customs that are fast disappearing, and for which there can clearly be no future. Well, apart from wanting you to understand what sort of person I was when I went to teach at Repton, and why, I am desperately anxious that you should understand Christianity, for that, when it comes to it, is what this letter is about; and there are things in Christianity, I feel certain, that can be better understood for a previous understanding of orthodox Judaism. I often wonder, indeed, whether a Gentile, however imaginative, can really live as a Jew can in the New Testament atmosphere. Time after time, while I was writing the previous pages, familiar passages came into my head. "The letter killeth and the spirit maketh alive." "But when ye pray, use not vain repetitions, as the heathen do; for they think that they shall be heard for their much speaking." "Not that which goeth into the mouth defileth a man; but that which cometh out of the mouth, this defileth a man." "The uppermost seats in the synagogues." "Which strain at a gnat, and swallow a camel." "The sabbath was made for man, and not man for the sabbath." "Ye hold the tradition of men, as the washing of pots and cups." "Let the dead bury their dead." "Which now of these three, thinkest thou, was neighbour?" "But rather give alms of such things as ye have; and behold, all things are clean unto you." "I fast twice in the week." "God is a Spirit: and they that worship him must worship him in spirit and in truth." "For when the Gentiles, which have not the law, do by nature the things contained in the law, these, having not the law, are a law unto themselves; which shew the work of the law written in their hearts." These and many more; but chiefly "There is no difference between the Jew and the Greek: for the same Lord over all is rich unto all that call upon him."

# CHAPTER XIII

## SOME QUALIFICATIONS

AND NOW HAVING GOT through a very unpleasant task I shall turn to something happier: to the qualifications, the other side of the picture. If you are a sensitive boy you will not have been deceived by some fun on the way into imagining that to criticise, even perhaps apparently to "guy", my parents' religion has been anything but painful to me: so painful that many times I have been tempted to abandon the whole enterprise in an access of self-disgust. And so it gives me now a feeling of great happiness, and of a burden lifted from my shoulders, to say that the orthodox Judaism I have been attacking is *in its intention*, in the impulse behind it, an exceptionally and in some respects a uniquely beautiful manifestation of the religious genius.

I am not referring to what would be described as beautiful, without any qualifying "in its intention", by almost everybody of average perception: the grand movement, I mean, of the story that begins with the iconoclasm of Abraham and ends with the birth of Jesus Christ. And not only its grand movement, but the many landmarks on its way—those eminences, to use a better word, that rise as high, in the perspective of history, above the cruelties and narrownesses and chauvinisms, the dull routine level of folly and wickedness, as goodness always rises, when viewed by the spiritual consciousness in that perspective, above evil.

I wish I could write a whole book on this subject. I should describe in it the slow reaching out to the conception of an all-loving and all-merciful God: with a quotation, by way of prelude, from Genesis—"And the dove came in to him in the evening; and, lo, in her mouth was an olive leaf pluckt off: so Noah knew that the waters were abated from off the earth"— and with another, by way of conclusion, from Jonah: "Then said the Lord, Thou hast had pity on the gourd, for the which thou hast not laboured, neither madest it grow; which came up in a night, and perished in a night: and should not I spare Nineveh, that great city, wherein are more than sixscore thousand persons that cannot discern between their right hand and their left hand; and also much cattle?"

I should describe, next, how the groundwork was laid for such a way of social living as, so many centuries later, no large-scale community has even yet come anywhere near to attaining. I might begin with what could be called, to make a false distinction, its more public aspect: "When thou cuttest down thine harvest in thy field, and hast forgot a sheaf in the field, thou shalt not go again to fetch it: it shall be for the stranger, for the fatherless, and for the widow: that the Lord thy God may bless thee in all the work of thine hands." "And six years thou shalt sow thy land, and shalt gather in the fruits thereof: but the seventh year thou shalt let it rest and lie still; that the poor of thy people may eat: and what they leave the beasts of the field shall eat. In like manner thou shalt deal with thy vineyard, and with thy olive-yard." "At the end of every seven years thou shalt make a release. And this is the manner of the release; Every creditor that lendeth ought unto his neighbour shall release it: he shall not exact it of his neighbour, or of his brother; because it is called the Lord's release." "And ye shall hallow the fiftieth year, and proclaim liberty throughout all the land unto all the inhabitants thereof: it shall be a jubile unto you; and ye shall return every man unto his possession, and ye shall return every man unto his family."

Then, still on this topic of social living, I might go on with what could be called its more private aspect: "If there be among you a poor man of one of thy brethren within any of thy gates in thy land which the Lord thy God giveth thee, thou shalt not harden thine heart, nor shut thine hand from thy poor brother: but thou shalt open thine hand wide unto him, and shalt surely lend him sufficient for his need, in that which he wanteth." "No man shall take the nether or the upper millstone to pledge: for he taketh a man's life to pledge." "When thou dost lend thy brother any thing, thou shalt not go into his house to fetch his pledge. Thou shalt stand abroad, and the man to whom thou dost lend shall bring out the pledge abroad unto thee." "If thou at all take thy neighbour's raiment to pledge, thou shalt deliver it unto him by that the sun goeth down: for that is his covering only, it is his raiment for his skin: wherein shall he sleep?" "Thou shalt not lend upon usury to thy brother; usury of money, usury of victuals, usury of

any thing that is lent upon usury." "Thou shalt not see thy
brother's ox or his sheep go astray, and hide thyself from them:
thou shalt in any case bring them again unto thy brother. And
if thy brother be not nigh unto thee, or if thou know him not,
then thou shalt bring it unto thine own house, and it shall be
with thee until thy brother seek after it, and thou shalt restore
it to him again. In like manner shalt thou do with his ass; and
so shalt thou do with his raiment; and with all lost things of thy
brother's, which he hath lost, and thou hast found, shalt thou
do likewise: thou mayest not hide thyself." "Thou shall not
deliver unto his master the servant which is escaped from his
master unto thee." "If thou meet thine enemy's ox or his ass
going astray, thou shalt surely bring it back to him again. If
thou see the ass of him that hateth thee lying under his burden,
and wouldest forbear to help him, thou shalt surely help with
him." "Thou shalt not avenge, nor bear any grudge against the
children of thy people, but shalt love thy neighbour as thyself:
I am the Lord." "But the stranger that dwelleth with you shall
be unto you as one born among you; and thou shalt love him as
thyself; for ye were strangers in the land of Egypt: I am the
Lord your God." Reading this last passage, side by side with
"If thou seest the ass of him that hateth thee", we tremble on
the brink of what is in one sense just a further stage in ethical
development, but in another is as the sudden emergence of the
divine and absolute in human relativities: "But I say unto you,
Love your enemies."

Then, in this hypothetical book of mine, I should describe
Hebrew prophecy. I should describe, first, the nature of it, as a
direct meeting between God and man unmediated by any law
or externality: "For this commandment which I command thee
this day, it is not hidden from thee, neither is it far off. It is not
in heaven, that thou shouldest say, Who shall go up for us to
heaven, and bring it unto us, that we may hear it, and do it?
Neither is it beyond the sea, that thou shouldest say, Who shall
go over the sea for us, and bring it unto us, that we may hear it,
and do it? But the word is very nigh unto thee, in thy mouth,
and in thy heart, that thou mayest do it." And I should
describe, secondly, the message that issues from this meeting
of God and man: "Wherewith shall I come before the Lord,
and bow myself before the high God? shall I come before
him with burnt offerings, with calves of a year old? Will the

Lord be pleased with thousands of rams, or with ten thousands of rivers of oil? shall I give my firstborn for my transgression, the fruit of my body for the sin of my soul? He hath shewed thee, O man, what is good; and what doth the Lord require of thee, but to do justly, and to love mercy, and to walk humbly with thy God?"

I should have something to say, too, before I ended, about the emergence of universalism: "In that day shall there be a highway out of Egypt to Assyria, and the Assyrian shall come unto Egypt, and the Egyptians shall serve with the Assyrians. In that day shall Israel be the third with Egypt and with Assyria, even a blessing in the midst of the land: whom the Lord of hosts shall bless, saying Blessed be Egypt my people, and Assyria the work of my hands, and Israel my inheritance." And I should end my book, I think, with the vision that always makes one long so that one's own heart were gentler and more loving: "They shall not hurt nor destroy in all my holy mountain: for the earth shall be full of the knowledge of the Lord, as the waters cover the sea."

But that is not the book I am writing; and what I am after now is to suggest that Jewish orthodoxy as I actually observed it round me in my boyhood, right down to the grotesquerie of not carrying a handkerchief (loose) on the Sabbath, was "*in its intention*, in the impulse behind it, an exceptionally and in some respects a uniquely beautiful manifestation of the religious genius." John Macmurray has written that "the Hebrew form of thought rebels against the very idea of a distinction between the secular and the religious aspects of life." Now I distrust generalisations about national or racial forms of thought, just as I distrust generalisations about national or racial "characteristics". The same Greece produced Plato and Aristotle, the one essentially a mystic and the other a forerunner of scientific rationalism; and though you could say, in a sense, that the minds of both of them were "Greek"—in the sense, though even this is going too far, that the area of attention was in both cases a Greek area—what divided them is far more important, for the history of thought, than anything they had in common. Again, the same Judaea produced Caiaphas and Jesus; but Caiaphas was a Jewish particularist who relied on the letter (to interpret him most favourably) as a safeguard for the spirit, whereas Jesus was a universalist for whom the spirit, which might sometimes express itself in the letter, was everything. Nevertheless, Macmurray's dictum is true, and, to use the title of his own book, a clue to history, provided that by "the Hebrew form of thought" we understand the general manner in which, during a great creative period of Hebrew life, the men who were most influential in giving it its direction were thinking and feeling.

The fact of the matter, as I see it, is this. In some way and from some impulse we can never understand, unless we adopt (as I adopt but with my own interpretation of it) the broad notion of a divine purpose, there arose in this primitive people the conception of righteousness, and the conception of it as the word of a Person who was neither what they found in their own hearts nor what they experienced as bearing down on them in the external world, but a mingling of both, and with those characteristics of nearness and farness, of immanence and transcendence, of power and love, which might be expected from the combination, and which invested him with the quality of awfulness and "the numinous". It was natural that, discovering this righteousness and discovering it as the word of this Person, the discoverers should experience their discovery as involving, or rather as being identical with, an election, a being chosen by the Person as a nation of his priests, and as involving, by the same token, a covenant between the Person and themselves: a covenant which inevitably presented itself as involving commandment on the one side and obedience to it on the other. It was natural, too, that the tribal tabus already existing should be incorporated into the commandment, partly because they *were* tabus and partly because they would now become rationalised as a mark of the particularist election; but, for that latter very reason, there would now attach to them, at the conscious level of thought and feeling (however much they might remain tabus in the unconscious), the notion of holiness in a new and higher sense, the notion of a being connected, and connected inseparably, with the righteousness—the real righteousness, the righteousness of not stealing or murdering or coveting or committing adultery—now discovered as the Person's word.

It follows that "the very idea of a distinction between the secular and the religious aspects of life" is not merely rebelled against, but just cannot arise. It is precisely *life* that is the subject of the covenant—and to talk about *aspects* of life, in such a connection, is meaningless. You either dedicate yourself or don't dedicate yourself. It is life itself, life as such, that becomes religious: by which I mean that it is life itself, life as such, which is unquestioningly lived in contact with the Person, and as a matter both for obedience and for gratitude. Nothing is excluded; more than this, the idea couldn't conceivably occur that anything *could* be excluded. Let me give you an extreme example, though you will understand, if you've understood anything at all of what I've been saying, that in fact there cannot be any question of "extreme". There is nothing more secular, you might imagine, than going to the lavatory, about which, when the amenities are insufficient, I have already commented. But in the Authorised Daily Prayer Book of the United Hebrew Congregations of the British Empire you will find something very interesting on page four, almost immediately after the beginning of the early morning service. A magnificat has been recited; the spirit and body have been commended to God at the dawning of the day; and thanks have been given for the commandment that we should sanctify ourselves by washing our hands. Then comes the following: "Blessed art thou, O Lord our God, King of the universe, who hast formed man in wisdom, and created in him many orifices and vessels. It is revealed and known before the throne of thy glory, that if one of these be opened, or one of those be closed, it would be impossible to exist and to stand before thee. Blessed art thou, O Lord, who healest all flesh and doest wondrously." The reference is to the processes of urination and evacuation. A religion that regards these processes as to be religiously rejoiced in is an integral religion.

I had a rather heated argument the other night with a dear Roman Catholic friend, which illustrates my point. We were dining with John Collins, the Canon of St. Paul's. John had invited me to preach at his cathedral, in the inconceivable event of his chapter and the Bishop permitting it. My other friend was scandalised at the suggestion, not merely because I was a Jew (which was bad enough) but even more because I wasn't a priest. With my "Jewish" point of view I was equally scandalised: wasn't a priest anyone who spoke the word of God from his heart, and for the purpose of speaking it what slightest difference could there be between St. Paul's and Henrietta

---

Street, or, for the matter of that, between St. Paul's and a brothel? I very nearly said that Christ would quite obviously have agreed with me.

Once, as a matter of fact, I did act as a priest. I have always been glad I was married in synagogue (and I will add, for the sheer pleasure of recalling it, the total irrelevancy that your grandmother—who is not a Hittite but a Philistine, and might have been made by a Praxiteles if God had not made her so first—looked indescribably beautiful in cloth of gold with white lilies). So I thought it a good idea that your mother should be married in one too, and she agreed with me. But the Rabbi of the synagogue to which I still nominally belonged had a scruple about marrying them there unless your father went in first for some Jewish instruction, which might have taken quite a long time; for he is only half-Jewish by birth. This suited no one: they wanted to be married at once, so that they could have you sooner. They were married, accordingly, by registrar; but when we got home I became a temporary Rabbi myself, for I had the temerity to marry them all over again before the assembled company, in accordance with the beautiful old ritual: blessings (in Hebrew, with English translations for the *goyim*) and canopy and wine-glass-breaking and all.

The Chassidic movement of the eighteenth century appears to have expressed most completely, during the comparatively short period of its apogee, this conception, or naïf realisation, of what must appear to the genuinely religious consciousness as an unquestionable fact: namely, that to talk of "the secular" or "the religious" aspects of life is to perpetrate a meaningless dichotomy. It was a Chassidic Rabbi, the saintly Pinhas of Koretz, who said: "If a man declares that the words of the Torah are one thing and the words of the world are another, he must be regarded as denying God." Another Chassid remarked that "Enoch was a cobbler; with each stitch of his awl that drew together the top and bottom leather, he joined God and his Shekhínah";* and a third was fond of saying that he prayed "with the floor and the bench". There is a beautiful passage in one of Martin Buber's books which, interpreting

* The Shekhínah is the Divine Presence in the world: where it remains "exiled" until "the restoration of all things":

R. G. IN THE THIRTIES

Chassidism, expresses the matter in words that anyone with a Jewish background will immediately understand: "One should, and one must, truly live with all, but one should live with all in holiness, one should hallow all that one does in one's natural life. No renunciation is commanded. One eats in holiness, tastes the taste of food in holiness, and the table becomes an altar. One works in holiness, and he raises up the sparks which hide themselves in all tools. One walks in holiness across the fields, and the soft songs of all herbs, which they voice to God, enter into the song of our soul. One drinks in holiness to each other with one's companions, and it is as if they read together in the Torah. One dances the roundelay in holiness, and a brightness shines over the gathering. A husband is united with his wife in holiness, and the Shekhínah rests over them."

Defining the word sacrament as the pledge of a covenant between God and man, you might call this view of life pan-sacramental. It is the true view, the view that corresponds with reality; and the Kingdom of Heaven means to live in the spirit of it.

But something else followed from the discovery of this primitive people, something other than a rebellion against "the very idea of a distinction between the secular and the religious aspects of life"; or the same thing, as perhaps one should rather say, but expressed in a different form. What followed was this. Every command of the Person was sacred, and every command of the Person was equally sacred; not in the sense that to seethe a kid in his mother's milk must be considered as grave a sin as to commit murder (I doubt whether any Jew at any period of Judaism would have said anything even remotely of the kind), but in the sense that deliberately to do either would for a religious man, in view of the covenant, be equally unthinkable. And every command was binding, and equally binding, for two reasons: first, because it *was* a command; and secondly because to obey it was to be true to your election, to be faithful to your calling as an individual in a nation of priests, to mark yourself out as separate and "peculiar", whereas to transgress it was a betrayal, a making of yourself just like everybody else, a cutting of yourself off from among your people. The dread of betraying is very deep and very instinctive among Jews. It was this, doubt-less, that decisively—for other emotions were involved, such as disgust at the idea of "ratting" from your ship—prevented Bergson from taking the final step into the Roman Catholic church; and it is certainly this that has changed the attitude of many Jews since the establishment of the State of Israel. Before, they felt it proper to "identify themselves" with Jewry, lest some-thing precious, the special contribution to civilisation of the Jewish people, might vanish from the world; now they feel no such obligation, and are ready to "identify themselves" with the England or the any other country that has captured their heart, or better still with mankind as a whole. And they do so with a sigh of relief.

I have repeatedly used the word "command", and I now want to emphasise it again, for it explains many things in orthodox Jewish practice which would otherwise be inexplic-able. You will remember that when the weather was too bad for walking on a Saturday we stayed away from synagogue sooner than ride. Now how could anybody believe that the negative act of not taking a 'bus was more important than the positive act of attending divine worship? The explanation is simple and, given the premisses, completely satisfying. There is a biblical injunction to rest on the Sabbath, but no such injunction to attend Sabbath worship. To rest on the Sabbath included, by authoritative interpretation, not taking a 'bus. So if it came to a choice between taking a 'bus and not going to synagogue, the matter was already decided. Saying your prayers was no doubt exceedingly important; but there was nothing particularly sacred about a synagogue, and you could say your prayers equally well at home. My father, in point of fact, invariably recited the whole prescribed service when he stayed away from synagogue on Saturday. This very lack of any particular sacredness about a synagogue is another illus-tration of the rebellion "against the very idea of a distinction between the secular and religious aspects of life."

Finally, while all the commandments were equally binding, it is clear that a special sort of atmosphere would hang about those of them which were really incorporated tabus. This explains, I believe, the peculiar horror of an orthodox Jew at the idea of eating pig in any of its metamorphoses, a horror which, as you know, I substantially share. This horror is of a type which distinguishes it, and quite unmistakably, from horror about stealing or coveting, or even, perhaps, committing murder. Neither the intellect nor the spirit are involved, except by way of rationalisation. Your gorge just rises at the thought of it. You shudder.

*Brimpton, March 10th*

*Something has just happened which illustrates what I have been writing during the last few hours, something as delightful to the critical intelligence, in the beautiful clarity of its revelation, as it is shocking to the spirit. John Collins has been on the telephone: he had just had a meeting with his Dean and chapter about the question of my preaching at St. Paul's, and wanted to report. Of the four Canons three had acquiesced, though without much enthusiasm, but the fourth had objected quite violently. Collins, it appears, had explained to them that he wanted to have a sermon on "the Christian response to the present situation"—we have all been saying for some time that war is not inevitable, which means very nearly the opposite—and that he thought I was well suited to deliver it. John is far too kind to me, but that is not the point. The fourth Canon, when asked to clarify his objection, began as follows: "I proclaim the inalienable right of a Christian to be a bad man." He went on to explain that Christianity was not a matter of goodness or badness, but a matter of being baptised into the Body of Christ; and that as I had never, he understood, been so baptised, I was automatically ruled out from taking any part in a Christian service. Now this is not so stupid as it sounds: I could argue a man's head off, theologically, in favour of it, and even in favour of the Canon's opening sentence: but it is quite as irreligious as it sounds, in my sense, naturally, of the word irreligious. However, my only motive in citing the Canon's apophthegm is to point a contrast. "I proclaim the inalienable right of a Christian to be a bad man." No Jew, provided that he thought of himself as a Jew by religion and not merely as a Jew by birth, could conceivably say "I proclaim the inalienable right of a Jew to be a bad man". He might be sadly mistaken, as the Pharisees were, about the nature of goodness and badness; he might even be, consciously, a very bad man; but to say that he had the right, and as a Jew, to be a bad man— such a thing would be utterly unthinkable. For righteousness, here and now and in this earthly life, is precisely what the covenant was*

*about. The Canon was in fact expressing, with startling candour,
a dualistic point of view of the kind to which "the Hebrew form of
thought", as Macmurray would call it, is wholly antipathetic.
This "Hebrew form of thought" itself paradoxically resulted, as
we shall presently see, in dualism of another type, though it may
come to very much the same thing in practice: in letter without
spirit, observance without intention, "religion" without religion;
but the result was due to mistaken applications of a true insight
into reality, and not to an initial schizophrenia. It is this schizophrenia which has brought so much of institutional Christianity
into well-merited contempt: it is this which has made the average
Archbishop a blesser of battleships, and will presently make him a
blesser of hydrogen bombs.*

*"I proclaim the inalienable right of a Christian to be a bad man."
What has this to do with Christ, who told men to be perfect even as
their Father in heaven was perfect?*

You will now understand, I think, why I described orthodox
Judaism, right down to its last formalistic absurdity, as in
impulse and intention so beautiful. For the intention is that the
whole of life, every moment and every thought and every action
in it, should be lived as something holy and sacramental: something sanctified by the covenant between God and man, with
its commandments on the one side and its obedience on the
other. Or, with a slightly different emphasis, the intention is
that Israel should never fail, Israel as the path-finder for
humanity, to play its part, which is seen almost if not quite as
an equal part, in an eternal act of divine-human co-operation.
Hence all the seemingly ridiculous minutiæ by which the Law
is interpreted and hedged around: hence all those daily
reminders, from "Magnified and praised be the living God" at
the break of day to "Stand in awe, and sin not: commune with
your own heart upon your bed, and be still" before the closing
of the eyes for sleep. Reminders of what? Reminders at once
of the covenant, the election, the holiness of life, and the perpetual presence of God.

How beautiful many of these reminders are! Consider one of
those that derive directly from the *Shemá*, itself a quite perfect
expression of the sense that every moment in life is sacred.
"Hear, O Israel: the Lord our God, the Lord is One. And

these words, which I command thee this day, shall be upon thine heart: and thou shalt teach them diligently unto thy children, and shalt talk of them *when thou sittest in thine house, and when thou walkest by the way, and when thou liest down, and when thou risest up. And thou shalt bind them for a sign upon thine hand, and they shall be for frontlets between thine eyes. And thou shalt write them upon the doorposts of thy house, and upon thy gates*." And therefore, just as the *tephillin* are laid "for a sign upon thine hand, and for frontlets between thine eyes", so the *mezzuza* is affixed to the entrance of a house and to the doorpost of every room in it: a little oblong box containing the verses I have just written out, and with an aperture revealing that same ‫ש‬, standing for *Shaddai* or the Lord our God, which is formed every morning on the fingers of the left hand by the leather thongs of the *tephillin*. I love *mezzuzas*, and have them on my own front door here at Brimpton and on the doorposts of several rooms in the house; and knowing how I loved them my office staff gave me one when your grandmother and I had been married for twenty-five years, a beautiful silver thing of unusual size and eighteenth century workmanship, which they got from old Mosheh Oved, who calls himself Edward Goode, at Cameo Corner near the British Museum. I put it on the drawing-room door, and next time you come here I shall show it you and teach you the word *mezzuza*. I wish everybody had *mezzuzas*, and really looked at them and thought about them as they passed in and out. For they signify that the house and every room in it, and every house and every room in every house, are temples of the living God: or—to put it in a way that you will perhaps think less sentimental, and it comes to the same thing—are or should be dedicated to the expression of all that is best in the human spirit.

There are many other "reminders" I could describe to you, such as the *arba kanfas*, the simple little sacred garment that is put next to the skin when dressing, under the ordinary vest. This consists of two oblong pieces, one for the chest and the other for the back, joined by a couple of shoulder straps: the four corners of it (the words *arba kanfas* mean "four corners") are fringed, and they represent the four corners of an earth that is God's and man's. I gave up wearing mine before I was twelve. But what I really want to tell you about—I have been looking forward to it for the last couple of hours, eager for the moment to arrive—is the series of blessings for every conceivable occasion, a few of which I have already quoted. "A man," said Rabbi Meir, who lived in the second century A.D., "should utter daily a hundred benedictions." What a different sort of place the world would be if we all did this, and did it, every time, from the heart! There are blessings over the bread and wine, to which Christianity owes its great sacrament; blessings over grapes and figs and pomegranates and olives and dates and herbs and eggs and cheese; blessings for the smell of fragrant woods and odorous plants and odorous fruits and fragrant spices; blessings on seeing lightning, or falling stars, or high mountains, or great deserts; and the blessing on hearing thunder, spoiled a little perhaps by the word "might"—"Blessed art thou, whose strength and might fill the world." There is the blessing on entering into possession of a new house, or on wearing a new suit, or on tasting anything for the first time in its season—a blessing I particularly like, and quite often recite to myself, especially over the first crop of asparagus: "Blessed art thou, O Lord our God, King of the universe, who hast kept us in life, and hast preserved us, and hast enabled us to reach this season". And there are two which surpass all the others, one of them for the simplicity of its praise, and the other for the way it mingles acceptance of the divine will with charity to our fellow men. The first is at sight of beautiful trees or animals: "Blessed art thou, who hast such as these in thy world". The second is at sight of malformed persons: "Blessed art thou, who variest the forms of thy creatures".

I hope I have proved my point about the beauty of intention in Jewish orthodoxy. What then was wrong? Why so sharp a contrast between what I have just been describing and the earlier description of my boyhood's environment? Let us see.

# CHAPTER XIV

# ORTHODOX JUDAISM: WHAT WAS WRONG

THIS IS WHAT WAS wrong: The vision of reality from which Judaism developed was a true vision; but the very whole-heartedness of the desire to live always in complete loyalty to it was productive of a technique which itself made the realisation of that desire impossible. The word technique is a valuable clue: to combine a technique, any technique, with freedom and spontaneity, which are the essential characteristics of spiritual living, is all but impossible. To use a favourite expression of Berdyaev, what took place in orthodox Judaism was a process of objectivisation. You grasp a truth: realising its preciousness, you draw up a series of rules and regulations to ensure your fidelity to that truth: and by the very fact of so doing you destroy the reciprocal relationship that is its essence. Everything is externalised. It is as if a man, falling in love with a woman, proceeded to elaborate a technique that would rule out the slightest possibility of anything going wrong between them. He would kiss her (so he would decide) in such and such a manner at such and such a time; he would sleep with her on this night in this way, and on that night in that; he would hang her portrait in his office, and "religiously" look at it every morning when he came in and every evening when he went out; and he would carry a lock of her hair over his heart, and would take it out, to remind himself of her, at certain fixed moments on his way to and fro. It is perhaps too much to say that a love so safeguarded would inevitably die; but it is certain that only a man with such a genius for love as could survive anything (or, in the religious analogy, only a saint) could preserve unimpaired by the mortification of this routine that immediate, spontaneous, wayward and inconsequential quality in the meeting between two persons, that infinite variety in the experience of their union, which is what we mean by human love.

An occasional symbol, an occasional "reminder", an occasional set occasion, these may be invaluable in the religious life: but multiply them until they occupy the field, and they stifle the impulse that gave them birth. No longer does the spirit of a man commune freely with the spirit of God which he finds always within his own heart, even in the very experiencing of it as also beyond; instead, he relates himself as subject to an object external to him, he bows down before an idol and worships it. Idols, these were what I felt around me in my father's house: the Sabbath, the Passover, the dietary laws, the saying of prayers, all were idols. It was an idol that Abraham broke when he left his birthplace "to follow the call of his invisible God"; and now it had come back in another form.

And yet so powerful was the religious genius of the Hebrew people that voices were never lacking to warn them against this idolatrous apostasy, and to use it as the occasion for a further advance. This is the meaning of prophecy:

"Wherefore have we fasted, say they, and thou seest not? wherefore have we afflicted our soul, and thou takest no knowledge? Behold, in the days of your fast ye find pleasure, and exact all your labours . . .

"Is it such a fast that I have chosen? a day for a man to afflict his soul? is it to bow down his head as a bulrush, and to spread sackcloth and ashes under him? wilt thou call this a fast, and an acceptable day to the Lord?

"Is not this the fast that I have chosen? to loose the bands of wickedness, to undo the heavy burdens, and to let the oppressed go free, and that ye break every yoke?

"Is it not to deal thy bread to the hungry, and that thou bring the poor that are cast out to thy house? when thou seest the naked, that thou cover him; and that thou hide not thyself from thine own flesh?

"Then shall thy light break forth as the morning, and thine health shall spring forth speedily: and thy righteousness shall go before thee; the glory of the Lord shall be thy rearward.

"*Then shalt thou call, and the Lord shall answer; thou shalt cry, and he shall say, Here I am.* If thou take away from the midst of thee the yoke, the putting forth of the finger, and speaking vanity;

"And if thou draw out thy soul to the hungry, and satisfy the afflicted soul; then shall thy light rise in obscurity, and thy darkness be as the noon day:

"*And the Lord shall guide thee continually,* and satisfy thy soul in drought, and make fat thy bones: and thou shalt be like a watered garden, and like a spring of water, whose waters fail not."

Had there been no idolatry to prophesy against, Isaiah might never have written that passage: and Isaiah was the forerunner of Christ.

And still I have the uneasy feeling that I may have been unfair. There were men in my boyhood of the most scrupulous orthodoxy whose saintliness was beyond question: men such as Solomon Schechter and Simeon Singer, to name only two. There are men of the same kind today. Is one simply to believe then that saintliness, which is rare, can use anything for its purpose, the law-abiding performance of inherited observances no less than the liberty of those who are a law unto themselves? Yes, I think one should believe that, and no more. But I am bound nevertheless at least to ask myself whether for men of a temperament very different from mine the existence, ready to hand, of a ubiquitous ritualism may not even be the occasion of a saintliness that nothing else could evoke. I am bound to go further, and to ask myself whether, saintliness apart, an ordinary observant Jew, a *Juif moyen sensuel*, may not have had with him, as a result of his observances, a sense of God's presence which otherwise would have been missing from his life: whether, when he "vainly repeated" without attending to the words, and in no true mood of worship, he may not, for all that, have been in some measure sanctified by the mere performance of a *mitzvah* with traditionally religious associations. And I must ask myself a final question. Jews clung to orthodoxy because, among other reasons, they were determined to remain separate from the Gentiles. They were determined to remain separate from the Gentiles because, again among other reasons and in so far as reason still entered into the matter, they had been chosen from among all peoples to be a nation of priests. Is it not possible that this safeguarding of their separateness by their orthodoxy really helped them to be better men, since by being better, more observant, that is, of the basic moralities, they would be proving themselves worthy of their election?

I imagine that in respect of a comparatively few indi- viduals, but of only a few, all my questions must be answered affirmatively. It is certain also that the sense of there being at least something to care about, a certain order and discipline and a doing or not doing because the doing or not doing was "right" and the reverse was "wrong"—it is certain that an atmosphere such as this was far more productive of decent living than the eat and drink and be merry of a careless paganism, if that must be imagined as the only alternative. This is what is meant by Christ's apocryphal saying: "On the same day, seeing one working on the Sabbath, he said unto him: Man, if indeed thou knowest what thou doest, thou art blessed: but if thou knowest not, thou art cursed, and a transgressor of the law."

But as to the general effect of ritualistic and institutional orthodoxy on Jews as a whole I can withdraw nothing of what I have written; and this means that it failed of its intention, and is important—with what an importance!—mainly as the parent of a Christianity which, in its revolt against that failure, was itself to encounter the old difficulty in a new form. But if traditional Judaism failed of its intention, the intention was of a beauty very rare, if not unexampled, in the history of religion.

# CHAPTER XV

# PORTRAIT OF MY FATHER

I MUST NOW ATTEMPT a little portrait of my father; for though it was above all his antifeminism and his orthodoxy that gave, through my reaction to them, such an arrowy direction to my life, there were nevertheless many other things about him that goaded me (if no doubt a particularly goadable me, a me who was waiting to be goaded from the day of my birth) into an opposition which is as fresh today, when I am close on sixty, as it was in my teens and almost in my babyhood. These other characteristics of his were very much of a piece with his antifeminism and his orthodoxy; and yet, though extraordinarily simple and homogeneous, he was not at all the sort of man that my previous descriptions of him may have led you to expect.

First, he was by no means a fanatic. On the contrary, he was above all a moderate, common-sensible, middle of the road sort of man. This was indeed one of the things that made him most antipathetic to me, and me to him. The Aristotelian mean was his ideal: for instance, as you already know, he was an orthodox Jew but not a *Shulhan A'rukh* Jew. When he took me to that first *Traviata* at Covent Garden my pleasure delighted him: when I went on my own, two or three times or a dozen times during the next couple of seasons, he still listened good-humouredly to my account of the performances, but was obviously a bit bored with my raptures and minutiæ ("and what *närrisch-heit*,* anyhow, to talk like that about Destinn; have you never heard of Adelina Patti?"): when, round about 1909, I began going every night, he made it clear that he thought I was cracked. He "swore by" *The Daily Telegraph*, as he frequently remarked, and physically we had to show the greatest respect to it; for this was his virgin, and if he found any issue even the least little bit *sufflikt* (a word of unknown and possibly onomatopoeic origin, which signified awry or in extreme cases, God forbid, with the pages out of order) the atmosphere would be heavy with his annoyance. Neither *The*

---

* A misbegotten word, meaning foolishness.

*Times* nor *The Morning Post* could ever have occurred to him as possible substitutes; he would have thought the former too official and the latter too extreme. And yet I am wrong in saying that the mean was his ideal, for to put it that way implies deliberation and choice, and these were quite alien to his nature. He was as simple-minded a man as I have ever known; he took the things that were in his make-up for granted, and what seemed to him right was right obviously and unquestionably. And I am wrong, too, in saying that he was no fanatic; he was a fanatic, but a fanatic for the commonplace.

I can best explain my father by calling him a Pharisee. Not a Pharisee as depicted by Christ, who is endowed by the gospel narrators, from time to time, with a divine gift for exaggeration; nor a Pharisee as idealised by Travers Herford; but something between the two. He was neither wicked nor adulterous nor viperish nor serpentine nor yet, in any conscious sense, a hypocrite; but then, on the other hand, he was not a saint either. His *mens* was exceedingly *conscia recti*, and I have already quoted to you his frequent asseveration, "Thank God I have never done anything wrong in my life"; but I cannot accuse him now, as I accused him then, of an intolerable smugness, for the objectivity of his appraisal was the nice thing about it. He was feeling thankful, on such occasions, for the easiness of his conscience, and saying so; and if you tell me, as I jeeringly told him, that nobody's conscience should be as easy as that, I shall reply that the "should be" is in the present context irrelevant, and that, if a man is so unsubtle as to take himself at face value and be pleased with what he finds, then there is something rather endearing about his having the grace to feel thankful for it. Unsubtle: this is the word. He could certainly have kept what he felt to himself, but that wasn't his way, for he was open and direct about everything. The truth simply is that he was deficient, if deficient is the right way of putting it (as I think it is), in a sense of sin. Or did he perhaps protest too much? Was his "Thank God" etcetera a sign of the "dead men's bones within"? Was he in fact not less hag-ridden but more hag-ridden than most of us? I doubt it, even after discounting my conviction, which I know to be nonsensical, that Freud and my father somehow don't rhyme. It is simply, I think, that he was temperamentally blind to a whole area in his make-up of which, in their own cases, others less simple are painfully aware. He looked very straight at himself, and with considerable frequency; but he never looked into himself. He was ordinarily decent in his life as a man and normally observant in his practice as a Jew: this is what he meant when he proclaimed his innocence: and he was pleased about it with the pleasure of an extrovert child.

He thanked God, not only for never having done anything wrong, but also for knowing what was "correct". Opinions were correct and behaviour was correct when they were the opinions and behaviour of the compact majority, of Jews in the Jewish field and of Englishmen in more general matters: of Englishmen rather than of men, for he was "staunchly patriotic" (just as he was "strictly observant") and was very proud of the fact that "never for a single moment had he left these shores". Anything unusual, independent, or minority was abhorrent to him. He didn't merely dislike such excesses: he thought them disreputable, and was as proud of so thinking as he was proud of his patriotism and his Jewishness and his integrity. For it was not a question, for him, of taste or opinion; it was a question of morality, and he liked being moral. "People don't *do* such things" was one of his favourite clinching sentences, and I felt a wicked glee when I discovered that Ibsen had said it too, but the other way round, so to speak. Commonest of all was his rhetorical question, "I suppose there *is* such a thing as public opinion?"

In one sense, as you know, he was violently intolerant, for over a wide range of topics he thought that anybody who differed from him must obviously be either wicked or *meshuggah*. The possibility that he might himself be wrong could never for a moment have occurred to him. But there were important exceptions—and important is the word, as you may remember from the case of Baron Y, with his bread-and-motza sandwiches at Passover. Nor was it only in such ritual matters that this largeness of mind was displayed. For if, more generally, a "big man" or "a great Englishman" or "a pillar of the community" either acted or thought in a manner to be normally reprehended, then either the report was false, or this was none of our business, or the crime might actually turn into its opposite. (Even, to give another ritual example, when *Kippur* was in question. It was unthinkable that an ordinary person like me should so much as clean his teeth during the entire twenty-four hours: but if Lord Justice so and so fasted "half a day" this was something else again—it was "really very nice".)

And yet if, in one sense and with these exceptions, my father was violently intolerant, in another sense his tolerance was remarkable. Certain as he was of his own correctness, he turned the blind eye whenever he could, unless, for instance, the incorrectness was actually committed in his presence: in part because he genuinely preferred to think well of people, and in part because if he once admitted to the perpetration of the offence the compact majority would by so much, in his mental image of it, be diminished. He rarely argued unless challenged or provoked, for he combined a certainty that he was right with a singular lack of intellectual passion: trying to convert a man, being anxious that truth, for its own sake, should prevail, these were quite outside his spiritual view, and when he found them in others, such as myself, he disliked them intensely. When he felt bound to argue, he did so by citing authorities and by appealing to public opinion; but most of all by the simple assertion, at frequent intervals, that what he himself thought was correct. What it comes to is this. Intellectually intolerant to the last degree, he showed a great deal of tolerance, for various reasons, in practice. How otherwise could he have put up with me for all those long years until I left home for Oxford? And how otherwise could there have been, with so much sulkiness and such gusts of anger on both sides, also so much adjustability, and, yes, as I look back upon it, so much groping affection, between us?

Among the excesses (as I am sure he would have classified it) for which my father had no sort of taste was what I must feebly indicate by the word spirituality. Religion, for him, was something matter of fact: it consisted of saying certain pre-scribed prayers, "keeping" certain days, performing certain *mitzvahs*, and perhaps (I am not sure about this—I am not sure whether it would have come under religion, though he would have thought the Canon's pronouncement quite crazy) living an ordinarily decent and law-abiding life. Anything mystical, or of the kind that might be suggested by such words as "religi-ous experience", was probably unintelligible to him: it was certainly repugnant, as savouring of exaggeration. "You can overdo religion too" was another of his favourite phrases. He did not mean by this that you could say too many prayers, or perform too many *mitzvahs*, or in general be too orthodox; though I rather think that if in my early teens I had suddenly insisted on obeying the whole *Shulhan A'rukh* instead of gradually abandoning everything he would have thought me equally *meshuggah*. What he meant was that there was a correct way in religion as in everything else: that this correct way was the way of observance: and that to import into something so sharply defined a highfalutin extra in the shape of "experience" would mean to be guilty of—well, to be guilty of overdoing it. I first heard my father use the expression when one of my sisters began to go off the rails. She was of a strongly religious temperament and became dissatisfied with orthodoxy; Christianity appealed to her, and at any moment, it was feared, she might decide to be baptised. My uncle Hermann, an orthodox Rabbi of enormous learning and little spirituality, was imported to deal with the matter; he repeated my father's phrases, and expounded the difference between religion and religious mania. His efforts were unsuccessful: the baptism took place. The treatment of my sister that followed, though shocking by liberal standards, is the mark of something very fine in the old man when the whole of his background is taken into account. Fifty years ago, it must be remembered, no Jew of his type could have brought himself even to pronounce Christ's name, except for purposes of scholarship; and in baptism was the horror of a final apostasy. One of the chosen people, by deliberate choice, had cut himself off from God. It was traditional in such cases, though I do not know to what extent the tradition was followed, for the father first to curse the apostate, and then to sit in mourning as if for the dead. My father, though tempted to do the first when my sister got baptised, did neither. He brought himself to see her as time went on, and increasingly towards the end of his life; and he even left her the proper share of his tiny estate—while in the Christian England of 1951, as I occasionally read, sons are "cut off" by their fathers for joining the Labour Party.

My father had an immense respect for wealth, but not if it had been dishonestly acquired. "A good solid man" meant an adequately rich man, and there was something in the old man's tone of voice as he said it that implied a sort of moral approval. Wills fascinated him; and he would often call up to my mother from the breakfast table, she not yet being "down", that old so and so, according to the *Telegraph*, had "cut up" for a quarter of a million. Speculations about potential "cuttings up", even during the lifetime of the cutters, were common: "they say Lord X is ill; I wonder how much he'll cut up for?" But there wasn't a trace of envy in his attitude; he was genuinely happy, for their sakes, about these people's success. Nor did he personally desire to be rich; if the thought of such a possibility had ever entered his head, as I am sure it didn't, he would probably have been alarmed by the prospect. He had begun as a small business man, and a small business man he remained till the day of his retirement: not so much by deliberate choice, as because that was automatically how he thought of his job. For with all his immense prides—his pride in being a Jew, his pride in being a Gollancz, his pride in being "correct"—there was something at the same time very humble about him. He knew he wasn't "big", and had no desire to be so. So he laboured unceasingly, leaving in the morning with his *kosher* sandwiches, picking up his stock at the office in Aldgate, driving in his brougham to the outer suburbs, and getting back at night as late as half past nine. This grind was unvarying, and the sole aim of it was to provide a decent life for my mother and us children, and to leave a few thousands behind him for our security. He could very well have done with more money, for there were many things that he enjoyed, though they rarely came his way: he was content, as it was, with an amphitheatre stall at Covent Garden two or three times in the season, an occasional treat such as a pigeon for dinner, and a party in the drawing-room when he felt we could afford it. And his discomfort must often have been great, particularly during those interminable rides in the brougham. A little man anyhow, he suffered from a curvature of the spine, which bent his back over in a humpish parabola; and he always wore a truss, for the bags he had carried when apprenticed as a boy had been much too heavy for him, and he was ruptured. Perhaps for this reason, or perhaps because he worked too hard and never took holidays, his health was poor; on two or three occasions he developed enormous carbuncles, and a persistent bronchitis was frequent: but though nervous about himself, like all the Gollanczes, I very seldom heard him complain. (And he lived into his eighties.) When still too unwell to get out to his office, he would work in the dining-room at home: taking stock, or

writing to his customers, or making up the books of account.
For he was his own accountant, and surely the most scrupulous
that can ever have existed. Shortly after I had started my own
business, when the turnover was already quite high, it was
reported to me that the books failed to balance by something
in the neighbourhood of a hundred pounds, and that the
auditors proposed to write the sum off. I was horrified. I
remembered how my father's books had once failed to balance
by less than a pound, and how he had sat up night after night
until he had discovered the source of the discrepancy. He
was an utterly honest man: meticulous literally to the last
farthing.

So his respect for the wealthy, and his moral approval of
them, is not to be explained by any enthusiasm for money-
making in the case either of himself or of others. It is to be
explained by the fact that a rich man, other things being
equal, was "solid", established, influential: not merely a
member of the compact majority, but a leader of it. He
thought of rich men exactly as he thought of famous men, or
titled men, or M.Ps., or R.As., or members of the Royal Family:
they "stood for something" ("I suppose the Royal Academy
*does* stand for something?"), and this was already, *prima facie*,
to be moral. What it really came down to was a question of
respectability. If a man was established, he was respectable:
if he was respectable, he conformed: and to conform was to be
a guardian of morality.

My father, for the rest, was honourable in all his dealings;
in politics, was a "staunch Conservative"; had actually, I feel
certain, "never done anything wrong in his life", in the sense
of never having deliberately injured his neighbour; was quite
unimaginative, and wholly incapable of entering into other
people's feelings; was consistently kind, but within the limits
just mentioned; smiled charmingly; was capable of taking his
meals by himself, after a particularly bad row, for days at a
time; was lonely; had a craving for affection, and too rarely
received it; and was the contrary, whatever the expression for
such a contrary may be, to a man of the world. Dirty jokes in
his presence would have been unthinkable. But he knew one
himself—only one; and he told it from time to time with a most
delightful combination of shyness and "what the devil do I
care?" He not only told it, he had assisted, aeons before, at its

inception. It concerned himself and a barmaid and a brand of biscuit: the kind called tops and bottoms.

Timothy, will you listen to what I am going to say? Will you remember that I might have behaved differently if somebody had said it to me? I cannot know how your relations with your own father will develop, though I can pray that they will develop most happily. But if, in the splendid hot-headedness of youth—I must interpose that, not so much in my own defence as in defence of rebel youthfulness everywhere, and of the whole scheme of things by which the world progresses—if in the hot-headedness of youth you find yourself at loggerheads with your own father, imagine what your grandfather must be feeling while he sits here and remembers, as he has remembered so many times during the last twenty years, what unhappiness he caused by his arrogance and harshness and lack of common charity. I am not asking you to compromise with your ideals: I am not suggesting that you should show any special respect to your father as such, for this I could never desire: I am only begging you to remember that to have been unkind to a human being with whom one has lived in such daily contact is something for which, long afterwards, one can ask—and how bitter that is!—only one's own forgiveness. I do not wish you to infer that my father and I were constantly quarrelling; for we rubbed along quite decently more often than not, and sometimes there was active affection. But the old man must have been agonised on a thousand occasions by my graceless invective against things he held sacred; and the pain I then caused is irrevocable. It was only when he lay dying that the barrier between us came finally down. I asked myself if somehow, without saying anything—for he was shy, as I have told you, and would have been embarrassed by a confession—I could get through to him at this very last moment and make him understand what I felt. And so, remembering the love of music that he had inherited from his own father and passed on, for my happiness, to me, I bought a huge pile of gramophone records: forgotten old things that he had heard in his boyhood and that you may never hear, such as "Casta Diva" from *Norma* and the shadow-song from *Dinorah* and "O Paradiso" from *L'Africaine* and the drinking-song from *Lucrezia Borgia*. Hour after hour, until he wanted to sleep, I would play them to him. It was the tiniest of reparations, which he paid back, in his turn, a hundredfold; for a day or two before he died he suddenly muttered to himself, not intending, I believe, that I should hear, "I never knew I had such a wonderful son".

He was a Pharisee; he was hide-bound; intellectually he was everything I most passionately reject. Nothing of this will I withdraw. But I understood as I heard him mutter those words, and am telling you now as the conclusion of the matter, that underneath all the accidentals—I mean everything that his background and environment and all the rest of it had contributed—the essential was what he then revealed: a gentleness, a humility, a gratitude, a willingness to forgive. There is a blessing appropriate to him that few of us could claim as appropriate to ourselves: "Blessed are the pure in heart, for they shall see God."

# CHAPTER XVI

# MY FATHER AND I

You will understand, without any lengthy explanation from me, how I reacted to those characteristics of my father which I have just described. Public opinion, respectability, conformism—I not merely thought them devoid of all value, I worshipped their opposites; and with a passion so fierce that I was compelled—really compelled, driven by a force that I couldn't withstand—to rise up in immediate defence of anything or anyone in any way unorthodox, by simple reason of their unorthodoxy and irrespective of what my own views might happen to be about the person or topic in question. There was something missionary in this passion; I had the burning conviction that if for a moment I were silent, if for a moment I compromised or hummed and ha'd or were anything but to the last degree militant, I should be guilty of most shamelessly betraying what, beyond any particular truth or falsity in the matter under discussion, was an overriding truth, or rather *the* overriding truth, at the very heart of reality: namely that everybody was not only entitled but categorically obliged to think, say and do (subject, in the last case only, to his not hurting others) what he himself might consider it proper to think, say or do. To stand quietly by while something that might turn out to be valuable was being stifled by tradition or public opinion—this I just couldn't bear. For how could anybody possibly tell that the thing being stifled wouldn't in fact turn out to be good? How could anybody tell that it wouldn't even turn out to be the very best thing in the world?

It was with a thrill of delighted recognition that I found what I was feeling in Ibsen. Recognition is the right word. Ibsen taught me nothing, for the more difficult plays, and the subtler passages in the easier plays, were of course at that time unintelligible to me. I am not sure that I fully understand *Rosmersholm* today. But *The League of Youth*, *The Pillars of Society*, *Ghosts*, *An Enemy of the People*, *A Doll's House*, *The Lady from the Sea*, and, a little later, *Peer Gynt*—when I read them for the first time in the old blue and gilt edition of the Walter Scott Publishing Company (which I can see over to my left in the bookshelves

just opposite me, treasures of my boyhood not a yard away from
the little Whieldon figure I bought only yesterday) I seemed to
be remembering, after Plato's fashion, things I had already
known in a previous existence, or things I knew and would
always know in an eternity from which the veil of temporalities
had been suddenly removed. The exposure of conventional
humbug! The satire against compact majorities! The hatred of
compulsion! The warning against betrayal of a self's uniqueness!
The clinching lines in particular, always towards the end and
sometimes at the very end of a play, got hold of me and caught
me up into a rapture of intellectual assent. The last words of
*The Pillars of Society*—"No, no; the spirits of Truth and Freedom—these are the Pillars of Society": Helmer's "You talk like
a child. You don't understand the society in which you live",
and Nora's reply "No, I don't. But I shall try to. I must make
up my mind which is right—society or I": Assessor Brack's
"Heaven help us—people don't *do* such things!": above all, Dr
Stockman's "This is what I've discovered, you see: the strongest
man upon earth is he who stands most alone"—time after time
I challenged with these words, sometimes silently and sometimes openly, my father's "I suppose there *is* something in public
opinion?" And there were longer passages that I knew almost
by heart and that mean as much to me at this moment as on the
first day I read them. There was, for instance, the moving dialogue in the fifth act of *The Lady from the Sea* between Ellida
Wangel and her husband, when Ellida is on the point of going
away with the Stranger—a dialogue that even the grotesque
translation, which reads like a parody of a parody of it in "Mr.
Punch's Pocket Ibsen", can do little to spoil:

ELLIDA (with increasing agitation) Wangel, let me tell you this
    —tell you in his hearing! I know you can keep me here!
    You have the power, and no doubt you will use it! But my
    mind—all my thoughts—all my irresistible longings and
    desires—these you cannot fetter! They will yearn and
    struggle—out into the unknown—that I was created for—
    and that you have barred against me!
WANGEL (in quiet grief) I see it well, Ellida! Step by step you
    are gliding away from me. Your craving for the vast and
    infinite—and for the unattainable—will drive your mind
    out into the darkness at last.

ELLIDA Oh yes, yes—I feel it—like black soundless wings hovering over me.

WANGEL It shall not come to that. There is no other way of deliverance for you; at least I see none. And therefore—therefore I—I cancel our bargain on the spot. So now you can choose your own path—in full—full freedom.

ELLIDA (gazes at him awhile as if speechless) Is this true—true—what you say? Do you mean it—from your inmost heart?

WANGEL Yes, from the inmost depths of my suffering heart I mean it.

ELLIDA And *can* you do it? Can you carry out your purpose?

WANGEL Yes, I can. I can—because I love you so deeply.

ELLIDA (softly and tremblingly) So closely—so tenderly have you come to love me!

WANGEL The years of our union have taught me to.

ELLIDA (clasps her hands together) And I—I have been blind to it!

WANGEL Your thoughts took other directions. But now—now you are fully freed from me and mine. Now your own true life can return to its—its right groove again. From now you can choose in freedom; and on your own responsibility, Ellida.

ELLIDA (clasps her head with her hands and gazes fixedly towards Wangel) In freedom—and on my own responsibility? Responsibility too?—That transforms everything!

[The steamer bell rings again.

THE STRANGER Do you hear, Ellida? They are ringing for the last time. Come away?

ELLIDA (turns towards him, looks fixedly at him, and says with decision in her voice) I can never go with you after this.

But my favourite among all the longer passages was Peer's farewell when he is to be melted down by the button-moulder as so much useless scrap, for he has never dared, either in good or in evil, to be his own real self:

> So unspeakably poor, then, a soul can go
> back to nothingness, into the grey of the mist.
> Thou beautiful earth, be not angry with me
> that I trampled thy grasses to no avail.
> Thou beautiful sun, thou hast squandered away
> thy glory of light in an empty hut.

> There was no one within it to hearten and warm;
> the owner, they tell me, was never at home.
> Beautiful sun and beautiful earth,
> you were foolish to bear and give light to my mother.
> The spirit is niggard and nature lavish;
> and dearly one pays for one's birth with one's life.
> I will clamber up high, to the dizziest peak;
> I will look once more on the rising sun,
> gaze till I'm tired o'er the promised land;
> then try to get snowdrifts piled up over me.
> They can write above them: 'Here *No One* lies buried';
> And afterwards,—then—! Let things go as they can.

Ibsen was a god to me, and still is; I find him untouched by time, and every so often, when I come up against one of those neo-orthodoxies which are for me the real *trahison des clercs*, I turn to him again with the feeling that I am going back to my own. He was one of the four round whom my reading centred, from the time I began reading at all (seriously, that is, for my own pleasure), right up to my going to Oxford. The other three were Shaw, Walt Whitman, and Maeterlinck. I am glad to find that many of the actual copies I then read are here in the library, including an edition of Whitman dated 1897, but bought of course later, and rebound at home in a linen cover with a paper label, which some forty years later is still in position. I am glad to remember, too, that I was allowed to touch Shaw at the very beginning of my intellectual life, when I read *Widowers' Houses*, and at the very end of his; for I received a long letter from him a few hours after reading in the press of the fall that proved fatal. I never lost my reverence for Shaw; many of his later views I abominated, but he remained for me, in spite of his extravagances about dictatorship and his letters to *The Times* on taxation, the divine gadfly that, even at the cost of perversity, goaded us into life more abundant. I doubt whether he will live by the quality of his thought; but I am certain that he will live by the passion of his morality. For of what was it born if not of moral passion, his unflagging determination to deliver us from indifference and complacency by putting, with a gaiety that masked his priesthood, "the case against"? His real greatness is in the sphere not of art but of religion.

You will understand without difficulty why Ibsen and Shaw

so delighted me, and why I found in their pages almost all my own reactions to my father's way of thought. And because they so delighted me I was determined that they should delight everybody else, my father included; for how could it conceivably happen that the truth should be shown to a man and he shouldn't recognise it in a second? So I talked about my authors incessantly; so incessantly that my father would turn to my mother, and say to her (in my presence) with a faint trace of the old Rabbinic singsong, "The Ibsen and the Shaw and the Whitman and the Maeterlinck—the boy's *meshuggah*". In the case of Maeterlinck perhaps I really was a trifle *meshuggah*. I doubt whether I could read him now; but he appealed to something in my make-up that was to send me hot in pursuit, then and continuously to this moment, of anything I might be able to lay my hands on about the hidden, the mysterious and the bizarre. One of my earliest publishing "flops" was Charles Fort's *Lo!* which I brought out in the late nineteen twenties. What a book it was! Minnows raining from heaven on an inland town: hands spirited away from a ship in mid-ocean: an elderly gentleman one minute in London and the next in New York: all certified by press-cuttings, and proving beyond question that the planets are very close to our earth, that their mischievous inhabitants enjoy nothing better than playing tricks with us, and that the one they enjoy most (known as teleportation) is to pick a thing up at one end of the globe and drop it down instantly at the other. Someone must have stolen my copy of this great book (or possibly it has been teleported) for I find it absent from my shelves here, which nevertheless carry a rich store: Charles Williams and Algernon Blackwood and Edgar Allan Poe and Monty James and Leslie Hartley and Sheridan Lefanu and Violet Hunt and Walter de la Mare and H. P. Lovecroft and Vincent O'Sullivan (with the Beardsley frontispiece) and Arthur Machen (who now, alas!, will never mix a white powder again, and refused before his death to entrust me with the recipe) and David Lindsay's *Arcturus* and Visiak's *Medusa*: and of course a whole long row of the gem-encrusted magus, M. P. Shiel. . .

I wouldn't dream of putting my boyhood Maeterlincks in this honourable company; they are tucked away among minor plays. My fourth idol, Walt Whitman, is another matter, for he has retained a large measure of my old respect. I loved him for

his *joie de vivre*, his pansacramentalism, his contempt for respectability, and his fellow-feeling with harlots and criminals; and
I found in him, more immediately perhaps even than in Ibsen
or Shaw, an expression, now blaring like a trumpet and now
gentle as a flute, of the social and political philosophy that
I was rapidly evolving in opposition to my father's. I thought
at the time that the opening poem of *Leaves of Grass* said
everything, and said it perfectly. I now know that there is
much it omits, and one thing of crucial significance; for it
says nothing about the place of suffering in human life, and
perhaps also, to speak by way of analogy, in the life of God. But
though there is a great deal I would add there is nothing I
would alter:

One's-self I sing, a simple separate person,
Yet utter the word Democratic, the word En-Masse.

Of physiology from top to toe I sing.
Not physiognomy alone nor brain alone is worthy for the Muse,
    I say the Form complete is worthier far,
The Female equally with the Male I sing.

Of Life immense in passion, pulse, and power,
Cheerful, for freest action form'd under the laws divine,
The Modern Man I sing.

The first two lines in particular, with the vital "yet", will help
you to correct an impression that you may have falsely received
from much that I have so far written. For my passion for individuality and uniqueness, my defence of minorities, and my
detestation of conformity and of subservience to public opinion,
by no means involved either a dislike of the masses or a repudiation of democracy. There was nothing Nietzschean about me.
I read Nietzsche at St. Paul's, and had some talk about him with
Oscar Levy, his translator; but while I admired him as a rebel,
and thought that there was an element of value in what he had
to say, his outlook as a whole was repugnant to me. Aristocracy,
an *élite*, supermen: I had no sympathy at all with these—no
more than with "solidity", "being established", respectability,
and wealth—for it was to democracy and the common man that
my heart had been given. If I disliked the tyranny of public
opinion, this was precisely because it made a myth of democracy;
for democracy meant the co-operation of free and equal persons,

and how could such co-operation exist if everybody followed blindly where "everybody" led? "Everybody" was not persons: more, "everybody" and persons had nothing in common. On the one hand were innumerable persons, each living and growing and particular and unique; on the other was a single force, "everybody", a something mechanical that had *happened* and was *there*. "Everybody" was over against, external to, the persons; and it was the persons who had all the reality. So a democracy where people said and did what "everybody" said and did was no true democracy at all: it was an enslavement of life to death, of spirit to matter, of the dynamic to the static, of reality to unreality. The true democracy was at the other extreme: its whole purpose being that the people, "common" people, every single man and woman that made up the democracy, should be, because it *was* a democracy, the most real men and women imaginable. Not only must they be free to think and feel and speak and act independently: they must be encouraged by their environment to do so. Thus life would be everywhere; and the life in each one would be harmonious with the life in each other; for the innumerable lives, by being true to themselves, were being true to what each had in common, since life as such, any life uninhibited, was ultimately the same life, the life of the One. And so the life of the One would be realising itself in the infinite richness of varied but harmonious livings. It followed that inequality of any kind, in the sense of anything that prevented a single human being from developing to the utmost all the potentialities within him, was an outrage against the life of the One as depriving that life of what otherwise might have added to its richness. Supermen were such an outrage, for they fed on the rest. The real superman was the free co-operator who was perfect in freedom and co-operation: everyone should be that sort of superman: but how could supermen of this kind develop from a society of dominators and dominated? In our own society, anything that prevented the fullest possible development of any single man or woman, whether positively by the exercise of power or negatively by encouraging subservience, was similarly an outrage; and so "big" men of every kind, including rich men, were to be deprecated, and any atmosphere of respect for them, of special respect, that is, because of their bigness and riches, was fatal to the democratic ideal. The question of leadership did not occur to me. If it had,

I think I should have answered what I certainly answered at Repton and should answer now: namely, that the true leader leads through a free recognition that his words and his actions are good, and that the freer this recognition—the more he encourages a refusal to take himself and his message uncritically—then the better his claim to true leadership. Even spiritual power may damn, if it derives from anything other than truth made evident.

I have tried to think myself back into my boyhood and, stripping off all later accretions, to set down as faithfully as possible what I then felt about democracy, public opinion, minorities and the rest. The basis of what I now feel is there, and there is nothing that I would modify in it so far as it goes; but one vital element, indeed the heart of the matter, is missing. This is: you must lose your soul to find it. Everybody's self-development is not enough; or, rather, the very essence of self-development—and therefore what the One relies on—is positive self-surrender. And community is not an epiphenomenon, something arising as an extra from the pursuit by personality of its own fulfilment; it is by community, rather, that fulfilment of personality can alone be achieved.

The difference between my father and me on the topics I have just been discussing can be expressed in the form of a sharp antithesis. Although I never heard him actually attack democracy as such—to do so would have been going too far, would have savoured of extremism—by instinct and in detail he was thoroughly undemocratic: but he almost literally worshipped public opinion. I was highly suspicious of public opinion, but a passionate advocate of democracy.

We clashed very early, as you will readily deduce, in the party political field. He was a Conservative, as I think I've made clear: not a Tory, or a Tory democrat, or anything finicky like that, but a good, honest, small-business-man, Daily Telegraph sort of Conservative—or Unionist, for that was how he always described himself, not only, I think, because this was the term most in use at the time, but also because there hung about it some special flavour of "staunch patriotism". I was a Liberal, with a very large L. I have rarely, in my life as a whole, been a good party man; my make-up is too independent, and the only Member of Parliament I have ever really envied since the first world war,

and would have liked to change places with, has been Eleanor
Rathbone. I was almost painfully anxious, it is true, that the
Labour Party should come to power in 1945, and had for
many years done everything I could to bring about this result; but to support a party because it's the only party to
support is quite different from supporting it because you and
the party are one. There has always been a certain detachment
in my attitude to the Labour Party. The reasons for this ambi-
valence are many, and I shall discuss some of them rather fully a
little later. But briefly: On the one hand, I see little hope for
humanity unless democratic socialism can be firmly established in this island, as a focus and model for the rest of the
world; and the only party that can do it is the Labour Party.
So I shall continue to support it. But it has been responsible, on the other hand, for a number of policies, and has
adopted, spiritually, a number of attitudes, which seem to me
detestable. So I shall continue to criticise it, unless it mends
its ways.

But bad party man as I have normally been, I was body and
soul with the Liberal Party (soul certainly, and body to the
extent to which a stripling could give it) from some grotesquely
early age, perhaps seven or eight, to the outbreak of war in
1914; and if after that my enthusiasm began to flag, it was still
with the Liberal Party, or that only true part of it known as the
Wee Frees, that I took my first job when the war was over and
I was already about to be married: working with Wedgwood
Benn in a basement near the House, suggesting "supple-
mentaries" for the harrowing of the Coalition, briefing Donald
Maclean on the Capital Levy, and circulating memoranda
on anything that might be afoot. I read a good deal
about socialism, and even made some study of it, at St.
Paul's; but though there were points about it that already
appealed to me, my allegiance to Liberalism remained
complete.

You must remember what the Liberal Party then was, and
how, being the boy I was, I couldn't fail to be seduced by it.
I detested poverty, as you know, and at any rate believed that
there was no sacrifice in the world I wouldn't make to abolish it.
And the Liberal Party, above all, was the party of social
reform. In the background it stood for freedom, and that alone
would have been enough to recommend it; but as foreground,

during the first decade of this century and particularly during the second half of it, what emerged most of all was the on-slaught it seemed determined to make on the poverty and insecurity that degraded so many millions of Englishmen. Lloyd George, I imagine, is hardly a name to you, for he was one of those who, in Vergil's phrase, defeated his own life by living—hung on when the splendour had departed, and some-how attracted to himself, already some twenty years before his death, an atmosphere of failure and even of sordidness. But I shall always remember him, and I wish the world would remember him, as the pioneer, in this country, of social reform: as the man who brought a little ease into innumerable hard lives by his various social insurances, and made a first serious effort at the redistribution of wealth in his great Budget of 1909. My wild enthusiasm for these measures was like nothing in politics I've experienced since: quite different in quality, for instance, from my sober happiness when Labour was returned in 1945, or from my intellectual approval when railways and mines were nationalised.

My brain is a rather slow-moving one, and it has always taken me a long time to penetrate to the bottom of an economic fundamental, even when I've eventually succeeded in doing so, as I frequently haven't. So I did not then understand, what I understand now, that the Lloyd George reforms were merely scratching at the surface, and that if the problem of poverty were to be seriously tackled something much more radical was required. And I doubt whether, if I had understood it, this would have made any difference to my enthusiasm. The man is doing something practical, I should have said; because of him, millions are a little happier than they would otherwise have been: isn't that sufficient?

There was another thing that made me worship Lloyd George. You know how I hated war. It was in 1899, when I was six, that I saw the appalling picture on our drawing-room table of the man at Balaclava with his head hanging off. It was also in 1899 that the Boer War broke out. Those days were very different from these. We now almost all think that war is iniquitous: and we live day by day in an agonised consciousness of it, and would do anything in our power to prevent its occurrence. This is only secondarily because of atom bombs; primarily, I am afraid, it is because war now threatens every

one of us, and—here the atom bomb comes in—with a particularly horrible fate. But very few Englishmen felt like that in
1899. You can have little idea of our sense of security, not only
then but right on into the summer of 1914. And sense of
security doesn't give you the atmosphere, either: it suggests
something positive, some actual reflection about our position,
whereas the possibility that *we* might be affected couldn't
conceivably have entered our heads. If Britain were to be
involved, we had an army: it was their job, and a very noble
one too, to fight and if need be to die for their country: as for
civilians—not that they were thought of as civilians, they were
the ordinary population of the country—they stuck little flags
into newspaper maps, and followed the campaign with appropriate emotions, and hung out bunting when we won. And
because we were personally unaffected, I doubt whether one
Englishman in a thousand, or perhaps in ten thousand (Quakers
excepted), ever had it on his conscience that war was a blasphemy: ever visualised the dead and the dying, and vowed in
his heart that any recurrence of such wickedness, anywhere in
the world, must be permanently rendered impossible. His
failure was not a failure of decent feeling: it was a failure of
imagination. The whole thing was so remote. Englishmen were
particularly liable to this failure, because war had never
touched our island, or not recently enough to mean anything;
but everyone, on the Continent and elsewhere, was more or
less affected by the same indifference.

Yet however rare it was, back in 1899, to hate war as such,
opposition to that particular war was quite considerable; for
many thought it aggressive and unjust, and a few even realised
what a villainous greed had been primarily responsible for its
outbreak. Conspicuous among the opponents was Lloyd
George, who was famous for a speech at the Birmingham
Town Hall and his escape by a door at the back from an
infuriated mob. It was this that first attracted me to him, for
his social legislation was to come later. In general, and rightly
or wrongly, I thought of all good Liberals as men of peace; as
anti-imperialists, too, and Little Englanders; and nothing
could have been sweeter to me than words such as those,
which were terms of abuse to my father.

The political centre of my life in Elgin Avenue was the
General Election of 1906, when I was thirteen. General

Elections were much more exciting in those days than they are
now, because polling was spread over about three weeks, and,
as people like to be on the winning side, earlier results might
affect later ones. And the election of 1906 must have been one
of the most exciting ever fought; comparable to 1945 in that
on both occasions there was a swing to the left of a magnitude
no one could have foreseen, but with daily fluctuations, hopes
and fears of a sudden reversal, and a long-delayed climax as
additional thrills. Somewhere or other in London—the picture
is very vivid in my mind—there were two enormous ladders,
one for the Liberals and one for the Tories; and on each of them
was a little man, who climbed higher, or stood still, as the daily
results came in. The little Liberal was soon soaring to heaven,
while the Tory climbed painfully a rung at a time as if his feet
had been caught in a quagmire. I cannot remember where I
saw these ladders, but I rather think in Piccadilly Circus, or
perhaps on the *Daily News* posters that covered the hoardings;
or in my own *Daily News*, for I took it in and read it religiously
in reply to my father's cult of the *Telegraph*. These ladders are
oddly confused in my mind with a contraption of tin I had
loved as a baby. It was meant for a tree: squatting at the base
was a black boy: you slowly got him up to the top: and hey
presto! down he came rushing, with a pineapple perched on
his head.

My father and I, in spite of our political differences, were on
specially good terms at this time, perhaps because I was shortly
to be *Barmitzvah*. On many nights during the election we went
together to a neighbouring tobacconist called Drucquer, who
had a telephone and was in touch with the Tory headquarters.
Being there thrilled me. I enjoyed listening to the results; but
what I enjoyed most of all was the atmosphere of life and bustle,
and the sense that I was no longer a boy but already involved
in those adult affairs that were going to be so wonderful for
me when I was properly grown up. The crowds of people: the
thick tobacco smoke: the repeated "Mr Montgomery Wilson?
Mr Drucquer" at the telephone—these were rapturous intimations of the things to come. I imagine that I was
the only Liberal there; and I gave my little cheers as the
Liberal victories came pouring through, and my little boo
at an occasional reverse. Everyone was very kind to me,
especially Mr Drucquer; we became good friends, and later

on, when I took to a pipe, he advised me with special pains about tobacco.

For the rest, my father's sayings, and the thinking I inferred from them, produced or reinforced in me a passionate loathing of intolerance, self-righteousness, and inability to put oneself in another man's shoes. You already know that I was myself guilty, and perhaps to an unusual degree, of these very faults that I hated so intensely in others; but you will be wrong, certainly if you imagine that my hatred of them was lacking in genuineness, and probably if you infer that I hated them so intensely in others merely because I was anxious not to hate them in myself. I am sure that I really did understand, as a matter of direct moral intuition, that consciousness of one's own weakness and fallibility; an endless sympathy with the weakness and fallibility of others; a repeated self-questioning as to how one would have acted oneself had one been in the other man's shoes: and the sense that, however certain one might be of one's own rightness and the other's wrongness, only God could know—I am sure that I really did understand that this was the essence of good living, and was desperately anxious, too, that life should be always so lived. But alas! there were two things of which I was incapable. I was incapable, first, of feeling tolerance for an inability in others to understand about good living what I understood; and I was incapable, secondly, of putting myself in the position of anyone I was personally involved with whose manner of living and thinking, in any particular, ran counter (as I thought) to the manner of living and thinking that this understanding (as I thought) must involve. Here is an example of the first inability: I believed in "Judge not, that ye be not judged"; I believed in it genuinely and passionately, and I believed that my belief in it involved my whole being; but if anyone had told me that he thought the injunction was folly I should have judged him most bitterly. And here is an example of the second inability: If a man was condemned to death for a particularly atrocious murder, I felt for him, lived in him, asked myself whether, given his background and circumstances, I might not have myself done the same; but if my father had said "Serve him right" I should have burst out into furious invective, and it would never have occurred to me to ask myself whether, given my father's background and circumstances, I might not have myself said the same. And my furious invective would have seemed to me to spring from an inescapable sense of moral obligation.

I was not self-rightous in the sense that I believed myself good. Such a thought never entered my head. I was sharply aware, on the contrary, of such moral failings as I was capable of recognising in myself: there were many of them, and they sometimes produced in me a painful feeling of guilt. But I was self-righteous in my attitude to other people's self-righteousness; and I was self-righteous in the sense that I was not merely indifferent to the unhappiness I caused by my ruthlessness in the advocacy of what I thought to be the truth, but was quite certain that I was behaving in this respect as any man of decent morality must obviously behave. Or this was so for the most part: from time to time, it is true, there were hours of remorse. The fact is that I hated unkindness, and regarded it, with heart and brain, as the worst moral failing of all; but what might otherwise have been a bitter self-condemnation for my own unkindness was swallowed up in my sense of mission. And I sometimes wonder whether that isn't the worst sort of self-righteousness a man can be guilty of.

This is not to imply that my embryo Christian morality was merely theoretical. The essence of it, on the contrary, was precisely that it was not theoretical. Morality, I believed, must engage a man's whole life; and in one sense it engaged the whole of mine. But not in the final sense, not in the only sense that ultimately matters. I had still to learn that what finally matters is not the *about* what but the *from* what: that an intellectual understanding of what goodness consists in, however just, and a desire for the triumph of that goodness, however genuine, and a determination to bring about that triumph, however passionate, are not yet in that order of reality where a single pure impulse lives eternally: that all battles are shadow battles except the battle a man fights in the innermost citadel of his own being: that until he has won this battle he is useless either as a sheet of glass for the flooding in of good to the universe or as a sheet of iron for the shutting out of evil: and that something must happen to him, some free acceptance of an offered grace, before this battle can be won. "Except a man be born of water and the Spirit, he cannot enter into the Kingdom of Heaven." This is why love is not love unless it can love, without taking thought, the unloving: this is why tolerance is not tolerance unless it can tolerate, without taking thought, intolerance. I was to learn all this, many years later, at the time of Munich. I know it now, but barely have the power to live in accordance with the knowledge; for still the old Adam is very strong within me.

*March 27th. In the train to London.*

*We've been spending a very happy Easter with you, Tiba (that's what you call yourself), or rather you've been spending it with us. The smiles that were round the corner last time you were with us have come out into the open, and you seem to be smiling all day now. You don't look the least little bit like a polymorphous pervert. I showed you the big mezzuza on the drawing-room doorpost as I had promised myself I would; and you liked opening the little doors and poking your finger through the hole and pushing in the parchment with the ש on it—the name of God!—and you learned to say mezzuza very quickly and accurately. Your grandmother is going this week to old Mosheh Oved in the hope of finding another one with doors, but that sort is rare, and you may have to be content with an ordinary one. Anyhow, you shall have a mezzuza of some kind for your own little bedroom at Harrow.*

*I suppose it was being for four days with somebody under two that made me suddenly reflect in bed last night that I am getting on for sixty, and have little time left to do all the things I want to do, and publish all the books I want to publish, and start all the movements I want to start, and, especially, write all the books I want to write. The sonnet of Keats came into my mind, and I was worried by not being able to remember one of the words in the second line; so your grandmother went to the library next door and found it for me:*

*When I have fears that I may cease to be*
*Before my pen has glean'd my teeming brain,*
*Before high-piled books, in charact'ry,*
*Hold like rich garners the full-ripen'd grain . . .*

*How wise "Back to Methuselah" is! If only we could repent and live longer!*

*I wish I could have been alive from the beginning of time, and could live for ever! Only once, for some months in 1943, have I had any sympathy with Wandering Jews and Flying Dutchmen and suchlike, and their stupid peripateticism in search of a pure woman's love that might save them from the burden of living. I should like to have been an aristocrat at the time of the French Revolution, and also a revolutionary leader: I should like to have been Max or Anatol in Schnitzler's Vienna: I should like to have been Gandhi: I should like to be Schweitzer: I should like, most of all, to be the man who will come at the end of the long human story—I should like to be the last man alive, even if the second law of thermodynamics is applicable to the spiritual as well as to the physical world, as I do not believe, and even if there will be a last man, with nothing but a featureless waste to follow him!*

# CHAPTER XVII

## QUIET JOY

QUIET JOY WAS THE background of my boyhood. All three
words, "quiet", "joy", and "background", are important in that
sentence. Joy was the background, not happiness and still less
sense of pleasure; for while my happiness was great and I could
fill a much bigger book than this with a record of my pleasures,
this happiness and these pleasures were not themselves the background of my life, but temporalities, with an eternal glow behind
them. And the joy was quiet: not leapingly wild, as in Browning's
"O the wild joys of living! the leaping from rock up to rock!"—
my pleasures were largely like that, not my background joy—
but calm and free, breathless with adoration. ("*My* background
joy", though, is wrong: the fact of its not being "my" is the
essence of the matter.) And the joy was a background, not only
to my pleasures and my happiness, but also to the agony that a
child suffers, or that I at least suffered, with an intensity very
rare in later life. Certainly I had my full measure of such agony,
and can live again now in the heart-broken sobbing, and the
strangled gasps that ended it, with which whole hours of my boyhood were occasionally filled; as when I felt myself unfairly
treated, or had a sense of outrage—for I sobbed then too—at
some wickedness, as I thought it, committed against others or
the world in general, or some statement or action that impinged
on me as blasphemy against self-evident truth. And I feel great
pity, as I look back at him, for that sobbing boy. A good deal of
glib nonsense is talked about self-pity: for just as we should love
ourselves as well as our neighbours, ourselves being persons too,
so we should pity what is truly pitiful in us, in the us of the
moment as well as in the different us which is the subject of our
reflection about the past. But though I suffered agonies that
made me sob so pitifully, these, like my pleasures and happiness,
seem but incidents against the background of my quiet joy. I do
not mean that I felt joy, even in the background, when suffering
these agonies: I mean that they were mere interruptions to
something steadily there—or steadily there but for a few dreadful months, when it vanished. And even during those few
dreadful months, prefiguring something much worse that was

to happen in 1943, the background was nevertheless still there: not as something present, but as a perpetual awareness of something forever lost.

I think that my distinction between joy and pleasure, and between joy and happiness, may not be clear to you—I say "my" distinction, because other people might not draw the distinction, or might draw it in a different way. In pleasure and happiness as such, and apart from what may completely transform them, there is always a specific accent on the self, even when no question of selfishness can arise. If you feel happy at the beauty of a spring day, the essence of the matter is that *you* are feeling happy—not greedily, not it may be self-consciously, but still *you*. And if you feel happy when you read of some beautiful and redeeming action, or when an opportunity is given you of doing something kindly yourself, the situation is still the same—the happiness is *yours*: not in any exclusive sense, not in the sense that you want to keep it for yourself instead of sharing it—sharing it is often the main element in such happiness—but yours none the less. Joy, on the other hand, is not yours. It is something that happens, some potential that is realised, when you and Reality are at one; and happens not in you but in Reality, or happens in you, rather, only because it happens in Reality, and you and Reality are one. Joy is not selfless: the self, on the contrary, is wholly involved: but involved in this way, that inevitably the joy must be there in the self, by the simple fact (and not at all at the idea) of the oneness of that self with Reality. None of which is to imply that the joy is this and the oneness that: no question can arise as of substance and property: the joy and the oneness are wholly one. You can speak indifferently of joy in oneness or of oneness in joy.

The nature of joy has never been better expressed than by Wordsworth in these few lines from *The Excursion*:

> In such access of mind, in such high hour
> Of visitation from the living God,
> Thought was not: in enjoyment it expired.
> No thanks he breathed, he proffered no request.
> Rapt into still communion that transcends
> The imperfect offices of prayer and praise,
> His mind was a thanksgiving to the power
> That made him; it was blessedness and love.

Everything is there—the grace, the quiet, the at-one-ness, the man's whole heart and soul and mind become love and blessedness and thanksgiving: and my own mind, as I remember and write these things, is just such "a thanksgiving to the power that made me"—not to say this would be churlish, for the power in question, for all we know, may like people saying things that he knows very well already. And I like saying it, anyhow.

But though pleasure and happiness are by no means identical with joy, joy may on occasion be mediated by them: for a creature may be rapt by the merest sensualities, such as the first happy puff at the first cigarette before breakfast, into "still communion" and its inseparable thanksgiving. Delight in a physical pleasure may occasion, may be simultaneously transformed into, union with all delight; and the very fact that the note is so personal—that it strikes so poignantly for *you*—may at once mean to live, as otherwise you would not have lived, in the whole symphony. I judge this experience to be comparatively rare, but it ought to be both perpetual and universal. If it is really rare, the words I have myself used, "merest sensualities", give a clue to one reason—one among many—for this rarity, and I have used them, not because I believe them to be suggestive of anything true, but by way of a recognisable shorthand. There are no "mere sensualities": the expression is stupid and gross, and could only be prompted by disrespect for the body, and by that fatal dichotomy of body and soul which makes living in wholeness impossible. "All Bibles or sacred codes," says Blake, who understood wholeness better, so far as I am aware, than any other Englishman, "have been the causes of the following Errors:—1. That Man has two real existing principles, viz. a Body and a Soul. 2. That Energy, called Evil, is alone from the Body; and that Reason, called Good, is alone from the Soul. 3. That God will torment Man in Eternity for following his Energies. But the following Contraries to these are True:—1. Man has no Body distinct from his Soul, for that called Body is a portion of Soul discerned by the five Senses, the chief inlets of Soul in this age. 2. Energy is the only life and is from the Body, and Reason is the bound or outward circumference of Energy. 3. Energy is Eternal Delight."

Mediation of joy by pleasure is rare among adults for another reason too, or perhaps for the same reason in another form. When pleasure mediates joy, it is the sharpness of delight that effects the mediation: from the sharpness of delight come the joy and communion, the joy in communion or the communion in joy. But commonly, as life advances, the sharpness goes: we suffer a blunting to the edge of our delight, and take wonders for granted when often experienced: with crass insensitiveness and careless ingratitude, for a wonder repeated is a wonder still, and a wonder not less wonderful but more. Remember the dreams of your youth, says Schiller, if you wish to be a man. Keep fresh, similarly, the naïf impact of young delight, if you wish, in later life, to know joy.

And if joy can be mediated by pleasure, it can also, and more obviously, be mediated by happiness.

There is something else, not itself joy, that can mediate joy—can mediate, that is, the "still communion" in which true joy consists. It is something very different from pleasure and happiness: suffering, I mean, and pain and grief. And not only can they mediate communion: they can mediate, I suspect, a communion more perfect than could otherwise in any way be achieved. Christ was in a communion such as we can never know when he prayed at Gethsemane "Nevertheless not my will but thine"—but after begging that the cup might pass from him; and again, supremely, on the Cross, when "My God, my God, why hast thou forsaken me?", the world's great cry of dereliction, was followed by "Into thy hands I commend my spirit", Paradise regained. Does it seem to you odd that I should talk about joy in the context of Garden and Cross? But you remember my definition: that it is in communion, in its thanksgiving and blessedness, that the joy we are speaking of consists. It was not for very many years, not till more than half my life was over, that I was to understand—I mean realise with my whole being, not intellectually understand—the relation between suffering and joy; and I understand it, even now, very imperfectly.

The joy in me or with me, which has persisted so graciously to this hour, was not quite the same in the days of which I am speaking as at those later times when it seemed most complete, 1917 and 1942. As child and youth I sang for joy, but silently: my heart sang, not my lips. At Repton I was no longer silent: praise came flooding out in a stream of verses, for the desire to express the adoration I felt had suddenly become irresistible. I was no poet, though I had the heart of a poet, and the verses I wrote at that time, often at the rate of one or more a day, are of interest only as naïf expressions of what I was then thinking and feeling. Most of them have long since been lost or destroyed, but I have a tiny booklet of "Sonnets and Poems by V.G." which was privately printed in 1917 as a wedding present for one of my best friends, and there are a few others which I can imperfectly remember. I shall quote one or two of them here, to illustrate the change from silence to speech that I have just described; and one or two more when I get back to Repton (by way of Oxford) on this circular journey, to illustrate the nature of the oneness I was feeling so imperative a desire to express.

There are a few lines of blank verse, printed in italics on the first page of my little booklet as a sort of key to what follows, which are interesting to me as I reread them for their expression of the change from silence to speech, as well as for the "stillness" that they seem anxious not to break:

> We are of them that feel and cannot sing.
> But sometimes, when a summer's day is done,
> And, wandering over field and hill, we see
> White clover in a wilderness of grass,
> Our hearts are bursting so with joy and love
> That words must come—and in the evening calm
> We cannot but stammer out, with faltering lips,
> A quiet hymn of thankfulness to God.

And there is a sonnet, the octave of which describes a passing mood of flatness, an inability, one day, to write the usual verses —and then, in the sestet, the reason for this temporary dereliction is queried:

> A day, and no song written. All the soul
> 　Gone out of books and fireside, where had been
> 　A sense that made them, as it passed between,
> The whispered hintings of a perfect whole:
> For self gazed out and trembled, as there stole
> 　The thought that each thing joyed in, each thing seen,
> 　Getting from all, and giving, sweetness keen,
> Itself was part, attainèd, of the goal.

Was it that when at last clear speech was won
After the silent joy of all my days,
And there was singing, singing everywhere
But never quiet sleep, I breathed a prayer
For respite from such agony of praise—
To God, Almighty in creation?

The last (very bad) line was intended to suggest that as it was
God's job to create, there was something properly punishable
in the effrontery of a man who prayed, for his own convenience,
that he might be spared, if only temporarily, the creative pangs
of self-expression: the punishment being that God had taken
him at his word, shut off the inspiration, and might never
restore it.

I find these verses full of the adjectives calm and quiet
("dawn's breathless quiet of joy" and so on); and there is also
a quartet of lines in which I was referring, probably, to the
"background" quality of joy, and transferring it to human
love:

Your love is his blue sky behind the trees:
And every moment, as it passes slow,
Is like some splendid tower that he sees
Against a dawning sun's eternal glow.

That really does express rather well what I have been trying to
say, during the last hour or so, about joy, happiness and
pleasure. The splendid towers are the happiness and pleasure:
the blue sky and the eternal glow—looking back a few pages
I find I actually used this expression—are the joy.

The difference in this matter, then, between the me of Elgin
Avenue and the me of Repton was mainly the difference between silence and speech. The difference between both those
mes and the me of 1942 was something much more important.
I can best describe this difference by mentioning separately
two ways in which it presents itself to me, though they are, no
doubt, merely two ways of saying the same thing.

In Elgin Avenue and at Repton joy was the background. But
in 1942 it was no longer only the background: it was background, foreground, everywhere, everything. I was wholly lost
—every minute, except that there were no minutes, only eternity,

and every bit of me, except that there were no bits and no me, only a totality: I was wholly lost, caught up, "rapt into still communion". It was not a question of happiness or unhappiness: this did not arise. There was one thing at least about which, in a sense, I was not merely unhappy but agonised; for 1942 was a time of war, as was 1917, and the war, on both occasions, was unutterably horrible to me. There is something very strange about the fact that joy has been most persistent in me precisely at these two times when other people have been suffering agony: agony that since the age of six I had felt, as if in my own person, to be worse than any other, an agony that I entered into, lived with, in the very midst of my abounding joy. I was trapped with the trapped in a basement; when the wireless announced that so many tons of bombs had been dropped on Germany, I saw the flying limbs and the mangled babies. And yet my joy was unaffected. I shall make no attempt either to explain or to apologise for this (I mean in my own sight and God's, not in yours or the world's); for though I have thought about the matter a very great deal, I have never been able to make up my mind whether there is anything to apologise for. Somebody or other said that all cares are private cares, and that no one has ever lost an hour's sleep over other people's troubles. This is a stupid piece of libel in general, and quite untrue as an explanation of my own case. I troubled the whole time, as did most other people, I imagine; and I lost a good deal of the very little sleep that I was anyhow in the habit of getting. And yet, I repeat, my joy was unaffected. It was as if the essential me was so completely in tune with a goodness and beauty which alone were really real that anything evil or wretched that might be happening to me or anybody else, including my own so frequent agony of mind, was happening in another and less real dimension.

But though I thought or rather felt myself completely in tune with ultimate goodness and beauty, in fact I was not. There was something missing, and this was to come. To 1917 no year of dereliction had succeeded, but 1942 was followed by 1943. It was an aftermath terrible at the time, but very gracious in retrospect; and I can now thank God for it.

The first way, then, in which I would describe the difference between my joy in 1942 and my previous joys is by saying that in 1942 the joy was no longer background but everywhere and

everything. And the second way in which I would describe it is
this. The living of my life in Elgin Avenue was grossly marred
by what I have long since seen as the mark of a particularly
fierce egoism; and I should feel worse about it, more self-
condemnatory, but for the knowledge, slowly won, that self-
condemnation of a sort, as opposed to a remorseful acceptance
of what one has been and perhaps still is and will continue to
be, can be egoism itself in disguise; and but for the comfort I
take in those words of F. H. Bradley that I quoted much earlier:
"It is connexion with the central fire which produces in the
element this burning sense of selfness. And the collision is resolved within that harmony where centre and circumference
are one." I like to think of this passage as granting me absolu-
tion: or not so much me, as the whole scheme of things that we
are apt to rail against so bitterly for making us what we are.

The fault or vice or sin which I now see as the mark of a particularly fierce egoism was spiritual greed.

Spiritual greed is incompatible with joy, and so there could
be none of it in 1942, when the background had become everything, and "the collision was resolved within that harmony
where centre and circumference are one." But there was a very
great deal of it during those earlier years: not when I was
experiencing joy, not when I was living in the communion
which is another name for joy, but in my attitude to this background of joy and communion. And the essence of the matter
was this: I was not content to live in joy when joy was vouch-
safed to me, and otherwise with that quiet acceptance of the
moment which, had I but known it, is precisely the same joy,
the same undifferentiated communion; but I must be forever
seeking joy, looking forward to it, unhappy and sometimes terrified at the idea that at some future hour I might find myself
without it. I think, indeed, that the qualification "not when I
was experiencing joy" ought perhaps to go, and that this greed
of mine may have been present even when I was living in communion, which would be another way of saying that I was
never truly living in it at all. For even when the communion
seemed quite complete, even when I seemed wholly rapt in
adoration and thanksgiving and blessedness, there was often,
and perhaps always, the shadow of possible loss: the desire,
mixed up with the joy, that the joy might continue for ever.

The secret of good living is to live always both in the moment

F

and in eternity: or, for this is the truer way of putting it, to live in the moment as eternity and in eternity as the moment: the two, for anyone who has mastered the secret, being one. I lived as a child and youth in the moment and in the future, and that is about as different from the right way as you could imagine, though the wrong way, as wisdom grows, may lead to the right. And not only did I live in the future as well as in the moment, but it was the future that dominated the partnership. "Looking forward" was perpetual: most often with a sense of ecstasy at the wonders to come, but sometimes, and particularly during a few terrible months, with foreboding and even despair. Pleasures and happinesses were qualified for me, in the very moment of enjoyment, by the fear that they might never recur. Not that there was anything lacking at such times in the intensity of my pleasure and happiness: the intensity, on the contrary, was most poignant, as with the intensity of something always newly discovered: but side by side with the intensity the fear was present, and it was the intensity that occasioned the fear. Let me give you a trivial and almost grotesque example of this "looking forward" that has just come into my mind. You know what music meant to me. Now one of the operas that enraptured me most when I was beginning to frequent Covent Garden was Verdi's *Aïda*: the magic of the Nile scene, in particular, held me breathless. Time after time, as the melodies unfolded themselves, I was caught up into a meeting between me and the music; and I recognised quite clearly that, as is commonly the way with young music-lovers, a freshness of recognition and rediscovery was one of the main elements in my rapture. And then gradually I found myself fearing that I might be getting to know this opera too well, and that soon when I heard it the rapture of recognition would be dulled. Just then the original exhibition was on at the White City, and I had a season ticket; and among the greatest of my pleasures was listening to the military bands that played in the open on summer evenings, with programmes made up largely of operatic pot-pourris. If *Aïda* happened to be included I wanted to keep away but couldn't; and then when I got home I would be seized by a dread that everything had been ruined—and for how little: Covent Garden was one thing, a military band another!—and would go through a kind of ritual counting in an effort to persuade myself that I hadn't really heard the work so often after all. The formula never varied, and was repeated two or three times on each occasion: "*Aïda*. Heard it nine times at Covent Garden: heard it three times on an M.B." M.B. meant military band. And I would do the same for other operas.

(Ritual counting in general, which has points in common with hand-washing and similar rituals, was one of my manias. If I was resolving to break myself of a bad habit, I would say, usually aloud, "I won't do it again after counting twelve", and then I would count very slowly and impressively, and feel for the time being secure. At the back of this oddity was, I think, the idea of a completely new start: the guilty past was dramatically ended, the *vita nuova* now clearly and decisively embarked upon. But you cannot magic away the guilt of your past: what you will do, if you are wise, is to become reconciled with it.)

Why do I call this "looking forward", this fear of deprivation, spiritual greed? Because it was joy, in the sense I have been applying to the word, that I was always seeking. I was looking forward to a life lived perfectly—next minute, next month and all my adult years: particularly all my adult years—in the joy I had already so often experienced. I cannot remember whether, or to what extent, I consciously thought in such terms, but I am certain it was this that impelled me, even when I was looking forward to, or fearing the loss of, what would ordinarily be described as physical trivialities: I looked forward to them, or feared the loss of them, because they could be mediators of joy. The tragic paradox of human life was here. With its love, the greater Self was working through me, in its own way, for at-one-ness: with my greed and egoism, I thought that *I* could achieve this at-one-ness, and I desired it for *myself*. Always one comes back to the central words of Christ: "Whosoever shall seek to save his life shall lose it; and whosoever shall lose his life shall preserve it."

The fear of deprivation was as strong in me as the "looking forward", and it has persisted during the greater part of my adult life. It has taken many forms: fear that I might do wrong, fear of having already done it, fear of a guilty conscience: fear, in general and above all, of not being good. It has been dormant from time to time for long periods, and I have been wholly unaware of it; and then suddenly, as something happened that gave it its opportunity, it would come leaping out and almost physically choke me. This fear, strongly egoistic, is almost certainly environmental or, more deeply, pathological in origin, and the chapter that follows may throw a good deal of light on it; but this does not affect the fact that it has always been essentially the same fear, the fear of losing Paradise. It reached its climax in 1943, which was total fear: perpetual fear: fear, as it seemed, in eternity. But 1943 taught me acceptance; and during the last few years my fear has been growing rarer and rarer, and now, if it comes at all, I can quickly feel its nothingness by receiving a sort of prayer. Fear will have vanished, I believe, before I die.

§ 2

Away with talk of fear! Away with metaphysical distinctions between pleasure, happiness and joy! Let us breathe together the air of my enchanted boyhood. Let me tell you of my young delights.

About the music you already know something, and especially about opera and Covent Garden. Ah! the look of the place before my eyes as I write: the smell of it in my nostrils! The enormous red curtain when the lights had been lowered: the people seen dimly: the moment of expectation: and the lemon squash man in our gallery, and the feel of my bottom on the cold stone steps as I read the libretto in preparation for the act to come! And I loved its past, just as now I am loving that past of it which I myself experienced. There was an old high box-room in the attic at home, full of packing-cases and black-domed trunks and discarded umbrellas and the like; and one day, to my immeasurable delight—I had just begun going to St. Paul's, so must have been about fourteen at the time—I discovered there a few old *Telegraphs* that had been taken up perhaps for some job of packing and thrown carelessly in a corner. Thrown away, such treasures! It became a favourite occupation, in summer when the sun was high, to sit reading in the full glare on our narrow balcony, and then to break off and go searching for still more copies of the *Telegraph* in the dimness and dust above. For those were spacious days for all who were not poor, and opera announcements were as different as you

could imagine from their present successors. The chances were
that after drawing a few blanks I would come upon some issue
with a summer date, summer having meant, from time immemorial, the operatic "grand season"; and there, by the left-hand
margin of the middle left-hand page, not all wretchedly
crowded up as today into a mean half inch but overflowing
for a generous foot, would be a dozen announcements of forthcoming performances, each with a good solid inch to itself
and each giving fully, down to the *Steuermann* in "Tristan" or
the *Messaggiero* in "Aïda", the names of the performers. The date
might be nineteen-hundred, or eighteen-ninety, or even one of
the late eighteen-eighties: five years back, ten years back,
twenty years back: and I became as familiar with the minor
names—I have the shape of them still in my mind, though not
the exact spelling—as with the Pattis or de Reszkes or Nordicas
that came popping out from the page every now and again to
give me a sudden stab of delight. The curious thing is that,
although I was only just beginning to go to the opera, I knew
exactly which role each one of these performers had been playing—or was playing for me at the moment, for that is how I
thought of it. This odd expertise was a product of unconscious
detection—comparison, elimination, etcetera—combined with
a masterly knowledge of operatic literature: libretti, I mean: for
there were lots of them about, and there was nothing I liked
better than reading them in bed at night, looking out on the
way for particularly famous arias, and comparing the English
with the Italian or German opposite so that, when I came to
hear the work myself, I might be able to follow it perfectly. For
there was no opera in English in my day, or only as an occasional eccentricity: we worked hard for our enjoyment, mastering in advance the original text. I have never cared for opera in
English: as often as not the musical line is ruined. But opera in
English is better than no opera at all.

The domestic stock of operatic text-books was supplemented
later on by a wonderful gift to me from my great-aunt Rosetta,
the Hastings aunt. She, already an old lady at that time, had
been a great opera-goer in her day, and had accumulated,
partly, I imagine, by inheritance, a magnificent store of the
small, closely-printed booklets in yellow and orange and blue,
published by firms in the Haymarket and Wardour Street and
St. Paul's Churchyard, that had been the ordinary libretti of

a generation or so before mine. She gave the lot to me, and I have them still. All the fine old classics were there, the *Sonnambulas* and *Dinorahs* and *Otellos* (Rossini's), the *Africaines*, the *Prophètes*, and the *Etoiles du Nords*: things already obsolete in my day, when the craze for "music-drama" was already at its height, and a taste for Bellini was considered a trifle grotesque. Occasionally—the libretto, in such cases, had clearly been bought at the actual performance—a small slip of paper, lightly fixed to the title-page, would set out the names of the cast: printed anyhow, as though of no great importance: but—the Ravoglis in *Orfeo*, Tamberlik in the *Prophète*, Albani in *Puritani*, Nicolini in *Robert the Devil* ("Carriages may be ordered for 11.50"), Patti, Scalchi and Maurel in *Semiramide*, Ella Russell, Nordica, Lassalle, Scalchi and Edouard de Reszke in *Ugonotti*: and—Mario! "Ah, did you once see Shelley plain?" Envy me, Timothy, my delight.

Covent Garden was the centre of my operatic existence, but I would go anywhere to hear what I wanted. It was at the Savoy, in a Marie Brema season, that I listened for the first of many times to the innocence and integrity of *Orfeo*; I sat in the gallery of the Holloway Theatre for a scratch performance of *Mignon*, which we never heard at Covent Garden; and these were the Drury Lane days of Chaliapin's majesty, and the bowmen leaping out at us in *Prince Igor*, and the white perfection of the winged *Sylphides*. Then there was the Old Vic, down amid the fly-blown tattoo shops and dingy sexualities of the Waterloo Bridge Road: suggesting somehow dirty railway compartments and tenth-rate pubs in ill-lit streets and underground lavatories, but the embryo of a *Volksoper* from which Sadler's Wells, now so soigné in its informality, was soon to develop. The place was genuinely proletarian in those days—you could get in for tuppence, I think: even the stage box cost only a shilling or so, and I sometimes sat in it with a party of friends to get a closer view of old Charles Corri, who conducted his squeaky orchestra of about a dozen, and the stage as well, with an extraordinary presence of mind that would cover up a thousand mishaps. It was at the Old Vic that I first heard *Don Giovanni*. The Leporello ate spaghetti (as part of his performance) while the stalls sucked oranges. I enjoyed it far more than many stuffed-shirt performances, but almost equally ill sung, that I have heard at Covent Garden during the last few years.

*April 6th*
*Ladbroke Grove, 5.30 a.m.*

*Laus deo! Laus deo! I don't know why I say it in Latin, except perhaps that the words have an immemorial ring about them, some grave and hierophantic sound that "Praise be to God" does not possess. "God", it may be, is too definite: it suggests an old man with a beard, not the ineffable I AM which is alpha and omega and the rain outside and the response in my heart. Anyhow, I have been lying awake for hours now, as I have lain awake for so many nights, thinking of what I shall presently be writing, and remembering more and more of my childhood; and dozing and waking and dozing again, and struggling with the temptation to prop myself up and start writing again immediately—I call it a temptation, because this sleeplessness is bad for my heart, and I have had one or two small bouts of my pseudo-angina recently: until now, with the thin line of light quite strong above the curtains that cover the great bow window (scraps of poetry keep coming into my head, this time "The lines of festal light in Christ Church hall"), I must put down on paper, for I can resist it no longer, the Laus deo! Laus deo! Laus deo! which has been throbbing so insistently inside me, or it may be in the world, like a swelling ground bass for the flutes and violins. In a few minutes now the morning tea will be up, and then there will be masses of figures at the office as we try somehow to beat the inflation; and my visit to Wormwood Scrubs, and a talk there with Doug, the prisoner of whom I have grown so fond; and home to Brimpton; and tomorrow, from eight to seven, with an interval for sleep after lunch, a steady getting down of these boyhood memories —in the library, pipe alight, with the downs outside: "the long day of love to come." Laus deo.*

*Breakfast at Brimpton,*
*April 7th*

*The sun is up, and the conservatory is blazing—with camellias and cinerarias and peach blossom and oranges; and the first flowers are out on the climbing geranium, and the first bit of yellow is showing on the million-budded mimosa.*

Apart from opera, the two great backgrounds to my musical life were the proms, when Covent Garden was over for the year, and the Sunday afternoon concerts at the Albert Hall. I should

have thought it impossible to miss a night at the proms, except
at first on Fridays, when I wasn't allowed to go; and just as I
had my own seat, B 49, in the Covent Garden gallery, so I
always stood in almost exactly the same spot at the Queen's
Hall, about a couple of yards from the bank of flowers that
hemmed off the orchestra, and a little to the left. It was the
occasional operatic arias, and the Monday Wagner, that thrilled
me most in my earliest season: the popular bits, too, such as
*Finlandia* and *Peer Gynt* and *Casse-Noisette*, and, specially, the ex-
cerpts from Berlioz' "Faust". Berlioz was to become one of my
favourite composers. There are moods in which I would sooner
hear *Voici des roses* than anything. There is an ache in it, as in
the Botticelli Venus, for an earlier, a sort of pre-moral beauty.
And time after time, whether he is being tender, as in *L'Enfance
du Christ*, or exalted and pitiful, as in *Les Troyens*, he expresses,
like no other musician, the pang of loveliness.

But soon, very soon, the great German classics were unfolding themselves and transporting me—Mozart and Haydn and
Beethoven and Schubert, but not, at all comparably, either Bach
or Brahms: and I realised, with a sense of continual expectation,
that day after day throughout the lifetime ahead of me there
would be a whole new world to grow familiar with. The
Beethoven symphonies were played one by one on Friday evenings, and this meant that I had to miss them till I broke the tabu:
but I heard them at other concerts, and there was a good deal of
Beethoven anyhow on secular evenings. The Ninth Symphony
was invariably shorn of its choral section; the last movement
was begun, but ended abruptly just before "O Freunde, nicht
diese Töne." So I was always looking for opportunities to hear
it complete.

I have retained, by the way, my reservations about Brahms
and Bach. Some of Brahms I think of as German in the stupidly
offensive sense, and often when I am listening to him I wish I
were listening to Bizet, who is his Gallic opposite. As for Bach,
even to mention the supremacy of his intellect and the perfection of his technique would be impertinent; and yet I find him
on occasion, in spite of his incomparable grandeur and much
beauty of the purest kind, rather cloyingly rich in his rhythmical
exuberance, as well as somewhat unspiritual in his religious-
ness: a little lacking, one might say, in what Soloviev would
describe as godmanhood. I fear this must sound paradoxical,

and I have crossed it out three times: but that is how I feel about
Bach, and I had better say so. Is he, perhaps, more than anything, a great churchman and a supreme mathematician?

My other musical background—Sunday afternoon at the
Albert Hall—was not only delightful in itself, but was associated
with a number of subsidiary delights. I used to rush away early
with my lunch half finished, and wait for a Marble Arch 'bus,
or a puffing green vehicle—propelled I think by steam, and of
a type that was soon to become obsolete—at the corner of Elgin
Avenue and Maida Vale, in the lull and remoteness of the deserted
streets; and the anxiety was, as I arrived at the hall and leaped
two at a time up the broad stone stairs to the topmost gallery,
whether any free places would still be vacant in the standing
room at the end of the sixpenny seats. There were about fifty of
these places, and if I was too late I would spend a precious sixpence and, looking down at the orchestra far below, divide my
time between listening to the tuning up, so heavenly a sound,
and reading over and over again the programme descriptions.
By some trick of memory there comes singing into my mind
now, to the exclusion of everything else, Tchaikovsky's *Capriccio
Italien*, all mixed up with the Mendelssohn Violin Concerto.

I usually walked home, through the park and up Edgware
Road: partly to save money and partly because I loved the
park and the streets and walking; and always, when I got to
Marble Arch, I would stop and stand listening to the orators:
sometimes for two or three hours, taking part, if a Tory was
speaking, in the heckling: but sometimes hurrying off to the
bandstand, where I would stand and listen, or sit and listen if
I could afford it, while the smell of cigar smoke hung mingling
with the summer heat. It was on these occasions, I think, that
I first acquired my love of cigars, though it was some years
before I was to smoke one; and now I enjoy them more than
all other physical pleasures, with one exception—more than
bouquet of wine, or the mellowest brandy, or food however
insinuatingly cooked: and sometimes I enjoy them most of all,
with no exception.

Covent Garden, the proms, Sunday afternoons at the Albert
Hall—these were the musical background; and against it,
occasionally, were the Philharmonic, and the London Symphony, and Pachmann, and Paderewski, and Culp in lieder
at the Wigmore or Steinway, and the first slow approach to

chamber music. But it was not till some years later that I was to hear, interpreted first by Lener and then by Busch, the beauty of music in, so far, its supreme expression—Beethoven's last quartets.

Why has no one ever included, among the various "proofs" of the existence of God, the musical? Music is as much μίμησις, imitation, as any other of the arts: Beethoven doesn't invent anything, he perceives something and tries to reproduce it: then how does it happen, what Beethoven tries to reproduce in, say, the E flat quartet? Can anyone imagine that it happens accidentally?

§ 3

My love of geology took its rise from the discovery when I was still quite small of a tiny duodecimo textbook, with only a hundred or so pages of letterpress but a few quite entrancing illustrations. My mother had a bookcase with glass shelves above and cupboard below, the latter normally kept locked; but occasionally she forgot, and then was my opportunity. In the shelves that were open to view were fat red volumes of George Eliot in the William Blackwood edition, and bound-up Dickens parts, and so on; locked away in the cupboard below were Ibsen and Huxley and Darwin, and Ouida and Rita yellowbacks, and paper-covered booklets, with the gayest of pictures on their fronts, called "Three Weeks" or "Five Nights of Love" or "A Bed of Roses". If one of the latter came to light, my mother would make haste to explain that she read them "to see what the most modern people were writing." She had other eccentricities of a similar kind. Very occasionally, at Saturday lunch, she would ask for a whisky and soda. Draining it, she would make a wry face, and shudder, and say "boo-ooo": then would turn to us children and proclaim very solemnly "I take it as medicine."

It was in these surroundings, jumbled up with Victoria Cross, that I found my little treasure one day, and begged to be allowed to keep it. My request was granted; and immediately I was caught by an enchantment that was to hold me for at least ten years—it holds me still, though I have forgotten almost everything I knew—and came very near to rivalling my passion for music itself. Soon I was progressing to more and more difficult textbooks: I was given, when *Barmitsvah* at thirteen, the great standard work by Sir Archibald Geikie in two volumes: and meanwhile I was venturing into palaeo-botany and palaeozoology and the other indispensable sub-sidiaries, all however without the slightest knowledge of botany or zoology themselves, for mere contemporaneities seemed tedious and flat to me—the Switzerlands or Canadas of life, with nothing romantic or "extra" about them. It was the world's magic past that so compellingly called to me: nostalgic with a nostalgia far surpassing mere home-sickness or longing for one's own petty past, I lived starry-eyed in the strange vast aeons that had preceded my arrival on earth. Pleistocene and Recent made little appeal to me: neoliths, palaeoliths, mam-moths—contemptible proto-modernities, not more than some millions of years old! I wanted the reptiles of the Mesozoic, winged for the air and armoured for the land and paddled for the coralline seas; I wanted the forests of the coal measures, darkling and steamy with eternal rain; but far more than these I wanted the real earlinesses—Devonian and Silurian and Cam-brian: trilobites: the immemorial worm-tracks; and so down at last to the bottommost gneisses, alone before the birth of life. What a glory, this journey through time, for a schoolboy not yet in his teens!

Incapable of mastering even the rudiments of those sciences with which geology is inextricably linked—chemistry and physics and astronomy as well as botany and zoology—I never-theless developed an odd expertise within the range of my own capabilities. My appetite for detail was immense. I not only knew, as a matter of course, what genera of fossils were to be found in the various strata: I might also know, and always wanted to know, the name and appearance of a particular species characteristic, say, of some band, perhaps only an inch or so thick, in the chalk of Dover or the limestone of Bath. To unravel the whole story of the earth's past: to find that seas had been here, land-masses there, mountains somewhere else, at this or that moment in mundane history: to visualise the appearance of the changing populations—the echinoderms and ammonites and belemnites and lepidodendra and ichthyosaurs and deinosaurs and palaeotheria and mastodons, down, in types that teemed, to the smallest variation in the latest subspecies—it was this that so fascinated me, so compelled me to go ever and ever forward and learn ever and ever more until at last I should have won, as I passionately desired, the last guarded secret of the stony record. I haunted the airy galleries, aromatic with bees-wax, of the South Kensington Museum; I pored over show-cases with pencil and notebook, and made feeble sketches, now of some tiny bivalve, and now, moving on, of the vast megalosaurus that bestraddled the length of a neighbouring room. Breaking off, I would eat my sandwiches in the grounds, on a seat by the stump of a fossilised tree, and then go hurrying back to my sketching. South Kensington Station, when nowadays I happen to pass through it, brings back to me, always, these holiday expeditions: airiness, and bees-wax, and summer afternoons.

I was found at my work one day by a man called Sherborne Smith, a kindly and bearded man, almost as big as the megalo-saurus, who was in some way connected with the Department of Geology. He made me free of the exceptionally fine geological library, and I spent many happy hours there in the months and years that followed, taking down notes, drawing up comparative tables, and copying illustrations of specimens unrepresented in the galleries. When I got home and told my mother how kind this man had been to me, she smiled with a sort of wistful gravity that I often remarked in her. "A world-famous naturalist and writer like that!" she said. "Really great men find time for anything—even for unimportant small boys. It's a sign of their greatness." There had been some confusion, I realised, between Sherborne Smith and White of Selborne; but I did not say so, preferring to trade on a spurious glory. I was equally lacking in forthrightness about my membership of the Geologists' Association, which I joined at the age of ten or eleven, at the prompting of the same Sherborne Smith, who wanted to make me a professional geologist. This was a delightful Association. It staged a weekly expedition for fossil-hunting to such heavenly places as Swanage or the Island of Sheppey; and though I could never go, partly because the event was always on Saturday and partly because I couldn't have afforded to anyhow, I looked forward eagerly to the monthly bulletin, which contained full accounts of the members' "finds". There was another feature of this little booklet that made it as precious to me, on occasion, as the libretto of a Meyerbeer opera. From time to time a member would investigate, band by band, the flora or fauna of some particular stratum; and the results would be published in the bulletin, under some such title as "Notes on the distribution of ammonites in the Lower Lias at Brackenmouth". There might even be illustrations! Here was something really expert, something a serious geologist must immediately take note of, something, above all, that filled in the picture. When a bulletin arrived with an article like this, I would have given up everything, save only the opera, to read it without a moment's delay.

Anybody could join the Association upon payment of a trivial fee. But when my membership of this body was confused at Elgin Avenue with a Fellowship of the Royal Geological Society, to which, it appeared, I had been elected at the age of ten, I was silent. The difference after all, I may have thought, was not so great. And I was the youngest member of the Association, anyhow. I occasionally signed myself M.G.A.—"Member of the Geologists' Association." Once or twice I may have made it F.G.A. But I am sure I never went so far as F.R.Geol.S.

My researches at the Museum bore fruit in my second or third year at St. Paul's. There was a prize there, known as the Smee prize, for what was described as "original work"; or rather a whole series of prizes, for my recollection is that some couple of dozen were awarded every year, of a value, to be taken out in books, ranging from a few guineas to a few shillings. Almost anything ranked as "original work". I recall water-colour sketches, and Buddhas carved in soapstone, and model engines, and collections of impaled butterflies, and electrical contraptions with lamps that went on and off, and poems: the only proviso being that you had to have made or written or painted or collected the thing by your own unaided effort. I entered for the prize with a huge piece of cardboard, about the breadth of a mantelpiece, entitled "The Age of Reptiles: A Diagrammatic Sketch of a Typical Landscape in the Jurassic Epoch (Original)". I searched for it the other night in a cupboard full of lumber at Ladbroke Grove, and found it: brittle with its nearly forty years of life, it cracked and broke as I propped it up against the library table. It is an extraordinary performance: comically ill-drawn, but done with such obvious devotion, such painstaking attention to the last detail, as really to be rather moving. An accompanying key classifies the various objects in appropriate categories:

aves, reptilia, pisces, crustacea, echinodermata, arachnida, insecta, mollusca, and vegetabilia—the latter subdivided into cycads, conifers, equisetaceae and filiciales: ninety-one items in all. There are pterodactyls in the air, ichthyosauruses in the sea, an iguanodon, among other monsters, on land: looking, this last, like a child's "dying pig" that has been heavily striated with ink. There are a couple of extensive beaches, with each grain of sand meticulously filled in; molluscs, and a fine assortment of my beloved ammonites, richly cover them. There is an array of cycads (divided, on the key, into "species founded on stems" and "ditto on leaves") with various spiders hanging low from their fronds (one of them "marked in the British Museum 'A spider from the lithographic stone of Bavaria' "); and there are rocks in the sea, with bryozoa sticking to them. But the centre-piece is a gigantic brontosaurus, with a sausagy neck, a half-witted gape, and an eye no bigger than a grain of my sand. The only visible leg looks like a swivelling attachment on a tin toy.

I got a prize—the last, for five shillings. I believe that everyone who entered got a prize. I was very much upset. Next year I tried again, with "The Age of Mammals. A Diagrammatic Sketch of a Typical Landscape in the Tertiary Period. (Original)". In this one the shells are drawn nearly half the size of a huge two-dimensional mastodon. Again I was awarded five shillings, whereas the man who carved Buddhas got a guinea. Nowadays, when a critic disparages one of my firm's masterpieces I say something in my mind about him. I said the same about the Smee prize examiner. *Amha-éretz!**

As you will gather from these Smee-prize cardboards I had a passion for "reconstructing". There was a great deal of talk by my mother about the alleged ability of anyone but a fool to reconstruct whole animals from single bones. I never attempted that; but I was always putting a line round fossil skeletons, and imagining that I had done something marvellous. Once I went off in another direction. I drew up a series of comparative tables, purporting to show in the greatest detail that certain geological epochs corresponded exactly to the Biblical days of creation. My mother was entranced: she said I was reconciling religion and science.

My own collection of fossils, which was the centre of my geological life, was necessarily a very poor one. To buy any would

* Ignoramus!

QUIET JOY 175

have seemed indecent, indeed the possibility of doing so would
never have occurred to me; and even to accept one as a gift,
apart perhaps from some special rarity I couldn't hope to
find for myself, would have been a little dubious. For the search,
the discovery and the careful extraction—cutting round and
prising out so that nothing might be damaged or lost—this
was the heart of the matter: the third term in a relation between
me as a person and the rocks, the holy spirit, which purchase, or previous possession by alien hands, would somehow
have robbed of its purity. But my opportunities for fossilising
were extremely limited, being confined to the occasional
summer holiday or a quarry I might hear of on the outskirts of London. Any opportunity that did occur I eagerly
seized, "tapping the strata", as I grandly described it, with my
geological chisel, which was an ordinary chisel, and my
genuinely geological hammer. Margate was my best treasure-
ground; I got some very nice echinoderms in the chalk at the
far end of Cliftonville, and a quantity of those small jointed
stalks, like miniature bamboo shoots, of which I never discovered the origin. I had excellent ammonites, too, many of
them with beautiful convolutions, and one that I loved above
all, for it shone with a patina of bright green like Roman glass
or peacocks' feathers. But my largest collection was of fossils
from the flint. Roads were constantly being made in our neighbourhood, and I became quite an expert at carefully weighing
up, from the appearance of a flint, the probability of there being
something inside. If I thought there might be, I would smash it
along the proper line, and was often rewarded by beautiful
sponges, and once or twice by the cast of a shell. I always tried
to discover where the flints had come from. My specimens were
carefully arranged, each with its own Latin label, in some cardboard nests of drawers that I had bought at a draper's.

I also collected minerals; they pleased me exceedingly, though
I felt about them, as a real geologist, very much what, as an
opera-goer, I felt about Russian ballet. My scruple about purchase no longer applied, for to find even the commoner minerals,
with one or two exceptions, would clearly have been impossible.
The exceptions were felspar, mica and small pieces of quartz,
for these were to be obtained by fracturing the granites that lay
everywhere about for house-building or road-making purposes.
I bought the rest of my specimens at a mineralogist's in the

Fulham Road, and formed a really beautiful little collection. There was kidney-shaped haematite—you made a blood-red streak with it on a white sheet of paper; and talc—you split it up into layers and at once bought another example; and asbestos—you plucked off its fibres, as slender as silk. There were the beautiful layered things, agate and onyx and sardonyx. There were two special crystals, a smoky and rather lopsided one, and a perfect rose-quartz, very sharp at the angles, that measured a good couple of inches. There were the deep solid colours, malachite and lapis lazuli: those more delicate, amethyst and turquoise and beryl and chrysoprase: vermilion cinnabar: sulphur for burning: the common things, garnet and gypsum and iron pyrites—"thunder-bolts"—the latter at a dozen a penny: and a lovely bit of matrix-of-opal, which was one of my three prime favourites. The other two were labradorite, with its play of rainbow colours as you turned it to the sun, and silken, shining cat's-eye. Mixed up with all these were (correctly) a piece of marble my Aunt Minna had brought back from the Parthenon, and (incorrectly—it should have been with the rocks) lava from Vesuvius. And there were the many pieces of limestone I had found here or there, their crevices coated with tooth-like crystals. I must have had nearly a hundred specimens in all.

Was my love of geology and mineralogy, of fossils and minerals, somehow connected with my love of earth? I think so. For I loved earth exceedingly, and anything that suggested it: the smell of violets, and the taste of medlars, and leaves lying sodden on autumn mould. There was a big spreading elder at the bottom of our garden, and under it, on Saturdays and Sundays one wet October, I spent hours making a huge rich mess of earth and leaves: stirring it up, digging it about, feeling its grittiness between my fingers. When, years later, a cousin of my wife found us a fine Leeds coffee-pot for a wedding present, with a couple of big red roses lying fresh and strong on a creamy ground, it was the beautiful earthiness of it, I am sure, which gave me the sense of an immediate welcome that I get from music: you could feel it, somehow, against your hand, you were common with it as if it were part of your own body, while you merely looked at its pleasantness. We soon found a teapot of the same type, very small and exquisitely potted, at a little antique shop in the Queen's Road; and so began our collection of Leeds pottery, which was to develop, after 1943, into a collection of English pottery in general. We have saltglaze, even closer to earth than the cream-ware of Staffordshire and Leeds, and with such a painting of butterflies and flowers, of ruined landscapes and Miss Pit drinking tea, as would seem to have been wholly absorbed into the matt surface, to have become or to have been from the first an inevitable part of it, without however losing a particle of its sharpness; and we have Ralph Wood figures, the Good Shepherd and the little chimney-sweep and the Roman Charity and the hurdy-gurdy-man, finely modelled and with superb translucent glazes, but already getting near, dangerously near as we think, to the character of porcelain. We much prefer the Astbury things, with rosettes and the royal arms and suchlike in creamy slip on a red-brown ground: and Nottingham ware, lighter in shade, shining, finely pitted—loving-cups, dated and inscribed, and tiles, and a silver-mounted teapot, and those little circular goblets, charmingly delicate, with double "walls" on the Chinese model. We have a huge bowl, too, of Bristol delft, said to be one of the largest ever made, and ringing like the Christ Church bell when you tap it; violet-tinged, and painted by Bowen: with houses, and boats, and a fisherman, and landscapes, and ladies and gentlemen talking—under a frieze, in *bianco sopra bianco*, of formalised flowers. We bought it at Bristol itself, on Christmas Steps. But best of all is the seventeenth-century slipware on the dining-room sideboard, and more of it on the ledge above the library shelves: a posset pot dated 1688, and a charger with a pattern of heads that look like Shakespeare's, and tygs from Wrotham with magnificently English dates, such as 1649, when Charles was executed, and 1660, the Restoration; and a very late jug, end of eighteenth century, with "John Joy for Ever" trailed richly over its thick brown glaze, clearly an election pot: all of them made of good red earth, so dark, in some cases, as to be almost indistinguishable from black.

We have never much cared for porcelain, your grandmother and I: the stuff is exquisite, of course, the Chelsea toys and the Sèvres cups and saucers and the Meissen figurines, but remote from reality and lacking in contact with common life: you live with pottery, live with it and almost in it, but porcelain you merely appreciate. That is why we would not trade our very special, inner, collection of "things with screws" for all their more precious equivalents in the world: not for the finest enamel or porcelain ones, not for *bibelots* of filigree or with inset of diamonds on gold. We have snuff-boxes painted with flowers, and a hand in the act of pinching, and dogs on cushions, and a booted foot, and a rich crimson rose, and a whole long row of ladies' heads with high eighteenth-century coiffures: all of them in pottery, with their screwed-on bases —for holding in the snuff or the patches or whatever it may have been—in pottery too.

There was another thing I loved with a love identical with my love of earth, and this was rain. I was a sun-worshipper, naturally, as most children are, and my pleasure was, on fine summer days, to sit unprotected in the glare, upturning my face to the sky: a habit that continued through most of my life, until, a year or two ago, I began to prefer the shade. But my love for rain was different in kind: with more of equality in it, more of something joint. I loved the rain on my face as, going out of the breakfast-room door on an autumn night, I would stand for a time in the garden and look up to the sky and sniff the air and do my little act of silent worship; but most of all I loved it at its point of meeting with earth, and with earth's common coverings—pavements in London, and grass and trees in gardens and parks and in what little country I knew. I loved morning dew, glistening leaves after torrents of rain, and pavements that dried, to a smell of stone, when a summer shower was over; and often I would watch as the circle of wetness—deep at the centre and thin on the edges—grew ever smaller and smaller, until suddenly, as if caught up into the air, the last little sixpenny had vanished. Is it fanciful to see, in this love of a meeting between earth and something from heaven, a dim foreshadowing of my later philosophy? Perhaps; and yet whatever may develop in us later must be present, embryonically, in our childhood.

I loved everything young: tightly packed buds that struggled to open; and my own birthday month of April—the smell, in particular, of garden mould as evening came on after sunshine and shower. The smell, too, of privet leaves, crushed between the fingers, from roadside hedges in London gardens. And sweeping winds. And ice and snow. And autumn mists—these especially—touched with gold. And cut grass (cricket, with doughnuts, at the Paddington and Maida Vale Recreation Ground!). And hay. And poppies. All seasons, all weathers.

I loved the spiritual solidity of things. Does this sound nonsense to you? I felt joy, I mean, at the existence, the life, of solid objects, joy because the objects were *there*: things like fenders and mantelpieces and walls; and my father's safe; and large thick books; and a table that stood in our nursery, with a rough deal top and "mahogany" legs. Not that I didn't like small things too; there was the absurd little poem I've mentioned about a scrap of paper in a classroom, and my feeling of happiness as it fluttered to the floor. But that was a joy in movement; my joy in these solider things was a joy in thereness. Only once, to my limited knowledge, has an artist got down with his brushes exactly the relation I am trying to describe: for Van Gogh saw the chair and the pipe on it, and answered them, exactly as I saw and answered my fenders and books.

I loved anything that suggested the adventure of life: what was coming, adulthood. Shops, for instance, because grown up people shopped in them and grown up people served you: very grand and important they seemed to me, these latter, particularly shopwalkers—I wanted to be a shopwalker myself, then decided to be a statesman instead—and yet not so important as little old Miss Buckingham, the lady who presided at a florist's near the Royal Oak. We did most of our shopping in Westbourne Grove (we, because on holidays I went with my mother as often as I was allowed) and always, when I knew I was going, I looked forward to the details. The smell of stuff: the bumping on the counter of the tall flat narrow rolls as length after length was unwound: the expert measuring on the long strip of brass that was nailed to the edge of the counter—"Let me see! I think I'll take five and a half yards": and the sound of the shears as they rushed at us, ripping the satin. And then, in the earliest years, came something very special indeed. A wooden ball, with the bill and my mother's coins inside it, would be catapulted on to a railway that ran along the top of the store. Soon it had rattled off and vanished. Returning, it successfully negotiated a whole series of trapdoors that were lying in its path; but, arrived at our counter, it suddenly fell off—a bit of the railway having incontinently dropped, on a hinge—and deposited itself, this time with the bill marked "paid" and my mother's change inside it, within convenient reach of our assistant's hand. I thought it a miracle, this choice by a ball of exactly the right spot to fall off at; and I am still very vague about the mechanics of the thing, in spite of all your grandmother's efforts, during the last half hour, to explain them to me.

My favourite store was William Whiteley's, because of the vastness of the place, the number of departments, and therefore the variety of smells. We would pass in a single hour from grand pianos (furniture polish) to soap, from provisions (bacon!) to flowers, from toys (tinny) to tennis balls. And there was always a most exciting question: should we be using the covered way, with its tiled floor and its looking-glass walls and its echo of clattering feet, that connected the premises in Westbourne Grove with those in Queen's Road? I don't know why using it was such a thrill; perhaps because all tunnels are mysterious, or perhaps because it meant that our shopping wasn't coming to an end and that the whole thing was going to be done properly. I have enjoyed such passage-ways ever since, particularly a carpeted one at the Charing Cross Hotel, where I occasionally stayed for a night or two early in the first world war: and this is odd, because I am slightly claustrophobic and dislike lifts—nothing would induce me to shut myself up in the lumbering little self-propelled monstrosity, only big enough to hold two, that mounts to the Flegs' apartment overlooking Notre-Dame.

Grown-upness hung even more romantically about the galleries, rather showrooms than shops—very *soigné* they looked to my inexperience, though I daresay they were pretty gimcrack really—that abounded at the White City. Some of these had French names, and women's perfume was always in the air.

*Saturday, April 14th.*
*Brimpton, 7 a.m.*
*Brimpton grows more beautiful with every week-end. The bricks of the long low engine-room at the back are red with the*

*unseen sun, and the frames to the left of them are blazing white,
but the field, lying lower, is still in shade: and brightness is
flooding into the library, catching the mahogany of the desk and a
claw of the pedestal table. The shadows on the carpet are long and
deep: and the prunus is in bloom outside.*

Grown-upness! The wonder to come! Chief among the
things that suggested it, and that accordingly delighted me,
were fog and trains. There has been no real fog in London since
my childhood; this is a fact, and not an exaggeration arising
from the tendency to see everything, as we first experienced it,
twice as big or twice as little or twice as wonderful as it actually
was. The explanation of this change, I am told, is that there
are fewer coal fires in modern London, and that motor-cars
with powerful headlights tend at once to disperse the fog and to
illuminate it. However that may be, we had real "pea-soupers"
when I was a boy. People tell you occasionally nowadays "I
couldn't see my hand in front of my face". This, unfortunately,
is picturesque nonsense; but fifty years ago it mightn't have
been nonsense—it might have been literally true. I often tried
the experiment when out at such times, putting up my hand to
within an inch of my nose; and if I could see even the slightest
outline of it, then this might be something else again, not
wholly unattractive, but had nothing to do with fog. I used to
go through the manœuvre with painful anxiety, and if the
result was unsatisfactory I always felt cheated. Still, one could
"look forward"; there was the possibility—even, perhaps, the
probability—that the darkness might get thicker and thicker,
or, as foolish people called it, worse and worse: and then the
real fun would begin. My father—we would be walking,
naturally, with the 'buses long since at a standstill—might
decide, and if matters were "bad" enough almost certainly
would decide, to bargain with a link-man, and, provided his
terms were not wholly outrageous, or even, when it came to it,
if they were, engage him to guide us home. These link-men
were very attractive: they carried enormous flares, smelling of
acetylene, which streamed in the wind of their movement like
the strands of a woman's hair. Sometimes the link-men were not
men but boys; and this was more satisfactory, because then they
could be hired more cheaply. Streaming flares, muffled footsteps,

mouths tightly shut: a murky smell, lights suddenly loom-
ing, accidental bumpings, scraps of conversation from people
unseen: these were enchantments, and each new enchantment
was more ravishing than the last. And the final one was still to
come; for suddenly, as we felt a wall with our hands, or peered
at a name-plate by the light of our flare, we might realise, my
father to his consternation and I to my delight, that we had
missed our turning and were lost.

> "Hastily rose our guide,
> Leaving us at the board; awhile we lingered,
> Then paced the beaten downward way that led
> Right to a rough stream's edge, and there broke off;
> The only track now visible was one
> That from the torrent's further brink held forth
> Conspicuous invitation to ascend
> A lofty mountain. After brief delay
> Crossing the unbridged stream, that road we took,
> And clomb with eagerness, till anxious fears
> Intruded, for we failed to overtake
> Our comrades gone before. By fortunate chance,
> While every moment added doubt to doubt,
> A peasant met us, from whose mouth we learned
> That to the spot which had perplexed us first
> We must descend . . .
> We questioned him again and yet again;
> But every word that from the peasant's lips
> Came in reply, translated by our feelings,
> Ended in this,—*that we had crossed the Alps.*
>
> Imagination—here the Power so called
> Through sad incompetence of human speech,
> That awful Power rose from the mind's abyss
> Like an unfathered vapour that enwraps,
> At once, some lonely traveller. I was lost;
> Halted without an effort to break through;
> But to my conscious soul I now can say—
> 'I recognise thy glory': in such strength
> Of usurpation, when the light of sense
> Goes out, but with a flash that has revealed
> The invisible world, doth greatness make abode,
> There harbours: whether we be young or old,

Our destiny, our being's heart and home,
Is with infinitude, and only there;
With hope it is, hope that can never die,
Effort, and expectation, and desire,
And something evermore about to be."

You will remember that I was with my parents. If I had been alone, half of me, at least, would have been terrified at the idea of being lost, even in infinitude: for the terror of being lost, alone, without human support, has been lurking in me, sometimes obsessively, throughout almost the whole of my life. But mixed up, or rather identical, with the terror would have been quite another sensation, a sensation of delight: of a delight that engaged—that more than engaged, that *was*—the very depths of being. But I was not alone, I was with my parents; and it was something quite uncomplicated—it was the rapture of anticipated adulthood, the sense that already, though still a small boy, I was committed to a grown-up adventure—that I was experiencing primarily, or that at any rate I thought I was experiencing.

It was not only an extremity of fog that I prayed for—literally, when six or seven, with "Dear God, let the fog get thicker": I prayed for all manner of other extremities—for the solidest ice, the deepest snow, the heaviest rain. There was a little old man with a beard who was paid a few pence by the neighbourhood for keeping the crossings in order. I hated his activities. First he'd spoil the snow, then he'd begin tampering with the slush, and finally he'd abolish the thick brown mud. There were others, even more pernicious, who practised on our own pavement: piling the stuff high in the gutter, scraping with their shovels at the hard bits underneath, and then going down the area steps for their pay (which was always forthcoming). Meddlers! What did they want to do it for? Why couldn't they leave well alone? All boys, I suppose, are like this. Or was I unusually extravagant?

As for trains, they were as good as fog, and better than ice or snow. I went through the usual routine of railway expertise, taking in *The Locomotive* and *The Railway Magazine*, and talking very earnestly about bogies, and engines of this or that type—the Atlantic is the only one I remember—and some numbering, such as 2-4-2, by which you could distinguish them. I was also greatly fascinated by points, which at first were as mysterious to me as that other sort of railway at the drapery stores; but later, when I grasped how they worked, I became ambitious, and embarked on a complicated diagram of the whole length of track between Westbourne Park and Hammersmith stations, with each set of points, and where they led to, clearly marked and labelled. Points had a special attraction if by accident I became personally involved; as when, missing the Hammersmith train and taking an Addison Road one instead, we swung to the left after half the usual journey—there never ceased to be some miracle about this, my knowledge of the mechanism notwithstanding—and curvingly descended an unfamiliar slope. Slopes in general were extra fun, or gradients, as I expertly called them: one in a hundred, one in fifty, perhaps, sensationally, one in twenty-five: and when nothing very special was afoot there were always the navvies, with their monster chisels, scraping up the grease that lay black on the sleepers and dabbing it on the side of the rails. But this was schoolboy stuff. What I really dreamed of was main-line magic: expresses, particularly, roaring through the night, with people inside them on their way to far places, busy with the world's affairs.

I remembered these dreams of mine on the long cross-country journey from Cambois in Northumberland to Repton, for an interview with Geoffrey Fisher before the job, my first, should be really and finally mine. Now at last adult life had begun: everything before had been mere preparation. The icy weather: the blackness outside: my first-class compartment (I was in uniform): the steamy windows: sitting up all night: the constant changing: buying buns at Manton at two in the morning: bath and breakfast at a Derby hotel—this was fulfilment. Memories of childhood came back to me, and I wrote a few lines, some of which I imperfectly remember:

> "Long years ago, when still a boy,
> I used to dream that, being grown,
> I'd talk to ladies with an air
> And catch expresses all alone;
> But never dreamed that flying wheels
> Could . . ."

I've forgotten the rest.

My delight in trains has persisted all my life. I specially like going to bed in them: in sleepers from Manchester, for instance, with a cup of tea and one small biscuit at six in the morning, and a taxi from Euston through deserted streets. There is something strangely fascinating, on such occasions, about arriving at Ladbroke Grove before anybody is up, and about undressing when you ought to be dressing, and having a bath. It is the strangeness of things on occasions like these that makes you see life afresh, and respond to it: an egg to your tea, or changing the position of a picture, has a similar effect. But while I like this sort of thing in life, I don't like it in art: I don't like surrealism.

Continental expresses are the emperors of travel. I sometimes hear people say "It was wonderfully quick; we breakfasted in London and lunched in Paris." They mean that they have flown. But what waste of a precious opportunity! A man might say, not a whit more coarsely, that he has "knocked down" a fine old brandy as if it were vodka, or smoked his cigar with such frenzy that it burned like a red-hot coal. The whole point of going to Paris, or at any rate the preliminary point, is precisely, if you leave after breakfast, to arrive not for lunch but for dinner. You settle down in your English Pullman with books and magazines and a pipe or cigarettes or (in my case) a holiday cigar. You drink your coffee and wonder about the weather; and soon, but not too soon, you are smelling the astringency of Dover Marine. And then, when you've mounted the gangway and surrendered your ticket and taken up your position and watched the manœuvring into Calais harbour, you hear, as if you had never heard it before, a first hoarse shout in the mother-tongue of Europe—"*Porteur, porteur!*" You are in France. Follows the discovery of your seat, in a Pullman this time French: and déjeuner, as usual—the same technique with bottles, the same *hors d'œuvres*, the same *tranche*: and Etaples: and Amiens: and Creil (you are now very near): and a glimpse, to the right, of Sacré Cœur: and a grimy wall, with "Paris Nord" and an arrow: and tipping the Pullman man, in the hope that he'll be quick with the luggage: and driving to the hotel: and cocktails in your bedroom: and then, only then, a careful weighing-up of the pros and cons about dinner—something cheap at a brasserie, or a full-scale affair at the restaurant you like best at the moment? This is travel. This is what trains are for. How could any sane man throw it all away for a featureless rush through the air?

Finally—for I must somewhere put an end to these memories of enchantment—I loved London. An early recollection is of Hamilton Terrace, and of bowling a hoop there with furious speed, and then stopping it in full career with a stroke of the stick on its further side: the great art being that, wobble though it might, you should keep it upright for the return journey. The plane-tree burrs—I began to collect them—and the long glass porches of the grand-looking houses, were a fairyland setting for this early enjoyment.

The magic of London captured me by stages. In 1897, when I was four, there was a great to-do about the Diamond Jubilee. The brougham was brought up from the City, and I rode in it with my parents for a view, not only of the decorations by day but, even better, of the illuminations by night. This latter seems extraordinary, given my age; but my memory can hardly be at fault (unless I'm confusing two occasions), for I recall many features in considerable detail. There were wonderful festoons in the Haymarket, draped above the roadway from side to side, and carrying down the centre a close row of crowns; and the Bank of England, the long low façade of Sir John Soane's Bank, looked specially lovely with its blaze of lights. There were fairy lamps everywhere, on railings and balconies: we were to have a great display of them ourselves a few years later, at the time of the Mafeking celebrations. The technique of fairy-lamps pleased me greatly: the small fluted candles, the melting of their bases to make them stick, and the pineapple surface of the lamps themselves.

A little later I was allowed, as an occasional treat on summer afternoons, to accompany my mother on her daily pilgrimage to Duke Street, Aldgate. I shall explain to you presently the reason for her journey. We went by 'bus, by a horse 'bus at first, but later, when motors came in, usually by a red Number One. The horse 'bus was best. We sat on top, in two of the front seats if possible; and mother pointed out to me the landmarks on our way. The whole journey, in the earlier days, must have lasted a good couple of hours, all in the heat and solemnity of a London August. The great turning points—I see them in an angular pattern, like dates: up to 1912, level to 1914, down to 1919, and so on—were Marble Arch and the General Post Office and the Mansion House: and I smell, in particular, the rank bubbly sweatiness of onions from tripe shops in the Edgware Road, and the cool grey stoniness of offices and banks in the City. Selfridge's was going up towards the end of this series of journeys: I saw the whole process, first the destruction of those decent little almost one-man shops, then the scaffolding, and finally the building completed. There was the cinema, too, on your left, just as you turned into Oxford Street from the Edgware Road: one of the first, perhaps the first, in the West End of London: with Flora Finch and John Bunny and a violet smell from pistony sprayers. Then I liked, extra well, the miracle of Holborn Viaduct, and the canal in Maida Vale, and the concourse of traffic at the Bank. However many times I did the journey, there was always, in the earlier years, the same impression: that of getting farther and farther from babyishness —Elgin Avenue, Maida Vale, Edgware Road—and deeper and deeper into strangeness and adventure—Oxford Street, Holborn, the City.

Other things that pleased me were standing on the parapet of the National Gallery, and gazing in the heat over Trafalgar Square, down to the House of Commons; and second-hand bookshops in the Charing Cross Road; and, very much earlier, "excursions" to Kensington Gardens, and to the sort of no-man's-land between Kensington Gardens and the far less attractive Hyde Park. These were whole-day excursions, with mustardy sandwiches and a box of precious water-colours; for I liked to try my hand, inexpert though I was, at Serpentine or lily-pond or bridge, and at numerous landscapes, so gentle and varied, of grassy slopes and trees like weeping willows.

In 1911, the year before I went to Oxford, *The New Machiavelli* was published. I got it at once, and came, in the first chapter, on the following passage:

"I look out from this vine-wreathed verandah under the branches of a stone pine: I see wide and far across a purple valley whose sides are terraced and set with houses of pink and ivory, the Gulf of Liguria gleaming sapphire blue, and cloud-like baseless mountains hanging in the sky, and I think of lank and coaly steamships heaving on the grey rollers of the English Channel and darkling streets wet with rain, I recall as if I were back there the busy exit from Charing Cross, the cross and the money-changers' offices, the splendid grime of giant London and the crowds going perpetually to and fro, the lights by night and the urgency and eventfulness of that great rain-swept heart of the modern world.''

A fine piece of rhetoric. I was thrilled. That was just what London, in my eighteenth year, had come to mean for me.

# CHAPTER XVIII

# HELL—I

But if there was heaven in my life at Elgin Avenue, there was hell too.

My mother, as different in this respect from my father as could be imagined—in spite of her complete subservence to him —was interested, during all the years I knew her, in anything, any idea or theory or movement of thought, that was a little, or even a great deal, off the main track; the main track not only of conservatism or orthodoxy in the more obvious senses, but also of that sane, solid, bourgeois approach that sees every phenomenon in a common-sensible or plain man sort of way, with nothing highfalutin or mysterious about it. Some of the things she was interested in were really "new": others, though already a little past their first bloom, she happened to have only just heard of. Her interest was of a curious kind. The attitude varied from a grave detachment (she herself, *bien entendu*, could no more be personally involved than with "Five Nights of Love") to a bland and long-suffering distaste (she took it as medicine). The medicine included mesmerism, evolution, Ibsen, the subconscious, Herbert Spencer, Liberal Judaism, and the Wagnerian system of leitmotifs. My father was affectionately contemptuous of these eccentricities, as contemptuous as of my mother's play-writing: "poor Nellie," he used to say, with one of his most appealing smiles. (This infuriated me, and inflamed my feminism.) Mother would smile rather wistfully in return. The fact is that beneath a very great terror of life, bound up with sex—I see her, when I think back, as the most terrified creature I have ever known, except, in some dreadful moments, myself—she had an eager, searching, almost radical type of mind, as well as such spiritual strivings as could persist in an atmosphere of conventionalised religion. Come to think of it, I'm not at all sure that she wasn't a saint—or an Aspasia—*manquée*: but very much *manquée* indeed.

Now one of the items that specially fascinated her was telepathy; and her interest, this time, was by no means Olympian, for she had experienced the phenomenon herself. Or so she said. I am bound to add this qualification, because another of her characteristics, itself springing from the same obscure revolt from the plain and the humdrum, was a habit of telling tall stories. But were they tall? There are people, much given to recitals of the strange or important things that have happened to them, whom somehow you cannot help disbelieving. As each new tale is told you, or as suddenly, amid the babble of a party, you catch the familiar ring of an old one being told someone else, you immediately think "Bloody liar!" And the odd thing is that as often as not they are telling the truth, or something like it. A famous professor, a very great teacher of his subject, walked into my office one morning during the recent war and said "Victor, I've just come from Downing Street: Winston has given me Palestine for the Jews." I nodded gravely, and jeered inside; for the things that Prime Ministers and Presidents had said to or done for him were already as familiar to me as if I'd experienced these favours myself. But I soon became convinced that I was being unjust. I concluded, on reflection, that my professor had in fact been to Downing Street, and that Mr Churchill, during the course of their conversation, had mentioned his fidelity to Zionism, and his determination, when occasion arose, to assist in the creation of a Jewish State.

So my mother's telepathic experience may, after all, have been a fact. One day, it appeared—the date was unspecified, but it was assumed to be before my birth—she had seen a vision and heard a voice. My father's bearded face—he did not shave, but clipped—had appeared in the air before her, and his voice had said "Nellie, Nellie, it's all right, it's all right! I'm safe, I'm safe!" The point was that he had gone to Birmingham on the day in question, and that the papers had reported next morning an appalling disaster to his train, and the loss of every single passenger save one, namely him. It never occurred to me to investigate the matter: to find out the date, look up the newspaper (which must surely have been preserved), and read the account for myself. My disbelief was too complete.

If the story wasn't true it was a beautiful example of the aetiological myth. The thing to be explained was the daily journey from Elgin Avenue to Duke Street, Aldgate, that I have already described. My mother's experience, it seems, had been a severely traumatic one: the vision and voice, in spite of their reassurance, the hours of terrible waiting, the ghastly news in the paper next morning, the far ghastlier news that, her imagination told her, would but for a miracle have been there—these had produced such a wound in her psyche that if ever again, she feared, she were to be faced with the prospect of waiting inactive for my father's return, terror that he might never come would drive her insane. So she would not wait: she would go to meet him. The arrangement was that he would always be in his office by a certain hour; and so her anxiety would be confined to the last few minutes of her pilgrimage— culminating in the breath-catching second when, reaching the Duke Street office at a painful run, she would peer through a window from which a thick yellow blind had been removed for the purpose, and assure herself that—yes, thank God, he was there. I understand all this perfectly. When you wait interminably you are out of control, a puppet in the hands of fate: on the move, proceeding to a rendezvous, you are taking the initiative yourself, and that helps enormously.

My mother's daily journey was sacred: as sacred as keeping the Sabbath, or fasting on the Day of Atonement, or not eating bacon. If I said that I cannot remember a single day on which it was missed, from as early as I can remember anything until the moment of my father's retirement, that would give a quite false idea of the atmosphere: for the notion that it might conceivably be missed could never have entered our heads. What happened, you may wonder, if my mother was ill? My father stayed away from the office.

If I have been writing lightheartedly, this is because I cannot help, at a fifty years' distance, seeing in this mania an element of comedy. But at the time it wasn't comic at all. My mother was in the grip of a terrible neurosis; and, what is important for this record, it had communicated itself, at I don't know how early an age, quite as terribly, and perhaps more so, to me. My earliest recollection is of standing on my bed one night in a sort of little boudoir that opened out of my parents' bedroom. It had just gone eight (I had a watch, and could read the time): my parents were usually back from the City at round about a quarter past nine. During the last half hour my anxiety had been growing: at eight it had become terror, and I had got out of bed, and, for some reason I cannot remember —perhaps with the idea of keeping awake—had begun standing on it. Then, appallingly, the terror developed into panic. I swayed in a horrible dance from side to side, lifting first one

foot and then the other: I sobbed dreadfully: I prayed, "Dear
God, dear God, please bring them home." And then I heard
the key in the door. I don't suppose I shall ever again experience the blessedness of sudden relief that I experienced at that
moment, and at hundreds of similar moments as the years went
by. It was as if the agony had never been. I was no longer
alone. I was secure. I went to sleep.

I have said that my mother's neurosis communicated itself to
me. I believe that this is so: that my terror was environmental.
But perhaps I am wrong. She had truly, perhaps, suffered some
trauma when carrying me in her womb, and had brought me
into the world with the mark of her agony in me. Or perhaps
my own trauma at loss of the womb, my own shock of loneliness
at the instant of banishment from paradise, was more painfully intense than is usually the case, so that her mania and
mine were identical merely because they were identical in
origin. However that may be, this one thing at least we had
in common.

I have never succeeded in conquering this neurosis, though
of recent years, like so many other things, it has grown far
less unmanageable than before. It has always taken in my adult
life precisely the same form as in childhood: panic that mother
would never come back, and that I might be doomed for
eternity to a blank aloneness. The mother, since marriage, has
been my wife. Love has little to do with the matter: the
emotion, or whatever it should be called, is almost wholly
self-regarding. I have never felt the slightest anxiety of an
abnormal sort about my children. But I have had panics about
Ruth as horrible as any in my childhood. One day in Paris we
tried an experiment in the hope of effecting a cure. She was
to go off to a tea-party; the time of her return was to be deliberately unspecified; and I was to wait quietly at the hotel, and
use all my will-power not to worry. The result was disastrous.
Almost immediately, and long before she could have arrived
at our friends', I was feeling vaguely anxious. Within half an
hour the possibility of an accident had come into my head.
Suppose, after all, something had already happened? Or might
happen on her way back to the hotel? This was Paris, and the
taxis were awful. If she took one, there might be a collision; if
she didn't, but walked, how did I know she wouldn't be run
over by one of those tearing maniacs? Then suddenly another

thought stabbed me. They drove on the right here instead of on the left. She would forget: she would step off the pavement and look the wrong way: she would certainly be run over. Why had I ever let her go? Why had we ever come at all to this miserable place? And what ought I to do? In London, dear, familiar London, one knew the ropes; one dialled 999, and if the police were no good one got on to the hospitals oneself. But here one didn't know whom to ring up; my French would get worse and worse, and there would be nobody to help me. I tried to control myself, but couldn't. Soon I was crying. When your grandmother returned, far earlier than I ought to have expected, I was in a state of hysterical collapse.

The whole experiment was based on a ludicrous but honourable misunderstanding. I am all for will-power, and dislike the flabby absence of it that nowadays—no, I musn't talk like a nonagenarian. But there are things you cannot conquer by will-power, and a neurosis of this kind is one of them. The attempt, indeed, must almost certainly make matters worse. For what is at the root of every neurosis is morbid self-feeling in one form or another: an unreal involvement with the self as a thing in isolation from its proper whole. But the use of will-power, prompted though it may and always should be by considerations transcending the personal, means the deliberate putting out in self-consciousness of personal and self-reliant effort. "*I* will do it." So the self becomes more fully involved. The way to conquer a neurosis is not to do something, but to receive something. What is wanted is an inner change, and when that has occurred all fears for the self, including the final fear, the fear of hell, become phantoms. But the something to be received must be received as truth, and not called in as a cure. "Seek ye first the Kingdom of Heaven, and all things shall be added unto you."

I had other hellish fears in early childhood, but these were rapidly to vanish. A lover of darkness under heaven—for this is a form of light, and there is none more beautiful—I was terrified of it in rooms, unless someone was with me; and before the incandescent gas could be turned down there must always be a night-light properly going by my bed. An effort was made when I was six or seven to break me of this habit, and for an awful few days I was deprived of my night-lights and told to be sensible; but my wretchedness from the moment I got up, and the agony that developed in me as bed-time approached, were so obvious that the experiment was abandoned. I loved my night-lights, not only for their comfort but also for their engineering possibilities. When I woke in the morning there would always be a wafer of wax at the bottom of the paper surround. These remnants I would carefully preserve; and when a really good store had accumulated I would melt them all beautifully down with a lighted match in a saucer from the nursery cupboard, and work up the resulting mess into a whole new splendid night-light, a little mis-shapen but monstrously large. My thumb-marks on the soft warm wax particularly delighted me.

§ 2

I have come now to a point which I have been thinking of and wondering about almost ever since I started this letter. When I made up my mind, suddenly one morning in January, to write it for you—though I didn't really make up my mind, for at one moment I was sitting idly by the library fire and at the next, without previous intention, I was writing almost automatically—my idea was to be absolutely honest, or as honest as I "knew how", about everything I said, but not necessarily to say everything. I anticipated no great difficulty, for at first all I wanted was to tell you what I felt about a number of particular topics, giving only such personal details as would make my opinions intelligible. Very soon, however, the element of autobiography was growing: clearly it would continue to grow: and then I began asking myself about sex. To be completely silent about it (I don't mean about sex as a topic, as something to be discussed, with whatever background of personal experience, from the outside—for that could present little difficulty: I mean about my own sexual life) this would be not only ridiculous but, if I was to succeed at all in my purpose, impossible. Every man is essentially a whole: even when you talk about a split personality, all you mean is that the essential he comes through in a split form. The sex in a man, the religion in a man, the art in a man, the politics in a man, these are the man himself; and though to some extent you must isolate them for descriptive purposes the process is always an artificial one, for it is only in the light that they throw on one another, and together on the man, that the ultimate secret is partially revealed. But never more than partially. In one sense, the writing of genuine autobiography is impossible—as impossible as describing music with words. The uniqueness of an individual can never be verbally expressed. The uniqueness is the living, and the living the uniqueness. The greatest autobiography in the world could do no more than provide a few clues.

It was clear, then, that I must say something about my sexual life. But I have made up my mind to say as little as possible: just sufficient for my purpose, and no more. This decision may seem curious to you. Why, you may wonder, do I feel myself free to say anything that comes into my head about my religious life or my political development, but not about my sexual experiences? Does a feeling of guilt inhibit me—the feeling of guilt for certain of my own sexualities that has been with me and sometimes tormented me during very long periods of my life? That, or the shamefacedness it implies? Perhaps, but I doubt it. The reason, I think—I have been puzzling it out—is that just because sex is peculiarly at the heart of life, the details of sex, when abstracted from the actual living of them, when not lived, as one might say, but verbalised, are like butterflies pinned to a board, or lamb at a butcher's that might have been a lamb in a field: always outraged and sometimes disgusting. So I shall stick to my decision, and be as reticent as possible.

At almost exactly the age of nine (Rousseau's age), late one morning just before leaving the Paddington and Maida Vale High School for lunch—it happened there, but the effect of it became more sharply defined during the short walk home down the sunlit street—I had a sexual experience. The school was mainly for girls, except in the kindergarten, where the boys and girls were roughly equal in number. I had been going there since I was tiny, and had stayed on, unlike most of the boys, till I was quite "grown-up"—it was not till I was round about ten that I left for a neighbouring prep-school. There were no male teachers, only mistresses, and the head was of course also a woman. She was a small woman, and I should judge her now to have been, at that time, of late middle-age. She always dressed in black. Her manner was grave—grave but kindly, not severe—and I, like all the other children, was rather in awe of her. I can definitely say—my recollection of her is sufficiently vivid for certainty on the point—that she was in no sort of way what would ordinarily be called sexually attractive.

It was in her study that the experience happened. But no, this is not quite right. It had begun to happen a few minutes earlier—at the moment at which, for some reason I cannot remember, I had been told I was to go and see her. I have mentioned Rousseau. I must make it clear, therefore, that no physical contact of any kind took place between me and the headmistress: that I desired nothing of her, as she desired nothing of me: that no word was spoken by her, and no gesture made by her, which even with my present experience I could imagine to have been remotely sexual, either in origin or in significance: and that it was of the situation and the situation alone—the being sent for by her, with me, the small boy, as the summoned, and she, the grown woman, the headmistress, as the summoner—that my experience was born.

It was a terribly sweet and poignant experience, and at first with no touch of shame in it. I thought it unique, this "feeling" as I called it: something I had been specially chosen for, something granted to me and to no one else. I prayed for its return, prayed literally, as I prayed for so many other things: "Dear God," I prayed, "give me the feeling again." And I tried to do my share in reproducing it. I thought myself back into the original situation, and when this succeeded I called up imagination from the depths where it slumbered, and invented situations similar to the one that had occurred but even more wonderful. The feeling did not stale with repetition: on the contrary, at each new recurrence it came flooding into my being with an added, a more urgent, intensity. Something pent-up and powerful beyond expression was struggling to be free. I have had, as well as joy and fun in good measure, a great deal of misery from sex—how could self-conscious adults in our stage of development, let alone a child, be expected to manage the thing properly?—but to deny, or not to praise, the glory of it as first I entered on my human heritage would be blasphemy.

You will understand that I did not connect my experience

in any way with sex, of which I knew nothing either at the age
of nine or for many years after. Precocious in my fashion, and
for all the sexuality that flamed in me so fiercely, I was yet
oddly deficient in an understanding of the body, not only
during childhood but also in my teens and beyond. I still have
strange patches of ignorance. You will hardly believe me when
I tell you that even today I know nothing of sexual physiology.
I know the words, of course, and like using them, for their
earthiness, during happy love-making; but if you asked me what
my own body looked like an inch beneath the external organs,
or by what inner mechanism in a woman the implanting of
semen is followed by conception and birth, I should have to
confess that I hadn't the faintest idea.

In sexual matters generally I was long without worldly
wisdom. One night, while I was at St. Paul's, I had come back
by 'bus from the opera, and had got off at the corner of Elgin
Avenue and Maida Vale. A woman came up to me and asked
if I would take her home. I said I should be delighted. I felt
immensely chivalrous, for I thought that what she wanted was
protection from the perils of the night. She lived, it appeared,
a little beyond us, at a flat in the Lauderdale Road; and as we
walked towards it through the summer darkness I fell to telling
her of the performance at Covent Garden: how miraculous
Destinn had been, how her soft high notes in the Nile scene had
been beautiful as never before. I asked the lady whether she
shared my enthusiasm for Destinn; she looked rather blank,
and said she preferred musical comedy. When we got to her
flat she thanked me, said good night, and went in. I stood on the
pavement for a moment and drank in great draughts of the
air, feeling very grown up and tremendously pleased with my
adventure. I was full of it next evening at supper, and was
puzzled by my parents' silence and the odd sort of look they
exchanged. But it was many years before I realised what my
lady, my gentle and chivalrous lady as I shall always remember
her, had really wanted of me. And the oddest part of the whole
affair was that I had already read Ibsen and Whitman, who
is very outspoken about prostitutes.

Day-dreaming was not to be the end of my experience in
the headmistress' study. Masturbation (long before puberty)

inevitably developed. The ecstasy it gave me was overwhelming. But I never practised it for its own sake: I should have felt that dishonourable. I am getting into deep waters, but I must put it like this: my surrender at the moment of my summons to the study—for surrender is of course the proper word for it— was how sex awakened in me, sex the bodily aspect of our destiny to merge: I was caught up out of myself, literally in ecstasy: I was loyal thereafter to that ecstasy of surrender: and masturbation helped me to achieve it. Masturbation without the surrender, if such a thing had been conceivable (and I doubt whether the practice is ever possible without fantasy), would have seemed to me disloyal and disgusting. And if anybody accuses me of highfalutinly dramatising a common or garden tendency to masochistic autoerotism, I shall reply that you explain nothing by labelling it; that my memory is excellent; and that I have been honestly living myself back, these last two hours, into an experience of early childhood. And if anybody, further, feels inclined to be disapproving (though God knows why), let him exercise his sense of humour, and remember what it is we are discussing: namely something that, without any initiative on his part, happened to a boy of nine. There are very many things in my life that I bitterly regret; but what I felt in the high-school study, and what I felt and did afterwards, is not among them.

I can't remember clearly when a change took place, and I began to have feelings of shame and guilt; but I rather think that it was at puberty, and that terror at the sight of my first small emission (which occurred just as I was waking from sleep) was the occasion for it. I remember that terror very clearly indeed. I thought, with a sudden appalling stab of apprehension, that I was desperately ill, and that masturbation was the cause of whatever complaint I was suffering from. I had no idea at all of what this might be: I just thought of it vaguely as something terrible. Shortly afterwards my father came up to my bedroom one morning while I was still in bed, and stood looking out of the window, half turned away from me, in great embarrassment. After a minute or two he was able to say "There's nothing to worry about in what's happened to you: it's nature": then tried to say something else, failed and left me. My terror was over, but self-accusation remained: and in respect, not only of masturbation, but of my day-dreams and their subject matter too.

I have said that fear at sight of my emission was probably the occasion for this new and troubling element in my sexual experience. It was at puberty, at any rate, that my feeling of guilt, if it had existed previously, became stronger, otherwise I should remember some earlier occurrence of it. Possibly, however, it was a sense of guilt, a latent one, that produced the fear, and not the fear that produced a sense of guilt: otherwise, why should I have feared at all? Well, I may have been frightened simply by the revelation of something unfamiliar and mysterious in which I was personally involved. But again this fear, I imagine, itself presupposes a sense of guilt: for all fear, ultimately—certainly all my fear—is a fear, a pathetic and faithless fear, of forfeiting wholeness (bliss, Paradise, God): and one fears one may forfeit it because one thinks (knows?) one isn't good enough to keep or win it, or has somehow betrayed it: and isn't that, after all, what we mean by a sense of guilt? Fear and a sense of guilt, in other words, may be interchangeable terms for the same spiritual defect; and this defect, no doubt latent in me already, may have been more fully actualised (if you can actualise a defect) by the stir of puberty. The Freudian or post-Freudian analysis, though apparently so different, is in fact very similar: for whether the explanation be in "psychological" or "religious" terms, union with, and isolation from, one's proper whole are always the underlying concepts.

It was precisely a sense of having isolated myself, cut myself off from what I have previously described as joy in communion or communion in joy, that masturbation produced in me after every new act of self-indulgence: the masturbation which, however inevitable it might in any case have been whatever the fortuitous occasion for it, had actually started from a passion to relive, and then again and again, a particular experience of this very communion in joy. (But it was no real communion that I had experienced on that occasion in the study: merely a distorted image of it: for surrender in dependence is something very different from, indeed almost opposite to, the free giving and free receiving, the undifferentiated mutuality, which is what genuine communion consists in.) Each time, when the thing was over, I felt that some link between me and everything had been deliberately broken by my own act: not merely a precious link but an essential one: and that now, by the breaking of it, the essence of me and of everything was somehow irretrievably spoiled. But my misery, at this period, was transient. After a time—perhaps a quarter of an hour or so—hope revived. Resolving never to do the thing again, I called upon my will with agonised insistence; then I ritually counted, put the past behind me, and felt clean. The shadow had gone: I was back again in joy. But all I had done was to suppress my sense of guilt: I had driven it under-ground, instead of accepting what I felt to be wrong in me and coming to terms with it. This suppression was to revenge itself, first during a period of months that was very soon to follow, then at various moments of my adult life, and most terribly of all in 1943. For the time being, however, joy re-mained the essence of my living.

The attitude to masturbation, I would add in passing—the attitude of many parents and schoolmasters in the days of my boyhood and later—was stupid and cruel beyond belief. The practice of it, when persisted in, was regarded by such people as a matter for punishment, and often for punishment of a most brutal and degrading kind, very likely to exacerbate what it was intended to cure—if that was really the intention. An epi-sode at a school I was once very briefly connected with—not Repton—was by no means as exceptional as you might imagine. Beating was much in vogue there, carefully graduated—in point not so much of severity as of impressiveness: there were house-prefect beatings, house-master beatings, school-prefect beatings, and, as zenith or nadir, headmaster-beatings. In the case of a school-prefect beating the reason for it had to be entered in a punishment book; and the reason for the one I am referring to was "self-abuse, when he knew it to be wrong". This was how the beating was done: The prefects were assembled: the boy to be punished was sent to the end of a corridor and told to bend over: one of the prefects took his stand at the hither end: stood poised for a moment: raised his cane: took a run at the bottom: and slashed it repeatedly. The caner, on the occasion in ques-tion, was a great beefy athlete.

But I am not one of those who regard masturbation as in itself unobjectionable, except during an early year or so, and even if it develops, as it normally does, into some form of other-regarding sexuality. Still less do I agree with the opinion, which I read the other day in a journal of sexology sent me for another purpose, that in certain circumstances the practice of it is positively to be recommended. (Though I must qualify this, and say that when sensuality is insistent, and when fantasy has proved irreplaceable and not to be satisfied in any other way, then the alternative, that of abstention, might be worse: provided, perhaps, that acceptance has taken place, and that feelings of guilt—but how can one be sure of this?—are genuinely absent.) Masturbation is objectionable precisely because, as I experienced myself, it outrages communion; and so except in the case of someone whose capacity for communion has been inhibited in the sexual respect, or who would outrage it even more by abstaining, masturbation, at any rate of the solitary kind, is sin. It was fashionable at one time, especially among flagellant schoolmasters, to describe this practice as the sin against the Holy Ghost. Strangely, they were right: for the Holy Ghost is betweenness, and it is betweenness that masturbation outrages. (But there are outrages of another sort against betweenness, and therefore sins of another sort against the Holy Ghost.) Masturbation, indeed, is the type and exemplar of all sinning: to sin being to grab for oneself, with pitifully inevitable self-defeat, what can only be won, not albeit for oneself but for the whole, by giving. "If a house be divided against itself, that house cannot stand." Sin is division, self-contradiction, in the house of life; and solitary pleasure is peculiarly typical of such division, because reciprocity, which is the meaning of all existence, is most patently, and almost as if to teach us what life is, the characteristic of sex. To put it in another way, masturbation is the most obvious unreality; and to be unreal, or less real than one might be, is to sin.

Or to put it in another way again, masturbation is waste. "Onan poured his seed upon the ground." How horribly sterile to waste what one otherwise might give: one's tenderness, one's love, one's physical self, one's semen! Birth-control similarly involves waste, though of another sort: and it is for this reason, among others, that since first I heard of it I have found it so distasteful.

But birth-control having cropped up, I dare not leave that sentence as it stands, for you might imagine that I oppose its practice. I do nothing of the kind. I want, on the contrary, to see a knowledge of it spreading rapidly through the world, and contraceptives so cheap that a peasant in China or India, starving on his handful of rice, could easily afford to buy them. Better still, they should be free—as free as air. Air is necessary for any sort of living; and contraceptives are necessary, over a very large part of the earth, for living of such minimum decency as alone would qualify, if people were imaginative enough, for the description of living at all.

Millions upon millions are born into a world unprepared to support them: sickly from birth, smitten very often by loathsome and disfiguring diseases, they drag out their few wretched years in pain and starvation, then die. And the fault is certainly not their parents'. The sexual urge is common to everybody: and only when life is full, only when richness of experience has captured and possesses the attention, does natural control—and then not always, by any means—become a genuine possibility. With things as they are, birth-control is quite indispensable for stopping such a pressure of population as must condemn a large percentage of mankind to the most abject misery. Nor is it a question of China and India, and similar countries, alone; if contraception were abolished, the same problem, though in a less acute form, would face even England.

I am one of those, as you will presently see, who are convinced that, birth-control or no birth-control, the standard of living could be improved in the suffering areas by a world-wide co-operative effort, and that such an effort, birth-control or no birth-control, is indispensable: and am even inclined to believe, without knowing enough about it to speak more positively, that, given such an effort, a still bigger population than the present one could be adequately maintained. But that does not affect the fact that, for the time being at least, widespread birth-control is an essential element in any genuine programme for the alleviation of primary poverty. And if the picture seems faintly ridiculous of an Indian peasant on the verge of starvation rushing for contraceptives, and if it be true, as it no doubt is, that nothing very much can be expected in the way of birth-control until some rise in the standard of living has given a little hope, nevertheless a beginning must be made, particularly with propaganda: the two methods, contraception and a direct attack on poverty, must go hand in hand: and so I was delighted to hear the other day a rumour to the effect that Dr. Abraham Stone, who specialises in sex and loving-kindness, had been appointed by the Government of India to advise them on this subject.

I am not going to argue the theology of the matter, though I should be happy to do so on another occasion. I am interested here, not in theology, but in religion. Well, there is a kind of religion, as you know from my description of orthodox Judaism, which I believe should be put in quotation marks: it should be described as "religion", not religion. A religion which, on theological grounds, would oppose contraception as such is to that extent of this nature. It is something abstract, in the air, cut off from the roots of concrete actuality: a construction, meaningless, unreal. For religion is the love of God and man— of God and man indistinguishably. And "He that loveth not his brother whom he hath seen, how can he love God whom he hath not seen?" You cannot agree with this sentiment, if meanwhile, in the name of God, you doom millions to misery.

And yet—there is something terribly wrong about birth-control, something in opposition to reality. Sexual intercourse is at its most real, is most itself, when spontaneity, inevitability even, most fully characterise it; indeed, it would not be too much to say that sex is a sacrament of spontaneity and in-evitability. But contraceptives mean wilfulness, planning, preparation: they shackle freedom—I don't mean this bit of freedom or that, but freedom generally, the freedom that's about in the world and glorifies existence. They interfere with the waywardness of spirit. So they spoil, not necessarily any individual act of intercourse (for perfect union, with or without contraceptives, is always possible), but the whole general scheme of things—the meaning, not so much in events, as between them. And when, by manipulating a contrivance, you stop something reaching its goal of which rushing to a goal is the essence, you are damaging integrity—again I mean in-tegrity as such, over and above particular instances of it; for you are deliberately making a thing deny its own nature. There is little difference in this respect (though a great deal in respect of physical satisfaction) between the use of contracep-tives and *coitus interruptus*; and I believe that the injury to nerves which commonly results from *coitus interruptus* is not only the aftermath of physical frustration, but derives also (if you can separate the two) from a shocked perception of spiritual impropriety. In both these cases, those of *coitus interruptus* and prevention by contraceptives, as well as in that of masturbation, you can imagine God saying "What a waste!"

Do I contradict myself, when I advocate birth-control at one moment and call it terribly wrong at the next? Yes, I contradict myself. And I do not know how to resolve the contradiction. Take the same remark as applying to all such contradictions in this letter as are real contradictions. (There are some which, if you think enough about them, you will find to be only apparent ones.)

The agony of my struggle against masturbation, which left so deep a mark on me by strengthening a sense of guilt perhaps in any case unusually strong, took what I imagine to be its normal course. I shall not describe it further, St. Paul having done so already. "For the good that I would I do not: but the evil which I would not, that I do . . . For I delight in the law of God after the inward man: but I see another law in my members, warring against the law of my mind, and bringing me with captivity to the law of sin which is in my members. O wretched man that I am! who shall deliver me from the body of this death?" What was terrible above all else was the stab of memory at the moment of failure. How honestly, how fiercely one had resolved, perhaps only a week or so before, "I'll never, never do it again"! How utterly convinced one had been that failure was at last at an end! And now, in spite of that certainty, in spite of the whole sickening series of resolutions that seemed to stretch endlessly back, failure had again occurred, and a failure that, appallingly, was irrevocable. If only it wasn't irrevocable! If only one could have another chance, be back again, with everything in front of one, an hour, even a minute, before its recurrence! Would the thing never end? Would one always go on like this, resolving, struggling, failing, till the day of one's death?

As the months went by, I intensified my old method of dealing with the trouble, but otherwise made no change in it. Wasn't one after all, I asked myself, one's own master? It was simply a question of resolving more fiercely, and of preventing, this time, the first faint insidious thought—that was the danger point—from entering one's mind. One might, for instance, tie a knot in one's handkerchief and feel it if temptation seemed

imminent: then one would immediately remember one's resolution, and be saved. Yes, this really would be the last time. And
so one continued to resolve: one ritually counted, as before:
sometimes one ritually washed one's hands: and, having done
so, one continued to thrust the whole thing deep down into
oneself, and imagine it gone.

"I thank God," says St. Paul, immediately after the outburst
I have quoted, "through Jesus Christ our Lord." These words
show what was wrong with my procedure, though St. Paul did
not mean what I mean by them, as is apparent from the dualism of the eighth chapter, which follows; or, rather, we only half
mean the same (or do we quite mean the same, but express it
differently—he in a dualistic and I in a monistic way?). I was
relying unilaterally on my own human will, whereas a grateful
co-operation was necessary: that co-operation between the human
and divine of which the words Jesus Christ are the final expression. I correctly, if obscurely, understood what in fact was sinful
in my habit, namely that it isolated me, drove me in on myself,
deprived me of communion with the whole and the whole of the
communion I owed it: and I proceeded to intensify this isolation
by the very ferocity of the self-reliance with which, not ignobly
but mistakenly, I was determined to abolish my sin. But it was
only by the communion itself that the sin could in fact be
abolished: it was only in the communion itself that what was
struggling for some form of expression could find a sane and
proper one, and thus emerge as sin no longer.

Nothing I have been describing so far was the hell which
gives this chapter its title. After each new occurrence of the
trouble the memory of it vanished from my consciousness, now
as in its earlier stages, and my perennial joy was unaffected. But
one day, in a classroom at St. Paul's, something was said to me
by the boy on my left. I cannot remember how old I was, and
this is very curious, in view of what immediately followed; but I
imagine, from the appearance of the room (which is vividly
before me) and my memory of what particular rooms I sat in at
particular times, that I was about sixteen. I cannot even remember exactly what the boy said, though I can see very clearly his
big, slightly bulbous green eyes, and can hear no less clearly the
distinctive lisp of his malevolent whisper. I make him look and

sound, you will notice, like the stylised villain in a hack melodrama; well, the conventions must have come from somewhere,
and perhaps, on the larger stage, there really is some typical
congruity, even in quite young people, between their physical
characteristics and the roles they are called upon to play. If so,
that is one more reason for never judging anybody.

He made me understand, whatever his actual words, that he
knew about my habit: that it was a wholly unforgivable habit:
that no decent person could ever associate with a boy who had
been discovered to practise it: that once contracted it could
never be got rid of: and that there was no possible hope for the
victim, who would rot and rot inexorably till he died a disreputable death. Salvation—he insisted on it—was out of the
question.

A choking terror caught me. The horror I had felt at sight of
my first emission came rushing back, and this time stayed. My
father's reassurances had become meaningless; I don't think
they even occurred to me, for something deeper was at work
than reason. You already know, my dear Timothy, what a
curious mixture I was: how unusually sophisticated in some
respects, how backward, how "innocent", in others. I had read
Ibsen's *Ghosts*, and been vaguely disturbed by the conclusion: "Mother, give me the sun"—what exactly did it mean,
with its terrible intimation of madness? I had studied a little
feminist pamphlet about the prevalence of syphilis and gonorrhœa, and felt shocked at the wickedness of men who thought
nothing, it appeared, of infecting vast numbers of women with
their own disgusting filth. And my mother, on several occasions,
had talked oddly about lavatory seats: you never knew, you
couldn't be too careful, you had much better wait till you got
home—all with her grave knowing look, all without a word of
precise explanation. And now these odds and ends, that had
been lying in wait, came hurling themselves at me with relentless accusation. One after another they mounted, each pressing
home the attack with a sudden new breath-taking stab, some of
them deliberately summoned as one plays with a nagging tooth.
And the burden of what they told me was this: "It is you that
the thing is about: you, the whole you, the you you are living
with and can never escape. It is you that has caught this disease, syphilis or gonorrhœa or whatever other filthiness it may be:
it is you that will slowly go mad, you that will suffer corruption,

you that will horribly die. And you have caught the disease, not from lavatory seats or from intercourse with women, but from your own wicked practices. You were right to be fearful at the sight of your emission: it is the one unmistakable symptom of a hopelessly incurable disease."

Unclean, unclean—that was not merely an adjective I applied to myself with conviction: that was what in my consciousness I was—was beyond any possibility of questioning. It was myself as unclean, not the thought of my uncleanness, that I lived with; lived with in the instant of shock, lived with for months to come, and imagined at the time, or knew rather than imagined, that I must live with for ever and ever. I thought on occasion of consulting my parents, but always dismissed the idea. What possible point could there be in consulting them about a certainty; and how, in any case, could I reveal my shame? As for books, at best they would confirm what I already knew. But what if they added fresh details? That, I was sure of it, I shouldn't be able to bear. So I avoided the text-books and encyclopædias; I even ran away—almost literally ran away—from any sort of book that might contain, it seemed possible, some casual reference to the subject.

So this was my hell, and it lasted several months. Or that is one way of expressing its duration; for you might equally well say that it lasted for eternity, or that it had no reality at all. The diagnosis, I imagine, would be a sense of guilt, sexual in its immediate occasion and emerging as syphilophobia. The fact that I had done nothing that could conceivably have infected me with syphilis is irrelevant.

*Brimpton*
*The chorus of birds is growing louder. It is a quarter past five on the morning of Sunday, May the sixth.*

I have spoken, I think properly, of my hell. But you are not to equate it, Timothy, with horror at my bodily fate. This horror was acute; and the aspect of it that caused me the saddest, the most remorseful anguish—for there is an anguish that is sad and remorseful as well as one that is bitter and desperate, and it was this sort of anguish that was mine as month after month went by

—what caused me the greatest sadness was the certainty that marriage and children, the dream of perfection I had cherished for almost as long as I could remember, was now impossible. (Ah, God's mercy! If a trouble one day comes to you, and you feel certain you can bear it no longer, be assured, little grandson, that sometime, perhaps soon, it may end; and that suddenly, when it has ended, it may be in a second as though it had never been; or, better, may still be within you, but now as an experience of which you can say "I suffered it for a purpose and am glad that I suffered it". I thought I could never have children; but on the Wednesday of this very last week I came out to Harrow and had tea with you on your second birthday; and you showed me the anemones—you pronounced the word beautifully, for your power over language is miraculous, and one day, I think, you will write in a way I shall envy—and stamped your foot, and pointed to the tool-house, and said very clearly "Papa"—you call me "Papa", as if you knew how much I'd wanted a son after the birth of my fourth daughter—"Papa, give Dutch hoe". I dare not speak for others, victims of concentration camps for instance, who have known things that mercifully I have never known; but remembering the past I keep ready in my mind, for use as occasion may arise, the words of Vergil: "O passi graviora, dabit deus his quoque finem"—"Oh ye who have suffered worse things than these, God will give an end to these too.")

My hell, I was saying, must not be equated with horror at my physical condition. The essence of my hell was outlawry. What I had experienced occasionally, and for only a few minutes at a time, from the day I had first felt guilty till the day I was whispered to in class, was now perpetual. By my own deliberate act, by the way I had contaminated my body (I am describing to you exactly what I felt), I had broken the links that united me with universal living: I was separate, alone, without lot or part in the everything. I had deprived myself, treacherously, of it; I had deprived it, quite as treacherously, of me. The smell of the grass was still there, but was now all the more alien for its sweetness; the sun still shone, but not for me. If only I could no longer care! If only my senses had died! But the terrible thing was that the opposite had happened. The sweetness was sweeter than before, the sun still more radiant; happier they were, more lovable than ever I had known them since first I had awakened to their blessing. The lull of the summer streets, which had always had sadness in its magic, was now like all sadness incarnate: like an intimation of Paradise lost, of a Paradise that could never be regained. Most anguishing of all was my relation to music. I had betrayed it. And perhaps because I loved music best, my concern in this instance was almost entirely for the thing betrayed and hardly at all for myself the betrayer. The shame I should feel in its presence was something I should be unable to bear. So I kept away.

(If only we could realise, when first tormented by the sense of sin, that wickedness is no monopoly of *ours*! If only, in the very act of praying for purity of heart, we might know our impurity as God's will, and offer our acceptance of it to him! "Shall there be evil in the city, and I the Lord not have done it?" When we begin to feel like that, we have made a start with the conquest of egoism.)

For three or four months my despair was complete. And then, on a late August day, came the first trifling breach in my certainty of damnation. Supposing, I suddenly thought, that things are not as bad as they seem? Supposing that somehow or other, after many long years, there is a faint possibility of finding a way back? Supposing I'm not finally damned? I dismissed the thought, but it recurred, and then again; and every time it came back it was stronger. And at last, by the grace of God, I took a resolution: I would consult our family doctor.

I must pause here for a moment, and attempt a little portrait of Armstrong: out of piety, you will understand, for his memory is dearer to me, on account of one common-sensible action, than that of any other of my many dead friends. He was a tall bony Scotsman, with a look of concavity, and large grey moustaches that seemed to interfere with his speech; for his voice was always low and a bit hoarse, as though he were forcing it through an obstacle. He laughed a great deal, but almost silently, and when he laughed his entire body shook. Women loved him; my mother, surreptitiously, among others.

He lived in Clifton Villas. I went there at ten one morning with a letter I had painfully written; for to bring the story out bit by bit, and to watch his reaction as he listened, would have been unbearable. I was asked to go straight to his consulting room, but refused; I sent my letter in by the maid and told her I would stay in the waiting-room while the doctor read it.

I shall say nothing of what I felt while I waited, for this, if you have any imagination, you will already know. I paced up and down in that heavy dark dining-room with its brown lincrusta and bulbous mahogany, and kept acting to myself what would happen when the doctor, knowing everything, should send for me.

He did not send for me. He came in. For a moment he said nothing. I looked at him. He was shaking all over.

*Et nunc gloria deo patri, gratiae pleno, nunc et in saecula saeculorum, amen.*

He came up to me, still shaking, and put his hand on my shoulder. He found the perfect first words. "Every boy does it," he said, "at some time or another. Or ninety-nine per cent do. If a boy's never done it at all, there's usually something wrong with him." He need have said nothing more. In a second I was peculiar no longer. Pariahdom had gone.

But he said a great deal more. He gave me a little lecture on physiology. He showed me just the books I'd been frightened to look at. He interpreted the diagrams (but they were rather beyond me, and I quickly forgot them). He even talked about syphilis as if it were the commonest of phenomena; and this, come to think of it, was exceedingly wise of him. He went a great deal further than my mother would have liked. "I should give up the habit, if you can," he said, "it's a bit weakening. But never mind if you can't. All this sex business adjusts itself a little later on. Men get married, or have a woman." He gave me a lot of other advice, on subjects not strictly germane. "You work too hard," he said. "Still, you've got masses of vitality. But you want to replenish it. Whisky and soda's the thing. Not now, perhaps; you're a bit too young. But when you're properly grown up make a point of a couple a day."

He showed me out. I turned my face to the sun and sniffed the stone pavement. I smiled. Hell was a myth, Paradise the only reality.

*Requiescat in pace Ricardus Stowensis Armstrong. Amen.*

I had one great love in my schooldays. This was for a boy, slightly younger than myself, whom I shall call Gilbert Joyce.

# HELL—I

I thought him exceedingly beautiful. Was he really so, or did love deceive me? I have been curious to find out, and made a long dusty search, a few days ago, for the photograph he gave me when, in nineteen hundred and twelve, I was elected to my scholarship at New College; but it seems to have disappeared, so my curiosity is unsatisfied. He allowed me to call him Gilbert, but never called me Victor. I remember the inscription on the photograph: "To V. G., on winning the only open scholarship to New College."

Homosexuality, let me say at this point, is not a matter of black and white. Homosexual love, when a substitute for hetero-sexual love, is terribly wrong for the reason for which onanism is wrong—because it means waste: since whatever the values that may issue from it, it clearly involves the frustration of a purpose for which our bodies are designed. But I hope I need not say that when both parties are, or have involuntarily become, homosexual by nature, I should use the word "wrong" with no accent of moral condemnation, but as implying that, if some people are made in a way that frustrates their human nature, there appears to be deep at the heart of things an inner contradiction, a flaw in the design, which is quite inexplicable in terms of human knowledge, but no doubt disappears in eternity. Condemnation of people for the way they are made, and in which they must accordingly express themselves, is both contemptible and blasphemous.

Corruption, whether of oneself or of somebody else, is another matter. Deliberately to abandon fruitfulness for sterility—a fruitfulness of which one is capable—for the sake of an *outré* experience, this is what I call corruption; and corruption is a matter for blame, if men should blame other men at all. Further, to corrupt someone else is worse than to corrupt yourself, not because, as a person, you are any less valuable than the other, but because you are interfering, by the use of power, with the other's development. Worst of all, for this reason, is corruption of the young. Even here, however, a caveat is necessary. Somewhere in the background of environment or development some influence or experience may lurk which, if only one knew of it, would show as compulsive what one had previously thought of as deliberate, and so banish condemnation.

But having said all that, I must add something. Though

devoid of homosexual leanings myself (since that one experience) and strongly sexed in the normal manner, I wonder
whether homosexual love may not sometimes be purer (purer
in heart) than average heterosexual love; and whether to give
everything and demand nothing, after the fashion of chivalry,
may not more commonly be the mark of it. My happiness in
marriage has been exceptional: tenderness and passion have
meant as much to me during the last forty years as to most
people: but no love in my life has been purer, in the sense in
which I have already used the word, more selfless and other-
regarding, than my love for Gilbert Joyce. By the same token,
there was a strong sweetness in it, an unfeverish intensity, a
quality of acceptance rather than of seeking, such as I have
rarely experienced since. It is common to make fun of schoolboy and schoolgirl "pashes" and "crushes". I wonder whether
they are not among the best things in life.

There is really very little more to say about my love for
Gilbert Joyce. I did him the service usual in such cases. I was
a bit the cleverer of the two, and helped him with his Latin
verses. I waited about in corridors when I thought he might
pass. Sometimes we spent lunch-time together, saying very
little. During holidays he wrote to me about once a week, and
I would stand outside our door, looking down the street, long
before the postman was due. My most vivid memory is of a
very long walk we took, one Sunday in late November, over
unexplored parts of London. It was a grey day, damp and
rather foggy; and as night was falling we found ourselves on
Willesden Green. I was greatly but very peacefully moved: by
the mist, and the coming of darkness, and a wetness as of a dew
on the grass, and the far-stretching space that was empty save
for me and the boy. Immortal longings—they come to us at
such moments: but longings for what—or for whom?

During the whole of our relationship, there was no slightest
sign, on my part at least (for I cannot speak for him), of any
physically sexual manifestation. No tremor stirred my body; I
did not desire to kiss him; I did not even desire to touch him.
If I am to speak of my body at all as a separate entity, I can
only say this: it felt specially at peace, was specially—this is
truer—unaware of itself, in his presence. Everything—he, I,
the world—was in harmony; no, was harmony.

I did not even recognise the experience as a homosexual one,

or as in any way connected with sex, until shortly before the
end of my schooldays. I had known about homosexuality for a
long time, not from the usual gossip, which curiously had never
come my way, but from Plato and Catullus; and yet, by that
oddity of disassociation I have already referred to, I had
somehow never made the connection. I don't think it was a
question of the awareness being present but suppressed; I think
it was a question of genuinely watertight compartments. But
one day, in my final term, a prefect made everything clear.
"You're an ἐραστής of Joyce, aren't you?" was the way he
put it. I asked him what the devil he meant. I called him a
filthy swine. I was very angry.

For the rest, I had tender and romantic feelings, when about
eleven, for a charming and willowy young girl, a few years my
senior, who wore a big bow in her hair and dressed in grey;
but though I wanted very much to be in love with her I was
really only in love with her name, which was Una. (I imagined
myself in love, a little later on, with another young girl who wore
a bow in her hair; "beautiful she looked, like a tall garden lily";
her name was Joy.) But though I felt tender about women in
general, and always looked forward to being married, I was untouched by sexual love of them till I went to Oxford; and I slept
with no woman till I slept with my wife. Only once in those
early years, so far as I can remember, was I stirred erotically
by anything feminine. This was one morning in Warrington
Crescent, on the way to synagogue with my father. A young
lady was walking in front of us; she was wearing a charming
lawn *caleçon*, and a black skirt too short for her age.

# PART II

# CHAPTER XIX

## OXFORD—I

"To lie abed, pretending noon is dawn,
  This is the Oxford morn.

"To read philosophy, and slumber soon,
  This is the afternoon.

"To talk with friends until the break of light,
  This is the sacred night."

So, when versifying at Repton a few years later, I wrote about Oxford; and if 'philosophy' is interpreted in the widest sense—so widely as to cover almost anything—the picture is essentially an accurate one. A picture, naturally, not of everybody's Oxford but of mine.

For the first time since I started this letter I have been feeling a disinclination to continue. I had been looking forward for days, almost for weeks, to arriving at this point, and had even wondered what the weather would be like: "I ought to be getting there," I had thought, "about Whitsun, and if it's fine and warm that will fit in perfectly." Would fit in, I meant, with the sunniness of thinking and writing about Oxford. But after getting home early a couple of nights ago and writing the word "Oxford" and my little trio of couplets on a fresh sheet of paper, I came to a disagreeable stop; almost as if the pencil was eager, but something was holding my arm. I wanted to press on, and wanted not to. I decided to go to bed immediately (it was only half past nine) and make a fresh start about three. But next morning, and the next, I found myself still in the same uncomfortable mood: I lay thinking indecisively till my tea came up, writing nothing. I felt more than merely reluctant to go forward: I felt afraid. Night-sounds, nondescript but beautiful—a moving branch, perhaps, or the muffled drip of rain—came from the darkness in front; for the curtains and the great Crittall window had been pushed right back, and the room lay wide open to the Square. As I listened to these noises, and later to the cooing of the pigeons, the question of mere procedure kept turning itself over in my mind. Wouldn't it be better, perhaps, to wait till the coming week-end, when I should have, by the luck of Whitsun, an uninterrupted three days? Wasn't there a danger, otherwise, of my finding myself compelled to break off at the very moment of getting into the swing? (On the other hand, mightn't the whole impulse go if I waited so long before starting?) I made one excuse after another; and then, as if in search of further justification for delay, I fell to musing on the previous chapters and recalling many pleasures I had forgotten when writing of my childhood: the earthiness of chrysanthemums and lavender, and horses dressed up for May Day, and the chestnut-trees in Bushy Park, and the tropical houses at Kew; and Krupp's great conservatory at Abercorn Place, with its boxfuls of pansies and marigolds; and how, when occasionally buying something there for my own special garden (which was two foot by three), I had always been delighted by the action of the trowel as it cut through the tightly packed mould, and by the appearance of the little white roots as my plant was pulled away from the rest ... And the remote and narrowing ends of station platforms, sordid and gloomy but all the more romantic for that, by which one passed from well-lighted everydayness into the mystery of night. And the deep blue clematis that had trailed across the iron of our balcony, and colour-prints of flowers in shop-windows in the Charing Cross Road.

Ruth, who is a good artist, paints very rarely. When I reproach her for this, and tell her she is wasting her talent, she always makes the same reply: that things are very well as they are and require no interference from her. She means that the landscape, or whatever it may be, is its own praise, so why should she praise it in paint? I thought of this idiosyncrasy as I lay there, and then an image came suddenly into my mind. An absurd image, I thought it at first—absurd in such a connection; but it recurred and recurred, as if demanding to be taken seriously. So I shall not refuse its request.

Will you have seen *Rosenkavalier*, Timothy, by the time you come to read this letter? My feelings about it have been constantly changing over a period of forty years, for I must have heard it first, with Claire Dux as Sophie, about nineteen

hundred and eleven or twelve. Sometimes—most often, perhaps
—I have found it ravishing: sometimes I have found it sickly,
sickly with the sweetness of decay. But there is one short scene
that I have never found anything but *himmlisch*—I use the
German word, because somehow it sounds better than
'heavenly': I mean the presentation of the Silver Rose.

A marriage has been arranged between the gross Baron
Lerchenau and the charming young Sophie von Faninal. The
equally charming young Octavian has been chosen as the
Baron's ambassador for the traditional ceremony of presenting
the Rose. The door is thrown open: to the music of celestas
Octavian enters—"dressed all in white and silver, carrying the
Silver Rose". Behind him are his servants in white and pale
green. Octavian advances "with high-born grace" towards
Sophie; but "his youthful features bear traces of embarrassment, and he blushes". Sophie, disconcerted by his beauty,
blushes too. Octavian presents the Rose "as a token of the
Baron's love"; Sophie takes it, and expresses her "indebtedness
in all eternity to your Honour". Then she smells it:

> *Sophie:*    Hat einen starken Geruch. Wie
>              Rosen, wie lebendige.
> *Octavian:*  Ja, ist ein Tropfen persischen
>              Rosenöls darein getan.
> *Sophie:*    Wie himmlische, nicht irdische,
>              wie Rosen vom hochheiligen Paradies.
>              Ist Ihm nicht auch?

("It has a strong sweet smell, like a rose—like a living one."
"Yes, a few drops of Persian attar have been poured on it."
"How heavenly it is! Not an earthly rose, but from Paradise!
Do you not think so?")

Well, that was the image that kept coming into my mind the
other night. Oxford was my Silver Rose; and my fear was that,
in presenting it, I might knock off the drop of Persian attar and
so rob it of its perfume. A strange conceit, for Oxford is not in
the least like a Silver Rose; was not, even, in the miraculous
summer of 1914. And yet, I don't know. I do sometimes see it
like that: like a miniature jewel lying in some compartment of
my brain, from Magdalen down the High to Carfax, and then
out to Tom and the Ashmolean. And sometimes it glows, this
jewel in my brain, with particular gentleness: as it glowed on

Saturday—the Idea in sympathy with its Image—when coming
from the Mitre (we had dined with some friends) we drove the
car round for a bit and saw buildings and towers illuminated
for the Festival of Britain: Tom and Magdalen and St. Mary's,
and the bell-shaped cupola of Queen's. I had thought on the
previous evening, when the Festival Hall was opened, that
nothing in the world could look lovelier than the dome of St.
Paul's all lit up, or the long low façade of Somerset House;
but Oxford aglow looked lovelier still. Or did I merely pretend
to think so, because I love it more?

Usually, however, I see Oxford as anything but jewel-like:
I see it as rough-hewn, and common with the earth and the sky.


Disinterestedness, but of what Schweitzer would describe
as a life-affirming and world-affirming kind, was characteristic
of the Oxford I knew. We worked hard: but whatever we might
happen to be officially "reading", and whatever the amount of
time we might devote to it—however much or however little—
our leisurely speculation, and the love with which we sought
after wisdom, were void of self-interest; for the primary aim of
our reading and thinking and discussing was not to pass our
Schools, or to get a good first, or to fit ourselves for some particular career, but to fill ourselves out, to make ourselves complete, to develop into the best types of person we were severally
capable of being. Not, however, in any spirit of detachment
from the world; but rather that we might live in the world,
and play our part in the life that lay ahead of us, with a proper
equipment for whatever, as it might happen, we should find
ourselves called upon to do.

To spend most of one's time mugging up one's set books, or
otherwise preparing for one's exams, wasn't at all the idea of
what an undergraduate was there for. One took such things in
one's stride. I was by no means singular (though perhaps I over-
did it more than most) in starting real work for my Schools only
about a fortnight before they were due. Once I *had* started I
hardly slept at all—hardly went to bed, I mean—until, a few
weeks later, the last wretched paper was finished. (But wretched
is only rhetorical, for I am devoted to the classics—other than
Demosthenes, whom I got a gamma for. This man, with the
pebbles in his mouth, had always bored me.) The *maître*

*d'hôtel* of J. C. R., George Bennett—a magnificently voluminous snob with Poirot-like moustaches, beetling eyebrows, and the face of a gigantic gnome, who rarely said anything but "Certainly, *sir*", superbly lisped—used to bring me a great pot of coffee before leaving at night for North Oxford. In the morning, after an hour or two's doze in a chair, I would go to the barber at the corner of Holywell Lane and have an electric massage to my head: I had the idea it would freshen me up. When the whole thing was over, the porter of Holywell Lodge expressed serious concern for my health: he thought I looked ghastly.

The Schools in question were Mods—Classical Moderations—which one took, about half way through one's time, as a preliminary to Greats. Mods were for the language and literature of Greece and Rome: Greats, in the main, for philosophy—the whole range of European thought stemming from Plato and Aristotle. The war broke out just as I was starting on Greats, so that was the end of them for me. My attitude to Greats, I am sure, would have been different from my attitude to Mods. The Greats school was a wonderful intellectual discipline, and required patient thought over a long period of time: it was also about the things that matter most. Its very renown as the greatest of Oxford Schools was typical of Oxford disinterestedness: for one read Greats not because one happened to be a classic, not to become an expert philosopher, and not to get a job, but to grow into wholeness as a man. And while taking our Greats very seriously (or history or theology or whatever it might have been), and studying it in a disciplined way, we should still not have regarded our study of it—our study of the subject as such—as our main concern. The vistas of thought that our reading of it might open up, the action this thought might suggest, and, more generally, learning how to live—these would have seemed more important.

I have enjoyed writing the last three paragraphs in this hundred per cent fashion, and wish I could leave them unmodified; but they are absurd as they stand, as I knew all along, and require very drastic qualification. What I have been trying to describe was certainly not applicable to everyone. Many thought of nothing but games, many thought of nothing but their Schools, many thought of nothing but having a good time. And no doubt everybody's motives were mixed. Nor exactly is it a question of motive, of an aim anyone self-consciously pursued: it is a question of the general atmosphere, of something we freely drew in with the genial air of the place. I have been painting, if you like, a picture of the ideal University, and suggesting that the Oxford of my day did in some degree approximate to it. And to the degree to which it did, it was the quintessence, not of England and the West as they are, but of England and the West as they will be when they have realised their potentiality; for life-affirming and world-affirming disinterestedness is what England and the West are for, being peculiarly fitted by their history to lead the rest of the world on the road that will end in it. England, during the last five years, has been trying, perhaps as never before, to advance on this road: half betraying itself, however, in the process, by a failure, as I shall presently complain, either fully to understand what it is after, or wholeheartedly to accept what that involves.

And I must hasten to add that there was a lie at the heart of the disinterestedness I am claiming for my Oxford. The condition for it was a spaciousness and leisure at University age, time to turn round in before making a career, which were prerogatives of privilege and were rendered possible, in the conditions of that day, only by the existence of privilege; and involved in the existence of this privilege was the denial of culture to all but a few. The great solid body of Englishmen, the labourers and peasants and clerks, were without lot or part, except by virtue of some special brilliance (and then only accidentally) in a spiritual and intellectual discipline so precious to those who had access to it: the cultured lived off the backs of the uncultured: and that is something to take note of in any definition of a culture that is vanishing—and something not merely to take note of, but to attack as intolerable. The disinterestedness, in a word, was self-contradictory.

We are in the process of changing all that. We are trying to build an egalitarian society. This in any case would mean (quite apart from the special pressures of our day, those contemporary economic developments which are likely to grow worse, from the point of view of the *ci-devant* privileged, rather than better) that everyone starting out in life is inevitably driven, unless checked by some rarity of temperament, to concentrate first on economic security. The old happy leisure has gone: the University is filled, and rightly so, no longer to an overwhelming degree with people of classes that are rapidly becoming extinct, but more and more with a genuine cross-section of England: and I imagine that the undergraduate of today keeps his nose far more closely to the grindstone, and thinks far more exclusively of his future career, than did the undergraduate of mine. To gain the knowledge that will help him in some definite occupation already decided upon, and to get a good class in his Schools, not as symbolising wisdom acquired but again with an eye to the future—this, I suspect, is his leading consideration.

A great deal of loss is clearly involved in this change. Yet the end of the process will be—I am sure of it—not less culture and disinterestedness, but more. On one condition, however. Let us guard ourselves from imagining for a moment, at a time such as this when we tend to commercialise everything, that absorption in the means to existence rather than in existence itself—to be preoccupied with earning a living, rather than to live more abundantly—can end, unless treated as growing pains, in anything but spiritual disaster. Let us keep alive somehow the old ideal, which was right in itself but wrong in the privilege it implied. Let us work for a society in which the atmosphere of world-affirming disinterestedness, purged of the lie that once marred it, may be the portion, not of a few, but of everyone on the threshold of affairs.

*Brimpton, May 10th*

*What an afternoon this is! Yesterday I suddenly determined to cut the office and come down here immediately, so as really to get going during the couple of days before Whitsun. Brimpton, on a Thursday, seems delightfully strange: like the house and the roads in my boyhood, when, at a time I should normally have been at school, everything at home seemed new and awaiting discovery. I wrote steadily all morning, and now, at three, have been out into the garden before embarking on my afternoon lap. Butler was mowing the lawn, and the smell of cut grass, and of a bonfire he had lit on the meadow, mingled with an earlier smell: that of doughnuts during cricket at the Paddington and Maida Vale Recreation Ground. The sun is ablaze, but a strong east gale is blowing; and as I came in just now past the Jew's-mallow trailed on our porch, it was violently tossing its burden of ochre and chrome.*

*And all this flaming turbulence will have been set for me, thanks to broadcasting, between two serenities: the miracle last night of Yehudi Menuhin's first note in the Brahms Violin Concerto, and a performance, coming this evening, of Beethoven's supreme affirmation—the Quartet in E flat, opus 127.*

It is by reference to liberalism, in the widest sense, that my own life at Oxford is to be understood. I can best make you realise what this liberalism meant to us by quoting a letter from Bernard Strauss, who, a son of my father's best friend, was closer to me than anybody else at Oxford, though a couple of years my senior. We had kept constantly in touch since the outbreak of war; and he had sent me a telegram, just before going into action for the first time, which had ended with the words GOODBYE LIBERALISM FOR EVER. I had read it as written, without stops, and must have remonstrated; for I received a long letter in reply, which I was to publish much later in *War Letters of Fallen Englishmen*. It is dated November 20th 1915, and part of it runs as follows:

"My dear Golgotha [this was one of my Oxford nicknames],
". . . Altho' I have forgotten exactly what I wired on the impulse of the moment, it was never a Goodbye to Liberalism. I think it ran *Goodbye. Liberalism for ever!*—a flaming watchword; no farewell cry of departure. Indeed, as you say, I could not say Goodbye, even if I wished to; for by Liberalism I understand everything worth living and dying for—that is why years ago I once said that you and I were the only two real Liberals in Oxford: to us it was a passionate religion embracing all life's activities, not merely a hotchpotch of political views— γνῶσις not δόξα*—it still is. With you, I share the conviction that nothing dies, except what is evil. That is why the thought of Death has no terrors for me: and if I fall, it will be cheerfully and with a good conscience, and with the passionate hope that the sacrifice will not have been in vain—indeed it will not have been."

He was killed two years later, at the age of twenty-five.

* δόξα (*doxa*) means literally "opinion"—one's view of or judgement about a thing: γνῶσις, familiar in our alphabet as *gnosis*, is untranslatable when used in the above sense, but might be loosely rendered "deeper knowledge." The O.E.D. defines *gnosis* as "knowledge of spiritual mysteries." The word gnosticism is of course derived from it.

"A passionate religion embracing all life's activities": yes, this is a good description of our liberalism: and to preach it, make others understand what it meant, work out its implications, equip ourselves for its future service, even, so far as possible, live it already—that, for people like Bernard and me, was what we were really at Oxford for. I was very much given to the joining of clubs and societies; and I used them all—this indeed was my purpose in joining them, or mainly so—partly for the conversion of others, and partly for the clarification of my own ideas. Already in my first week at New College I had joined the old Russell and Pam, which met in undergraduates' rooms—every good Liberal traditionally joined it: and later I was to take part in founding, above a café in George Street, a Liberal Club that was the first to have rooms of its own. Then there were the various debating societies, and two in particular: a New College one called the Twenty Club, and the Union. A frequent performer at the Twenty Club was A. P. Herbert, speaking exactly, to the last mannerism, as he was to speak many years later in the House of Commons; but the star turn was J. B. Raju. This was a tall Cingalese, a Christian and already a professor in his own country, who had come up to Oxford as an undergraduate at the age of about thirty. He was a master of that formal eloquence that you hear very often in cultivated Indians; they talk like Burke, with a rhetoric and a perfection of rhythm that an Englishman couldn't help feeling ashamed about. Standing *exalté* at the end of a half-hour's speech, with the great black beard on his prognathous face thrust out at you from across the table, he would always wind up with some variant of a stock peroration: "As I look down the vista of the past, scattered with the ashes of my ancestors . . ." He stemmed, so he once or twice told me, from the Kings of Ceylon. Nearly thirty years later, in 1941, I was thrilled one day when his name was announced to me at Henrietta Street. He was returning to the East, it appeared, and found himself financially embarrassed, but only quite temporarily. I was fortunate enough to be able to give him some trifling assistance. I was rather offended, remembering what his speeches had meant to me, when he swore by the ashes of his ancestors that he would repay me the moment he got home. . .

A sinister legend was current about Raju at Oxford, or possibly I invented it myself. His name was mysteriously coupled—

H

not *in sensu obsceno*—with that of a particularly pale Englishman, who was known as Raju's White Man: mysteriously, because, so far as could be ascertained, no one had ever seen them together. If Raju was there the White Man wasn't, and *vice versa*. One day the rumour got around that Raju had shaved off his beard. Later, a heavy black growth was seen sprouting on the White Man's chin. The natural explanation was scouted: why, if it was an ordinary beard grown in the ordinary way, did it look so exactly like Raju's? A horrid story: there was nothing in it.

But the Twenty Club, after all, was parochial, rather like a performance in English during the autumn "off season" at Covent Garden. The Union was the thing. I was constantly there, not only on Thursdays in the Debating Hall, but almost every day of the week in some part of the building or another: writing letters, for instance, in what is now the billiard room— one initialled the envelopes and posted them free; and this made me feel very important, so that often, when there was nothing in particular to write about and nobody in particular to write to, I would think up recipients and topics for the mere fun of scribbling my initials; and I wondered quite recently, when noticing "E.B." on the left bottom corner of a Foreign Office envelope, whether Mr Bevin felt the same. But better than anything were the long slow winter afternoons, spent amid the haze of tobacco smoke in the reading room upstairs. The armchairs were deeper than any in the world, the fires like fires in a railway engine. I was always amazed by the prodigality of the attendants with these fires: they flung on great bucketfuls of coal, one after another, and when you thought they had finished they had only just begun. I would sit there from lunch till nearly seven, reading, dozing, eating much hot buttered toast; and as likely as not "the Britter" would be snoring nearby. The Britter was one of those oddities that Oxford has always collected, like the man with a big square face who, three decades later, could be seen any day in the Broad, baring his teeth and screaming at the passers-by. The Britter was very old and very round, and dressed like a better-to-do labourer: Britter was short for British Working Man. He was the world's first authority on the Basquish verb. He had been appointed, I believe, ages before my time, to teach the subject. He had no pupils.

I attended the debates very regularly, spoke often, and looked with great longing at the green leather benches to left and to right of the President's chair. They were reserved, primarily, for members of the Standing Committee; and membership of the Standing Committee could be the prelude to office, or its aftermath. These great ones lolled about negligently, legs stretched, hands in pockets, huddled low. I saw them then as imitating the front bench at Westminster: now I see the front bench at Westminster as imitating them. But my longing was in vain, for my Union career was not a success. I spoke well— much better, I think, than several of the men who won office: but passionately always, in the heaviest of manners, without elegance or cynicism or wit. My style was a little like Cicero's, or Raju's, though I never attained the perfection of these masters. Moreover, I was without charm of manner, had little intellectual distinction, dressed badly, and, at the beginning, didn't even know how to dine: when asked what I'd drink at my first small dinner-party at Buol's, I said "port". Most damaging of all, I was socially an outsider. But my vote, at any rate, was considered of value. Gilbert Talbot, a very big man just standing for the Presidency, smiled at me once on the Union premises; and within hours of my maiden speech (I got a few words in the *Isis*: "Mr Gollancz, New College, also spoke") the breakfast invitations were beginning to arrive. They became a regular feature of my life at appropriate seasons. Three for the same morning were not uncommon. I made a point of going to them all. Kedgeree, and large flattish omelettes with hot tomato sauce, were usually on the menu.

But I don't want you to think that my failure at the Union was a ludicrously unqualified one. Lurking rather dustily in the wings, far from the white ties and tails of the presidential stage, was a body called the Library Committee, though expertise in librarianship, or even the ability to read, was in no way a condition for membership. Once you got on to the Library Committee you might, theoretically, get anywhere; and I did get on to it in my sixth term, which—but only by the accident of the times—was also my last. (My last, that is, for serious purposes: I went up for a month or two in the autumn of 1914, and am not at all sure that I didn't become an unofficial sort of Secretary— of a bogus Union in a bogus Oxford.) It is not excluded that, if there had been no war, I should have reached the heights. Mr

Leslie Hore-Belisha, after all—his rooms, Prince Rupert's at St.
John's, were among the most delightful in Oxford, and so were
his luncheons—Mr Leslie Hore-Belisha, my contemporary and
friend, got no farther before the war than I did, if I remember
correctly: did not even, perhaps, get as far: but he returned
when the war was over, and soon became President. I did not
return, being eager for the world; and I had to wait twenty-
eight years—till 1942—for my first real Union success.

1942 was the time when Jews were being incinerated by the
million, and a Committee had been formed, the National Committee for Rescue from Nazi Terror, to do something about it;
for we believed we had a practicable scheme for saving a few
hundreds or a few thousands, and that nothing but Government
unimaginativeness prevented its realisation. I was helping in
this work, which my friend Eleanor Rathbone had inspired; and
when a debate was being prepared at the Union, on some such
motion as "That in the opinion of this House His Majesty's
Government is doing everything in its power to rescue the victims of Hitlerite terror", I was asked to oppose. Of course I
agreed. I was down to speak last on the order-paper, seconding
the opposer; the general debate would then follow. My style, this
time, was appropriate to the occasion, for cynicism and elegance
would not have been in place. When I had finished and sat down,
the mover, an undergraduate, rose: "Mr President, sir," he said,
"I can no longer vote as I intended. I wish to cross the floor."
Then, with a gesture to the benches behind him, he crossed, and
all but a dozen or so followed him. The debate, in effect, was
over. Nothing of the kind had ever happened before: this was
Union history. I have always felt proud of that occasion: proud
of my part in it, but prouder of Oxford.


Incinerators and 1914—they don't fit at all. If you are to
understand the political atmosphere of my Oxford, and the
manner of our debates at the Union and elsewhere, you must
realise, if you can—it will not be easy for you, unless things
have greatly changed by the time you come to read this letter—
that the shadows which now darken men's lives, and have dark-
ened them, moment by moment, for a full twenty years or
more, were wholly absent: the shadow of totalitarianism, involving, in many of its varieties, an explicit rejection of freedom,

and, in all its varieties, the deliberate infliction, on a mass scale, of misery, imprisonment and death; and the shadow of war.

There was terrible misery—destitution, unemployment and the like—in those earlier days, both at home and abroad, and I and my friends were appalled by it: we felt it, as I have already told you, in our own persons—that, among other things, is what made us such passionate liberals. But this evil was the result, in all but a few special instances, not of purposeful cruelty but of carelessness and inertia and egoism and greed; and far from oppressing us with a sense of despair it inspired us with a passion for reform. That six million people could be poisoned, of set human purpose, by noxious gases, and burnt up in ovens specially constructed for the purpose—the idea of it would have been literally, and I mean literally, inconceivable. Even Czarist oppression, which we hated—and our hatred of it was powerfully to affect, a few years later, our reaction to the Russian Revolution—was different in type from Hitlerite and Stalinist inhumanity: or so at least we should have said, and I think rightly, if we had known, at the time, what was coming. For we saw the iniquities of Czarism, pogroms and all, not as the deliberate embodiment of an awful and previously unheard of political theory, but as the desperate expedients of a regime that was putting up its last hopeless fight against the downfall that inevitably awaited it. Cruelty and oppression, in 1914, seemed relics of an evil past; cruelty and oppression, since 1914, have been making their bid for the conquest of the world.

But you may wonder, remembering 1914, how the shadow of war could have been absent. There were portents enough— Agadir and the Lloyd George speech, war-credits in Germany and three years' service in France; and I had read, for my own part, though very superficially, some Marxist literature, and must have encountered the analysis, which I was later wholeheartedly to accept, that the clash of competing capitalisms would inevitably end in disaster. Nor was I indifferent to war, as you know from an earlier chapter. The fact is, nevertheless, that in 1912, 1913, and up to the very eve of disaster the threat of a European war was without actuality: to me certainly, and, I am almost as certain, not merely to my friends and contemporaries but to the overwhelming majority of Englishmen.

There are two explanations for what must strike you as a curious aberration. A forty years' period of unbroken European peace is the first. The second is still more important: we were wholly absorbed by the tremendous domestic conflicts of our time.

And even if we had been utterly convinced that war was coming, there could still have been no shadow on our lives of the kind that is with us today; for we could have had no idea, no approach to an idea, of what modern war would be like. If I had seen in a vision, any time before 1914, the trenches at Passchendaele, and then, thirty years later, the horror at Nagasaki and city after European city not a city but rubble and dust, I should have imagined—and I assure you I am speaking with precision—that I was gazing at the nightmare obscenities of an alien planet. It could never even have entered our heads that one day we should be living, or that our children would be living, under an ever present threat of universal destruction.

Nor could we have believed, we liberals and socialists, that anything really precious in the old civilisation was dying. Vast changes were afoot, and we rejoiced in them; for what they promised was this—that the oppression, whether of peoples or of classes, would soon be ended, and that the possibilities of good living, which had slowly been increasing down the ages, would be open, and for that very reason in a purer form, to all. (And I still think, to anticipate, that everything since 1914, gas chambers and atom bombs and all, may be seen by generations to come as a terrible road—a road we could have avoided but for the hardness of our hearts—which was to lead us, through repentance, towards salvation.) What the Tories felt I do not know. But certainly on the Continent of Europe there was anguished regret, as disaster approached, for a day that would soon be done. Such an accent of heart-breaking sadness sounds again and again in Gustav Mahler's *Lied von der Erde*, and I never hear its *Abschied*—the Farewell that ends it—without calling to mind, in a mood as regretful as its own, those long afternoons on the Cher in the summer of 1914. *"O Schönheit! O ewigen Liebens—Lebens—trunk'ne Welt!"* "O Beauty! O Eternal Love—Life—drunken World!" And then, at the close, two syllables so lingeringly repeated that you think they will never end: *"Ewig . . . ewig"*, "Ever . . . ever".

But we felt nothing of this in the pre-war days, my friends

and I. It was a time of tempestuous political strife—wilder than anything that England has experienced since; and we threw ourselves into it, verbally at the Union or elsewhere and occasionally by way of action, with the gayest enthusiasm and hope. There was a great to-do recently when Mr Aneurin Bevan, regrettably I thought, referred to people he didn't like as "vermin": well, look up the Limehouse speech, and get an idea of what, forty years before, political abuse had been like. Between 1906 and 1914 a first decisive breach was being made in the citadel of privilege, which has now largely fallen; and the fury of onslaught was paralleled by a fury of resistance. Civil war, which by 1914 was to have developed, over the issue of Ulster, into a physical probability, had long been latent in the moral and intellectual atmosphere.

Consider all the ground that had been won during the years just before I went up, and that must now be held! Supertax had arrived with the Budget of 1909, which, rejected by the Lords, could be placed on the statute book only when the January election had given a rather dubious mandate. By the second of these 1910 elections the Lords had been finally crippled. The programme of social reform had culminated, a few months later, in the National Health Insurance Act, and this had been followed by a violent but unsuccessful campaign to engineer a strike of the medical profession. Irish Home Rule had been launched through the Lords on its way to the Statute Book. This was no decaying civilisation: there was much more about it, for anyone who was young enough, of "very heaven".

"The honourable gentleman from New College is out of order." I was frequently pulled up by the President, as I dragged in such topics at debate after debate that had nothing whatever to do with them. Then there was Indian independence, and colonial emancipation in general: E. D. Morel's *Red Rubber*, exposing King Leopold's atrocities at an earlier period of Congo misrule, was one of our favourite textbooks. Meanwhile organised labour was marching. The miners' strike of 1912, a tram-strike at Oxford itself, Jim Larkin in Dublin, the formation during 1914 of the Triple Alliance of railwaymen, miners and transport-workers—as liberals, not as socialists, we passionately supported them all. And yet a struggle was in progress that engaged me more narrowly still: this was woman suffrage. For it symbolised everything we stood for.

I shall not tell again, for you can read it elsewhere, the story of suffragist militancy. But one episode I must mention. On Derby day in 1913 a middle-aged lady, called Emily Wilding Davison, threw herself before the King's horse as it galloped round Tattenham Corner. I don't know what you'll think of her protest, which was dangerous for others as well as for herself: but she was very brave: and she died of her injuries. You have a link with her, Timothy; she was wearing, for disguise, your great-grandmother's wig.

Though I ought to be ashamed to talk of it in the same breath, I did something myself for the suffragist cause that was really rather brave in its own grotesque way: for I have always been physically timid, and so fearful of violence to my person that footballers of either sort, and racing motorists, and airmen, never fail to elicit in me a bemused admiration. Now Eights Week at Oxford is an event like no other on this earth. The sun shines, young women wear summery dresses, and everyone is happy. The heart of it is a contest for headship of the river. Well, Laski and I, with one or two others, had chartered a launch for the Eights Week of 1914; and we steamed up and down—I rather think while the races were actually in progress—shouting "votes for women" through a megaphone. So far, so good: but what next? Next, undoubtedly, would be a bad beating-up by the bloods. So I hid in the classical reading room, which the bloods, one could be sure, had never heard of: under a very low table, at the very far end, for I wanted to make doubly sure. Sympathisers brought me food, and I emerged, a bit stiff, when the affair had blown over.

In the more peaceful field, I planned, just before coming down, a small volume of feminist essays. Maude Royden and Eleanor Rathbone wrote for me, and "The Making of Women: Oxford Essays in Feminism" was issued a few years later by Messrs Allen & Unwin. I was not only the editor and a contributor, but, for contractual purposes, the author as well; and I had an exciting interview with Sir Stanley Unwin (not yet knighted) to negotiate an agreement. I had always understood, of course, that the publication of such a book couldn't be considered a commercial proposition: so I undertook to buy a considerable number of copies myself—three hundred, to be exact—or to hand in before publication orders from contributors, the Repton Bookshop, or various suffrage societies for the equivalent number. Although the three hundred were to be free of royalty, a really generous one was to be paid on copies disposed of in the ordinary way of business; and I was very happy about it all, especially as the three hundred were to be supplied at quite a reasonable discount (about twenty-five per cent), so that any I might take up myself could be sold at a profit. But I proved too optimistic, for I had to destroy the remnant of my copies—quite a little pile—when moving from Ladbroke Road to Ladbroke Grove in the middle twenties. I have always been very grateful to Allen & Unwin for giving me this start. I happened on the contract only a few weeks ago, slipped between the pages of a book by Sir Stanley himself, called "The Truth about Publishing".

I also wrote a feminist play, called "Daughters". I was the hero. Given every advantage by my sex, I had just been appointed Home Secretary, and was on the eve of presenting a Bill for the abolition of capital punishment. Given every disadvantage by her sex, the chief female character was slowly going mad through frustration. It was not a good play, though I thought very well of it at the time, and still think its doctrine fundamentally sound, though no doubt rather exaggerated in expression. A Sunday society, one of several that existed at this period and specialised in single performances, was willing, and even eager, to produce it if I, on my side, would put up eighty pounds. I had no eighty pounds. I have rarely felt so wretched. The thought crossed my mind of applying to the Spoo for a loan, but I dismissed it.


The Spoo—I must tell you about him. This was W. A. Spooner, our Warden. He was a beautiful albino—beautiful from the albino point of view—with the usual albino eyes, which he was always blinking. I didn't know him at all well, and my impression of him may be untrustworthy; but, remembering him with affection, I shall give it for what it is worth.

I think of him as gentle, very gentle indeed; but also as very strong when occasion arose, and of great, even exceptional, moral courage. He was famous, of course, for his spoonerisms, such as "Will you take me?" instead of "Will you make tea?", with marriage unexpectedly resulting; but all these old chestnuts were probably myths, and I never heard him talk so myself.

Once, it is true, a contemporary spoonerism was reported on the day it had allegedly occurred. He was preaching, so they said, in New College chapel, on the topic of sin and its blandishments. "When temptation assails you," he advised, struggling with 'misled' in his script, "do not be mizzled. No, not mizzled. Mished. Well, mizzled or mished." It was also alleged that he habitually referred to Russell Brain, now President of the Royal College of Physicians, as Brainy Russell. But if literal spooner-isms were myths, intellectual ones were common. He had sent for me one day, and began, as always, by endeavouring to find out who I was: his memory for faces, or for my face at least, being oddly defective. His courtesy was great, and his method accordingly roundabout. "Ah, let me see," he said; "what is your initial?" "V." "And V stands for what?" "Victor." There was a little pause: then he looked at me, blinked his eyes, and asked, in a voice that somehow sounded albino too, "Victor what?" The moment I had told him he plunged right in. "Ah yes," he said. "I know what I wanted to see you about. I wanted to congratulate you for making that magnificent century. The college is proud of you." What he really had in mind, or rather hadn't, was a speech at the Union that had got a few lines in the *Isis*.

His oddities were numerous. I was to dine with him alone one night, and, arriving rather early, was asked to go straight to his bedroom, and talk to him while he finished dressing. I found him struggling with his tie. We chatted a little. The door to an adjoining room was slightly ajar, and I heard a low drone coming from it. Presently the tie was satisfactorily adjusted, and we were just about to leave when "Wait a minute," he said, "I'd forgotten." He went to the door I have spoken of, opened it wider, put his head in, and said, almost peevishly, "Very bad, very bad indeed. Write for next week on the Epistle of St. Paul to the Ephesians." Then we went down and dined.

I had personal experience of his beautiful consideration. He sent for me in 1913, when I had been up a term or two, and after the usual preliminaries showed himself clearly embar-rassed. "I hear," he said, "that you're rather poor. Is that so?" I said yes. "Does that mean," he asked, "that you often feel a bit pinched for money in your life here at New College?" I again agreed. "Well," he said, "I'd like to make you a loan. Here's a little cheque. Pay it back, please, some time." The cheque was for fifty pounds. It was the recollection of this kindness that made me wonder whether I might ask him to subsidise "Daughters".

His attitude to my own eccentricities was very wise. "Mr Gollancz," he said to me once, "Mr Henderson tells me you go to no lectures, and are generally slack in your work. When he's given you a composition to do you turn up with nothing, and explain that you've been very busy. Busy at what? At your clubs and societies, he tells me. Well, I shan't interfere. If you pull off a first, I shall congratulate you. If not, I shall take away your scholarship and send you down." But I'm not sure that there was anything particularly spoonerish about this: it was typical of Oxford.

I have mentioned his moral courage. When you visit the New College chapel, you will find two stone tablets at the entrance, in memory of New College men who died in the first world war. One of them, the normal one, is very big. The other is much smaller. The inscription on it is something like this: "In memory of the men of this college who, visitors from another land, returned to their homes at the call of duty and laid down their lives for their country." The names that follow are German. I do not remember precisely when this tablet was put up: in 1917, I think, when the war was still on: certainly, otherwise, soon afterwards, while feeling against Germans was violent. Now I have been told that there was strong opposition to the proposal, and that it was Spooner who insisted. I like to think that this is true—Spooner's part, not the rest of it. I have also been told that he preached on the subject in New College chapel, and wept.

Whenever I go to Oxford, I like, if I can, to visit these memorials. I think mainly of my many dead friends, but also of W. A. Spooner.


You must not imagine that I tried my hand at nothing but feminist topics, or that all the clubs I frequented were exclusively or mainly political. We had a delightful little Society called The Midwives, because we assisted at the birth-pangs of one another's compositions. We were very exclusive indeed, limiting ourselves to about a dozen from various colleges: others being C. W. Stewart, who was presently to be associated with

Faber & Faber, Hubert Phillips, the puzzle man, John Crowe Ransom, the poet, Elmer Davis, and Christopher Morley. We owed our masterpiece to Morley. He had found a forgotten letter, signed Kathleen, in a blotter at the Union, with a number of crosses and "These are from Fred" as a postscript. The novel we composed on the basis of this fragment, writing a chapter apiece, was a miracle of deduction. Morley specialised in Sherlockiana, and was regarded by experts as the first of authorities on Baker Street. He was also the author of some lines that have stuck in my memory. Descriptive of a minor poet, they ran:

> ". . . . . and lay the rhymester's switch
> Across the rosy buttocks of the Muse."

The image has always seemed to me a very pretty one.

Still more exclusive than The Midwives was the New College Essay Society, which I was never invited to join. It was intended, really, for men of somewhat heavier calibre. But I went several times as a guest, and usually enjoyed myself. The proceedings opened with a fascinating ritual, but when my own turn was coming to bow, receive the loving-cup, drink, face about, and bow again, I always felt afraid that I should giggle nervously and ruin everything. Military drill, a little later, was to affect me similarly. My company commander in the Inns of Court O.T.C. at Berkhamsted often had occasion to bellow "What's that stupid-looking man in the rear rank laughing for?" This always made me worse.

*Ladbroke Grove, May 21st*

*There is something awfully wrong about this record—not the Oxford bit in particular, but the whole enterprise—and I feel very strongly tonight that I should like to abandon it, though I know perfectly well that I cannot—the matter is out of my hands. There is not something wrong, there are many things wrong; they have been uneasily at the back of my mind every now and again since I started, and something happened to me tonight—a combination of moods—that has brought them compulsively to the foreground. I have been feeling as sad all evening as Mahler's ewig, though not at all for the same reason. And in one sense I have been feeling the reverse of sad. As I walked down to Bow Street for the opera at a quarter to seven in the late fitful sunshine, all the old familiar joy of mingling and becoming one with the world's beauty was in me again: I looked "as with heart first awaking" at the spires to the east, and at a little toy post-office van, and a lorry of brilliant green, that sparkled at the end of a vista against a white façade. And coming home in a taxi after supper, where I had no longer been able to keep what I was feeling to myself but had talked of it to Ruth and even, obliquely, to the maître d'hôtel, I felt as Traherne once felt—"the stones of the street were as precious as gold to me"— as we passed Trafalgar Square, so lovely in its flood-lighting for the festival. I suppose, really, that a specially poignant apprehension of beauty, of something good and rare and precious at the heart of things, is what has induced my present mood—this, combined with the news from Persia, and all that it indicates of ever-increasing hatred and strife.*

*The first thing I feel to be so terribly wrong about my letter is this: I am writing about the good life instead of living it. I cannot explain why I feel as I do, because I know very well that books and pictures and music have been messengers of God to the world like few others, and that self-expression, if a man has something to say, is every bit as much a part of the good life as any other way of living it. Would I be without Beethoven's music? And yet I do feel it: I feel that I am being false, committing just that sin against the losing of oneself, against spontaneity, that I am so desperately anxious to explain as the chief thing, the only thing, that prevents us from living in Paradise. I feel that a single unknown act of charity is worth more than all the hundreds of thousands of words that this letter will eventually run to, and that somehow all this brooding and writing and elaborating prevents me from performing it. What I mean is that the beauty of the world and the ultimate goodness at the heart of things notwithstanding, there is misery everywhere—moral misery even more than physical misery: and that nothing can cure it but an absoluteness of good, expressed moment by moment in one's daily life, over against that misunderstanding called evil. An absoluteness of good for its own sake, with no calculation about the consequences—not even with the calculation that it will conquer the evil, not even with the hope that it may do so.*

*Let me give an example or two of how writing about the good life prevents me from living it. Appalled last December by a seeming inevitability about the drift to war, I sent a letter to the papers advocating a two-point programme on which everybody of good will might agree—determination to negotiate at every opportunity and in a real mood of peace, and an English initiative for the launching of a world-wide plan to abolish hunger. I asked anyone who agreed to send me a postcard with the word "yes" on it. The response was remarkable, and an Association for World Peace resulted. We have done a few things during the two or three months that have elapsed since its foundation, and I have had spurts of energy about it; but my heart isn't in it as my heart was in "Save Europe Now", not for months but for years; and you make a success of a thing when your heart is in it and not when it isn't. "Where thy treasure is, there thy heart is also"; and my heart is in the writing of this letter, not in the Association for World Peace. I tell myself that we are doing as much as we can, that there is really very little that we can do, and that if suddenly a way seemed open of turning our Association into a genuinely effective instrument for the preservation of peace I should drop everything else, including this letter, and throw myself into the effort. All that is largely true. But it isn't completely true; for I know that if it were not for this letter I should find ways of making the Association as effective as "Save Europe Now" was. I was passionate about that: I am not passionate about this, although there is really nothing I wouldn't do to prevent another outbreak of war. And it is the writing of this letter, I repeat, that prevents me from having the passion I ought to have.*

*It is the same with the letters I still get in very large numbers from Germans in distress, asking me for help of various kinds—some of them have been deprived of their homes by the occupation authorities, others want to leave Germany and join their parents or children overseas, others have a little money in England which would save them from misery and want to find a way of getting hold of it. Success in such cases is always difficult, and for the most part impossible: but it is possible occasionally: only, however, if the most devoted care is given to each application. Well, I don't ignore these letters: on the contrary, I spend a good deal of time on them and "do what I can"; but there is all the difference in the world between "doing what you can" and being utterly absorbed, as I should have been utterly absorbed a year or two ago, until either a solution has been found or one has convinced oneself that a solution is impossible. And the explanation for the difference, again, is my absorption in this letter.*

*The word "absoluteness" which I used just above points to all the other things that I feel to be so wrong about this letter, and that make me want to abandon it—or at any rate to lay it aside until at last I can speak single-mindedly. I don't know for how many years now I have been struggling against the conviction that my whole spiritual and intellectual position is false, and I have been growingly aware of this falseness whenever I have called to mind, for the purpose of this letter, my ideas at various periods of my life. I feel this falseness, for some reason or another, more acutely than ever tonight. Can I correct it before I shall have finished? When I come to the final page, shall I find that I have at last been able to conquer whatever it may be in me, "wretched man that I am", that prevents me from accepting intellectually, and living spiritually, the truths which, deep down in me, I believe I have always known, known since early childhood, to be truths that conscience, or apprehension of reality, or whatever you may like to call it, demands that I should accept and live?*

*What I am trying to say—and pray God that I may find such words to say it in as may make it all clear to you—is this. I look at the world around me, and at my own life. At the world of atom bombs; at the hatred between East and West; at the vileness of the press; at the sadism of films; at the murder of children and old women; at murderers hung by the neck until they are dead; at millions and millions starving miserably, and no one caring anything about it; at my own wretched efforts to make profits for my firm and provide for my own present comfort and my future old age. And I know, I have long known, with every atom of my being, that there is only one answer: absolute pacifism, absolute communism (not in the Stalinist sense, but in the early religious sense of holding all things in common), an absolute living of the Christian ethic.*

*We were at Fidelio tonight, and when I unburdened myself to Ruth, at supper, of what I have just been saying, she asked me "But was Leonora wrong to threaten Pizarro with the pistol? She saved her husband's life." She couldn't have put the dilemma in a more agonising form, for Leonora's pistol and the simultaneous trumpet-call had long seemed to me the perfect expression of divine-human co-operation, and I had put the trumpet-call on the half-title before the section "Man, fellow-worker with God" in my anthology "A Year of Grace". But I had to answer "Yes, she was wrong." To interpose her own body, of course this would have been right: to threaten with the pistol was far better than just to have been indifferent, just to have done nothing about it: but to retaliate against*

*violence with violence—this, absolutely, was wrong. And the abso-*
*luteness is everything. I do not believe that you can approximate to*
*Christian ethics: that is why Christ told us, not merely to love our*
*friends and do no injury to our enemies but positively to love our*
*enemies, and not merely to be as good as we could manage to be but*
*to be perfect as our Father is perfect. The question is not one of*
*degree. You cannot be more or less of a Christian, just as you cannot*
*be more or less of a lover. You either love or you do not. When*
*absoluteness is reached, you are suddenly a Christian; before, how-*
*ever close you may have got, you have not been a Christian at all.*
*And this absoluteness is the only possible road to the Kingdom of*
*Heaven: it is the Kingdom of Heaven itself. Whether or not Christ*
*actually said what he is quoted as saying in a Gospel fragment, he*
*might very well have said it: if ye keep not Sabbath for the whole*
*week, ye shall not see the Father.*

*I have never been able to understand, so evident does this seem to*
*me, how people could possibly think otherwise. When, some time*
*early in the war, I wrote "Shall our Children Live or Die?" in reply*
*to Lord Vansittart, I included the sentence "It is necessary to love*
*Hitler." I wrote it as I might have written "one must eat to live".*
*But my friends implored me to cut it out, for they feared a scandal,*
*and I weakly complied.*

*It follows that whether or not such absoluteness will "succeed"*
*is utterly irrelevant. I don't mean only in the short run; I don't*
*mean only, for instance, that it's utterly irrelevant whether total*
*disarmament, and love in our life and in our hearts for Stalin and*
*the Red Army and the G.P.U., would either hinder a communist*
*conquest of the world or mitigate its horrors when it came. I mean*
*in the long run too; I mean that whether or not, ages hence, the con-*
*dition of the world might appear, in human judgment, to have been*
*improved by such behaviour is utterly irrelevant too. The thing suc-*
*ceeds, in the real sense, by the fact of it happening: it is there, good,*
*eternally, God realised and incarnate. Perhaps, as Samuel Alexander*
*might say, it makes God. I am explaining this badly; perhaps I am*
*trying to explain something one can only feel utterly convinced about*
*but can never explain to others. Let me make another attempt.*
*Elizabeth Pilenko, a Russian living in Paris, took the place of a*
*Jewess who was going to the incinerators and was burnt in her*
*stead. It happens that her action is known. But if it had never been*
*known; if no one had witnessed it; if the Jewess had herself been*
*killed immediately afterwards; if, therefore, what Elizabeth had*

done could never possibly have become known to anyone—nevertheless she was doing the only thing that can answer the world's evil, and her action lives and reigns eternally, whether or not, to mortal seeming, the world is a better place for it. And as irrelevant as this last consideration is the fact that, as I have little doubt, Elizabeth's life, in the ordinary sense, was a far more valuable one than the Jewess's, and that, if she had lived, she might have given spiritual strength and physical comfort to thousands.

I feel exactly the same about communism, in the sense in which I have used the word, as I do about pacifism. Meister Eckhart wrote, "He who withholds but a pennyworth of worldly goods from his neighbour, knowing him to be in need of it, is a robber in the sight of God. Further I declare, who spares a penny for himself to put it by against a rainy day, thinking, I may need that for tomorrow, is a murderer before God." I am utterly convinced that he is right.

And now do you see what I am getting at? Do you understand why I stated that the whole intellectual and spiritual position that this letter is slowly unfolding is fundamentally a false one—though there is just a possibility (the slenderest possibility, I fear) that I shall have found strength, been given grace, to become the real me by the time I am done? For I said, and I meant it, that I believe with every atom of my being in absolute pacifism, absolute communism, an absolute living of the Christian ethic: I know that they are right. I knew that they were right when the positions I honestly held, and shall honestly describe in later chapters—positions that I still largely hold—were the positions neither of absolute pacifism nor of absolute communism. You will have noticed immediately that I use the word "false" one moment and "honestly" the next, and you will consider the paradox a startling one. But the paradox is the point: both "false" and "honestly" are exact.

Take, for purposes of clarification, my present position on pacifism and Christian communism. I am not—not yet—a pacifist. Why, if I know it is right? Because, fighting with this deeper knowledge, is another kind of knowledge that I cannot deny—a δόξα, as Bernard Strauss might have called it, in contrast with γνῶσις. I know, with this other kind of knowledge, that but for armed resistance to Hitler fascism might have conquered the world; that freedom might have vanished everywhere; and that, worst of all, generation after generation might so have been conditioned that freedom might have vanished not only everywhere but for ever. And this knowledge, the knowledge of a possibility so horrible that I am unable to face it, is like a great *lump of lead shutting down what is both deeper and more real in me, and preventing it from occupying my whole being. (But isn't all this utterly faithless? Isn't such a fear nonsensical, seeing that (a) the eternal God is freedom, and (b) there cannot be anything "wrong" with the totality of things?)*

*It is the same with Christian communism—which, for individuals in our present society, would mean following the spirit of Eckhart's words. I run a business for profit; and though I give away a good deal of money, I am careful to keep enough of it to ensure that I shall live very comfortably both now and in the future. Why do I do it, knowing deep down what I know? Not only from selfishness and greed, though those of course come in. But also because I know, honestly with the other kind of knowledge, that to publish the sort of books I specialise in is a valuable service to the community: that power in this way to advocate a better society is more likely to assist in achieving it than the abandonment of such power: that no business can survive, in present conditions, except on the basis of profit-making: that, family considerations apart, if I give my last penny away I may make myself a burden to the community: and that I am the sort of human being whose personality would shrivel up, be robbed of any value it may have, not only in conditions of penury but even if deprived of the country and travel and books. (And in the very act of writing these words I half know that I'm making excuses, and then again I half know that I'm not.)*

*Well, there is the dilemma, and it agonises me. You will find an answer of sorts, so far as public affairs are concerned, in Reinhold Niebuhr's "Moral Man and Immoral Society". I admire Reinhold Niebuhr as much as I admire any man now living, but I reject his dualistic relativism utterly. His point of view is based, among other things, on a sharp differentiation between this world and the next: on a contrast, seen as basic and inevitable, between the individual man and the collective man (whereas, for me, the assumption of this inevitability is the cause of half our evils, and derives from a muddle-headed, bogus-mystical, unrealistic taking-it-for-granted that there is something in society, something ultimate, other than the men and women who make it up): and on a profoundly pessimistic estimate of human nature. "The demand of religious moralists" he writes in a typical passage "that nations subject themselves to 'the law of Christ' is an unrealistic demand, and the hope that they will do so is a sentimental one. Even a nation composed of individuals who possessed the highest degree of religious goodwill would be less*

*than loving in its relation to other nations. It would fail, if for no
other reason, because the individuals could not possibly think themselves into the position of the individuals of another nation in a
degree sufficient to ensure pure benevolence." But that is to beg the
whole question. Side by side with this passage may be set a peculiarly
horrible statement by Martin Luther: "It is indeed true that
Christians, so far as they themselves are concerned, are subject to
neither law nor sword, and need neither; but just take heed to fill
the world with real Christians before ruling it in a Christian and
evangelical manner. This you will never accomplish, for the world
and the masses are and always will be unchristian." I don't want
to be melodramatic, but really you can almost hear the nails on
Calvary.*

And now I want to tell you a little about my reading at
Oxford, and in the years just before and just after—for dates
are jumbled up in my memory. It was wide in its way, and
yet confined, in the main, within what might almost be described as professional limits: my profession being, as I saw
it—I must put all this pompously, if I am to give you a picture
of my mind—that of equipping myself, as efficiently as possible,
for liberal or progressive world-citizenship. I was fascinated, it
is true, by the beauty and rhythm of words, and often tried my
hand at translations of various kinds, turning "The Shropshire
Lad", for instance, into Latin hendecasyllables and a lyric or
two of Shelley's into appropriate Greek metres; but my interest
in ideas, and my eagerness for knowledge of a particular kind,
were so persistent and intense that little time was left, by comparison, for the enjoyment of literature as such.

I was eager to understand how the world-machine functioned
—how the wheels of the world went round. Wages, prices, production, money, shops, rate of interest, banking, credit, trade,
"business", foreign exchange, gold points, tariffs, employment,
supply and demand, entrepreneurs, taxation, middle men, five
pound notes—what, in hard fact, did they *mean*, these and a
hundred more like them? How did they work out in practice—
a detailed, daily practice that I could understand as immediately as I understood how to eat and move, or that I could
touch, I might almost have said, as I touched my own body?
And how, more important than anything, did they all fit

together? I wanted, very passionately indeed, to get a clear tidy picture of the whole involved process, with every detail filled in; and I wanted to do this, partly because it seemed stupid and undignified, almost slavish, not to understand things with which anyhow one was inevitably mixed up, but also, and above all, because one couldn't possibly alter what one didn't understand, and I was anxious, most anxious, to alter what I felt to be evil. So, difficult and sometimes repulsive though I found this research—for my mind has always turned naturally, not to economics, but to metaphysics and the philosophy of religion—I read anything I could discover on the topics that absorbed me, from pamphlets, popularisations and volumes in the Home University Library to Marshall and Pigou, Bastable and Mill, Bagehot and Jevons. I was particularly anxious to understand the theory and practice of money, banking, stock exchanges, and the like, for I felt that deep down in them lay the clue I was constantly seeking; and though my attitude to business was a snobbish one, for I thought of it as banausic and indeed, to be candid, as disreputable, it was at Oxford that I began playing with the notion of going into business myself (for the shortest possible period that would serve my purpose) with the object of discovering at first hand just how everything dovetailed. I had no idea then that the business would be publishing, or that I should remain in it, more or less, for ever.

I ask myself in passing whether my attitude to business as such was really a snobbish one.

I have been looking up the word 'snob' in the Oxford Dictionary. It may mean, I see, 'a shoemaker or cobbler; a cobbler's apprentice', which is charming but irrelevant. Its main meaning is given as "one whose ideas and conduct are prompted by a vulgar admiration for wealth or social position. Also *transf.* of intellectual superiority." If my attitude to business was, and in some degree still is (though I am in business myself), such as might reasonably be described as snobbish—and my attitude to the business aspects of publishing must nowadays be included—the snobbishness in question is clearly intellectual in type. For I have no admiration, vulgar or otherwise, for wealth or social position; the contrary is the case. Have I, then, a vulgar admiration for superior brains, and do I denigrate business as being exclusively an occupation for half-wits? No. The question is a moral or spiritual one; and while my admiration for spiritual excellence has always been great, I can see nothing vulgar about it.

While, when at Oxford, I had certainly not accepted the idea that profit-making as such was immoral—not accepted it with conscious acceptance—and was even doing battle against it, I am sure that it was lurking, as one day to be inevitably accepted, somewhere in the depths of my consciousness; and I am equally sure that this idea, which for so many years now has been the basis of my socialism, is what really explains my vague feeling at Oxford that business was essentially disreputable. So I wasn't being snobbish at all; I was showing the first indication, oversimplifying of course and self-righteous as usual, of a moral ideal that was struggling to express itself. And if I now feel a passing astonishment at something I happen to learn about the background of Lord Z—a banker, let us say, who turns out to be a Fellow of All Souls—what I am really wondering, perhaps, is how a man such as this, with brains on the one hand and the advantages of education on the other, can be deliberately giving himself to profit-making when he might be remaking the world. The fact is that I am absurdly ambivalent on the subject of original sin: my painful awareness of it, in myself and others, is always colliding with a conviction that knowledge is virtue. And I am no less surprised about my own case, as you know from a recent outburst, than about Lord Z's: excusing myself, however, quite honestly at one level of honesty, by the reflection that publishing and business are not, after all, quite synonymous. But no doubt Lord Z, if it occurred to him that there was anything to excuse, would excuse himself similarly.

To remake the world: that was the mainspring of my urge to understand it. So, simultaneously with my reading of economics and the like, I went from one exposition to another of scheme after scheme for putting an end to the various human miseries, and particularly to poverty and war. The range was pretty wide. Detesting authority, worshipping self-direction, I should in any case have been powerfully attracted by the

writings of Henry George; but my interest was additionally
stimulated by the fact that Bernard Strauss, and the whole of
his family and group, were fanatical single-taxers. It was at
a single-tax dinner, just after I'd gone up, that I first met
Ruth. The liberalism of the single-tax people was liberalism
at its finest. Their hatred of oppression was not something that
occasionally swept over them, it was something they couched
with. A wonderful story is told about a millionaire called
Joseph Fels, proprietor of fels-naphtha soap, who belonged to
this circle. A congress of Russian revolutionaries—a subsequently world-famous congress, for the bolsheviks and men-
sheviks were to split at it—was being held in 1903 on the
outskirts of London. Lenin, who attended, was looking for
funds. Joseph Fels, detesting Czarism, gave him a cheque for
a thousand pounds. "I'll repay it," said Lenin, "when we win."
Seventeen years later Leonid Krassin came to London for the
purposes (a) of reopening trade relations between the Union of
Socialist Soviet Republics and Great Britain, and (b) of paying
a thousand pounds to Joseph Fels. But Fels had died in the
meantime, so his executor was paid instead. I hope I've got
the story right, and that it's true; for I like hearing things of
that kind about anybody, and dictators in particular, whose
conduct is normally detestable. I heard an equally good story
the other day about Mussolini. Sir Charles Walston, a Cambridge archaeologist famous among other things for his pro-
jected excavation of Herculaneum, had died when on a cruise
off the Italian coast, and was to be cremated. Mussolini, hearing of this, sent an urn from Herculaneum for the reception of
his ashes.

But while keeping an open mind about the doctrines of
Henry George, so attractive in their promise of liberation by
the easy enactment of a single reform, I was unable to escape
the conviction that such easiness was altogether too easy, and
that somewhere in those pages a fallacy must lie hid. So I fell
to investigating simultaneously every possible method of
socialist reconstruction, in an effort to discover whether any of
them might perhaps prove consistent with my liberal faith.
Syndicalism (which, attractive for its hatred of bureaucracy,
I immediately rejected for its violence), marxism (at second
hand, however, except for the Communist Manifesto and a few
odds and ends like that), fabianism, guild socialism, Babeuf's

conspiracy, the theories or utopias of Morris and Saint-Simon and Lassalle—these and many others were the subjects I read about. Guild socialism was specially in my thoughts. It had a journal of its own: the astonishing *New Age* which, edited by A. R. Orage, who was often to be seen hanging about in the old plush-and-gilt Café Royal, had a brilliance unapproached, then or since, by any other paper of its kind. I had only one complaint against it. The music critic, a man called Kaikhosrau Sorabji, or the other way about, was lukewarm about Destinn.

I must mention one book in particular, since its influence, not so much on my thought at the time as on the future development of it, was particularly great. This was J. A. Hobson's *Imperialism*. It shook my Liberalism a little, though at first did no more than that. But its arguments came back to me later when I was moving decisively in a socialist direction; and I was to draw the deduction, which the author, so far as I remember, had himself never drawn, that poverty could not fail to result from a maldistribution of purchasing power inherent in capitalism as such, and could accordingly never be abolished except by the abolition of capitalism itself.

For the rest, I read anything, in prose or in verse, that rang with the praise of freedom: or sang for joy: or was instinct with a feeling for human dignity and universal brotherhood. Shelley I had been fond of at school, but I fell in love with him now in the air of an Oxford that was fresh, for all its repudiation of him, with his own generosity. How often, as I walked to my rooms from a whole night of talk at Ralph Rooper's fireside, or, when summer had set in, by his window wide open to the quad, did my mind thrill again with the words, or my lips utter them, of "the first of poets, were it not that there is one yet greater than he, the mystic William Blake":

> "Thrones, altars, judgement-seats and prisons: wherein,
> And beside which, by wretched men were borne
> Sceptres, tiaras, swords, and chains, and tomes
> Of reasoned wrong, glozed on by ignorance,
> Were like those monstrous and barbaric shapes,
> The ghosts of a no-more-remembered fame,
> Which, from their unworn obelisks, look forth
> In triumph o'er the palaces and tombs

Of those who were their conquerors: mouldering round,
These imaged to the pride of kings and priests
A dark yet mighty faith, a power as wide
As is the world it wasted, and are now
But an astonishment; even so the tools
And emblems of its last captivity,
Amid the dwellings of the peopled earth,
Stand, not o'erthrown, but unregarded now . . .
The loathsome mask has fallen, the man remains
Sceptreless, free, uncircumscribed, but man
Equal, unclassed, tribeless, and nationless,
Exempt from awe, worship, degree, the king
Over himself; just, gentle, wise: but man
Passionless?—no, yet free from guilt and pain,
Which were, for his will made or suffered them,
Nor yet exempt, though ruling them like slaves,
From chance, and death, and mutability,
The clogs of that which else might oversoar
The loftiest star of unascended heaven,
Pinnacled dim in the intense inane."

There were other great passages that I could summon, not
too faultily, at will: Bertrand Russell's

". . . undismayed by the empire of chance, to preserve a mind
free from the wanton tyranny that rules his outward life;
proudly defiant of the irresistible forces that tolerate, for a
moment, his knowledge and his condemnation, to sustain
alone, a weary but unyielding Atlas, the world that his own
ideals have fashioned despite the trampling march of unconscious power."

And Walt Whitman's

"I say no man has ever yet been half devout enough,
None has ever yet adored or worship'd half enough,
None has begun to think how divine he himself is, and how
    certain the future is."

And the anarchist's speech in Lowes Dickinson's *A Modern
Symposium*:

"England! No, not England, but Europe, America, the world!
Where is Man, the new Man, there is our country. But the

new Man is buried in the old; and wherever he struggles in his tomb, wherever he knocks we are there to help to deliver him. When the guards sleep, in the silence of the dawn, rises the crucified Christ. And the angel that sits at the grave is the angel of Anarchy."

And many, very many things of Blake:

"The Angel who presided at my birth
Said,—'Little Creature, formed for joy and mirth,
Go love, without the help of anything on earth.'"

And

"For the tear is an intellectual thing,
And a sigh is the sword of an Angel King,
And the bitter groan of the martyr's woe
Is an arrow from the Almighty's bow."

And

"Let every Christian, as much as in him lies, engage himself openly and publicly before all the World in some Mental pursuit for the Building up of Jerusalem."

And

"No bird soars too high, if he soars with his own wings."

Yet another thing I loved to recite was the Platonic affirmation, which Socrates expounds, with such solemn tranquillity, at Agathon's drinking-party:

"ἀλλὰ αὐτὸ καθ' αὑτὸ μεθ' αὑτοῦ μονοειδὲς ἀεὶ ὄν ('absolute, simple, separate, and everlasting)"

but also the passage that breaks in on it—as though, amid the quiet of some cathedral, you were to hear, with a blissful inexpectancy, the pipes of a Pan come to free you from heaven itself:

". . . when suddenly there was a great knocking at the door of the house, as of revellers, and the sound of a flute-girl was heard . . . A little while afterwards they heard the voice of Alcibiades resounding in the court; he was in a great state of intoxication, and kept roaring and shouting 'Where is Agathon? Lead me to Agathon', and at length, supported by the flute-girl and some of his attendants, he found his way to them. 'Hail, friends', he said, appearing at the door crowned with a massive garland of ivy and violets, his head flowing with ribands. 'Will you have a very drunk man as a companion of your revels?' "

Yes, this is a passage that has always delighted me. For though there are times when I'd like to be a monk, there are others, now growing rarer, when I wish I were a carefree and conscienceless pagan.

One or two of these quotations might have led you to believe, but for earlier chapters, that I was an atheist at Oxford. I was very far indeed from being that. I passionately believed in the splendour of man, and should have said with Paracelsus, if I had read him at the time, "Man is a sun and a moon, and a heaven filled with stars". I believed in his infinite dignity and worth, and in his ultimate power, if once he could be freed from human shackles—shackles imposed on him by human institutions and a misunderstanding of his own nature—to reach a point only a little lower than "the loftiest star of unascended heaven" or, in biblical words, only a little lower than the angels. It was this vivid sense of human possibilities that attracted me to Russell's "A Free Man's Worship", and not "the trampling march of unconscious power". For I believed in God as passionately as I believed in man: not as an entity demanded by logic or dogmatics, for dogmas of any kind had long been repulsive to me, but, by an immediate and unquestioning apprehension, as something good and loving at the heart of things, as some gentleness and joy which were alone the final meaning of existence. I did not attempt to harmonise my worship of man and my worship of God, for it never occurred to me that they needed harmonising: I instinctively thought of them as identical. But one thing was missing in me, and without it no true harmony is possible. This was acceptance: not obedience to God's will, for, as you know, I dislike the connotation of "obedience"—a sort of slavishness it implies in the obeyer and a sort of power-mongering in the obeyed—but the freely given, co-operative acceptance of divine reality: or divine-human reality, for that is the meaning of Christ. It is precisely in the moment of this acceptance that man becomes most splendid: more truly dignified, more freely himself than otherwise he could ever be, and capable, then, of oversoaring even the loftiest stars that are "pinnacled in the intense inane".

And still I have not told you about another kind of reading that often absorbed me when I was unable, for some reason, "to talk with friends until the break of light". This was the reading of plays. I read very few novels at Oxford—only the Russians, Wells, Conrad, a George Moore or so, Chesterton, Poe and Blackwood, a little Hardy and Meredith (but his novels far less enjoyably than his poems), and, with special pleasure, the *contes* of Henry James. I daresay there were several others—I have just remembered "Peter Ibbetson" and "The Crock of Gold"—but the list is not a long one. For plays, on the other hand, my appetite was enormous. There were several reasons for this peculiarity. I have a streak of impatience in my make-up, which shows itself particularly when I start to read anything fictional: and though I sometimes have moods, as on long summer days in the sunshine of Italy or France, when my special delight is to read a big volume, if it is well enough written, with an almost exaggerated slowness, and to enjoy every word as I enjoy Mozart's music, more often I press forward in an effort to absorb the whole work with an impulse as continuous as possible. The impulse can be quite continuous in the case of a play. Then again I am fond of the drama, rather specially fond of it, but except on rare occasions find performances disconcerting: more often than not there is something false about them, like singers or fiddles off the note. But reading a play at home you have your own performance, and this is nearer the ideal, being played in the theatre of your imagination, than any but a great one on the stage: which is better still, for drama ought to be a communal act, and requires, for its perfect realisation, the audience as well as the performers.

But these were not the reasons which chiefly attracted me to play-reading. The years before the first world war were dramatically the post-Ibsen period, when the drama was a principal vehicle for exposing social shams and furthering the work of human emancipation. (I write that sentence, in the present neo-reactionary climate, with particular pleasure.) This was the time of Miss Horniman's theatre in Manchester, of Sunday societies in London, of repertory companies everywhere, and of the wide publication of dramatic literature, often when the plays so printed had never received, nor were ever likely to receive, an ordinary public performance. Foreign dramatists, too, were being translated in great numbers: Strindberg and Tchekoff and Andreyeff and Hauptman and Sudermann and Schnitzler. I found in all these plays, both English and foreign —the Englishmen included Galsworthy and Granville Barker and Stanley Houghton and St. John Hankin and Harold Brighouse and Allan Monkhouse and dozens of others—both an echo of my own ideas and an aid to their clarification. I remember, in particular, what an impression was made on me by Galsworthy's *Justice* and *Strife*. (How stupidly this fine writer and man is underestimated today!) And once play-reading had become a habit the field opened out to include every variety of contemporary drama: the Irishmen in particular, J. M. Synge and Yeats and Lady Gregory and Lennox Robinson, for the Abbey Theatre in Dublin was then at its zenith. Pinero came in, too, from a slightly earlier period, and Henry Arthur Jones: *Cyrano de Bergerac* and D'Annunzio's *Francesca da Rimini*: Oscar Wilde: and then Sheridan and Farquhar, Ben Jonson and Beaumont and Fletcher. . .

Most of the specifically "modern" plays by English authors were published by Messrs. Sidgwick and Jackson, in a uniform series the colour of pale fuchsia. I acquired them nearly all, and the collection became quite famous in our circle. My gentle friend Ewan Agnew, who died in the early twenties from a horrible paralysis contracted during service in Egypt, would often come in from next door to borrow "a mild Sidgwick and Jackson". He meant by "mild" that I was not to give him anything violent: the reference being to a play called "The Doom" (or something similar), in which a number of lives were terminated, with simultaneous abruptness, under stress of an intolerable environment. I had many happy times with Ewan Agnew, and dedicated "Daughters" to him. He lived in a very large house near Weedon, and I often spent some days there during vacs. On one of these occasions we went over to Northampton, where a company headed by a man called Bonaparte (who looked like Bonaparte and acted like Bonaparte and must certainly, we thought, be descended from Bonaparte) were performing a melodrama. Partly in tribute to the excellence of the show, and partly because we wanted to meet Bonaparte, we spent a good deal of time in drafting a telegram, which we sent off soon after our return. "Much struck by performance," it ran. "Glad if whole troupe would lunch here tomorrow." They neither replied nor turned up. This was stupid of them, for the food at Littlecourt was wonderful, even by the standard of 1914. Ewan told me afterwards that he was glad on the whole they hadn't come: he had feared for the spoons.

Harold Laski was another occasional borrower of my plays. I did not much like his attitude to them. He came round one evening and told me he had been working very hard: "I want to slack a bit," he said. "I should like to read one of your plays." I enquired whether he'd like something lightish or heavyish. "I don't care in the least," he replied. When I'd looked something out that I considered suitable, he glanced at it hurriedly and asked for three more. "I'll bring them all back in the morning," he said.

Realism was the note of these plays. The sardonic and very lovable Douglas Jerrold—I like joking with him better than with any of my other old friends, in spite of his detestable politics —published, or threatened to publish, a parody of them. It was entitled "Their Own Life in Their Own Way", or something of the sort, and the text ran as follows: "The curtain rises and discloses three old women crouching over a fire. It falls again immediately, because they have nothing to say." He also published, or threatened to publish, an Eights Week magazine called "What Oxford is Thinking". Inside was a blank sheet of paper.

One of my happiest memories connected with play-reading is of a kindness Ralph Rooper once did to me. Knowing that I was eager to read "The Three Sisters", which alone of Tchekoff's plays had never been done into English, he got hold of a German version (which I couldn't have understood) and, though exceptionally busy with his Schools, made a complete translation for me. Ralph was a pacifist. He volunteered for service with the French Red Cross, received the *croix de guerre* for exceptional heroism, and was killed while on duty with his ambulance.

*Brimpton*
*Friday night, June 1st*
*Hardly a day passes now without my reliving some episode of my boyhood. When I woke up in London this morning, and saw the thick*

*green curtain all dappled with shadows, thrown athwart them by
the sun from behind—unexpectedly, after so many days of cold and
rain—I remembered how I had loved this chiaroscuro when seeing it
first as a child, and with what a catch of the breath, a few years
later, I had come on a description of it in* D o r i a n  G r a y: *"and
now and then the fantastic shadows of birds in flight flitted across the
long tussore-silk curtains that were stretched in front of the huge
windows, producing a kind of momentary Japanese effect, and making him think of those pallid jade-faced painters of Tokio who,
through the medium of an art that is necessarily immobile, seek to
convey the sense of swiftness and motion. The sullen murmur of the
bees. . . ." And as I came down from Paddington just now, by a
happy coincidence the track was agleam with some saplings of
"honey-coloured" laburnum, on the margin of a buttercup meadow
that flowed endlessly on to the sky.*

*Saturday*
*And at Brimpton this morning the first peony—of the old-
fashioned, claret-coloured, ballet-skirted kind—is out in the
garden, smelling softly warm with the sun.*

## § 2

And now I must deal more systematically with the conflict
that was developing in my mind between socialism and liberalism, which is the conflict of a whole generation; or rather—for
my essential liberalism has never changed, from early childhood
to the present moment—between socialism and social reform.
Where had I got in this conflict at the time of my residence at
New College?

I need not rely on memory. It happens that the subject of the
Chancellor's Prize for Latin Prose, which I won in 1913, was
"A Dialogue on Socialism". I have the printed copy before me,
and shall run through it with you, hurriedly and roughly
translating. (I shall cut a great deal, but shall fill in a point or
two which I remember to have been in my mind.) I wish you
could read it for yourself—could read Latin, I mean. Not because a study of it is useful in a number of ways, teaching people,
for instance, to write grammatically and with some sense of
rhythm; but because it's far more useless than useful. Besides, if

you knew Latin you could read *Vivamus, mea Lesbia* in the original. But you won't know it. I am already trying to teach it you, and the moment you see me you say "amo, 'mat"; but I shall be defeated in the end by the different intentions of your charming but scientific father, whose will-power, I discover, is quite as strong as my own.

The dialogue is introduced by a letter, headed "Athens", from one Titus Pomponius to his friend Cicero. The writer had been entrusted with two faded and obviously antique manuscripts by a dying Greek; and when, by a lengthy process of analogy and deduction, he had managed to translate the at first unintelligible language, he had found to his wonder and delight that there before his eyes was a literary relic of Atlantis. (I have always believed passionately in Atlantis, and the very sound of it produces the same effect on me as Atzcapotzalco or Quetzalcoatl; indeed I was at one time so fond of disclosing how my own paternal family, itself Atlantidaean in origin, had since time immemorial met all the other Atlantidaeans once every hundred years or so in secret conclave, that I became thoroughly convinced of it myself. But "Gollancz" is not Atlantidaean; it is the name of a village in Poland.) In one of the manuscripts, writes Pomponius, is a detailed description of the Atlantidaean constitution; this he rapidly summarises; and we discover in a second that the Atlantis of 10,000 B.C. and the England of 1913 are identical. By this (I cannot help thinking) really rather happy device, we are enabled to take it for granted, when we come to the second of the manuscripts—the dialogue on socialism—which Pomponius encloses, that in fact we are reading about ourselves: though I should be bound to agree, if challenged, that the working-class conditions described more closely resemble those of 1850 than those of 1913, shocking though these latter were.

The dialogue immediately follows. It records a discussion between Sosiades, a generous young socialist (in whom I see a good deal of myself, in spite of the fact that I conclude on the Liberal side), Cleanthes, a presumably middle-aged Liberal, and Epiondes, a crusted old Tory. The scene is a suburban villa, built high on a hill and in reach of the pleasant sea breezes. The time is midsummer. The party is strolling one afternoon under a canopy of elms with Tanio, their host; and as suddenly they come out into the open, Phera, "most splendid of cities" (London), lies clear before them. Cleanthes (in whom I see a good deal of myself, at this stage at any rate of the dialogue) is immediately moved to express his emotion. I like his opening speech: I shall translate it in full.

"Your gardens are delightful, Tanio. What a pleasure to enjoy simultaneously such rural amenities and such urban magnificence! For I confess that, seduced though I am by the harmony of birds and streams, I am as happy amidst the roar of the market-place. The air is sweet here with the fragrance of flowers, and drowsy with the murmur of bees; but in the city— ah! some vital force seems stored up in its being which it communicates to us, so that our hearts leap within us even when we see what is ugly. To my last hour nothing will ever be dearer to me than royal Phera: magnificent with its smoke and rain, urgent with the flow of its crowds, splendid by night with its torches, it is more than the capital of our island—it is the heart of the whole world!"

"And in that same city," Sosiades retorts, "nothing could be more wretched than the condition of the workers."

Old Epiondes, who seems hardly more probable, on a re-reading of the dialogue, than our own Sir Waldron Smithers, now delivers an attack on the secular inexperience of youth, which has always imagined that there's nothing you can't improve if only you try hard enough. Economic inequality is a matter of fate; and if you attempt to put an end to it you'll merely turn the world upside down and destroy civilisation. "So take an old man's advice, and stop quarrelling with the inevitable. The workers' condition is certainly bad enough; but it's not as bad as you think, and the poor are contented because they've never known anything better."

This infuriates Sosiades:

"Really? I don't agree. I've lived among the poor, and I know very well what they suffer. But even if they were utterly content with their poverty, would that excuse *us* from never resting for a second until so horrible a plague had been banished from the earth? We are enjoying at this moment every possible delight that the world can offer us: must *they* be forever shut away from the fields and the sea, and live out their lives in a prison? And what lives! All day long they toil in great barracks of factories, some of the children as well: and yet they earn so little that they often half die of starvation. Do I need to tell you of the hovels where a man and his wife and five children may be living in a single room? Of the wretched diseases that contaminate our squalid streets? Of the crimes to which many of them are driven when they can find no market for their labour? How shameful that we should allow them to suffer so, when all this happiness is ours!"

"I suppose," says Epiondes (very like my father at this point), "that such things can be altered?" "They can." "How?" "By placing the conduct of business exclusively in the hands of the people as a whole." The cat is now out of the bag; and Epiondes, who has long been verging on apoplexy, "excuses himself with a plea of old age" and disappears finally from the dialogue. The remainder settle down to discuss Sosiades' proposition.

Cleanthes begins by asking Sosiades to explain himself. "The conduct of business," he objects, is an obscure expression. The people as a whole, replies Sosiades, will own the factories, the land and the instruments of production: will decide what goods to produce, and in what quantities: will conduct all foreign trade. "Then people will have nothing of their own?" "Oh yes they will. They will have no interest from capital, no rent from land, no profit from another's labour; but what anybody has earned will be his, to do what he likes with. The only personal wealth will be wages; and these will be increased by everything that in present conditions goes to rent, interest and profits. Just and adequate wages are impossible without nationalisation; for when business is in the hands of a few they accumulate capital, and capital, private capital, is nothing but robbery of the workers. You must understand this point, for it is the centre of my argument; so I shall first briefly demonstrate why the few now possess a vast capital, and shall go on to prove that this indeed implies robbery."

A short exposition follows, on marxist lines, of primary accumulation, the division of labour, the rise of factories, and the growth of employment; followed by an account of the Industrial Revolution, with all its advantages accruing to the capitalists. People who had bought the machines could produce far more cheaply than others, dispose of the product in far bigger quantities, enormously increase their labour force, and so build up huge fortunes which again would automatically be increased by their profit-making possibilities. So capitalists became astoundingly rich; for not only was the conduct of business entirely in

I

their hands, but nothing could prevent them, by very reason of this fact, from demanding a maximum of labour for a minimum —and what a minimum!—of return.

The labour theory of value is now expounded by Sosiades in proof of his contention that capital means robbery of the workers; and his account of it concludes as follows:

"A labourer may have worked all day, but may have added before twelve in the morning a price to the material equivalent to the total of his wages: from twelve till sunset, therefore, isn't he a downright slave, compelled to give his labour for nothing to a tyrannical master? Tyrannical, yes: how mean and greedy and inhuman these capitalists are! Not only are children hired out to them at a diminutive wage but the fathers are paid less than before, on the theory, if you please, that they ought to be content if death can be staved off by the earnings of the entire household. The only cure, I repeat, for this robbery of the workers is nationalisation."

Cleanthes now asks him to explain in detail how a socialist society would work out. Sosiades does so, quite elaborately. There is a good deal of painstaking stuff here—I remember I nearly broke my head over it—about payment by labour-tokens and pricing by labour-hours, the balancing of currency and goods, safeguards against the reintroduction of exploitation, and so on; but what it all boils down to is this. Control, planning and management of industry and trade are in the hands of government officials. Everyone gets a fixed salary on the basis, no doubt with exceptions, of so much for every hour worked. There is some variation in the rate per hour (but within comparatively narrow limits) as between various categories of workers by hand and brain, with the unskilled worker at one end of the scale and various high officials at the other: but not as between individuals *in* a category. The rates are fixed periodically in accordance with the total of available wealth. Officials are democratically elected as follows (I am simplifying): Every shoeshop chooses a head: these heads choose a regional head: and the regional heads choose a national head. So with every other trade, and with doctors, teachers, lawyers and so on; and a similar method is employed for distribution and foreign trade. All these various heads form the cabinet, which has thus been elected by the people as a whole in a far truer sense than at present.

"Such, then, is the society in which all will receive what they have earned by their labour. When everything that now goes to capitalists as rent, interest and profit is added to the workers' wages, only the idle will be poor. Spacious dwellings will rise everywhere in place of slums: squalid alleys will become broad highways: many will leave the grime and smoke, and settle in field or by stream. Beautiful cottages, filled with good things, will climb this very hillock, where a handful of agricultural labourers, paid a few sesterces a week,* now live like animals; and when the west wind brings with it the singing of birds and the smell of cut grass, their hearts will leap up with the pleasure of being alive.

"Nor will bodily goods alone bless the workers, but spiritual and intellectual ones too. I can scarcely restrain my emotion when I think of their condition today: how they labour till nightfall without joy or hope or solace, and so spiritually and intellectually blunted as to have become more like beasts of the field than those divine men and women in whom—yes, in all without exception—God has planted a spark of his own fire. When we have overturned this hoary State of ours and built a new one on its ruins, the greatest of all our glories will be this: that neither hours nor conditions of labour will any longer be such, as to hamper a man's spiritual and intellectual development. The voice of religion will be heard where it must now seem a mockery; the pleasures of literature will have ceased to be the prerogatives of a few; and theatres will have become Temples of Humanity for a whole people, in which men and women, as they sit side by side, may be moved to every generous emotion. Then at last will gracious living and love of beauty be the lords of our republic, not squalor and love of money."

So Sosiades concludes; and he does not speak again. Everyone looks towards Phera. "Her towers were glistening in the sun, and joy seemed everywhere; but we all knew that under the surface were misery and filth." A long silence follows, and then Cleanthes takes up the challenge.

He immediately lays stress on his own sincere sympathy with the workers, while asserting, as a thing he must prove, that they would suffer even more under socialism, and that something far less drastic can make them happier. He dissociates himself completely from Epiondes, "who wishes to keep everything as it is":

* They were paid eighteen shillings at the time I was writing this.

the issue is between Sosiades, "who wishes to change every-thing", and himself "who wishes to make a number of improvements". He and Sosiades are proceeding to the same goal, but by a different route.

After a refutation of the labour theory of value, which is of no interest for my present purpose, and some effective hay-making with Sosiades' differential salaries on grounds of logic, justice and practicability (if, for instance, any differences at all, why only small ones?), Cleanthes proceeds to his two grand arguments. The first concerns the level of production; the second concerns freedom.

If the officials in charge of planning and management at the various levels, he insists, are in receipt of the same modest salaries whatever their efforts, with no prospect of improvement except the sufficiently remote one of sharing, by their own small percentage, in a general and anyhow highly speculative advance, they will feel they have nothing to gain by straining every nerve to make production efficient, in point both of maximum volume and of minimum expense. But if the heads are slack, everything will at once go to pieces; for planning and management will count for far more than the effort of workers by hand. Those in supreme control of the State, moreover, will be much more timid than private individuals in view of their enormous responsibilities; they will hesitate to sanction the employment of improved machines, and "ingenious men", meanwhile, will have very little motive for inventing them. So everything will deteriorate: the movement towards plenty will be reversed: and destitution will seep through the whole body of the republic, instead of being confined, as at present, to one member of it.

But you may object, continues Cleanthes, that the officials will put country before self, and be content with a moderate wage. I shall quote in full his reply to this objection:

"Really? Are you going to change human nature? I don't believe it; for all men are essentially such that no passion is so constant or so strong in them as love of self. It is this that makes us labour day and night, give up pleasure, suffer every worry and inconvenience; and though you can moderate its intensity you can never completely get rid of it. With good reason: for our own personality is so much the centre of existence for us, that we sometimes think of it, not merely as a god looking out on the universe, but as the universe itself. We *know* that we exist: everything else is a matter of opinion."

After this essay in a very primitive kind of liberalism, Cleanthes addresses himself to the working-class aspect of the matter. Here the argument is identical. Where is the incentive for a worker to give of his best if his salary is the same for the same hours of work whatever his application to the task—and when no one, provided he just jogs along, need ever be in fear of the sack? So the rot up above will be paralleled by a rot down below.

Cleanthes now comes to the question of freedom:

"I find it difficult to keep my temper about working-class slavery, which will be far more oppressive and intolerable under your dispensation than under ours. Think of it! Your socialised workers will be forced to obey without question the smallest command of your officials, for, if they once refuse, the whole foundation of your republic will be destroyed. They will often be compelled to leave their homes and migrate to some remote place or other, so that a bigger quantity, say, of ploughs can be produced, or a smaller quantity of spades; and all those links that bind a man to his homestead and neighbourhood will be broken at the nod of an official. The workers, in a word, will become mere machines, every one of them identical with the rest: human beings no longer, but a featureless mass of pawns or automata."

One question remains to be dealt with—that of the highest officials, or, as we should say, of the cabinet. Cleanthes picks up a sentence with which Sosiades had concluded his description of the method of selecting them—"on the virtue and wisdom of these men, vested with supreme power, the fate of the republic will depend"—and comments as follows:

"It will indeed! So much so, that none but the wisest and most experienced ought even to be thought of in connection with so colossal a task. But your men—heavens, what an unbelievable way of selecting them! You may find by such a method the best cobbler, the best butcher, the best clerk; but can't you understand that we're not looking for butchers or clerks to direct our affairs, but for philosophers and statesmen? We want the sharpest wits: we want trained intelligences: we want men with a knowledge of history and an understanding of human nature. And what do you offer us? A college of carpenters and smiths, to whom, by way of balancing their inexperience, you add a few doctors and dentists!"

The dialogue ends with a plea for the middle way:

"Since your promises are so empty, and your dream, even if you could realise it, would mean nothing but unspeakable misery, would it not be wiser to preserve our present system of production, while correcting all those evils that afflict us? The State is like a building for which we have an equal concern; but you are all agog to destroy the foundations, while I would make suitable repairs. 'I know those repairs,' you will say; 'hot fomentations instead of the knife!' Put it in that way if you like; fomentations will at any rate not destroy the whole body, as you would at a stroke. Is this to imply that our sympathy with the workers is any less genuine than yours? Not at all; but sympathy, let me tell you, hasn't blunted our wits. We are hampered in our task by you and your wildness on the one side, by Epiondes and his sloth on the other; but we are determined to follow the path we have entered on, for we believe that thus alone can poverty be banished from the State. No, not banished but lessened; for so long as men remain as they are, there will always be a number who by criminal instincts or weakness bring misery on themselves and others. We go slowly, I confess; but remember that the goal is a distant one, and that there's no short cut to it. I shall not live to see the day when our hopes will have been fulfilled; but that day will surely come, and the world will understand, when it does come, that it was prudence and not timidity that restrained us."

During Cleanthes' last words—

"The sun was setting, and Phera was ablush with its rays. Her myriad voices mingled with the rustling of leaves, and with all the low counterpoint of sounds that hover so sweetly over the countryside. Suddenly a shepherd was heard, leading his oxen to their stalls. We sat for a while in silence; then rose, and returned to the villa."

The contestants in this dialogue, so young, happily young, in many of its details and yet showing every now and again some understanding of the issues involved—except the most import-ant, the basically moral one—are stating a case, and I am not to be imagined as having even so much as sympathised with every argument used during the course of it. My view of human nature, for instance, was very far from being that of Cleanthes, antisocialist though I was. Here, nevertheless—not in one character or the other, but in the clash between them—is a picture of my mind as it warred with itself in the summer of 1913. It is the picture of a liberal horrified by poverty: seeing it as a barrier to the development of personality that liberalism longs for: turning to socialism as the only cure: reacting against socialism as itself inconsistent with the liberal criterion of universal freedom: but fighting an antisocialist battle which, in the very moment of attack, is already regarded as lost. For I cannot read that closing speech of Cleanthes, with its clear low note of sadness and even despair, without hearing it as a swan song.

It would be impossible for me to say, by reference to a particular month or year, when I "became a socialist". The phrase in quotation marks is indeed a misleading one, for it suggests that at some time or other I ceased to be a liberal. This is not so, as I have said. The fact simply is that insensibly, by a continuous, indivisible, moment-by-moment process, my liberalism, which was learning as it went along, unfolded as socialism while remaining liberalism: my kind of socialism, naturally, not anybody's, and always with liberalism as its meaning and essence. You can no more put a date to the winning of particular positions than you can specify the moment at which dawn becomes day. But though my first political job, in 1919, was with the Independent Liberals, and I cannot remember whether I actually called myself a socialist even so late as 1926, when I walked to my office every morning in token of solidarity with the General Strike, I was probably committed to socialism within a year or so of my Latin "Dialogue", and certainly before I went to Repton. It was the socialist in me, as well as the liberal, that thrilled to the Russian Revolution; and I helped in establishing the 1917 Club, which was almost exclusively socialist. (But I avoided the place, as a wretched come-down from the armchairs and fires of the Union. If I went there at all, it was to worship from a distance the most beautiful woman I had ever seen or was ever to see to this day. She was one of those for whom the Hebrew benediction was invented: "Blessed art thou, O Lord our God, King of the Universe, who hast such as these in thy world!" Her name, which I record here in gratitude for such radiance, was Vera Mendel.)

I shall take the opportunity of carrying my "Dialogue on Socialism" a stage further: of looking at socialism from the standpoint, not of an Oxford undergraduate who was aware, forty years ago, that the question was by no means a simple one, but of a now oldish man who is still more alive to its difficulties, and yet utterly convinced, not that socialism alone is the cure for a world racked by suffering, but that without a sort of socialism—the right sort of socialism—no cure is possible. I do not propose anything systematic, or logically planned, or covering the ground, or with all the holes stopped up; I shall say anything that comes into my head in any order, and then get back to Oxford (for I've not yet quite finished with her) when I feel ready. And I daresay I shall deal largely with conflicting goods, and shall raise many more questions than I shall answer.

But first a word or two about "practicality". If you are going to grow up the sort of person who is always saying "we must be practical", "that's all very well, but it can't be done", "what about human nature?" and so on, you had better skip everything that follows and pick me up again when I get back to Oxford—which wasn't "practical" either when I knew it, as I've tried to explain, and I hope still isn't. There is nothing more mean-minded than this cult of a bogus "practicality", and I shall be horrified if you turn out to be addicted to it.

People misuse words so vilely. They call a nation peace-loving if it happens to be backing them in a war. They call a man sentimental if he doesn't talk and behave like a cynic, cynicism being the seediest expression of that emotional shallowness in which sentimentality consists. They talk about toughness when what they mean is brutality. They characterise an attempt to behave like a Christian as soft. If they "believe in" a dogma, such as that of eternal hell, which others may think unreasonable, or an insult to the deity, or both, they describe a sharp integrity in thinking, or an uncompromising refusal to be seduced into immoralities, as woolliness. And to be unpractical, according to this type of terminology, is to take anything but the lowest possible view, which is a false view, of human potentialities, and to go a millimetre outside the radius of what the humdrum take for granted because they've never made the effort to think for themselves.

For God's sake let's get straight about it all, Timothy. To be practical, genuinely practical, is more important than anything else in the world; and what it means is this: to do away with that breach between the so-called ideal and the so-called practical, to abandon that lie at the heart of our living, which has brought us to such a pass that we are busily preparing, at this very moment as I write, for the final practicality of ending human existence by atomic inventions: by inventions which have issued—and here is the heart of the matter, this is the breach to be healed—from that purest, most "ideal" characteristic of human nature, the search after truth. Oh, how can I make you see it? To be practical is to be revolutionary, as the gospels are revolutionary: to turn everything upside down— all the values of this world—as Christ recommended: to rate the first as last, and the last as first: to bring heaven down to earth and take earth up to heaven: to stop fighting against God: to establish the Kingdom. There is no other practicality: everything else is self-contradiction and self-destruction.

CHAPTER XX

# MY SOCIALISM

WHAT A MORNING TO embark on an essay—even a rambling, inconsequential sort of essay—about socialism! For this is the day of which Meredith wrote in *A Diversion Played on a Penny-whistle*:

"Away with Systems! Away with a corrupt World! Let us breathe the air of the Enchanted Island.

"Golden lie the meadows: golden run the streams; red gold is on the pine-stems. The sun is coming down to earth, and walks the fields and the waters.

"The sun is coming down to earth, and the fields and the waters shout to him golden shouts. He comes, and his heralds run before him, and touch the leaves of oaks and planes and beeches lucid green, and the pine-stems redder gold; leaving brightest footprints upon thickly-weeded banks, where the fox-glove's last upper-bells incline, and bramble-shoots wander amidst moist rich herbage. The plumes of the woodland are alight; and beyond them, over the open, 'tis a race with the long-thrown shadows; a race across the heaths and up the hills, till, at the farthest bourne of mounted eastern cloud, the heralds of the sun lay rosy fingers and rest."

That passage has been singing in my head ever since the fine weather started a week or more ago. England in June has dawned upon Ruth and me as fresh as in the days of creation, for this is the first year since 1947 that we have been about our garden at a time when the poppies are in bloom, and the beds on the verge of the daisy-lawn are agleam with mingled lupins and day-lilies, and down near the pond flowers a clump of those little prim irises, called water-irises, that remind me always of the bow in my first love's hair. Those other Junes we have been in America. I feel wonderfully happy to be here now, sitting by the library window and gazing across many-hued greens over to the Berkshire downs: happy, but sad as well, with that sadness inseparable from beauty—from the sight of a beauty which tells us that we are exiles still from our proper

home: and there comes into my head another fragment, which
year after year I have remembered as I have sat in the orchard
with summer already at its height, and have gazed at those
same distant downs through the dappled leaves of the fruit-
laden trees:

σύννομα μᾶλ' ἐσορῶν
τὰν Σικελὰν ἐς ἅλα

I cannot even remember whom the lines are by: Theocritus,
perhaps; or what they mean—though I translate them, maybe
wrongly, "looking over clustering apples, out to the Sicilian
sea". But on a morning like this I should rate even Sicily—even
Palermo by the one sea or Girgenti by the other—as nothing
of an exchange for my Berkshire green.

I had been saving up those Meredith lines for the little description, which I still have in store for you, of Oxford in the
summer of 1914: golden it was, more golden than anything
that had ever happened before, more golden than anything that
has ever happened since: but I could not keep them back any
longer, so have written them down for you at once. And on
this morning of gold how I long to be at play in the garden
instead of writing about Systems: about curing, as speedily as
we may, our so beautiful, our so corrupt world!

And yet it is on just such a day as this, and with just such
emotions as these, that one ought to be writing about socialism.
On a similar morning, a month or so ago, I was riding in a
taxi from Paddington to my office in Henrietta Street; and I
remember thinking, as my eye fell on a down-and-out in
Trafalgar Square, that no one could be a socialist in the fullest
sense, or at any rate in my sense, who did not feel as intensely
as I felt the joy and the wonder of life: so intensely, that a
system which doomed many millions, or many thousands of
millions, to monotonous and poverty-stricken lives, without
access, in the main, to gracious and interesting things, must at
once seem intolerable. I contrasted the day that stretched
before me with the life of a lift-man or miner, a scavenger or
clerk; and I was conscience-stricken at the thought of such a
contrast, as I am conscience-stricken a dozen times a week.
There must always be much sordid and monotonous work to be
got through if the wheels of the world are to turn? Possibly:
though if atomic energy could be used to do it for us instead of

cooking human beings alive or exploding them into dust the problem might be solved. But if tedious and repetitive and even disgusting jobs are inevitable, we should see to it at least that the people employed on them work for far fewer hours, and get far higher pay, than any others: then they would have extra leisure to set against the monotony of their work, and money enough to make the best possible use of it. But capitalism rules otherwise: business men and lawyers—or publishers, for the matter of that—are immensely "better off" in a capitalist society than packers or dustmen.

I say in a capitalist society; but in socialist societies—in societies, that is, which are technically socialist, or technically advancing towards socialism—the same topsy-turvydom exists; and this alone should make you understand how corrupt modern socialism is. The gap between typical incomes—between the incomes, let us say, of a general and a scavenger—is bigger, it appears, in the Soviet Union even than in America itself; and while in Labour Britain the gap is now rapidly diminishing between working-class incomes and the rest, this is largely the result of a mere readjustment as between classes brought about by the exercise of working-class power. The basic point of view—about what should govern the distribution of incomes—is essentially unchanged: for I see no sign of a conception, in circles of the skilled working class (it is almost a class), that the gap between the skilled and the unskilled should at any rate be similarly reduced. Quite the contrary. I happened to be talking at a Labour Party meeting a short time ago while a strike was in progress: its object was to maintain an existing disparity between the skilled and the unskilled (in a particular trade) rather than to benefit the skilled: and I took the opportunity of proclaiming that in a state of society just preceding the abundance of Utopia—I was careful to talk about Utopia, by way of cushioning the shock—dustmen and packers and suchlike would be paid a very great deal more than compositors and engineers, while in Utopia itself everyone would be paid the same. The majority thought it quite a good joke, and laughed appreciatively: a minority clearly thought I was mad. And yet nothing could be more self-evident, to my way of thinking: there is patent injustice in giving more to the skilled than to the unskilled, to the clever than to the dull, for the clever have their cleverness already, and the skilled their skill, as elements of

value in life. To deny that the rule under socialism should be
equality of incomes if there's plenty for everyone, and priority
for dustmen if there isn't, is to show a disastrous misapprehen-
sion of what socialism implies. Or I suppose I oughtn't to say
that, for anybody can call himself a socialist if, on whatever
grounds, he believes in "public ownership of the means of production, distribution and exchange." So for "what socialism
implies" read "what my kind of socialism implies"; and make
a similar emendation, if the context permits, wherever the word
socialism occurs in the rest of this letter.

[I have been discussing all this with my friend Stephen
Appleby-Smythe, the famous Labour Party economist and politician. He "couldn't agree less". He is far from convinced that
equality of incomes (which I learned, I imagine, from Bernard
Shaw, though I should have believed in it anyhow) is even a
thing we should work towards—and of course I'm not saying
more than that we should strive with passionate conviction to
bring it into being at the earliest possible moment. "I still consider," he says in effect, "that Marx and Engels thought most
clearly about all this, and accept their position, namely that we
should aim at abolishing inequality only in the form of *class
privilege*. Then when we've got a classless society—in their definition, not Stalin's—let's see whither humanity will go." (Inci-
dentally, "in their definition, not Stalin's" gives the show away.
Russia exhibits very clearly what can happen to a country when
people are obsessed with the class issue and forget the ultimate
objective.) I rub my eyes. Isn't it good socialist doctrine that in
the final society we shall pay a man "according to his need"?
And must I really explain why? Very well, then: we should pay
a man "according to his need" because that society is best in
which every single member of it is encouraged by his material
circumstances, in so far as his material circumstances can encourage him, to live most abundantly as a creature of God.
Some, no doubt, require more, in a material way, for this
abundance of life, and some less, and in a society marked by
perfect insight more or less would be given accordingly. But
until that stage has been reached, if ever, equality is the only
safe rule—the only thing to aim at: equality in worldly goods,
equality in external instruments for developing the inner personality, equality in everything that human resources can provide: an equality modified, never by inequality in the means to

achieve it, but only, as it may turn out, by inevitable variations in physical or spiritual or intellectual endowments.]

I have slid accidentally into this talk about equality of incomes—or perhaps not so accidentally, because belief in it is the test, in my opinion, of a genuine socialist faith; and having done so I may as well reply at once to an objection I am certain will be raised. Some, no doubt, will agree with me that the final society will be characterised by "to each according to his need"; but haven't I forgotten, they will ask, that "to each according to his work" is a necessary transitional stage? Well, I might take the objection more seriously if I saw any indication that equality for all—hard monetary equality, not equality of opportunity—really was any longer the goal, however distant, of socialist endeavour. But I see nothing of the kind: I see the opposite. Whether in Russia, which calls itself socialist, or in England under a labour dispensation, people are constantly declaring, as I read in the papers, that "socialism doesn't mean equality"; and it is clear from the context that they are talking about monetary equality, and referring, not to any transitional stage, but to the final one. When they say things like this they show that they are socialists no longer. They have grown weary as the years have gone by, and the vision has faded. A few, here and there, still profess the ideal of equalitarianism, but for the most part with lip-service only: how rare to find a man who believes in it with a passion that informs his whole life! People often remark that everyone is a socialist today: this is a lie: they might say far more truly that socialism is in danger of extinction, with totalitarianism in attack on the one side, and ameliorative social reform—very valuable in itself, but not socialism—on the other.

But suppose I am wrong: suppose people who call themselves socialists really still do believe that an ultimate equality is desirable: is it true, then, that "to each according to his work" is a necessary step on the road to this goal, or the best possible method of winning it? Let us examine the argument. The prerequisite for an equalitarian society, it begins, is plenty. But you will not get plenty, it continues, unless everybody strains every nerve; and no one will strain every nerve unless he sees that it pays him to do so. Very well then, it concludes, bribe him; for that is what it amounts to when stripped of its camouflage of justice, this slogan of "to each according to his work". Do you recognise the argument, my dear Timothy? You heard it only half an hour ago. From my socialist Sosiades? Not at all: from my liberal Cleanthes, in his attack on the whole socialist position.

There are two separate assumptions in this argument. The first is that a man will not give of his best unless he is bribed to do so; and the second is that you can usher in an equalitarian society (or a society based on public service, or calculated to encourage altruism, or describable in any way as decent or Christian) by appealing more and more insistently meanwhile to the motive of self-interest. Both assumptions are false.

The first of them, the old Cleanthes argument, three quarters of me, nine tenths of me, knew to be false when I put it into the mouth of my character: no, the whole of me: and if I made use if it then, this was partly for debating reasons, and partly because it expressed, in a highly erroneous form, my belief at the time that socialism as such was a deadening thing, and that all individual initiative, all the thrust and drive and eagerness of self-expression, must inevitably be shackled by it. If I erred at all when young in what I really believed about human nature my error was on the other side: I believed too naïvely that all men were in essence good and peaceable and altruistic, absolutely and exclusively so, and that you only had to free them from the dead-weight of accumulated traditions, from all those influences and institutions of society which interfered with the spontaneity of their development, to bring their latent original virtue into actuality. This belief lay at the back of my work with the boys at Repton, to which I shall presently return, and the success of it proved conclusively, at any rate to my own satisfaction, that my view had a great deal of truth in it, was far better based than cynics and sceptics might believe. I was in fact Rousseauite, far more Rousseauite than Pauline, in those days, and this in spite of my own sense of sin and my own guilty conscience. Life, and a growth of knowledge about myself and others, have taught me that the facts of human nature are very much more complex than I had imagined. But I still believe passionately that though good and evil, not accidentally and environmentally only but originally also, are both very strong in us all, the good is so much stronger than the evil, so much stronger in its own right,

by reason of its very nature as something positive and meaningful and light-bringing, that if only you appeal to it wholeheartedly enough, with no admixture of baseness in your
appeal, it can conquer and banish the evil by its own inherent
goodness; and when this has been done the evil will be seen as
having only that measure of reality—a measure of reality I by
no means deny—such as exists in a terrible fear that is afterwards shown to have been baseless. In one sense the fear is
real, more appallingly real at the time than anything else in
the world, and I have very good reason for knowing it: but it
is a fear, for all that, about something that has no existence:
and being about the non-existent and unreal, being based on,
all mixed up with, non-existence and unreality, in that sense
it has no reality itself. And while life has taught me how
powerful is evil, in the sense I have tried to describe, it has also
taught me on a thousand occasions, and in big things as well as
in small, that the appeal to good can be far more compulsive,
can be far more successful in eliciting good and banishing its
opposite, than I had dared to imagine even in my Rousseauite
days; or rather I imagined it then, but know it now. My experience with Germany in the immediate post-war years would
have banished any doubt in the matter, had it existed. And if
you knew what I know: if you had read the many hundreds of
letters that Germans, "hardened" Nazis among them, wrote to
me at the time of our Save Europe Now campaign, any scepticism you for your part may have in the matter would immediately be at an end. As a Jew I had felt that these Germans,
active Jew-baiters included, were also my brothers, and that I
must do them such service as I could; and they understood
what I was doing, and why I was doing it, with an immediacy
of knowledge very different from the bogus reality of their
febrile adherence to Nazism. So the good in them responded.
And remember that I am a very ordinary person, very weak
and fallible and with a great deal of wickedness in me. Imagine,
up against Hitler, for instance, a man of real spiritual power!
Imagine not me: not George Lansbury, who once tried to plead
with him: not even Gandhi. Imagine Christ!

I am convinced, then, that old Cleanthes was wrong, and
that whatever they may do for self-interest people will work
their heads off in the public service and to benefit humanity as
a whole, if only the right appeal is made to them and made to

them in the right way. But when it's made at all nowadays it's commonly made in the wrong way and with the wrong motives. For the appeal, to be effective, must be made with a real belief in its efficacy, and must be made without compromise: not wishy-washily, not in a half and half fashion, not with a lavish admixture of appeals to self-interest ("Do it because it's right: do it because it will help others: but remember that it will also help you."). Just as we cannot *nearly* be Christians, so a qualified altruism is not altruism at all. These are matters of a hundred per cent. The essence of altruism is its absoluteness. Appeal to it absolutely, and its absoluteness has a chance of responding: appeal simultaneously to self-interest, and self-interest alone can respond, for you have established no contact with altruism. Moreover, you must patently be attempting to alter those conditions, in your society and the world, the very existence of which, *unless* you are attempting to alter them, must make nonsense of your appeal. It is no good a rich man appealing for altruism to a poor man, while clearly unprepared to make the heaviest sacrifices himself: if you talk to a man about the sacredness of freedom in a prison, you must forgive him for being sceptical. And when you appeal for public service and the good of humanity it is these that you must really be after, if people are to be moved by you: not your own private gain, not a class advantage, not "the national interest"—that subtlest of disguises in which selfishness masquerades as altruism. All of which is another way of saying that statesmen and journalists (and anybody else with access to the public ear) must become a little less like statesmen and journalists, and a little more like prophets.

But nowadays, whether in Russia with its so-called marxism on the one hand, or in England with its democratic socialism on the other, it's not even a question, by and large, of the right sort of appeal being made in the wrong sort of way: for there can rarely have been a time when the appeal, to the working class at least, has been more openly and insistently in terms of self-interest. Consider, in Russia, Stakhanovism. Somebody produces more than the average: he is rewarded accordingly—with money, not with honour and decorations alone, which would be bad enough: others are encouraged to emulate him: so a few grow as wealthy as film stars, while, down at the other end of the scale, charwomen, let us say, can hardly get enough to keep

alive on. The theory is that they are working, these Stakhano-
vites, for their country, and that being of such value in con-
solidating socialism they deserve to be conspicuously enriched.
Can you imagine a more ludicrous paradox? Or a piece of more
distasteful hypocrisy? If service to their country were really their
motive would it be necessary to bribe them with money? And it
isn't a matter only of Stakhanovism: the whole system of production in Russia is based upon bribery and fear.

Things are not as bad in England, not as bad by a long chalk,
but they are bad enough. I don't know whether I am right in
detecting an immense proliferation nowadays of piece-work,
payment by results, and all the other devices which we regarded
in my youth as typical of capitalist degradation—and correctly:
for they rob an artisan of his professionalism, reducing everything to the level of cash. But I am sure that socialists in office
show a tendency to rely on these devices such as formerly they
would have regarded as alien to the socialist spirit: that their
policy is to bribe: and that bribery is bribery, irrespective of
whether the bribers are capitalists who are bribing in the
interest of profit, or directors of socialist policy who are bribing
in the interest of general prosperity. If you are to bribe at all,
it is better, no doubt, to have "socialist" than capitalist bribery,
for the motive—the motive of the bribers—is a better one; but
that is not at the moment my point. Isn't it even possible that
during the worst of the pre-war years the working class, on the
whole, showed a greater generosity of motive, in a groping sort
of fashion, than they are showing today? There were vile incentives, of which the vilest, with unemployment widespread, was
fear of the sack; but there was also, quite often, a sense of pride
in the job, and a loyalty to the firm, which I find growing rarer
today. Such loyalty was by no means of a kind to be welcomed
without qualification: frequently it had more in common with
the kow-towing gesture of yokel to squire than with a dignified
and self-respecting equality. But at the bottom of it, for all
that, was an element of something other-regarding. A sense of
public service should have taken its place: I cannot see that it
has done so. I am far from blaming the working class for all
this: the history of its exploitation must be taken into account,
and how can you respond to an appeal never made to you? I
blame the politicians and journalists. For they do not content
themselves with indirect appeals to self-interest by the whole

machinery of piece-work, heavy overtime rates, and the rest: the appeal is often blatantly direct. Here are a couple of examples that come to my mind as I write, and I could find you hundreds more if I looked up my files. A year or so ago, on the occasion of some legislative change—I cannot remember what it was, but it may have been the budget—the *Daily Herald* came out with a huge banner headline, in letters half an inch high, on its opening page: a five-word headline, with one of the words, as I remember, heavily underscored: WHAT IT MEANS TO YOU. And the *Daily Herald* is something more than just a socialist paper, it is the only official one. The thing hit me in the face as I read it with the force of a blow or a vulgar insult; and a vulgar insult it was, an insult to the whole working class. Earlier, when Englishmen had to be told that they must forego any hope of an immediate rise in the standard of living, even Sir Stafford Cripps made essentially the same appeal. What he said in effect was this: "I ask you to give things up. Why? Because you'll get all the more, if you do so, in a few years' time". The speeches of Sir Stafford Cripps, taken as a whole, give a fascinating illustration of what happens to a man when he wins high office in the atmosphere of modern materialism. He is a genuine socialist, and a Christian-in-action of a type very rare among statesmen; and often, in the House of Commons or elsewhere, he has ended what he has had to say with an appeal to the best in his hearers. But these perorations, in which the real Cripps is speaking, always seem incongruously tacked on; in the body of his speeches there is usually an appeal to something lower than the best, almost as if that were an obvious necessity of practical politics—and then comes the afterthought. The only prominent politician of our day who has consistently and uncompromisingly made the Christian and socialist appeal is Sir Richard Acland.

["All this business about bribery," says Appleby-Smythe, "is really astonishing! Why is it bribery to pay A $2x$ if he chooses to work either twice as fast or twice as long as B who is paid $x$? Why shouldn't the consumer be given the choice of having leisure or commodities in any ratio he chooses?" This sounds very clear-headed, but isn't; it's really quite specious. The basic facts are (*a*) that you passionately *want* the man to work harder; and (*b*) that he *ought* to work harder, as things are, in the interests of society: and you assume he'll work harder only if

you make it "worth his while". So you make it worth his while.
What on earth is that but bribery? What has it to do with the
socialist motive of public service? "Anyhow," retorts Appleby-
Smythe, a bit irritated, "you can't have democratic socialism
without—what you call bribery. The alternative is totalitarianism. If you don't 'bribe' you must compel." Well, that's to beg
the whole question of human nature, already, for the time
being, disposed of.]

So the first of the assumptions that seek to justify bribery as
a means of transition to equalitarianism—the assumption that
men will work at their hardest only if moved by self-interest—
derives from a view of human nature which experience, or
mine at least, has shown to be false. The second of these
assumptions—that a society to be based on public service can
be brought into being by appeals in the meantime, ever increasingly reiterated, to personal greed—also derives from a fallacy
about human nature, but from almost an opposite one. If it is
true that the more you appeal to the best the more you are likely
to elicit the best, it is equally true that the more you give play to
the worst the more you are likely to strengthen the worst. Sudden reversals in a settled way of feeling are rare: character, for
the most part, is a matter of year by year, hour by hour, minute
by minute development: and thoughts and emotions persisted in
become more and more fixed as a pattern. There is a time in
most people's lives when an inner conflict between selfishness
and selflessness is either constantly or spasmodically proceeding;
and each of us knows, knows as a matter of immediate experience, that, every time selfishness wins, its victory on a subsequent
occasion is made a little more probable thereby. So almost
insensibly a man becomes, not what he might have been, but
what he is. If, therefore, the entire community grows more and
more accustomed to putting private interests first: if struggling
to get the most for onself becomes more and more taken for
granted as the natural way of life: if speeches, sermons, details
of the system, the sanction of public opinion all combine more
and more effectively to represent that struggle as proper or at
least as inevitable—is it credible that such a community should
pass into its very opposite, into one where above everything
"the most for oneself" is tabu? It is as if you expected a forest,

leaning uniformly westward as the result of a century's winds, suddenly to find itself leaning eastward when the westward inclination had gone far enough.

Reflect on that simile, I beg you, because the truth it illuminates is the very pith and core of everything I shall be saying in what I fear will be this very long chapter. Nothing could be more disastrous than to consider socialism, socialism as a political and economic system, in isolation from the people who will be operating it. For while a good system, a good piece of social machinery, can make it easier for men to be good, yet unless men are good the best of all possible systems can be used for the vilest of ends, with, in that event, a worsening instead of a bettering of human behaviour over the entire field as an inevitable result. In the present context, people who have grown increasingly accustomed to think in terms of self-interest, and to make others think in them, are unsuitable stuff, whether as leaders or rank and file, for any valuable sort of socialist society: including trades-union officials of petty-capitalist mentality, and those ordinary men and women who, in a corrupt atmosphere, may regard the Welfare State as merely a device for getting something, and not, what it should be, as that minimum basis of well-being which alone can enable them to give themselves in the service of all.

This vicious circle that we've suddenly come up against—no good men without good use of a good system, no good use of a good system without good men—and its allied one—how introduce a good system at all unless men are already good enough to want it?—is the fundamental problem of organised society. I shall have a good deal to say about it later; I will say only one thing now. See to it, as you get power and opportunity to introduce each new bit of machinery, that you foster the spirit this machinery is intended to serve and not its opposite.


So much for equal incomes, differentiation in favour of scavengers, and various questions arising therefrom. Except perhaps this—about "practicalities". It's not a question, as I've said, of equalising everybody's income, in the England of today, overnight: it's a question of whether we think such equality proper, and test every bit of relevant legislation, every appeal we may make, every effect we may have on the spiritual and intellectual climate, by the criterion "Will it help, or will it not, in establishing an egalitarian society?" There will be other criteria as well, but this is a vital one; and we must refuse to be put off it for a moment by chatter about our economic crisis, or to fall for the propositions that (a) we'll get increased production only by appealing to greed, and (b) we'll put an end to our crisis only by increased production (an argument that will have been blown sky high long before you come to read this letter, though you'll still have a crisis). Clause (a) is untrue; as to clause (b), people would realise, if once they could stop being obsessed by the next half-hour, that our economic crisis is a world crisis or more truly a world problem, being the problem of malproduction and maldistribution in the world as a unit: that it is therefore a continuing crisis: that it can be solved in the long run only by an international socialism that will solve everyone else's too: and that it *ought* to be solved only on the basis of "fair shares" as between nation and nation and with no question of our maintaining a favoured position, and so only in an international setting. Attempts to reach a solution on obsessively nationalist lines are grotesque as well as wicked. Cut your imports, expand your exports, that is the cry; and when everybody else follows suit a lot of quite clever people seem flabbergasted. I shouldn't be surprised if the thing started presently within the Commonwealth itself: just as, or so I'm told, we are at the moment making our own atom bombs at enormous expense, because we don't really trust even our ally America when it comes to it. Marxists are quite right when they talk about the contradictions of capitalism; only they don't understand that capitalist and pseudo-socialist contradictions are not merely a matter of mechanics, but symptoms of a profound moral disturbance.

There is an awful lot of humbug, anyhow, about this crisis. Whose crisis? The overwhelming majority of Englishmen are immeasurably better off than in 1851, when the Great Exhibition was signalising our "prosperity": and within a few years of which a county magistrate was describing in Nottingham how "children of nine or ten were dragged from their squalid beds at two, three or four o'clock in the morning and compelled to work for a bare subsistence until ten, eleven or twelve at night—their limbs wearing away, their frames dwindling, their faces whitening, and their humanity absolutely sinking into a stone-like torpor utterly horrible to contemplate". You often hear people explaining how dreadfully the working class will suffer if the crisis isn't solved, owing to the resulting unemployment (which isn't at all improbable): and saying in the very next breath that they could do with a taste of unemployment, to make them work harder. I listened to all this only a few nights ago at an otherwise very agreeable dinner-party.

With so much by way of introduction, I shall talk a bit now about socialism under three main headings—socialism and poverty, socialism and freedom, socialism and goodness; though there's bound to be a lot of overlapping, as it will all be in fact about freedom.

> *Brimpton, Saturday, June 16th*
> *One of the pleasures of a garden is its unexpectednesses, when you get back to it again from a Monday to Friday in London. I am not thinking of what you might call the ordinary new things that are suddenly blooming after a week's interval but have been forgotten about since last year: all the purples and blues, for example —the veronicas, and grandiflora geraniums, and tradescantias with paint-blobs of gold, that are everywhere round me as I stroll about lazily, unable to begin the day's work: but I have seen, with a stab of quite different surprise, a many-branched clump of sweet-william. Its tufts of strong hair are still almost entirely green; but on five of them a single white flower, all crumpled before unfolding, brings the colour of July to my eyes and its smell to my nostrils. And on one of these little white packets a lady-bird is resting.*
>
> *It is odd that, as the weeks go by, I find it more and more difficult to get on with the main body of this book unless I write something first about the garden. Or perhaps it isn't odd: perhaps this is like starting one's morning prayers, as one always should, with Hallel—with thanks and praise. Anyhow, a bit about the garden appears to release something in me; and reluctance to sit down at my desk is suddenly replaced by desire to press forward.*

## § 1. SOCIALISM AND POVERTY

When I declaimed against poverty at the beginning of this chapter, I was clearly assuming that you couldn't cure it without socialism. I must now try to prove this; otherwise Cleanthes, or a Cleanthes with more valid arguments, is in possession of the field. But first I must deal with a red herring, a *soi-disant* religious red herring, about poverty itself.

Last Christmas I wrote, in collaboration with John Collins, a pamphlet called "Christianity and the War Crisis". It began with a description of what an atomic war might be like, and then came the following passage: "We are not going to say that, awful though this physical agony would be, more awful still would be the spiritual corruption. We are not going to say it, because no word of ours shall suggest that there can be anything worse than broken bodies and smashed faces and torn nerves and the final pangs of hunger. We shall simply say that the spiritual corruption must also be reckoned with." The *Catholic Herald*, which I usually admire, suggested in effect that there was something materialistic and irreligious in putting physical evils, however extreme, on a par with spiritual ones. The writer's sensitiveness escapes me. We were speaking, John and I, primarily about extremities of pain: but what we said about extremities of pain applies equally to extremities of poverty: and when comfortable people, making a much-needed stand, as they may imagine, for spiritual values, attack socialism as materialistic because it talks so much about things of the body, I confess I turn a bit sick. You know very well, from what I have written in this very chapter to say nothing of what has preceded it, that as a socialist I am mainly concerned, when one comes to finalities, with the spiritual unfolding of a man's whole personality; but quite apart from the fact that a sense of bodily well-being can not only mediate spirituality but in a fully integrated life can and does become fused with it, can and does become itself spirituality, the point of course is this: for the mass of human beings, a constant background of poverty, hunger, filthy conditions and worry about the future is wholly incompatible with spiritual development: just as a man does not think about God when a nerve is being severed without anaesthesia (I give this example because I once had it done to me at Salzburg), whatever he may have thought about before or may think about after. I doubt whether there are any but the rarest exceptions to this rule, so far as moments of the acutest pain and hunger are concerned: then, there must nearly always be an utter absorption in physical sensations, or virtual

unconsciousness. When a more general background of less violent agonies is in question there may indeed be quite numerous
exceptions: I saw people in Germany who were showing themselves better than their best in conditions (but for a year or so,
not for a lifetime) of lingering hunger. It might be thought, also,
that the extremer austerities of hermits and monks, whose spiritual life has been developed not in spite but by means of these
austerities, disproves my point. But this is not so. They have been
people of a particular temperament, who have deliberately
chosen a particular method for achieving their spiritual aims;
and have used it in so far, but only in so far, as these aims would
be furthered by it. No parallel can be drawn between people
such as these and those of a quite different temperament who
are forced into a poverty that is none of their choosing. And we
are talking, in any event, not about rare individuals, but, to
take an example, about millions upon millions of starving
Chinese.

Christ, who knew everything, is the safest guide for us here. In
some words that he uttered at a moment of quite central significance—a moment between the wilderness and Calvary, a moment
to be understood, not only in the light of the Cross, but in the
light, just as much, of his having chosen a path that must lead to
the Cross—he tells us very clearly that physical suffering, considered in itself, is a thing to be avoided if it may be. When he
prayed in the garden, he did not simply say "Thy will be done":
he said "O my Father, if it be possible, let this cup pass from me;
nevertheless not as I will, but as thou wilt." He was referring, if
we may dare to interpret him, to a future experience of spiritual
dereliction: but to an experience, none the less, that would
come to him, as he knew, through the medium of physical
suffering.

None of this is to deny that hunger or pain can be, on occasion, not merely neutral in their effect on people's living, but
positive sources of spiritual good—the extremes of them very
rarely, the lesser forms of them in the case of a larger minority.
It might even be said that when pain, experienced by humanity
as evil, coincides with a heroic and self-forgetful bearing of it,
something is present in the coincidence which intimates dimly,
as perhaps nothing else can, that our evil, like Blake's destructive sword, is but a portion of eternity too great for the eye of
man. So Christ, having prayed that the cup might pass from

him, triumphed on the Cross; so Beethoven, out of his agony at
Heiligenstadt, wrote by far the greatest music, and among it the
most serene, that the world has ever known; so sufferers from the
hell of cancer may sometimes show us, by their physical courage
and spiritual courtesy in moments of all but the acutest suffering,
what heaven really means. But does that absolve us for a moment
from the duty of making cancer impossible? Blake, who justified
the destructive sword, was the same Blake who asked:

> "Can I see another's grief,
> And not seek for kind relief?"

We should indeed at once identify ourselves with others in
this matter, and differentiate ourselves from them. Suffering,
though never to be sought, should be regarded, if it comes to
ourselves, as an opportunity; but in the case of another we
should think of it as wholly evil—should endeavour to experience the sum total of it, by a compassionate sympathy, in our
own person, and then, made active by imagination, struggle
with all our power to relieve him of it. This, and not a sermonising religiosity about the wickedness of putting physical
evils on a level with spiritual ones, is the truly religious attitude.

I had a thrill of rather malicious delight when, a few days
after reading that review in the *Catholic Herald*, I came across
this paragraph by the Catholic Coventry Patmore:

" 'I cannot help thinking,' said General Gordon, 'that the
body has much to do with religion.' Here spoke the man of
saintly life, who had attained to an obscure Catholic apprehension, without knowing it, of the mystery which is celebrated in
the Feasts of the Assumption and Corpus Christi. And, in
answer to the question, 'Is life worth living?' the cynic replies,
'That depends on the *liver*.' He would probably be greatly surprised at hearing that his pun, meant to be wicked, is fully
justified by the teaching of St. Thomas Aquinas, who declares
that the life of contemplation, which is the discernment of God
by the spiritual senses, and which he also declares to be the only
'life worth living', cannot co-exist with any present sensible
trouble."

Coventry Patmore, and apparently Aquinas, go a little further
than I would, but I am glad to be, in general, confirmed by
them.

*Sunday, June 17th*

*My five little flowers have uncrumpled, and are now lying flat
in the sun, with violet at their centres; and not a single green tuft
but is speckled with pushings of white.*

And now, having got rid of the religious red herring, I must
prove my contention about socialism as a cure for poverty. But
you must understand clearly what it is that I am trying to prove.
(1) I am talking, for the moment, simply about the cure of
poverty as such, not about the creation of a good society, which
is a larger question; (2) I am suggesting, not that socialism is
certain to cure it, for I think nothing of the kind, but that
socialism is the *sine qua non* for its cure; (3) by socialism I mean,
at this stage, the indispensable machinery of socialism and nothing more—what Sir Richard Acland used to call common
ownership of "the great productive resources" of a country.

Or, put more fully: an indispensable *condition* for the existence
of a good society is the abolition of poverty: poverty cannot be
abolished without the introduction of socialist machinery: it *can*
be abolished by the use of socialist machinery: and it *will* be
abolished if, but only if, a number of conditions other than the
introduction of socialist machinery are also fulfilled. Chief among
these are (1) an initial determination to use this machinery for
the purpose in question, and (2) a progressive lessening (or sublimation) of that selfishness, aggression, and lack of imaginative
sympathy with others which, given the undeniable fact that we
now have the technical means for abolishing poverty, is the cause
of its continued existence: a lessening or sublimation which
the introduction of socialist machinery can itself facilitate, but
also—and this is crucially important—can do no more than
facilitate. All this may sound very tentative and complicated;
but the establishment on earth of the Kingdom of Heaven is
no easy affair.

The poverty in question is world poverty: it is world poverty
that, I have been saying, cannot be cured without socialism.
Forget, for a moment, England: forget Europe and the United
States: consider, if you have the imagination to do so, the condition of humanity as a whole. If you have the imagination to
do so: for few of us can get outside our little streets, our little
rooms, our little moments, and attempt to gather up into our

own beings, as if we were God, the agony of the world. It wouldn't be a bad idea, sometimes, really to imagine that we were God: this might help us to realise, if only for a second, both our utter insignificance and our terrible responsibility. I spent a wretched afternoon and evening yesterday, unable to get on with this letter, unable to read office manuscripts, horribly ashamed of my stuff about the garden and a lady-bird and sweet-williams. The newspapers, page after page, and the wireless, minute by minute, conjured up the picture of a world that was stark with suffering. In China the communists had just held a series of mass trials for "counter-revolutionary" offences, and had sentenced hundreds to be executed on the spot and hundreds more to be done away with in a year or two's time—while thousands sat around and yelled for vengeance. In South Korea, the chairman of a committee of the National Assembly had reported that 50,000 South Korean conscripts had died from starvation and disease in military camps since December: that several thousand more had deserted rather than face death in the camps: that 80 per cent of the fewer than 350,000 survivors were physical wrecks, incapable of working: and that during three weeks of a "death-march" 300,000 men had deserted or died along the way. In India, a former secretary of the Congress Party had painted an appalling picture of general misery: "there was no relief," he had said, "even in the primary needs of the people for food, clothing and shelter." In Hungary "whole families at a time, with old people and children included, are being transported by cattle trucks to concentration camps. These are said to conform to the pattern stamped on Europe's memory by the Nazis, with a few refinements introduced, such as the refusal to provide food unless the prisoners pay by selling their few transportable possessions." From column after column of another newspaper emerged a hint of conditions in Africa, or parts of it, a good deal less bearable than the better-kept slavery of Greece or Rome. All this on a single day. Well, inhumanities such as these, which are merely the selected items that wireless and press think worth bothering about for their value as sensational news, are perhaps not too difficult to visualise—to think yourself and feel yourself into—for they stare you in the face from the columns of print. But I tell you this: that these things are nothing, nothing at all from the statistical point of view, when compared with that day by day, hour by hour, moment

by moment misery of world-wide hunger and disease which is
so completely taken for granted that it rarely even enters our
thoughts.

"If you are born coloured [as are over two thirds of all man-
kind]," wrote Stringfellow Barr recently in his pamphlet *Let's
Join the Human Race*, "the chances are overwhelming that you
will be chronically sick all your life—from malaria, or intestinal
parasites, or tuberculosis, or maybe even leprosy. You have
a reasonably good chance of suffering famine—to the point that
you will be glad to eat the bark off a tree. But this chance is
extremely hard to calculate. You have only a one-in-four chance
of learning to read. You are most likely to live in a mud hut,
with a dirt floor and no chimney, its roof thatched with straw."
And here are a couple of details, taken at random. Fifty per
cent of Chinese mortality is directly or indirectly caused by
chronic malnutrition; and in Cuba a family of five has to live on
a daily energy total sufficient only for one.

But perhaps Cuba and China seem very remote? Perhaps you
think, which God forbid, that the coloured, after all, don't
suffer like whites? Then go to a public library and have a look
at some volume that describes how people live in Southern
Italy, by our own Mediterranean Sea. If you want a single
round figure, take it that out of the two thousand two hundred
million human beings now alive in the world more than a thousand five hundred million are hungry.

And do not imagine that things are improving. The contrary
is the case. Population is increasing appallingly; and it is a
measure of our blasphemous mishandling of the world's affairs
that I must use the word "appallingly" in such a connection—
must use it of the coming into existence of more and more
human beings who might enjoy the beauty of earth and the
miracle of living. Do you remember what I wrote about
vegetarianism—how the real argument in favour of it was that
by killing animals for our own selfish pleasure we were diminishing the chorus of praise? And now I must describe as appalling an increase in the birth-rate, not of animals that we
slaughter for food, but of men and women, a little lower than
the angels, whom we suffer to die of starvation. But it *is* appalling, for the gap between world population and world food
supplies is constantly widening, and the situation, even by the
time you are old enough to read this letter, will be very much

more disastrous even than it is at present, as Lord Boyd Orr, and so many others, have repeatedly warned us. Unless we do something about it.

We *can* do something about it. Here, from people of unquestionable authority, are two categorical statements. The first is by Dr Charles Kellogg, Director of Soil Survey in the United States Department of Agriculture. The second is from a Uno report, entitled *Measures for the Economic Development of Under-Developed Countries*:

"The scientific evidence leads to the view that the world has enough resources for its food supply, provided modern methods are used generally for systems of sustained production."

"The belief that economic development must inevitably be dissipated in population growth causes pessimism in some quarters. We do not share this view. . . . The problem is difficult but it is not insoluble."

I am no expert on this subject, which is an exceedingly complicated one. I do not know what may be the limit of possibilities. I could not say how, when world standards are raised, the resulting shortage of raw materials will be remedied —though presumably, if we become sane, by the inventive ingenuity which is at present devising new weapons of destruction. I am certain that birth-control must have a place in any reasonable programme: while suspecting, though there are differences of opinion on the subject, that higher standards of living would lower *ipso facto* the birth-rate. But that the possibilities—of abolishing hunger by positive economic development—are immense I have no doubt whatever.

That, then, is the situation. It is not a question of this or that country abolishing poverty within its own frontiers, irrespective of what is happening elsewhere. Individual countries, or groups of countries, might be able to do so, may even already have done so, and could conceivably maintain, more or less permanently, a decent way of living for all; but apart altogether from the close interlocking of economies in the modern world, which means that, by and large, what happens in one place vitally affects what will happen everywhere else, it is surely obvious that the vast backward areas can be given even a moderate prosperity only by the deliberate aid of the more favoured ones: only if the latter, whose resources are relatively enormous, will employ them for the abolition of other people's poverty at sacrifice, meanwhile, to themselves. And don't be deceived, once again, by our "disastrous economic crisis" into forgetting that England, to say nothing of the British Empire, is relatively so prosperous that to complain of our difficulties is an insult to millions who are starving. The Statistical Office of the United Nations, analysing the income of seventy countries in 1949, found the average income per head in the United Kingdom to be fourteen times what it was in South and South-east Asia; it also found that the nineteen richest countries with only sixteen per cent of the population enjoyed just over sixty-six per cent of the total income, while the fifteen poorest countries, with just over fifty per cent of the population, had to live on less than nine per cent of the total income. Those are the types of fact you must either face or, if you think fit, shut your eyes to: you can't explain them away.

And do not forget, either, what sort of aid it is that the situation requires. Not charity: not wholesale investment, placed with one eye, or both, on the profit of the investor—though a measure of investment, without the motive of profit, will be necessary: but the right kind of technical assistance, and large-scale provision for the expansion of educational facilities and social services. To help these areas develop themselves—and many of them have very rich resources—that alone must be our aim.

First, then, it is a question of a great concerted, unselfish, world-wide attack on hunger and disease. Secondly, there are the strongest grounds for believing that the attack can be carried through with at any rate a measure of success.

Now is it conceivable that a really effective part could be played in this attack by any country with a capitalist machinery of production? That a single-minded, unwavering effort could be made by such a country—for nothing less compulsive would succeed, given the immensity of the task—and carried through to the end: to the end, not of the diminution, in greater or lesser degree, of disgraceful conditions, but of their total abolition? For this must be our aim, whatever our degree of success.

It is inconceivable, for two reasons. To begin with, the very existence of a capitalist machinery of production means that men in the mass must instinctively think first of their own advantage, not of some starving Malay: this is the mental climate, the ubiquitous background of their lives: and though they may to some extent modify their self-regarding habit of thought, they cannot, unless they are of a very exceptional type, substitute for what is almost necessarily their ruling motive a diametrically opposite one. Understand clearly, please, what I am saying. I am not referring at this point (though I shall do so later) to men's "private" lives: I am referring to how, whatever their function or class, they cannot help but relate themselves to the *processes of production* by which they earn their living.

If only, therefore, by reason of the ruling psychology, it is quite inconceivable that a capitalist country could play any decisive part in the abolition of world hunger. But it is inconceivable for another reason too, and not a psychological but a mechanical one. Our hypothetical plan for the development of backward areas requires a planned employment of the whole buying, producing, and distributing machinery of a country, in concert with that of other countries, for the end in view. How can that be done if capitalists, intent on profit, are competitively in control of the various separate bits of this machinery? The impossibility is obvious: need I argue it?

So I hope I may take my case as proved: I hope we may agree that without the introduction of socialist machinery no country can play a really effective part in the abolition of world hunger. But I must remind you at this point—it is vital for my argument as a whole—that this isn't at all the same thing as saying that our socialist machinery will necessarily be used for the purpose I have just been describing.

For clearly it can be used—nationalisation and the rest—for very different ends. It can be used, internally, for either the power or the enrichment, or both, of a ruling clique (which can become a class) governmental or managerial in character; and for the consequent enslavement of those wretched men and women whom marxists are so fond of describing, and who under totalitarian conditions can be so aptly described, as "the toiling masses". The machinery of socialism, in other words, can serve as the instrument of a tyranny viler than capitalism could ever have imposed. It can be used, again, not for bringing aid to others, but as a peculiarly efficient engine in the preparation of aggressive war. It can be used, finally, "for the national interest":

for increasing prosperity at home, with juster distribution and
"fairer shares" for all, but without consideration of appalling
conditions elsewhere, and sometimes at the cost of intensifying them. And these three evil purposes can be variously
combined.

"Evil purposes", I call them; and evil they all are, though in
different degrees—the first two wholly evil, the third half evil
and half good. That we should distribute more justly, using
socialist machinery to do so, is obviously good: that we should
concentrate on national prosperity, instead of genuinely
thinking in terms of mankind as a whole—genuinely, for self-
deception is easier in this context than in almost any other ("a
model for the world", "we must be careful not to jeopardise
our own unique socialist experiment", and so on)—is as
obviously, or ought to be as obviously, evil. It is a pity that the
expression "national socialism" has become identified with the
villainies of the Third Reich: otherwise there could be no better
description of what, if not the vilest perversion of genuine socialism, is the one we have to guard against most vigilantly in the
case of our own country. As I think I mentioned before, people
have sometimes wondered why, having longed so passionately
for the triumph of Labour in 1945, I have criticised it so unspar-
ingly ever since. Well, there were several considerations which,
shortly after I had finished my Dialogue on Socialism in 1913,
were committing me, as a liberal, more and more definitely to
the socialist position. Some of them I shall deal with later in this
chapter, though one of them was to become decisive only in view
of the world economic crisis of 1929, the rise of Nazism, and the
international developments that followed. But already in 1914 I
was beginning to see in socialism—socialism as a whole way of
life—what was finally demanded by a belief which, ever since
my revolt against my father's antifeminism and the poverty of
Notting Dale, I had felt to be involved in my liberalism: or
rather, not so much a belief as something taken for granted,
something as much part and parcel of me, as little to be argued
about with myself (though very much, by the same token, with
others) as my own hands and feet: the belief, namely, that in
God's sight no possible difference could exist—no difference in
worth—as between persons of one nationality and persons of another, and that if God thought about it like that then a man
who thought otherwise and acted accordingly would be

K

spiritually lying. So I was already an internationalist; and it was the outbreak of the 1914 war that set ringing in my head what we should now call the slogan "No internationalism without socialism". For, partly under the influence of J. A. Hobson's *Imperialism*, much more under the influence of H. N. Brailsford's *The War of Steel and Gold* (which was published on the eve of the war), and most of all under the influence of events, I saw the greed of competing capitalisms not only as at the bottom of that particular war and potentially of any future one on any sort of scale, but also, in a more general sense, as the muck and slime that clogged up the fountains of international brotherhood. This view was naïf. It concentrated too mechanically on systems: it isolated one kind of greed from all the other kinds: it isolated greed itself from the whole complex of passions, with power-mongering the chief of them, with which greed is involved: and it looked at the problem too negatively —in terms too exclusively of egoism and hate, and with inadequate consideration of what is really of far greater importance, the frustration of altruism and love. But it had a great deal of truth in it, and still has. Yet the majority of contemporary socialists and nearly all ex-communists (who love to throw away the baby with the bath-water) either cold-shoulder it or ignore it completely.

So you will easily understand why, with this internationalist background, I cannot abide national socialism, or the element of it which, mixed up with a great deal that's very much better, such as our policy in India, mars the record of Labour in office. When Senator Vandenberg announced in the Senate, soon after the first Labour victory, his "reluctant but firm conviction" that the proposed loan to Britain would "contribute to the continued well-being of the American people", and added that it was only on the basis of "intelligent American self-interest that the credit could be defended", he seemed not merely a typical but even a symbolic figure: for, almost by definition, the idea that there is something immoral, as well as unintelligent, in the deliberate pursuit of self-interest by a nation as a nation, must appear to the average citizen of an America so proud of its capitalism as criminally insane. Yet Mr Herbert Morrison, at about the same time, was speaking with the identical accent of economic chauvinism, and with less of enlightenment in his selfishness. "Industrial Britain," he said, "set out to win prosperity for its people led by a Government with a programme to bring certain basic industries and services under Government ownership. . . We are able, if we would, to tackle our industrial problems in a spirit and with a drive superior to any other country in the world. . . We started our drive with an impetus that was surely irresistible. . . We could, if we would, raise our standard of living to a height never before enjoyed by the bulk of our people." The speech as a whole simply reeks of national egoism and complacency, of a blind concentration on national prosperity: and was delivered at a time when the misery on our doorstep—across the Channel— to say nothing of China or India, was appalling.

As the Government settled down, such speeches, and the policies implied in them, became increasingly common. But it was a socialist Prime Minister who was to reveal, in the most explicit manner, a national-socialist psychology. A petition had been presented to Mr Attlee, signed by seven or eight hundred of the most eminent and representative people in the country, begging that general rations here should not be *raised* so long as there was distress on the Continent of Europe. '*It would not be possible,*' said the Prime Minister in his letter of refusal, '*for any Government to make the standard of life of its people dependent on conditions, however brought about, in countries over which they have no control.*'

I could refer to much else in the Government's record had I space or inclination, such as its hostility, or, if you prefer, the feebleness of its stand against working-class hostility, to the introduction of foreign labour, even when, to cite the narrowest consideration, our domestic economy was in desperate need of it: but worst of all has been its hamstringing of European unity. There are no doubt valid arguments, from an honestly socialist point of view, against a close integration of ourselves and the Continent; but these are not the arguments that have genuinely weighed with our Government. It is clear from statement after statement, and from one above all, that what they really reject, and reject with a passion that shows where their hearts are, is the smallest abrogation of national sovereignty: not its practicability or desirability here and now, not this or that measure of it in these or those circumstances, but the very idea of it as such. And willingness, indeed eagerness, to abrogate national sovereignty is the hallmark of a true internationalism. The fact is that socialist Britain has been swept, after its own comparatively decent fashion, into the tornado of nationalism that is destroying the world.

Nationalism! Of all the evils I hate I think I hate nationalism most. Nationalism—national egoism, thinking in terms of one's nation rather than in terms of humanity—nationalism is evil because it concentrates on comparative inessentials (where a man lives, what sort of language he speaks, the type of his culture, the character of his "blood") and ignores the essential, which is simply that he is a man. It pursues a spurious and abstract "national glory", which is devoid of any actual existence, and has nothing whatever to do with the glory, or with the daily and hourly happiness and well-being, of the nationals in question. It is partly an invention of ambitious and unscrupulous politicians, and partly a drug from which the populace derives, not individual peace of mind or the fulfilment of the genuine needs of their human nature, but a kind of bogus and vicarious satisfaction. It makes one set of people hate another set that they haven't the smallest real occasion for hating: it leads to jealousy, expansionism, oppression, strife and eventually war.

I am sitting by my window as I write this, looking out over my garden to the downs. I am happy for two reasons: the warmth of the sun and the smell of the grass are beautiful, and I am engaged in an activity that fulfils the needs of my nature. Doesn't that make me kin to every man and woman in every country? Doesn't everybody want the same—enjoyment of the world and self-expression? What does it matter, in comparison with this, that I speak English and somebody else speaks German, that my skin is white and a Negro's black, that I am a Jew and my neighbour a Gentile? What does it matter that I live in Berkshire, but a second man near Budapest and a third by the Rhine? What does it even matter that my "culture" is partly English and partly Jewish, while others have some other tradition that is the result not only of settled life in some particular region for a number of generations, but also of innumerable contacts between the various peoples of the world since the beginning of history? Let us, in the name of all reason and good sense, forget these differences, and remember our common humanity.

That is not to imply that the preservation of a particular tradition is, even relatively, of no importance. On the contrary, we may rightly consider it, as I consider the preservation of our western tradition, of an importance difficult to exaggerate. But the way to preserve a tradition is to live it whole-heartedly, and to hope that others will come by contact with it to recognise its merits.

All this would simply not have been worth writing forty or even twenty-five years ago, for it would have been thought too commonplace. There was nationalism then as there had previously so often been, and in many places it was rampant. But the general view among spiritually educated people was that it was something to be deprecated, a defect we must endeavour to eradicate. Now the mood, very largely as an aftermath of Nazi practice, is all the other way. Nationalism is again something good, glorious, "sacro", something that it is unpatriotic or disreputable to denounce.

Of all forms of nationalism, racialist nationalism is the worst. Territorial or cultural nationalism at any rate corresponds to a fact; but racial nationalism is wholly and perniciously unreal. What in Heaven's name can it signify, for the actual daily lives of men and women, whether they are of Slav or Teutonic or Magyar or Jewish or Aryan or no matter what sort of special race or special blood? Even if there were really anything "special" about it—even if the purity of races were not a childish and exploded legend—the unreality would still be complete; but the whole thing being mythical, the unreality is even greater, or would be if that were possible.

With the world as it is, certain instances of nationalism are no doubt necessary evils. Where a group, recognisable as a group, has been oppressed or ill-treated, or thinks it has been oppressed or ill-treated, by some other and more powerful group, usually in the name of the latter's national pride or egoism or glory, nationalism may be the only way out of an intolerable situation, and a necessary prelude to international harmony. Irish (and perhaps Jewish) nationalism has been of this type. So are the "native" nationalisms now emerging everywhere, for they bear the marks, mixed up with other less desirable characteristics, of a genuine struggle for freedom from alien exploitation. But while all this is true, it should nevertheless be recognised that even in such cases the nationalism, though necessary, is an evil; and the evil can clearly be seen in the fact that such movements, originally defensive, only save themselves with difficulty from the development of those arrogant, exclusive, chauvinistic stigmata which are typically nationalist in the baser sense.

I have recently heard nationalism applauded by democratic socialists, on the ground that the more we can get of it the less likely is Stalin to win: witness the Yugoslav resistance. Well, nationalism is one thing and a sober determination to preserve one's national freedom is another, though the latter may degenerate into the former with startling rapidity. But in the long run, it must surely be clear, neither nationalism, which is evil, nor determination to preserve national freedom, which is negative, can satisfactorily answer the Soviet challenge. For the dynamic of Soviet communism resides largely in this: that though no longer internationalist in any true sense of the term, and though both nationalist itself to a very high degree and appealing to nationalism wherever that may suit its designs, it aims, nevertheless, at world unification. And world unification is something good. The future is with it. Eventually, in whatever form, it will come. And we certainly shall not get it through nationalism, which fights against it. We shall get it either through Soviet communism, and this might well be disastrous, or through our own internationalism of a purer kind.

The communist movement, remember, arose very largely as a protest against the evil of nationalism. "Workers of the world, unite!" It was a valid protest. Marx, viewed by history, will be seen as reaching out, from a narrowly economic starting-point, towards the ideal of Christian universalism. That ideal is the hope of mankind. If communism has now dreadfully betrayed it, largely owing to something false at the core of the marxist position, then we must pursue it all the more wholeheartedly ourselves, and not foster its antithesis.


I have been making this brief reference to British national socialism in practice, with a coda about nationalism tacked on, because I have wanted to illustrate the fact, however obvious it may be, that the existence in a country of socialist machinery by no means guarantees the use of that machinery for the abolition of world poverty; and that, however right the machinery may be, it will fail of the purpose for which I have claimed it as indispensable unless the men and women in charge of it, which ultimately means the whole population of a country, are also "right". I could have illustrated the point more easily, doubtless, by the case of Soviet Russia, where the perversion of socialism has taken a quite different form, and one devoid of all that counterbalancing good—fairer shares at home, and so on—which, in spite of everything that must be said by way of criticism, is to be found in our own semi-socialism. But now I want to turn in my tracks: I want to remind you that this talk about national socialism, the use of common ownership as an instrument for tyranny and war, and all the rest of it, was introduced solely by way of caveat, and that the original proposition remains unaffected—namely, that without the existence of socialist machinery world poverty cannot be abolished. This must be emphasised again after what has just been written in criticism of socialist practice, because a considerable number of people, some stupid and some exceptionally clever, are feeling so let down by goings-on in the Soviet Union, and even in England, that they spit masochistically on everything they rightly once believed as well as on everything they wrongly once believed, and, abandoning in an access of self-hatred the whole socialist bag of tricks, turn to Gaullism or Groupism or "religious" anti-socialism (with particular emphasis on doctrines of total depravity), or even plain Toryism: or proclaim that meanwhile there is nothing in the world worth bothering about except smashing the Soviet Union, by atom bombs if necessary. These people, when not simply neurotic, want everything too easy. They should remember Spinoza: *Quam praeclara, tam difficilia.*


But if you cannot abolish world poverty without socialist machinery, must we then conclude that nothing can be done in the meantime? Not at all. Most people's characters, if you could project them as a film, would be seen even in their self-conscious aspect—even apart from what is happening in the depths of unconsciousness—as a ceaseless flicker of varying and often conflicting emotions. Preoccupation with personal interests would be dominant: but you would see, breaking into and out of it, big and little idealisms, moments of self-abandonment, willingness, on occasion, to make even the last sacrifice for the good of others. So already today, with miserable half-heartedness and in the spirit more of a rearguard action than of a great offensive, a movement is starting up, even in government circles, which has as its aim some improvement in the standard of living throughout the world's backward areas. There was the Colombo Plan: there are the Uno Special Agencies: there is Mr Truman's Point Four, implemented though it has been with such contemptible niggardliness—while fear of the Soviet Union, and the necessities of defence, had only to become vivid in America for sums such as the mind cannot grasp to be voted overnight. It is the same thing, really, here: can you imagine even Sir Stafford Cripps proposing, two or three years ago, that we should spend on behalf of China a tiny fraction of what we are spending today on rearmament?

The motives behind these initiatives have of course been mixed. Altruism of a sort—sudden spurts of it, with no staying power, and always with the "other things being equal", "national interests mustn't suffer" provisos: strategic considerations: an obscure understanding that communism may win the dispossessed unless our part of the world gives them succour and hope, and that it is accordingly in our interest to do so—one or other of these, or a combination of them, has been the meaning of these various proposals. If America, as we hope, makes a quite serious effort to implement Point Four during the next few years, it is concern for her own economy that will for the time being have pushed her into it; for she may fear a slump, particularly if rearmament slackens.

Still, the movement, whatever its motives, is there. Meanwhile men like Boyd Orr in a number of countries have been campaigning with single-minded enthusiasm, and without any admixture of the motives that move politicians, for world prosperity: and the minority of men and women who see in an international "war against hunger" our best remaining hope of saving everyone from a war between nations is no longer quite as negligible as it was. Somehow, the thing is in the air. A bold initiative—a call from one country (and I wish it could be ours) to all the rest, a proposal that the nations should get together with nothing but "the conquest of hunger" on the order-paper —might meet with a response that would surprise people. This does not mean, and I must say it again, that the problem can get anywhere near solution until many at least of the great nations have become socialist in structure and internationally socialist in spirit. (America too? Yes, America too. I by no means rule out such a development during your life-time if not during mine: compare the England of today with the England of my boyhood:

and when the final elimination of world hunger is in question we must combine a sense of desperate urgency with thinking in terms, not of years, but of decades.) But a beginning might be made; and the very fact that the nations were co-operating, however partially and with whatever calculation about the national interest, in an international task, might, and I believe would, produce a change in the atmosphere favourable to the coming, in one country after another, of international socialism itself.

And finally, don't let's have any nonsense, in this connection either, about "practicality". In addition to what I've already said about it, remember that (a) there's nothing practical about destroying humanity by an atomic war; (b) to get people co-operating over the elimination of world hunger, even if the Soviet Union doesn't come in at first or at all, is one of the best ways of preventing such a war; and (c) the argument that we must first set our own house in order won't wash, because we can't set our own house in order except in the context of an international plan.

But having written the word "finally" I suppose I oughtn't, after all, to leave a quite serious argument—against the whole point of view I've been outlining—unanswered. "If, as a result of any sacrifices we had to make," say the objectors, "our own standards of living were to be seriously reduced, what would happen to culture?" Appleby-Smythe is particularly anxious about this: he believes that what is vital, with the world in its present condition, is to preserve cultural "strong-points" —particularly our own—against the onslaughts of barbarism.

Well, here is the short answer. You can't have read this letter, Timothy, without realising what "culture", and music above all, have meant to me. And yet I say, with all the sincerity of which I am capable, that if I were faced with the alternatives of throwing every existing copy of all the nine Beethoven symphonies into a furnace, and then erasing the memory of them so completely that they could never be reconstructed—if I were faced with the alternatives of that on the one hand, and of letting a single child starve, as the price of not doing it, on the other, I should jettison Beethoven without a moment's hesitation. I did not, as a matter of fact, invent that dilemma myself:

Bernard Shaw did, unless I'm mistaken, and he gave the same answer. What sort of "culture" is it that depends for its existence on the misery—the final misery, a having-nothing-to-live-for-or-hope-for sort of misery—of countless human beings? There is a lie at the heart of it, as there was a lie at the heart of the Oxford disinterestedness I spoke about earlier—when stressing, you may remember, the overwhelming importance of the very culture in question.

Secondly, to suggest that culture can suffer, in any but the shortest run if in that, from the transformation of innumerable creatures who live like beasts of the field into creatures who live like men, is about the queerest sort of nonsense I have ever had to listen to.

Thirdly, what produces a vigorous culture is highly debatable; but there is some reason for believing that the most favourable soil for it is either a settled tranquillity, or a vigorous uprush of adventurousness, on the part either of a whole people or of some group or class in it. If so, that may explain the condition of our culture today. This is a period, in most countries, of disillusionment, fretfulness, and even despair among people of almost every condition and class; and too much contemporary art—the books being written, the pictures being painted, the music being composed—is *outré*, morbid, cynical, extravagant, cliquy, divorced from "the folk", and preoccupied with evil rather than with good. "Popular" art—the sort of art that most people can understand and enjoy—is almost non-existent; and nothing could be unhealthier than that. Isn't it possible that if a whole people could be lifted out of their own narrow interests, and could feel themselves dedicated to a grand unselfish adventure, there might be one of the greatest renaissances in artistic history?

Fourthly, "God will provide". I mean this quite seriously. Culture is the expression of man's divine creativity. It cannot vanish, and it cannot suffer from men and women doing good.

*Henrietta Street, June 27th*
*All the business about absolutes, pacifism, etc. leapt out at me again last night at the House of Commons, where a little dining club meets every Tuesday to discuss that very topic, the war against hunger, which I have just been writing about. A debate was going*

on in the Chamber around the banishment of *Tshekedi Khama*, an African chief; and so we found ourselves talking mostly about Africa at dinner, before getting down to our proper business. *Gilbert McAllister*, a Labour M.P., took the view that Labour people were inclined to be far too critical of our African administration, and told the story of something that had come to his notice during a recent visit to those parts. Some tribe, it appeared, had been on the point of breaking out into a dangerous riot, and whoever was in charge—the District Commissioner, I think—had ordered the police or military to fire into the crowd, with the result that several people had been killed. He had been severely criticised for this action, the argument being that shots should have been fired over the heads of the rioters instead of into them. But his brother, also a District Commissioner, had previously been faced with a similar situation in another locality: and he, instead of ordering any firing at all, had advanced unarmed "*in the true Christian spirit*" and been clubbed to death. The rioting had gone on in this case, and a great number of people had been killed; in the other case the threatened disturbance had been quelled in time. Surely, said McAllister, the pacifist had been wrong and the non-pacifist (whom he knew to be equally a pacifist by instinct) had been right. You had to measure these things in terms of the total amount of suffering involved; and there could be no doubt that the firing had produced less and the Christian gesture more.

And as I listened I felt with utter certainty, with what you will remember I called γνῶσις as opposed to δόξα when I broke out on the subject after that evening at *Fidelio*—with a sense of naked meeting between a truth that was within me and a truth "somewhere up in the heavens"—that the man who had gone out unarmed had been absolutely, beyond any possibility of argument, right, and the other wrong. I almost physically saw, in that dining-room looking out over the terrace, a sudden flash of lightning making everything that had been dark clear and vivid to the last detail: I almost physically heard the voice of him whom, at this moment, I wish to acknowledge as my Master, saying "*resist not evil; but whosoever shall smite thee on thy right cheek, turn to him the other also*". Beyond any possibility of argument, that is the point: for the moment you begin arguing about the question, not with other people but, where every real argument takes place, within yourself, all the familiar doubts recur. For instance: I am as sensitive as Gilbert

*McAllister to human suffering, and, if statistics must be brought in, would passionately desire, like him, that a hundred and not a thousand should suffer: how then can I support a course that, ex hypothesi, means suffering for the thousand rather than the hundred? And yet my conviction of last night remains unshaken a dozen hours later. I doubt whether it will remain unshaken much longer: I suspect that very soon the old struggle inside me will begin all over again. But just at this moment I believe beyond any possibility of argument (I cannot help repeating those words) that the only thing to do, if we are not to "mar utterly this fair garden we might win", is without calculation—without calculation even of the suffering we may thus bring on others—to help spirit gain additional strength in its struggle for victory in human affairs. And not only without calculation of the immediate suffering: without calculation—I feel this as strongly as I did on the Fidelio evening—of the total amount of suffering that in the longest possible run will be caused to the world as a whole. I am saying this: While I think it probable that every pacifist gesture will mean not more but less total suffering in the long run, whatever may be the immediate effect, nevertheless if I thought the opposite my view—my view of the moment, which may not be my view tomorrow morning—would remain unaltered. Even that Meredith quotation about marring the garden strikes a false note: even that suggests an element of calculation that we ought, in this context, to keep far from our thoughts.*

## § 2. SOCIALISM AND FREEDOM

Ever since I began this rambling disquisition on socialism during the first days of perfect weather two or three weeks ago I have been talking about poverty. But you will have understood that the theme has really been freedom, as it has been the theme of my whole conscious life: the friend and wife and mistress that has drawn me, as with a bodily presence, for almost as long as I can remember. I am the most unwebbian person in the world: for the spirit of my socialism you must go, not to *Industrial Democracy*, but to MacCarthy's great outburst in *A Modern Symposium*:

" 'May God forgive me,' he cried, 'that ever I have called myself a socialist, if this is what socialism means! But it does not! I will rescue the word! I will reclaim it for its ancient

nobler sense—socialism the dream of the world, the light of
the grail on the marsh, the mystic city of Sarras, the vale of
Avalon! Socialism the soul of liberty, the bond of brotherhood,
the seal of equality! Who is he that with sacrilegious hands
would seize our Ariel and prison him in that tree of iniquity
the State? Day is not farther from night, nor Good from Evil,
than the socialism of the Revolution from this of the desk and
the stool, from this enemy wearing our uniform and flaunting
our coat of arms. For nigh upon a century we have fought for
liberty; and now they would make us gaolers to bind our own
souls. 1789, 1830, 1848—are these dates branded upon our
hearts, only to stamp us as patient sheep in the flock of bureau-
cracy? No! They are the symbols of the spirit; and those whom
they set apart, outcasts from the kingdoms of the world and
citizens of the kingdom of God, wherever they wander are
living flames to consume institutions and laws, and to light in
the hearts of men the fires of pity and wrath and love. Our city
is not built with blue books, nor cemented with office dust;
nor is it bonds of red-tape that make and keep it one. No! it
is the attraction, uncompelled, of spirits made free; the shadow-
ing into outward form of the eternal joy of the soul!' "

Spirits made free. To free spirit—it is this, this always for
which I have longed to abolish poverty: I have longed, by
abolishing poverty, to remove one at least of the obstacles that
prevent a man from realising the joy of his soul, and from
helping God to realise his. Of course I know very well, as I
said near the beginning of this letter, that MacCarthy's way is
too easy: like that of the philosophical anarchists in real life,
who prefer to stand aside from the political battle and imagine
they have done everything required of them when they have
registered their protests, in a superior sort of way, against
anything that may smack of interference with personal liberty.
Without blue books and office dust you can do nothing. If a
system is in force that prevents the overwhelming majority of
people, and perhaps everyone, from realising their potential
selfhood—from being like the buds in my garden that blossom
into perfect flowers when the soil and the air are genial—is it
really sufficient to attack incidentals of the system? Is it really
sufficient, either, wholly to destroy the system, without putting
another in its place? If I could indeed live for ever, it is true,

I should not be content with the progress of humanity until the last lingering trace of the best possible system had vanished from the earth, and nothing remained except love and spontaneity. But it is surely the mark of a contemptible escapism to ignore or deny what is clearly our present requirement: the substitution, namely, of a system that would facilitate the development of human personality for one that obstructs it. And this demands office dust and blue books.

Yet MacCarthy's great protest, which thrills me every time I read it and even more every time I recite it, is nevertheless an all but final expression—quite perfect indeed except for the one word "wrath"—of the only true socialist spirit: and it gives two specific warnings which British socialism, as it comes to more effective power, should keep daily on its mental desk—like that little framed notice, with the date of an execution on it, which Home Secretaries must have ever before their eyes, for they must ceaselessly be considering, before it is too late, whether a last-minute reprieve should be granted. It warns us, by implication, against the cult of efficiency: and it warns us, explicitly, against the nightmare of a bureaucratic State.

True socialism (or, once more, my kind of socialism, if you prefer) has nothing to do, *in its essence*, with efficiency. Or less than nothing: because there is a nasty, mean, commercial sound about the very word that reminds you of a capitalist counting-house. I have never had much stomach for the "efficiency" school of socialism, with its talk about five competitive milkmen perambulating streets where one would be enough, and of how much "better off" we should be if waste and overlapping were eliminated. I like waste and overlapping, not for their own sakes, but because they suggest richness, variety, prodigality, spontaneity, devil-may-careness, a general spilling over of things: they are more of a kidney with the orchard where I am writing this diatribe, its masses of hay lying carelessly all over the place (for the first time this year, my Timothy, I am "looking over clustering apples"—but no apples yet—"out to the Sicilian sea") than with the neatly ruled lines, the red and the black, the hideously meticulous handwriting in an office ledger. Are we simply to replace one kind of commercialism by another? Is that to be the end of our socialist striving? The trouble is that capitalism, and pseudo-socialism of the kind I am complaining about, derive ultimately from one tainted source: they are rooted, the two equally, in western materialism, by which I mean an obsession with the machinery of life, instead of a care for life's quality. Matter at the service of spirit, matter become one with spirit, that should be the aim of our socialist commonwealth: free play like a fountain's blown about by the wind, not tidiness, order, a paralysing statistical exactitude.

I want to see the socialism of our day repudiating more and more the values of western materialism, and reaching out more and more to the idea of goodness. This is why I hate so intensely that reliance on capitalist incentives, characteristic of the last six years, which I previously discussed: this is why I hear with such nausea the counting-house phraseology that drops with such mechanical regularity from the lips of our socialist politicians. Let me give one example only. For more than a year now a horrible war has been devastating Korea. Let us assume for a moment that the enemy alone is at fault: though the facts are not as simple as that, and our easy assumption that they are is a mark of the national egoism already complained about. Still, assume the hypothesis that here, as never before, was an act of unprovoked aggression. Now what have our socialists said when some turn of events, an offer of peace terms perhaps, has required them to make a pronouncement? You can safely bet a hundred to one that it has been something like this: "they must learn that aggression doesn't pay". They must learn nothing of the kind. They must learn that aggression is wrong.

Some time in the twenties, if I remember rightly, a system called scientific management was very much in vogue. It was a capitalist invention for squeezing the last drop of profit not only from the bodies but also from the characters and minds of the industrial workers. The exact amount of energy required for each operation, the exact type of reaction exhibited by particular temperaments to particular stimuli, the exact measure of rest or recreation that in every given case would keep the human machine in good trim—all were carefully determined by an army of investigators, and then assembled and combined as the basis of a plan for achieving the maximum production. You are either disgusted by such an outrage or you are not. If you are not, my whole point of view will be unintelligible to you; but if you are, then you will share my horror at the vision of what I sometimes see in store for us. Are we moving, I ask myself, towards a scientific management not capitalist but pseudo-socialist in type? Towards the organisation of our society with one sole objective: no longer of winning profits for the few, but of achieving an ever greater prosperity, a purely material prosperity, a prosperity so exclusively pursued as to outrage spirit, for the whole general body of its people? It would no doubt be a change for the better, since the slaves would be more comfortable. But they would be slaves none the less—slaves to "a high standard of living". And I do not like slavery.

There is only one possible excuse for scientific management of whatever kind, and this is that it should so reduce the hours of labour as to make more abundant leisure a characteristic of the society in question. But more abundant leisure should not be our paramount aim: our paramount aim should be joy and creativeness in work. I was not one of those—even at the time, forty and more years ago, when a group of men and women was seriously discussing the possibility—who believed that we could put back the clock and return to the craftsmanship of the mediaeval guilds. We should anxiously be seeking, none the less, for some equivalent in modern conditions: for techniques and procedures, that is to say—and one of them will shortly be discussed—through which far more men and women than at present could achieve, in their working lives, the reality of self-expression. The question is really one of emphasis: and provided that self-expression through the job, and not more abundant leisure, is steadily held in view as the chief consideration, anything that reduces the hours of such labour as must necessarily be disagreeable is, other things being equal, to be warmly welcomed.

Having unburdened myself of all this I want to make quite a lot of things clear. I said that socialism *in its essence* had nothing to do with efficiency, or less than nothing. I was referring to the quality of human living that true socialism sets store by, and works to see realised in the society it would bring into being: I was referring to the sense of values that should inform us as we work for such a society, and that should be kept ever fresh and strong within us. I was not suggesting anything so stupid as that efficiency, if held strictly to its place and never allowed to become an obsession or the object of a cult, is devoid of all value as a means to the socialist end. On the contrary, its value is immense. Until every man, woman and child in every country of the world (including our own) is properly fed, housed and clothed, we dare not waste a single farthing, or permit half an unnecessary milkman, when the price of so doing is the continuance, wherever it may be, of sheer physical want. Quite apart from the qualification I have already made in my attack on it, even a socialist scientific management becomes defensible (highly dangerous though it must always be, as tending to degrade and enslave people) if adopted by a community, not in pursuit of false aims for itself, but to relieve the suffering of others. All this, however, is something quite different from making an idol of efficiency: from imagining there's some magic in the thing itself, apart from the purposes it may serve. And I see very definite signs of this idol-worship. I often hear socialism praised and capitalism condemned because the one is more efficient than the other, and in such a way as to suggest that the efficiency is the final criterion. I shall be told, no doubt, that the necessary qualification—my qualification—though unexpressed is always there. I doubt it: means have a fatal proclivity for becoming ends.

And now I am further prepared to admit that even in my own final society, even in the very last stages of my own private Back to Methuselah, efficiency will have its place; for while I should always prefer some slight element of inefficiency in affairs, as being somehow more human, more compatible with the vagrancy of spirit—men and women are men and women, not clockwork machines—nevertheless efficiency by and large, and if taken in one's stride as a thing that just happens by the way, is by no means to be despised: I am even free to confess that too little of it is a trifle disreputable. A cult of inefficiency would be almost as deplorable as the cult of efficiency. I should regard it as contemptible, for instance, to be forever bothering myself about ways of increasing the efficiency of my publishing business: but I should regard it as disgraceful if its mere dead wheels didn't properly turn. Our attitude to efficiency, in fact, should be exactly the opposite of an intellectual's attitude to his brains. He is always fussing about them: he should take them for granted, as ordinary people take theirs.

*This is the best day of the year. Ruth planted the whole sunk garden with nothing but annuals this spring, and now they are all coming out like a Botticelli carpet of flowers. There are snap-dragons richer in hue than the darkest claret: stocks, mauve and white, all happily double: early pink cosmea: a new kind of lemon-yellow daisy, its petals curving over in a movement of peculiar grace: and annual chrysanthemums, daedalian with vari-coloured rings. There is a wonderful array of nemesia, like so many miniature pansies clustering on a single stalk: orange ones mostly, but others too: the colour of rose-quartz pink, and forget-me-not blue, and red as in renaissance velvet. But better than anything are the clumps of clover growing wild on the little brick wall: I smell them, and am back again in the large rough field off Elgin Avenue.*

*I should like to write a whole essay on smells, constructing for frontispiece a sort of spectroscope of flower and plant smells, with lilies and those little wild cyclamens at one end of it and grass at the other. Clover, and perhaps nasturtiums and snapdragons, would come nearest to grass. I should have something to say, too, about the special delight to my nose of tar and even petrol. The peculiar quality of my pleasure in these various smells, and in that of the privet flowers which make me so happy as I pick them these summer mornings on my way down to Holland Park station— does it derive, I wonder, from something in my make-up that explains a lot of other things too: my delight, for instance, in pottery?*

*A little red insect, all length, is rushing down a blade of grass, and then up and down, up and down, in the sunlight. What a pity that I can't be inside it to share its feelings! And what a pity, by the same token, that it can't be inside me! What a pity that there must be these divisions!*

*And now something charming has happened. The little creature, which turns out to have wings, has suddenly flown on to the pile of manuscript by my side: as if it knew what I was writing, and sympathised.*

MacCarthy's other warning—"Who is he that with sacrile-gious hands would seize our Ariel and prison him in that tree of iniquity the State?" and "Are these dates branded upon our hearts only to stamp us as patient sheep in the flock of bureau-cracy?"—is even more important.

I have been claiming, so far, that the machinery of socialism, by abolishing poverty (if it is used for that purpose) and simply by this, can be a means to that self-expression in which freedom as I define it consists—consists, that is, provided that the word self-expression is properly understood, and not confused with self-centredness and egoism, which are in fact its opposites. But apart from this negative though immensely important function, socialism can enhance personality, by the detail of its machinery, in a very much more positive fashion. I do not yet refer to that fostering of co-operation and altruism which will be dealt with in the following section: I refer to the achievement of the particular kind of self-expression I mentioned just above—*self-expression in men's working lives*. But socialist machinery can just as well fail to do anything of the kind: it may even, while failing to do it, in addition rob working-class lives, by a beastly regimentation, of a great many freedoms they would otherwise possess. If that happened, abolition of even the grossest poverty would lose, I shall never say all its value, but certainly a very great deal of it.

Do you remember Cleanthes' indignant outburst in my Latin Dialogue?

"I find it difficult to keep my temper about working-class slavery, which will be far more oppressive and intolerable under your dispensation than under ours. Think of it! Your socialist workers will be forced to obey without question the smallest command of your officials; for if they once refuse, the whole foundation of your republic will be destroyed. They will often be compelled to leave their homes and migrate to some remote place or other, so that a bigger quantity of ploughs can be produced, or a smaller quantity of spades; and all those links that bind a man to his homestead and neighbourhood will be broken at the nod of an official. The workers, in a word, will become mere machines, every one of them identical with the rest: human beings no longer, but a featureless mass of pawns or automata."

It was the whole of me—of the socialist me every bit as much as of the liberal me—that was protesting in that passage, which of course I should phrase very differently now. Centralised, bureaucratic State socialism is a thing that has always repelled me, if not so violently as capitalism. It has repelled me, partly for its power to do the things that Cleanthes upbraids it for, and partly for its failure to secure the particular freedom we are at the moment discussing. Appleby-Smythe seems to think that when I attack it I am attacking democracy. Nonsense: I am attacking the pallor of its democracy. State socialism, when democratic in the broader political sense, gives everyone, as a voter, some share of control, if a long-term, rather remote, and very fractional one, over the conditions in which he lives. Even such democracy as this, for all its limitations, is of priceless value. As to democratic State socialism in comparison with democratic capitalism, the former, other things being equal, is immensely preferable: for it guarantees, or at any rate ought to guarantee, a freedom from poverty that capitalism cannot guarantee. But in respect of another and most precious freedom, the one we are now concentrating on, what smallest difference can it make to a man whether his employer is a capitalist or the centralised, bureaucratic State, however politically democratic? What smallest difference can it make, I mean, to the possibility of self-expression in his workaday life? We must get down to realities in such matters: not think theoretically, but in terms of how life really impinges on a man as minute after minute he works at the bench or digs coal from the face of a mine. The fact that once every five years or so he may help as a citizen in choosing the Government is wholly irrelevant to these vivid realities. I am all for democracy: but I want to deepen and broaden it, bring it right into the passing moment. I shall say something, soon, about methods of doing so.

Consider, in the meantime, not a man's daily life at his place of occupation, but his mobility, his power of choice, his freedom, no doubt within the limits imposed by his training and environment, to decide what he is to do and where he is to do it. Here, he may be even worse off under socialism than under any form of capitalism except a fascist one, notwithstanding the intolerable harryings to which capitalism has consistently submitted him: for your socialist Government, at a given stage, is more or less the sole employer, and this means that the effective *power* to regiment is greater than it could ever be under non-fascist capitalism, though the *wills* might be identical. That is why a socialist must be specially, almost desperately scrupulous about regimentation of any kind, and must beware, not only of the final totalitarianism which characterises regimes that are fascist or pseudo-communist in type, but of so very much milder a phenomenon, once exhibited for a few wavering months in our own country, as direction of labour. I want to say a word about this latter, partly because it is the shape in which, given certain pressures, totalitarianism might threaten us, and partly because it illustrates the sort of problem that liberal socialists will have to face as socialism comes increasingly to power.

The moment you touch such a question you are up against one of those contradictions that are constantly occurring in human affairs, and can be resolved only in part, when at all, by the ordinary processes of logic.

What do you do about it? You first of all work out, by a balancing of pros and cons, some measure of compromise. To take the case in question, direction of labour is essentially evil. It strikes at the inner citadel of a man's creativeness: it may compel him to leave undone what God—all the upsurge within him—may require him to do, and may sterilise, by what it positively forces him to do, something thrusting for expression in his unique individuality. This is vile. And yet there are circumstances in which it might have to be supported. Our plan for the abolition of world poverty, for instance, might require for its successful implementation a certain and perhaps a high measure of direction. If so, I should support it wholeheartedly, with a qualification to be presently given. So, I think, would most other people, if the case were properly put to them. The sense of a freedom lost would be swallowed up in the sense of a freedom gained—gained by the acceptance of that loss for the sake of others: especially if we had reached a stage at which a socialist spirit of the truly international kind had become characteristic of the entire community. Then, we may hope, men and women would be eager to come forward and do whatever might be required of them for great ends—as the Armada of little ships put out eagerly to sea when it knew that our men at Dunkirk were waiting to be saved. (What an evening that was! What a vision it conjured up of the heights men and women might rise to if once they could think of the world as they think of their country—but of their country, even, only in its moments of danger!)

My point, however, at the moment is that, believing direction of labour to be evil, one may still think it necessary in certain circumstances. What, then, does one do? Well, as I said, one works out, for a start, some measure of compromise: deciding, by a balancing of pros and cons, in what circumstances and on what details one will support the thing, and in what circumstances and on what details one won't. But now the question of absolutes comes in. I was discussing this question of absolutes the other day with Canon Raven, who told me that it had taken him fifteen years to find his own answer. You have to decide, he said—this was his solution, if you can call what is beyond logic a solution, after all those years of spiritual turmoil—you have to decide which are the one or two questions you are going to be absolute about. He decided to be absolute himself on the question of peace or war: he became a pacifist. Perhaps he was right: I am becoming more and more certain that he was right. And perhaps, in general, his solution, or whatever you may prefer to call it, is also right.

In the matter under consideration, anyhow, you arrive at a point when it's no longer a question of pros and cons: when, however valid the counterbalancing considerations, you say "*this* I shall never agree to." (What is happening now isn't of a piece, as might appear, with the ordinary pro and con business: balancing has gone: the decision is of quite a different type.) I am clear, in my own case, about at any rate one of the things I could never agree to. I can conceive of circumstances in which, if a man refused to do a particular job of work that had been assigned him, I should agree (though not without a great deal of fury) to his being debarred from doing any job of work at all—or anything that could officially be regarded as such. But what I should never agree to in any conceivable circumstances is that a man who, for reasons of his own, refused seventy times seven to do the work he had been told to do, should forfeit his liberty as a result. If a man will not work, neither shall he eat: very well then, let him starve, or escape starvation in his own way. Let him roam the countryside if he wishes, eating hips and haws or the grass, or maybe begging his bread from the cottagers or doing odd jobs in return for a meal. Nature and human beings are more genial than the leviathan State. To compel a man not to do what he wants is bad enough, but to compel him to do what the State wants, or else go to prison, is intolerable. The final freedom, more truly final even than freedom of speech, is freedom to be a tramp. A society in which there is no longer any place for a tramp is no longer, either, a society for decent men and women.

*Ladbroke Grove,*
*5.30 a.m. July 6th*

*We went to the Meistersinger at Covent Garden last night, Ruth and Livia and Francesca and I, because Beecham was conducting, and we thought that the playing might be exceptional. I couldn't keep away, but had feared I'd be dreadfully bored, for Wagner, who used to make me starry-eyed when I was getting to know him as a boy, has long seemed almost intolerable to me, and when we recently heard Tristan with Flagstad I could hardly sit it out. I did feel bored during the first two acts, especially with all the Beckmesser stuff and Sachs's interminable heartiness as he cobbles under the elder: it is as tedious, this four-square melody, as Siegfried's at the forge, with which it could easily be interchanged. I have a good deal of sympathy with Eduard Hanslick's description of it—as ostensibly comic but actually reminiscent of a peevish hyena rather than of a merry cobbler. I thought of leaving after the second interval. But fortunately I didn't; and from the opening bars of the prelude to Act III, played, as I have never heard it played except under Toscanini, with that justness of time in which all great conducting consists, I succumbed completely. I often couldn't see for my tears, which were not only tears of memory. With what a prodigal outpouring is beauty made present to us in those last two scenes, if only we give up resisting it! And how perfectly it was realised last night—Eva's pretty confusion about links and rechts while she stands with her foot imprisoned on the Meister's stool, and her break into confident rapture as Walther von Stolzing, all ready in his knightly clothes, appears on the balcony opposite. Beckmesser at Sachs's desk, the Preislied within an inch of his nose, and the orchestra, piano, telling us just that and nothing more—no device could be imagined of a rarer intellectual beauty: but best of all, the quintet! Theatrical conventions are forgotten, Sachs leads Eva to the middle of the stage, the figures become stylised, and music for a moment reigns unchallenged—as it reigned once before, in the canon quartet in Fidelio, and as it was to reign once again, in the Rosenkavalier trio. Yet the scene still to come is a true climax. Apart from all the special things—the*

*Preislied at last in its continuous perfection, the homage to Sachs, the chaplet on Sachs's brow—a luxuriance of elaboration in the intermingling of motifs shows the overture, which now comes to mind again after a five hours' interval, not as the anticipatory summing up it had then appeared to be, but merely as a starting-point for further development. I have hardly slept all night; I have seemed to be asleep, but I knew when I woke up just now that my brain had been alive every minute of the time with the heavenly bustle of the closing music.*

We concluded, before the bit about direction of labour, that socialist machinery would not necessarily facilitate self-expression in men's working lives. It must be socialist machinery of a particular kind if we are to achieve the result we desire: of a kind that has seemed necessary to me for close on forty years. For of the various factors that from the beginning of 1913 were almost insensibly converting my liberalism into liberal socialism I would put among the first a concern for the very self-expression in point: a realisation that without it the freedom of many must be partial and negative: and a growing conviction that it could be achieved on a significant scale only by combining common ownership with a new kind of industrial organisation and indeed a new kind of democracy. For my socialism, as I developed into a socialist, was of the guild and not of the State variety, and still is: I believed in functional democracy, and still do. Guild socialism and functional democracy were what Sosiades was groping after in his description of how government should be organised: "Officials will be elected as follows. Every shoeshop will choose a head: these heads will choose a regional head: and the regional heads will choose a national head. So with every other trade, and with doctors, teachers, lawyers and so on; and a similar method will be employed in the case of distribution and foreign trade. All these various heads will form the Cabinet, which will thus have been elected by the people as a whole in a far truer sense than at present." The picture is naïvely over-simplified and the proposal grotesquely inadequate; but the root of the matter is there.

We were all guild socialists, those of us who were socialists at all, when I was young. The movement, much influenced, in its origins, by French syndicalism, had already been getting under weigh two or three years before the outbreak of the 1914 war, and was to have lost all its impetus within two or three years of the end of it. Its great personalities were G. D. H. Cole, William Mellor, A. W. Penty and S. G. Hobson. Mellor was the evangelist of the movement, as Cole was its brains: a heavy, rude, violent-seeming man, with stubble on his cheeks as black as the Forest of Dean's (whom you will presently meet) and rather like a dawn when the storm-clouds are gathering; and indeed there was a good deal of dawn about the national guilds movement in general—our attitude was Wordsworth's, at its more generous, to the French Revolution.

Our conferences were held at the Memorial Hall in Farringdon Street; and Mellor, who talked mostly with his fist in a furious gesture of hammer on anvil, especially when pounding out the slogan "Industrial power precedes and dominates political power", always seemed part and parcel of a place—one of its fixed appurtenances, or something growing out of it—that was mainly associated with boilermakers and engineers. But he was really very far from being violent: son of a nonconformist minister, he was a kind-hearted Christian in revolt, like Kingsley Martin or Michael Foot, whose backgrounds are similar. He subsequently declined into the editorship of *The Daily Herald*, and then rose a little again into that of *The Tribune*, when he founded it with Sir Stafford Cripps and a few others in the middle thirties.

The guild socialist argument proceeded on lines that are already familiar to you from my criticism of State socialism as we know it today. "Once every three years, or two years, or six months," it ran, "the railwayman casts a vote, and so takes a share in deciding what group of people is to control the policy of his country. The number of issues before him is necessarily enormous: foreign relations, education, mining policy, and a thousand and one other things. He must strike some sort of balance and vote for the party with which perhaps on the most vital issue, or on the majority of issues, he is in agreement. But now think, not of that moment which comes once in six months or three years, but of his daily life. For a great part of his time, and over a great part of his personality, his most real concern is with his work as a railwayman. Where is his liberty in relation to this work? It does not exist. It may be his opinion that a new line should be laid out to open up a remote district; he may see the possibility of building a station here, of shutting up a station there; he will think perhaps that the regulations for the safety of passengers are inadequate, that it would be advisable to test a new brake or to proceed with electrification. And if he does not feel or desire any of these things, then he ought to feel and desire them. He ought to look upon himself as a member of a great profession, the railway profession, practised in the interests of the nation. You say that he is free because he elects Members of Parliament, and because from the majority party so elected come the directors of public policy; we say that his freedom is fatally limited, because, as a railwayman, he is completely sub-servient to an external authority, instead of being a rational, self-governing human being. You reply that he helped to elect the authority, and that the principle of self-government is therefore fulfilled? Well, there may, at the last general election, have been some point of railway policy before the electorate; but it will have been confused with other issues, and so the railwayman will have been unable to cast a direct vote on that point alone. Moreover, it will only have been a point; it is the permanent Civil Service that controls ordinary workaday policy. What would you think if the Government were to impose rules of medical etiquette on doctors and surgeons? Would you pretend that the profession had really imposed these rules on itself, because every doctor has a Parliamentary vote? So with indus-try. We by no means propose that the individual railwayman should be free to do whatever his fancy may dictate—working fifteen hours on Monday and not at all for the rest of the week; we are proposing that he should, as a railwayman, obey a rail-way authority which he has united with all other railwaymen, and with railwaymen alone, to set up, and which he may unite with all other railwaymen, and with railwaymen alone, to depose."

It was this idea of self-government in industry, as the way to make freedom more real, which was at the root of guild-socialist doctrine; and so far there was little to distinguish it from the syndicalism out of which it had sprung. Guild socialists desired to see each separate industry (there was a difficulty about the 'separate', but this was faced) democratically con-ducted by a self-governing body consisting of all the varied workers in that industry, and acting professionally for the public interest. No longer would mine-owners be buying for a paltry wage, or for a big one either, absolute control over the labour-power of individual miners, who had no voice in the management of their industry and no control over its product; nor would they be replaced by a mining department of the State, which would similarly hire miners for a wage, who would similarly be voiceless; but a single national guild of all the mine-workers—manual, technical, intellectual—would manage the industry on self-governing lines, appointing and dismissing officials from among their number, and so bringing real liberty and real democracy into the work which constituted so important a part of their lives.

But guild socialists were by no means content, like the syndicalists, with attempting to make liberty and self-government real in the matter of production alone: they wished to make them real over the whole of life, with its manifold interests and duties. And in order to do so they elaborated the principle of functional democracy. "The miner," they insisted, "is not only a miner; he is also a consumer of food, and perhaps an 'enjoyer' of the park in a neighbouring town and a user of education for his children. Just as he must have liberty and self-government as a miner, so he must have liberty and self-government in these other relations too. But in these other relations he will obviously organise for purposes of self-government, not this time with miners, but, for instance, with enjoyers of the park and users of national education. A great complex of organised bodies must be developed, each one carrying out, by means of democratic self-government, its own peculiar function."

It was no part of the guild socialist purpose to paint a detailed picture of the final Utopia, for the latter, it was held, must necessarily depend on developments, and so could not be foreseen; but guildsmen were always working out simplified sketches of what a self-governing society would be like. One of the earliest was this: Production is carried on by national guilds, each guild consisting of all the workers, whether by brain or hand, in a particular industry. The various guilds send delegates to a National Guilds Congress, which acts as a co-ordinating authority on the side of production, and which thus represents the whole community organised in accordance with their functions and interests as producers. Over against this Guilds Congress is the State or National Parliament, elected on a territorial basis, and therefore again representing the whole community, but this time organised as consumers. Guilds Congress and National Parliament are coequal authorities, and any conflict between them is resolved at a joint session. The State owns the means of production, which it leases to the various guilds. Each guild carries on production by authority of a charter of incorporation; and it is by a levy on the guilds that taxation is raised.

Many other schemes were worked out, some of them by guildsmen in revolt against the idea of coequal authorities and some of them by guildsmen opposed to the State altogether; but their interest is now only an historical one, and I shall pass them over.

I have been describing the guilds movement in some little detail for two reasons. First, it forms part of my autobiography: for several years my political thought was largely dominated by it, and it was one of the roads for me from Liberalism to socialism. But secondly, the spirit of it is of crucial importance today. Nothing could be easier than to make fun of the trim little Utopias we thought up, to point out obvious difficulties, and to prove satisfactorily that a lot of these devices wouldn't "click". But the basic position was, and still is, unassailable. Unless you get self-government in industry, socialist machinery will have failed to be the instrument of freedom in one of its most valuable aspects, in an aspect of it indispensable for good living; and this aspect of freedom can be realised, in turn, only by means of socialist machinery—only on the basis of national ownership. We are living today under a regime partly socialist in machinery, but without even an approach to industrial self-government. Labour people, here and there, are getting uneasy about this, the question is being discussed, pamphlets are appearing; but the hierarchy appears untouched. When two or three years ago a small-scale agitation arose, Sir Stafford Cripps, who must have been far more sympathetic than most with its spiritual meaning, said in terms, and I thought rather brutal ones, that the workers were as yet quite unfit for a share in industrial management, and that all such demands must be opposed in the interests of higher production. Efficiency again. I am not sneering at Sir Stafford: he had an important job of work to do, and knowing very well, at first hand, how difficult it is to overcome an autocratism native to one's temperament, I sympathise with people who hate seeing their efforts mucked about with. But how on earth are we ever to progress towards a real living socialism if we are always saying "first things first"? It is the same thing here as with the use, by a socialist government, of capitalist incentives. We simply must make a start. And it is no good waiting for a sufficiently insistent demand from the working class itself; or at any rate the bourgeois (to use the hideous terminology of socialist agitation) must do everything they possibly can to encourage that demand.

Self-government in industry must be real self-government in industry, however gradual the approach to it and however pedestrian its beginning. Joint councils under State socialism can be useful in their way, though they can also be little more than paternal sops. But so-called "joint control" under capitalism, with the profit-sharing or copartnership which are commonly linked to it, is another matter. Occasionally, no doubt, employers responsible for such schemes have been genuinely anxious to give their workers a significant share both of profits and of control, and may even once or twice have succeeded. But, by and large, these are nothing but devices for perpetuating capitalism, and for infecting the workers, still more completely than at present, with the spirit of it. The "control" is usually bogus, and its intention, not to facilitate a workers' control of the genuine type, but to side-track it. As for profit-sharing and copartnership of various kinds, it should be unnecessary to say anything in exposure of them. For their effect, whatever their aim, is to put a premium, from the workers' point of view, on higher profits: they substitute for an employer's sectionalism that of an employer-employee complex: and they appeal, not to the motive of public service which is always the concern of true socialism, but to greed.

I want to say a word at this point about the relation of trades unionism to workers' control. Trades unions, it is clear, are the embryos from which our national guilds, or whatever we may nowadays call them, can alone develop; but they will be so completely transformed as to be hardly recognisable. For their present ethos derives from the capitalist past; they are rooted, like capitalism itself, in commercial materialism. There is little moral difference between the Publishers' Association, to which I regretfully belong, and my packers' Union. Both are solely concerned, or essentially concerned if you prefer, with the protection of their members' "interests": with getting the best possible deal for their members, which is to say for themselves, irrespective of what may happen to anybody else: sometimes, no doubt, within more or less decent limits, and sometimes not. The Union is there to protect my packers from me; the Association is there to protect me and my fellow-publishers from packers, booksellers, authors, the purchasing public (which means ourselves in a different relation), and one another. There are similar Associations to protect booksellers from publishers, and authors from everyone whomever; including the literary agents whose job it is to protect them from me. But I never heard of any Association for literary agents themselves. . .

Trades unions, become organs of industrial self-government, will be concerned only in a far wider context than at present with rates of pay, working conditions and the like: their function will be to manage their industry, in association with all other industries, for the general good.

I have nearly had my say now on the topic of self-expression in men's working lives. But I should like to add this. If we are to get down to actualities, as we did when we realised that the establishment of bureaucratic State socialism wouldn't make a hap'orth of difference, and in so far as it is already established here hasn't made a hap'orth of difference, in this particular respect, then we must also realise that workers' control, while capable of achieving a great deal for many, is no panacea. Take the case of a man who works a lift in an hotel. His working life, under workers' control and functional democracy, would be very different from what it is at present. Not only would he be concerned with lifts in general, and the no doubt innumerable problems connected with them—security, for instance, and proper balance between the handling of them by automatic devices and the handling of them by human beings: not only would he take a genuinely democratic part in the management of the larger industry or industries, whatever they may be, of which lift-running and lifts form a part: not only would he be a responsible, self-governing person in respect, to take our old example, of the neighbouring park and of national education; but he would also be actively associated—with cooks, waiters, laundry-women, chamber-maids, gardeners, reception clerks, etcetera—in running the hotel. This would be a very great deal. But his actual work in pressing the

button and depositing his passengers on their various floors
would be as dull and monotonous as ever. (Not but that a lift-
man can be actively happy even during these operations: I know
of one, getting on for sixty, who takes as great a delight in
observing his passengers' idiosyncrasies and speculating about
their characters as any novelist could—and then a certain type
of man, whatever he may happen to be doing, can just enjoy
being alive.) There are only three solutions to the problem of
what to do about inherently unpleasant or tediously repetitive
work. The first, which is applicable, at best, only over a very
limited field, is to get away from mass production and back to
workshop practices in which craftsmanship is feasible. The
second is to reduce the hours of people engaged on such work
by the highest possible percentage. The third is to abolish it
altogether by atomic power or some other sort of power or in
any other way you prefer.


And now, having finished with this topic of workers' control
for good and all, let us consider for a moment how apart from
it, and apart too from the safeguards derivable from a fundamental bettering of men and women (which is the real crux),
we can lessen the danger of our socialist machinery producing,
not more freedom, but less. Several ways occur to me—mostly
negative ways, things not to do—applicable to our present situation a few miles on the road towards socialism, and a couple
more, applicable to full socialism itself. Here is the former lot:
  We must see to it with the utmost vigilance that every freedom we at present possess, except only the freedom to exploit
others (which is a bogus sort of freedom), is preserved without
the smallest modification. Anything that in any way derogates
from the processes of parliamentary government, formalises
them, robs them of their holy ghost, must be avoided like cancer
or war. I hate Orders in Council, notwithstanding the proviso
that you can "pray" for their annulment. I hate all-night sit-
tings a week at a time, such as we have recently been witnessing
during the passage of the Finance Act this June: you have only
to look at Members sprawling comatose on benches in the
basement, or smoking with their eyes shut and suddenly bursting out into maddened irritation, to realise what this means in
terms of parliamentary debate, to say nothing of health and

character. I hate the strict party discipline that increasingly sends people into the lobbies, day after day, to vote in favour of what they loathe and against what they've been passionately advocating for the whole of their political lives. I am aware that these things may be necessary, and that without them you might be unable either to get through your parliamentary business, more especially in view of the massive legislation that State control, among other things, demands, or to preserve party government, which is the *sine qua non* of our British democracy. All I say is, watch out; do everything you can to modify these tendencies; otherwise you may find that, in your zeal, which could never be too great, to institute "fair shares" and extend economic freedom, you have reduced parliamentary government to a farce.

Meanwhile we should be anxiously determined—just because we are socialising, as we must, but realise none the less what perils the process involves—not merely to avoid any further restrictions of an unnecessary kind on personal freedom, but to abolish, wherever possible, existing ones. I should like to see the Government appointing a watch-dog, or a whole little department of watch-dogs, whose entire *raison d'être* it would be to examine every bill, scheme, proposal etcetera in their earliest stages, with a view to detecting any unnecessary illiberalities contained therein—just as the Treasury examines every item of proposed expenditure today; and then not merely to report them, but to harry the Government, on the Government's own instructions, in an attempt to get them removed. The job should go to a fanatical laissez-faire Liberal, who should be treated much as policemen are said to be treated: their chances of promotion, I understand, depend on the number of their arrests.

Similarly with red tape and bureaucracy. Nationalisation inevitably involves, for the time being, some measure of these nastinesses, but that is all the more reason for cutting them down to a minimum. Here I should like to see the Government doing something really imaginative—or extravagantly dramatic, if you like. Why, for instance, shouldn't they try the experiment of abolishing altogether the whole army of ticket-collectors and ticket-inspectors that infest our railways? I doubt whether they would make a loss on the transaction, for the present cost of wages must be enormous, and the saving on it might very well counterbalance any damage to revenue that might result from an increase in bilking. It's surprising (to some, not to me) how well people will behave when put on their honour: nobody takes a newspaper from a box, when the man's gone off to lunch, without putting down a penny. The amounts involved are not comparable, but the fundamentals are. I don't believe, in fact, that there *would* be a loss: there might even be a profit. Practical politicians will no doubt think all this *meshuggah*. A little *meshuggaas* of the kind is precisely what these gentlemen could do with.

Then, freedom of speech and assembly, not only for Englishmen but also for anybody else whom we can allow or not allow to say what he likes, should be guarded with an almost agonised fanaticism. Nothing of the sort appeared to characterise Mr Chuter Ede's decision in the matter of a World Peace Congress which was recently to have been staged at Sheffield. He prevented a whole lot of people, some of them highly distinguished in their way, from entering the country. Of course the Congress was bogus: of course it had little to do with peace: of course it was communist in origin and aim. But what sort of comparison could there be between the possibility of contamination by a few dozen foreigners under the noses of M.I.5, and the certainty of blotting our own precious copy-book— of spoiling our tradition as one of the few great countries in the world where any bloody person can bloody well say what he pleases? If I had been Prime Minister, as I occasionally wish that I might be, I should have welcomed the Congress with open arms; should have ensured for its speeches a positively ostentatious publicity; and should at the same time have seen to it that in so far as I thought them pernicious they should be countered with equal publicity. But then I am still of the opinion that the only proper method of dealing with lies is to disseminate truth.

And here is my couple of suggestions applicable to full socialism; or rather, now I come to think of it, not quite to that, but to socialism at various stages between the present regime and a socialism that can properly be called full, which is to say Christian communism:

First, I would retain for many decades, and if need be for centuries (but I hope that would be unnecessary), an appropriate sector of "private enterprise". This is not because there

L

is anything good about private enterprise in the sense in which the term is here used, as synonymous, that is to say, with production for personal profit: on the contrary, it is bad: but the fact of its always being possible could undoubtedly do a very great deal to prevent tyranny, besides keeping alive the idea that there's nothing more valuable than "go" and initiative as such. This sector, however, should be neither of a size nor of a kind such as to involve any serious risk of its infecting the community with the spirit of greed, or spoiling the general tone of public service. I should hope, indeed, that it would become thoroughly unpopular, but that so long as it were necessary at all there would always be an army of volunteers who would be willing, however reluctantly, to engage in it from motives of public service, namely to safeguard liberty: just as, among the Arapesh—see later—people reluctantly take on jobs of a nauseating prominence from patriotic motives. I should hope also that, living in a society from which greed would have all but vanished, they would give away any extra proceeds either to people who for one reason or another were in particular need of them, or to the State.

Secondly, an old suggestion by Bertrand Russell is well worth reviving. He proposed to safeguard freedom by paying everyone an annual income sufficient to guarantee the means of bare subsistence, whatever work he might be doing or not doing; and he further proposed that these incomes should be paid in the form of money valid only for one year—a method which, while enabling a man to save for a summer holiday, would prevent such an accumulation of riches as might threaten a reintroduction of the capitalist system. An admirable proposal: though we oughtn't even to consider it until the problem of world hunger is at any rate on the road to solution. But even a device such as Russell's would be unnecessary in the final society, under conditions of Christian communism: for the principle of truly decent living—"to each according to his need"—would there at last reign unchallenged.


I want here, at the end of these two sections on poverty and freedom, to express the remorse I've been feeling, on and off, at my cantankerousness about the Labour Party and politicians in general. I don't withdraw anything I've said: but I realise that it's easy for me to talk, and that choosing what you're going to do from time to time in politics, and then doing it at your own pace and in your own way, as I do it, is something very different from the day by day sweat of the professional politician, with all the compromises and limitations it implies. I am sometimes filled with humble admiration when I watch some of these men, half dead with fatigue, toiling away at an endless mass of detail that must bore them stiff, and doing so, not from personal ambition, but in the service of socialism: and I know very well how tormented they often are when they are faced with two evils and must choose the lesser, or when they feel, rightly or wrongly, and I nearly always think wrongly, that they must even acquiesce in what they regard as outrageous, because otherwise, they tell themselves, the party would be driven from office and deprived of its power to do good. Not that I want to whitewash them all: some do little but hang about the smoking-room and bars, and others are mainly out for themselves. But the amount of self-sacrificing devotion remains great, and not only on the part of M.Ps. but also of innumerable "little" workers in local labour parties and the like; and it is by the grind of men and women such as these that socialism is built. The only value of people like me is that, from our position unencumbered by trees, we can call attention to the wood.

We are ready now for the third and last section of this chapter; but I shall seize the opportunity, before passing on, of copying out a few sentences by my friend Ernest Newman, the first of music critics, in today's *Sunday Times*. I do so because they express far more eloquently than I can, and certainly far more briefly, much that I have been trying to say in this long disquisition on socialism, and indeed in this whole letter; or much, at any rate, of the emotion behind them. I hope the great old man will not mind my quoting him: he calls himself, I imagine, a High Tory.

"I have often been saddened," he writes, "when coming out of a theatre during the interval of an opera, at the contrast between the ideal world of beauty I have just left and the real world I am facing, between, let us say, the tenderness and pity of 'Parsifal' and the machine for grinding out punishment that is symbolised in the building on the opposite side of Bow Street, or between the exquisite dream-world of 'Così fan tutte' and the clutter of mean streets and ugly houses surrounding the King's Theatre in Edinburgh.

"Must this antinomy between the spiritual riches of some of earth's more favoured beings and the spiritual poverty of others of them remain unresolved for ever? Is no positive thinkable without a negative, and as the latter painfully edges closer to the former must the march of civilisation spring a further gulf between the two? Covent Garden always seems to me to sum up civilisation in the simplest of equations: on the one side of Bow Street, the Police Court; on the other side, directly opposite, Sing-Sing. Always, as I survey the wondrous scene, I am reminded of the people in the tale who, ship-wrecked on an unknown coast, wondered if they were to fall into the hands of savages, until, to their relief, they came upon some bodies hanging from a gibbet, 'and they knew they were in a civilised country.' "

## § 3. SOCIALISM AND GOODNESS

Freedom will still be the theme in this last section. The ultimate freedom.

I cannot remember, as I have already told you, even an approximate date on which I might have said to myself "I am still a liberal, but I am also now, quite definitely, a socialist." Nor can I remember which of the various relevant considerations, if any one of them alone, was decisive. Did I "become" a socialist when, brooding on the topics discussed in the last section, I realised that self-direction and self-expression in men's working lives would be impossible, by and large, so long as capitalism persisted? Or was it a connection in my mind between capitalism and war, that first detestation of my child-ish spirit, that chief detestation of my adult spirit now, which gave me the effective push? I do not know. But suppose some-one were to ask me "What was it that, at a definite moment of your life whether you can remember the moment or not, made it utterly impossible for you ever to think of yourself as anything but a socialist again? What weighed with you

then, what weighs with you now, as final and absolute—
in the sense that, though you may in fact have owed your
conversion to something quite different, you would still be a
socialist, you would still have been a socialist from the moment
I am asking you about, even if every other argument had
tumbled about your ears or were to tumble about your ears
tomorrow—even if, for instance, you had realised, and were
still to realise, that capitalism and war are wholly unconnected,
and that self-direction and self-expression in men's working
lives are far more easily attainable, when everything has been
said, under your hated capitalism than under any conceivable
form of socialism which the wit of man could invent?" Well, if
someone were to ask me that I should not hesitate for a second
about my reply. I should say "I can never be anything but a
socialist, because capitalism is flatly immoral."

I am always amazed at the hardihood with which Christians,
speaking professedly as Christians, defend the profit motive
as such. I was recently invited by John Collins to address
a week-end conference of "Christian Action" at Oxford. In
fact he wanted me to open it by presenting the audience with
what, on such occasions, he always calls "a challenge": the
theory being that I am a Jew, that Christians would be offended
if I talked Christianity as one of them, and that I must therefore
be presented as a gadflyish outsider. I am getting a little
tired of this humbug, and so is John, who likes it no better
than I do. But in any event the proposal was stymied; because
some really big people insisted on resigning if the idea were
proceeded with—even more, I gathered, because I was a socialist
than because I was a Jew. So I was slipped in for the following
evening, when I should be less conspicuous. I spoke, as I thought,
with studied moderation; but as the whole object of the conference was to pursue ways and means of living Christianity in our
daily lives I could hardly avoid expounding the ethical case for
socialism. You must understand that no one was there but
avowed devotees of Christian Action; and Christian Action had
been started—only a few years before, so that the time for
decay had been short—with the single objective of applying
Christian ethics to national and international affairs. Anyhow
I spoke, I feel quite certain, unprovocatively.

When I had finished a man got up and asked me a question
at once awkward and pleasing. "Do you imply," he said, "that

an antisocialist can't be a Christian, or a Christian an antisocialist?" Observing at least one well known Tory in the
audience, I formulated my reply very carefully as I slowly
advanced to the edge of the platform. "A good Christian," I
said, "a Christian far better than I could ever dream of imagining myself to be, can be an antisocialist provided—provided a
number of things: (*a*) if he is stupid; or (*b*) if for one reason or
another he has never really thought the thing out to its end;
or (*c*) if, as a professional man perhaps, he has had no vivid
experience of the motives that necessarily operate in capitalist
production and distribution; or (*d*) if being clever, wise, and
himself engaged in some business enterprise, he is persuaded
(quite erroneously in my view) that in the present stage of
human development the supersession of capitalism by socialism
would inevitably mean, not less free play for egoism, but free
play for it in another and perhaps more evil form; and that
while the profit motive as such is base, and while we must
work for its eventual disappearance, we must beware meanwhile of intensifying, by a socialist revolution before the time
is ripe, all those emotions of envy, malice and hatred which
are even more detrimental to a decent way of living than the
economic selfishness inherent in capitalism itself. These are a
few examples," I continued, "of the type of man who can be an
antisocialist while remaining the best Christian in the world,
and in one case at least by very reason of being a good Christian. But nobody can be a good Christian who, not being stupid,
advocates the profit motive as, apart from circumstances,
proper and even valuable in itself. Surely that is obvious?" No,
it wasn't at all obvious. I noticed a certain atmosphere of
constraint at the coffee and buns that followed my address;
and when I asked John to tell me frankly whether I had
dropped an appalling brick and ruined his conference, he
replied that while the majority were with me—but rather
tepidly, I thought, to judge from demeanours, for there are
usually one or two on such occasions who rush up to me and
greet me as the Messiah, and nothing of the kind was occurring
—a quite small but influential minority was furious. This
included the publicity manager of a great film combine and a
well known Judge. The latter would be taking part in one of
the many small conferences at which, after the coffee and buns,
the main address was to be discussed. I sought permission—not

directly, of course—to attend this conference and explain my point of view more fully. The Judge's reply was that if I put in an appearance he would immediately leave the room. I must add, in tribute to him, that he realised later the dubious Christianity of this, and withdrew his veto. No similar change of heart occurred, as I gathered, in the film man. Even a young journalist well known for his "advanced" opinions remarked to John at lunch next day that he had been "amused" by my "obvious nonsense". And I was severely trounced by a respectable, if slightly fossilised, Church paper, which remarked that "Mr Gollancz, who appears to have learned nothing, still talks in the language of the Left Book Club". And why not? Did they expect me to talk in the language of the Primrose League?

We motored back to Brimpton after the conference, and I spent the night in turmoil. One of the things I've retained from my boyhood is intellectual passion, and one of the things I've retained from my remote ancestors (if that's really the explanation, which seems highly improbable) is proselytising fury; and I tossed about till morning in agony, horrified that anybody could be in such spiritual and intellectual error. I mooted to Ruth when the tea came up the desirability of returning to Oxford, getting John to abandon the Sunday programme, and organising a debate on what after all, in view of yesterday's revelations, seemed the only thing worth bothering about. Ruth, who wanted me to get on with this letter, and anyhow thinks less highly than I do of the whole Christian Action caboodle, dissuaded me. I wish she hadn't: I hate to think of the Judge, the journalist and the film man still in limbo.

(Ruth often says "no". She has a stronger sense of human limitations than I have. Wanting to describe the garden this morning, and despairing of success—for the blaze of it, of its lychnis and nemesia and rose campion and sweet-william, is at least twice as brilliant as it was in the same sort of sunshine last week—I begged her to paint me a little corner for the embellishment of this letter. "Reproduce in dull paints," she replied, "the light of the world?")

I can understand people saying that Christianity is nonsense. I can understand them not saying but thinking it. I can understand them, better perhaps this time than most people, admitting its truth but finding it too difficult for themselves or anybody else; and in case that is your own opinion, hang on to the thread of my argument while you let your mind linger for a moment on some beautiful sentences of François de Sales:

"But you see that the mountain of Christian perfection is extremely high. Ah! my God, you say this: how then shall I be able to climb it? Courage, Philothea! When the little bees begin to take shape they are called nymphs, and do not know yet how to fly over the flowers, or on the mountains, or on the neighbouring hills to gather honey. But little by little, nourishing themselves with the honey which their mothers have prepared, these little nymphs take wing and become strong, so that afterwards they fly to gather honey through the whole country. It is true that we are still little bees in devotion, we do not know how to climb as we would, which is nothing less than to attain the summit of Christian perfection. But if we begin to take shape by our desires and resolutions, our wings will begin to grow. We must therefore hope that one day we shall be spiritual bees, and shall fly. And meanwhile, let us live on the honey of the precepts which devout people of old have left us in so large quantity, and let us pray God that He will give us feathers like doves that not only shall we be able to fly in the time of the present life, but may also rest in the eternity of the future."

"The honey of the precepts which devout people of old"— and one in particular—"have left us in so large quantity." For whatever else I may come to understand I shall never understand this: how people who profess themselves Christians, and are often far better Christians than I could ever hope to be in what are usually called personal relations, can defend a profit motive, in itself and as such, which is clearly and flatly opposed to Christ's teaching, to the whole of his life, and to his death on the Cross. I am not going to start bandying texts like the people who, in arguments about pacifism, are forever trying to stump you with the money-changer episode: not realising that Christ, who had a few human weaknesses, was capable of losing his temper, and even committing violence, when up against so final an expression of capitalist immorality as trafficking in the Temple, without bringing into question, however, the pacifism of which his whole life was a revelation. No, I'm not going to start bandying texts, for everybody knows that what I'm saying is true. What did Christ come to save us from? From a sterile preoccupation, a morbid growing-together, an incestuous marriage with a self that we ruin by loving as separate (which in fact means not loving it at all): from pride, self-centredness, greed. And what did he come to save us *for*? For community. Is it suggested, then, that to seek your own profit is to be anything but greedy? Or that a system which depends on the profit motive is not morally legitimising selfishness? Or that playing for yourself is community? Capitalism, indeed, does more than merely legitimise selfishness: it consecrates it.

If my every other reason for being a socialist (though every reason is the same reason, ultimately) fell to the ground: if my every other reason suddenly appeared as the opposite of a reason: if, to postulate the inconceivable, I were persuaded by a superior intelligence that socialism would inevitably not merely fail to yield the fruits I have claimed for it but would yield their opposites; nevertheless, and in spite of everything I have said about the spiritual evils of poverty and the spiritual good of self-expression in men's working lives and so on, my socialism would remain quite unshaken. For here, once again, we are in the realm of absolutes. There is a final sticking-point. You *cannot* base society on the ultimate evil.

I know I shall be told by marxists that capitalism, and therefore the profit motive, have been "historically progressive". They may have been—I don't know. Perhaps the world, now on the verge of destroying itself by an atomic war, would be a better place if capitalism had never existed. People similarly talk about Napoleon having been "historically progressive"; and I have heard a left-wing intellectual say the same about Hitler, on the ground that what he did will eventually lead to the unification of Europe. But the whole question is irrelevant. God can no doubt use everything, human greed included, for his own ends. But that does not absolve *us* from the duty of listening to the truth which he has put into our consciences and revealed to us through Jesus Christ, the truth, namely, that greed is evil, and that we may not, and in the true sense cannot, live by it. So when Appleby-Smythe finds my attack on the profit motive "amazing", and says that our job is not to abandon it but to retain it and harness it to the public good—he does not even mean for a few decades, he means permanently—I am

confirmed in my view that marxists generally, and most ex-
marxists as well, understand very little about ethics. I will go
further, and, at the risk of appearing to trail my coat, will confess that, in spite of his brilliant insights and the fruitfulness of
his analyses, I have never thought of Marx as a real socialist—
by reason, but not only by reason, of this very attitude of his
towards capitalism.

*Brimpton, July 15th*
*Two quotations, "on the occasion of waking at Brimpton early
on a summer morning." About the world:*

> *"ere the high lawns appeared
> Under the opening eyelids of the morn."*

*About oneself, looking at the little early-Victorian gold and lacquer
chairs, the row of books, the Lucien Pissarro water-colours, the
chest of drawers, the Leeds horse, and so on, as the light comes
flooding through the curtains of the east window:*

> *"Her waking infant-stare"*

Now there are only two ways, fundamentally, of ordering
society. One of them is to base your productive and distributive
system on private profit-making, whether in a modified form or
not. That is the capitalist way. The other is to base it on everybody seeking always, first and last, directly and indirectly, the
general good, with no Benthamite nonsense in the offing about
the general good resulting, with a beautiful sort of Blake-like
casualness, from everybody seeking his own. That is, or ought
to be, the socialist way, and socialist machinery is in any case
the *sine qua non* for it. But to repudiate capitalism because the
profit motive is a bad motive, and to advocate the right kind of
socialism because seeking the general good is a good motive, is
not quite the same thing as advocating the right kind of socialism because the right kind of socialism can make it easier, in my
old phrase, for men to be good. But I am anxious, above all, to
show that it can, and shall now try to do so.

When I say that the right kind of socialism can make it easier
for men to be good what I mean is this. Most human beings,
perhaps all human beings, are the battle-ground for a struggle

between self-regarding impulses, issuing in greed, fear, strife, envy, jealousy, malice and hatred, and other-regarding impulses, issuing in unity and peace. Or this, rather, is how the matter presents itself to human consciousness, for I do not believe that there are two ultimate principles at work in reality. Somehow there is a rift in the created world, or reality, or existence, or whatever you may prefer to call it. How, when (if it is a matter of time) or why this rift occurred or occurs no mortal man can say. There are hundreds of explanations, stretching all the way from somebody's doctrine of a pre-mundane Fall to the latest psychological theorising. But whatever the explanation, the fact is a matter of unquestionable human experience. I can best express the background of my own thought on this question in the form of a theological myth. God was (or should we say, in the more appropriate language of eternity, is?) undifferentiated. But he perceives differentiation, concreteness, Blake's "minute particulars", as supreme value. He therefore creates (splits himself up into, produces as emanations?) these concrete particulars. But, by a law of reality, multiplicity involves relation, and a concrete particular, if it is to be a concrete particular, must have being and the potentiality for growth within itself. Each particular, therefore, being and growing, must be in relation with every other particular, also being and growing. Now the particulars, not being God (though being of or from God), cannot feel or know perfectly meanwhile—though they can and do have intimations about it—how the value of individual being and growth, and the value of relation, may be realised not as two conflicting values but as the one value which in fact they are: for individual being can be perfect only when there is perfect relation, and relation can be perfect only when there is perfection of individual being. The particulars cannot feel or know perfectly how to manage this, I said, "meanwhile": during the intermediate stage, that is—to use again the perhaps inapplicable language of temporality—between the undifferentiated God and the God become a unity of innumerable rejoicing particulars. The goal, if the word can be used when eternity is in question, is beautifully illuminated by a sentence from the Zohar: "When mankind is at one, God is One."

God, desiring this consummation (which may or may not be involved in the historical process), can help men understand how to live by the intimations he gives them; but he cannot do more than help; for if he did more he would be derogating from the value of individual being, which is the point, as it were, of the whole business.

There is nothing, by the way, "unscientific" about this theological myth. It is consistent with biology's "struggle to survive", and with a great many findings of psychoanalysis.

Let me put it in another way. All men desire the peace of home—the same peace of the same home, always. Some of them know they can win it only by losing their lives—by co-operation, by altruism, by love: and they, even, commonly achieve no more than a few passing victories on the outskirts of the central battle—the battle against a way of life they know to be ruinous. Others think, but usually with a mingling of wiser thoughts, that they can win their desire by concentration on self. They do no worse than misunderstand. God, I am sure, forgives them. He forgives Hitler; he forgives Stalin; he forgives you; he forgives me. He is, after all, at least jointly responsible. "The last prayer, *forgive them, for they know not what they do*", wrote Ian Suttie, "seems to imply that forgiveness is not a condescension to an unworthy object, but a recognition (on somewhat Socratic lines) that evil is merely error, not to be met by retributive error."

Always forgive, Timothy. Never let people put it over you that pity and forgiveness are soft and debilitating. Look into your own heart: see yourself, and forgive. You could do worse than memorise, for use in moments of forgetfulness, Walter de la Mare's poem, "One in the Public Gallery":

"The Seraph scanned the murderer in the dock—
    The motionless Judge, beneath the court-room clock,
    The listening jury, warders, counsel, Clerk;
Ay, one and all who shared that deepening dark:
        And then, as I shunned to see,
    He turned his burning eyes and looked at me."

And now I find I cannot let the opportunity go without saying something more about forgiveness, and the well-wishing and reconciliation that are involved with it. The important thing is this: Forgiveness must be, both in its inner completeness and in its non-discrimination about objects, unconditional forgiveness: well-wishing must be, both in its inner completeness and in its non-discrimination about objects, unconditional well-wishing: and reconciliation must be unconditional reconciliation.

Let us examine for a moment only two of the limitations which it is commonly thought right or necessary to impose upon the practice of forgiveness and well-wishing; and please note that I say "thought right or necessary", for I have in mind, not the weakness of anyone who, like myself, is unable to rise to the full height of the argument, but conditions and limitations that are deliberately imposed. You sometimes hear it said, for instance—I have heard it said by a famous leader of religious thought in this country—that to wish a man well would be not only unreasonable but downright immoral, if he has wronged you or someone else or humanity in general *beyond a given point*, or if you judge him to have been guilty, *beyond a given point*, of cruelty or faithlessness or whatever wickedness it may be. One might retort with an adaptation of some famous words, and ask "If ye love only the obviously lovable, what reward have ye? Even the spiritually careless do the same". The moment you make this kind of distinction in your well-wishing, it is clear that you do not begin to understand what well-wishing really means. To wish a man well is to wish that as a personality, as a partaker in the universal personality, he may have life, spiritual life, in greater abundance. How can it be relevant whether he has harmed you or others, or transgressed the moral law, beyond a certain point? Or rather it *is* relevant: because his revolt from love and reality demands from you, and precisely in your meeting with him, a correspondingly greater loyalty to them: the more his lack, the more you have to give. It is *he*, he in his immortal essence, he as an everlasting personality, with which you are concerned: but the moment you begin judging, the moment you begin weighing and measuring, you are not with him but with yourself. It is surely by no means a paradox, but the simple truth, to say that it is far more important to wish a man well whom you judge to be very wicked than to wish a man well whom you judge to be rather wicked, and to wish a man well whom you judge to be rather wicked than to wish a man well whom you judge to be a saint. Or to put it another way, it is precisely the hater who has most need of our love: and if we can really love him unconditionally, if we can really love him in spirit and in truth, the hatred will go and love take its place.

I will give only one more example of the conditions and limitations which people impose on well-wishing. It is sometimes

said—this also was said a year or two ago by one of our
great religious leaders—that you cannot and ought not to forgive a wrongdoer until he has repented. There is here a quite
radical misconception. What is in fact being said is that until the
other has become good you ought not to be good yourself. How
then can a start ever be made? I said before that to wish a man
well whom we judge wicked is more important than to wish a
man well whom we judge good: I will now go further and say
that it is more important to wish a man well who has not
repented than to wish a man well who has. It is precisely his
repentance, his reunion with love and reality, that we desire to
produce: and it is by loving him, we believe, that we produce it.
To say that we will love him only if he repents is to propose a
sort of bargain more relevant to the counting-house than to
spiritual reality. I would add that while an expression of sorrow
for having wronged, and perhaps restitution, are due to the
wronged one, repentance is to God: only God can judge of it:
and for a man to demand repentance, or to weigh up its quality,
is Satanic presumption, and a breach of the commandment that
forbids us to take the name of the Lord our God in vain.

What it all adds up to is this. We are called upon to love our
neighbour: and our neighbour means not merely the good man,
or the repentant man, or the man in the next street—indeed not
chiefly these—but just man—man indifferently, man everywhere.

Humility also comes in. Unless it is in utter humility that we
hold out our hands, the other will not grasp them: he cannot
grasp them, because, in spirit and in truth, they are not there.
Genuine charity is an act of complete self-surrender: if we are
really to meet the other, we must cut and cast away our last
moorings. If we judge the other, if we compare the other to ourselves, if, with whatever worthy motive, we play the schoolmaster or even the loving father and guide, there can be no
spiritual meeting: for we have by no means cut our moorings:
we have stayed on our own shore, and beckoned the other to us.
He will not come.


I had been hazarding a guess, before that interruption, as to
why men are the battle-ground for a struggle between self-
regarding and other-regarding impulses. But whatever the

explanation, the fact is one of everyday experience; and I am suggesting that socialism, the right kind of socialism, can help in this struggle. It can help negatively and it can help positively. It can help negatively, simply because it does away with the atmosphere of competitive capitalism. In all capitalist societies, and in a society such as ours which though semi-socialist in structure is still mainly capitalist in spirit, business psychology sets the tone (civil servants, professional men, artists, scientists and so on notwithstanding, and in spite of the professional element, when present, in business itself): and sets it increasingly, as we become more and more commercialised. A principal in business has his eye fixed on profits: profits are the rationale of his business life, whatever other motives may be present and whatever he may really put higher in his own scale of values. On the first day of January and from morning till night he must be thinking of what the balance-sheet will look like on the last day of December: to buy as cheap as he can and sell as dear as he can for his own advantage, directly or indirectly—that is the basis of his whole activity. The manager, if not so directly concerned with "making money"—can you think of a more disgusting phrase? —must identify himself, in his own interest, with the competitive interest of his firm. The shareholder watches his dividends. And working-class people, even if you could imagine them unaffected by the miasma that spreads from the top, would still have to fight for themselves by relentless trades union action—fight tooth and nail to extract every shilling, or else go under. So most people are either positively encouraged, or more or less compelled, to think first of themselves and their families, which are an extension of themselves.

It is hateful and corrupting, this climate of competitive capitalism. Sometimes when I travel down to Reading in a first-class compartment, and listen to the conversation around me, I am appalled by the beastliness of which decent men and women are capable. I recently heard a prosperous-looking man abusing, very foully, the whole working class because trades union action had forced up the wages of his men from five pounds and something a week to five pounds and something a little more. He didn't stop to consider what life on such a wage for a man with a wife and three children must be like. And the rest of the compartment apparently agreed with him.

I have been in business myself now for close on thirty years,

and, though I love publishing, and should hate to exchange it
for any other occupation in the world, except schoolmastering—
for I am really a schoolmaster *manqué*, as you've probably discovered—I have never ceased to detest, almost daily and with
the whole of my being, the commercial necessities that life at
Henrietta Street imposes on me: to detest and feel degraded by
them. This may sound mealy-mouthed and affected; you may
think there's a ring about it of "*I* am too fine for *this*, *this* is too
sordid for *me*". Perhaps there is; but then the "I" and "me" are
not the "I" and "me" who is Victor Gollancz, but the "I" and
"me" who is a human being. "What is the worst thing the Evil
Urge can achieve?" asked Rabbi Shelomo of Karlin; and
answered, "To make man forget that he is the son of a king".
The son of a king does not figure out on little bits of paper how
much money he will make if he pays such and such a royalty to
an author, and how much less if he pays such and such: and
then decide to pay the smaller percentage, irrespective of the
relative needs of himself and the author, because if he pays the
larger he will fail to make an adequate profit or perhaps make
no profit at all, and you can't run a business under capitalism if
you fail to make profits. I suppose I've been as decent a business
man as most. But decency in business is merely relative: the
thing itself is indecent. You cannot serve God and Mammon.
    And I know that my attention to profits (a necessary atten-
tion with things as they are), combined with other people's
attention to profits or various "interests", makes me worse than
I might otherwise have been. I should like to give myself wholeheartedly in service, in loving-kindness to my fellow men: I
do so only casually, only in fits and starts, only, as the Greeks
would have said, ἐκ παρέργου, because my thoughts are so
often elsewhere. And a quality waxes in proportion to its
activity: employ it seldom, and it atrophies. Moreover what
other people are thinking and doing has a powerful effect
even on a rebel: one follows the norm, by and large, even while
protesting against it, and even if one lives in active opposition
to it over a relatively small area. The fact that I was born into
a capitalist society makes it easier for me—I don't put it more
positively than that—to keep the greater part of what I "make"
for myself and my family, while millions are starving: which is
plainly disgusting, if you get outside the atmosphere for a
moment and think freshly about it.

It is in America, which is the model of capitalism, that people are most conspicuously encouraged by their environment to think first of themselves and their families. I should be sorry if you thought that I disliked America, and was anxious to attack it: I like people of all nationalities, and Americans, in some ways, particularly, and I detest the anti-American agitation that is fashionable at the moment in some left-wing circles. Left-wingers who work up ill feeling against any race or nation whatever are no true left-wingers at all, for to be a left-winger means, or should mean, to love humanity. Moreover, to dislike a man for characteristics that his background and history have made all but inevitable is stupid and coarse; and American history, starting with a revolt from oppression and with an onrush of pioneering, adequately explains American characteristics.

So it is to illustrate and not to attack that I say what I say about Americans. I am shamefully generalising, for I know only a fragment of the country, New York City and Connecticut in the main, and only a limited selection of the people who live in it. And even within that selection I know quite a number who walk untainted, "fresh as the dew on flowers", through the perilous atmosphere. For perilous it is; and the poison that infects it is an inversion of values that sees viciousness as virtue. To aim high—for oneself; to get on; to arrive: these, for too many Americans, are ethical imperatives; and though no American would quite put it like this—there would be a clash, if he did so, between a norm almost instinctively accepted and a Christianity explicitly professed—a good man, in the popular ideology, is a man who "makes good".

*Brimpton, Saturday, July 21st*

*A Bulletin of the Schweitzer Hospital Fund arrived in this morning's post, just as I'd come to "who makes good" when running through what I'd written last night. Do you know about Schweitzer? He is eminent as a philosopher and theologian, and plays Bach superbly; but people think of him chiefly as a man who, while still in his thirties, went out to Lambaréné in French Equatorial Africa, and, from then till now, has doctored a few hundred Africans. That is all: he has doctored a few hundred Africans. There has been nothing large-scale about his work: it*

*has gone on in the same modest way for—it must be now for close
on forty years. There are hundreds, even thousands, who have cured
men and women, or relieved human suffering, on a far greater
scale. And yet I should say that Albert Schweitzer is loved—by the
relatively small number of people to whom his name means anything—in a way no other person is loved who is living today:
loved as a man can be loved whom one has heard of or read, but
never known. "Christ" wrote Oscar Wilde "does not really teach
one anything, but by being brought into his presence one becomes
something." So a man becomes something by being brought into
Schweitzer's presence: simply by the consciousness that he is a fellow
human being with Schweitzer.*

*You know, Timothy, these few sentences aren't really irrelevant,
as perhaps you may think them to be. For this letter is the record of
a search, and at the same time a search itself: a search for a
manner of living that will enable human beings to be true to the
best that is in them. What could be more relevant than the example
of Schweitzer? He would not pretend that, theoretically, he has
solved the problem. He leaves it, in a sense, unsolved. He tells us
that, in human conditions, we cannot help doing wrong—doing it
not once or twice, but times out of number. We must turn a man
out of his job, for instance, when he is ruining our firm, for if we
failed to do so hundreds would suffer. We have to strike a balance:
we are involved in relativities. But let us always obey, Schweitzer
says, two imperatives. First, never let us pretend that when we are
doing a wrong we are not doing a wrong: let us not pretend, for
instance, that when we turn a man out of his job we are doing
anything but outrage to the law of charity. Let us not call such
behaviour ethical: let us call it unethical, and confess that we see no
way of avoiding it. Secondly, let us never do even the smallest
wrong unless we are certain that it is quite inescapable. "The
farmer who has mown down a thousand flowers in his meadow to
feed his cows, must be careful on his way home not to strike off in
thoughtless pastime the head of a single flower by the roadside, for
he thereby commits a wrong against life without being under the
pressure of necessity."*

*Schweitzer's ethical theory is criticised by many as inadequate
and inconsistent. His critics may be right: though he seems to me,
who have no technical competence in the subject, to get very near
the truth, with his recognition of a final insolubility under human
conditions—of something remaining over which impinges as self-*

*contradictory. What is important, however, is his practice, not his theory: or not even his practice, but a spirit in him that, quiet there in Africa, exists, because of him, in the world as a whole. He has lived his "reverence for life" to the uttermost, accepting only the limit imposed by human necessities: and people all over the world, by that law of correspondence which justifies reality, have given love for love: love in Germany, and America, and this little Berkshire village, for his love in Africa.*

*I have never met Schweitzer, and have only once had a letter from him. It contains the most genuine expression of unaffected modesty that has ever come my way. In "A Year of Grace" I had printed a good deal from his writings, including the whole chapter on "Reverence for Life" from "Civilisation and Ethics", and had sent him a copy when my book was off the press. I got a reply about a couple of months later, on a flimsy sheet of paper with his name and address rubber-stamped on it. "I always thought," he said, "that there was something in my ethic of Reverence for Life, but I never expected to see it acknowledged in this way." I have the letter framed on my library desk, in the window overlooking the downs; opposite it is a photograph of Schweitzer himself, with two antelopes nuzzling his arm. There is nothing else on the desk except the first few bars of the bridal march from L'Oiseau de Feu: Stravinsky wrote them out for me over dinner at the Langham one night, after I'd told him that Ruth and I had decided to get married, without saying so to one another, while this music was being played at Covent Garden.*

*(How bad it would be for us if beauty were perpetual! There had been until this morning—it is now Monday, and I am back in Henrietta Street—about ten blazing skies in succession, and we had got used to them: then came a tropical deluge, darkening everything. But as I woke from my afternoon rest a few minutes ago the sun was shining again: shining through my office window as it must have shone for Adam.)*

*And now I must tell you of what delighted me so about the Bulletin that arrived on Saturday morning. There was an account in it of Schweitzer's seventy-sixth birthday party earlier this year, written by someone who had just returned to Europe after a stay of several months at Lambaréné. She describes how at dawn there was singing outside Schweitzer's house; first by a choir of boys from the Protestant Mission, then by the lepers' choir, and then by a choir of other patients. And the organised songs were not the end of it, for soon everyone was singing—in Baloa and in Pahouin. A procession formed up next, of patients bringing gifts to the Doctor. Some small native children carried plates piled with maize or bananas or ground-nuts; others brought an egg, or branches of wild flowers from the jungle. One old woman struggled with an enormous basket of char-coal which she had prepared herself, knowing it was precious for the hospital. An old hospital servant came last with an egg still quite warm—he had waited for the hen to lay it.*

*Late the same night the Doctor was still working on his manu-script. The parrot Kudeku sat motionless in its basket. On the bed by his piano the three young antelopes, who are probably children of the antelopes in my photograph, stirred gently in their sleep. Below, in the theatre, the doctors were performing an emergency operation on a native woman; and, in their huts beyond, the four hundred patients were sleeping. . .*

*There is also a delightful description of Christmas 1950 at Lambaréné. It was celebrated before nightfall, in the clearing under lofty palms before the Doctor's house, by almost the whole popula-tion of the Hospital—orderlies, staff, and as many of the patients as were able to attend. The Doctor read the story of Christmas from St. Luke, and everyone sang hymns. Then the Doctor spoke, very simply. He said that Christmas was the loveliest of all the feast days, and that the presents we give one another are symbols of the goodness of God and of his great gifts to us. He then gave a present to everyone there. The men got basins, a kilo of rice or a leather belt, and the women got handkerchiefs for their heads, a piece of soap or a length of material. The evening ended with the singing of the lepers.*

It is difficult to return from Schweitzer to capitalism and socialism; but having shown, as I hope, that the machinery of socialism—public ownership—can help negatively in the struggle between self-regarding and other-regarding impulses simply by superseding capitalism, I now have to ask, can it help positively too? Can it, apart from merely removing an obstacle, positively encourage the other-regarding impulses? Can it positively, in some degree, promote human virtue? The words "can", "help", "encourage", and "in some degree" are important. For the reply will be, not, unconditionally, that it *must* do this, nor again that it can ever do *more* than this—

more, namely, than "help", "encourage", and promote "in some degree": the reply will be that it will certainly do this *on one condition*. The condition is that the introduction of socialist machinery, in the given case, shall have resulted in a system of production and distribution under which people do genuinely produce and distribute, in some co-operative manner, for ends that are broader than the selfishly personal ones, and feel they are doing so. Or, to put it more briefly, the condition is that the introduction of socialist machinery shall have resulted in what I shall call for the rest of this section the co-operative commonwealth, the word co-operative being used in a restrictedly economic sense. If this condition is fulfilled, then, as I shall claim, the general atmosphere of co-operation for narrowly economic ends, the habituation of people to consider, during the ordinary processes of "earning their living", not their own but a larger interest, will encourage the other-regarding impulses over a far wider field, and so help to promote human virtue.

We cannot, unfortunately, take the fulfilment of our condition for granted, any more than we can take for granted, as we have seen, that socialist machinery will be used for the abolition of poverty or world hunger. But why can't we? Isn't the co-operative commonwealth what socialist machinery is there for? Doesn't a passion for it explain the whole socialist movement? Well, only to a certain, though to a highly significant, degree. For the movement towards public ownership or collectivisation in one form or another is also, in part, an almost automatic process of history, a brute, steamrollerish sort of thing more or less independent of human motivation. This is not to imply that history results from anything but the interplay of human consciousness and the physical environment, realising the will of God: but the innumerable thoughts, aims, impulses and actions of innumerable men and women, in combination, may produce a force, a current in the historical river, which sweeps on, as one of the factors to be reckoned with, all but independently of those separate activities. Whoever built the first modern factory was not consciously working for collectivisation: nor was the inventor of railways or of internal combustion engines or of electric telegraphs or the like: but the work of them all, combined with a great many other things, was to make this result, not inevitable, but far more probable than it would otherwise have been. And there is clearly no reason why the movement towards collectivisation, in so far as it is to be explained by a factor akin to brute force, should any more result in a co-operative commonwealth than in fascist totalitarianism or in Mr Burnham's Managerial Revolution.

There are many other things, too, which make it impossible for us to assume the fulfilment of our condition. For instance: The ideas and emotions which consciously and directly inspired the modern socialist movement in its initial stages were varied and largely inconsistent. There was the ideal of human brother-hood: there was the desire to hasten forward an historical process: there was the demand for justice by or on behalf of the working class; there was furious indignation at their wrongs: there was envy of the more fortunate: there was greed, which is the same greed whether you find it in rich or in poor: there was lust for power: there was irritation at capitalist inefficiency ("five milkmen for one street"): there was the pathological reaction—and this is even truer of middle-class than of working-class pioneers—to thwarted desires and thwarted affection: there was longing for a more genuine, a more widely diffused, freedom: and, what is not necessarily the same thing, there was detestation of tyranny. There was much love, but there was also much hate. Many of these ideas and emotions were simul-taneously present in the same person; and sometimes what masqueraded as love was really hate. It was clearly not inevit-able that a co-operative commonwealth should result from such a mixture of origins.

Again, the socialist movement developed very largely in the atmosphere of capitalism and western materialism. This is true, for the most part, even of Russia; for the effective element in Russian socialism was an importation from the West, and carried with it a great deal of the western climate. It was probable, therefore, that the socialist movement, as it ran its course, would be seriously affected by the capitalist virus; and there was always the danger that it might result, not in a co-operative commonwealth, but in a capitalism standing on its apex, in a new sort of capitalism of a new set of people with a capitalist mentality.

Moreover, there seems to be something in the very nature of legislation which prevents a full realisation of the spiritual ends which historically have motivated it, and sometimes positively defeats them. It is not merely that men may have grown weary by the time they arrive at the legislative stage: it is not merely that corruption may have intervened between the impulse to legislate for a particular purpose and the embodiment of this impulse in legislative action; it is, above and beyond both of these, that legislation itself, which is formal, almost mechanical, in character, tends somehow to despiritualise—to dry up the fountain of spirit in—the processes that produced it. Legislation might almost be described as fossilised spirit: or as the residue, the rather meagre and pathetic residue, of spiritual striving. That is not to deny its desirability: you can do little without it to modify the structure of society: I am only pointing out that human ideals, when concretised in legislative enactments, seem to lose *ipso facto* a great part of their life-giving quality. Nothing could be more urgent than to struggle against, and over-come, this tendency: and that can be done only if we keep flaming always—even when legislating about drains—the torch of the spirit.

But the final reason—the final reason why we cannot take the fulfilment of our condition for granted—is the most important of all. It is to be found in the existence of that vicious circle which I mentioned at the beginning of this chapter on social-ism. By and large, you cannot have good men without good systems, nor good systems without good men. Just as, if the men are not good enough, you cannot assume, as we found, that our socialist machinery will be used for the abolition of world poverty, so, if the men are not good enough, you cannot assume that it will be used to establish the co-operative common-wealth. And yet the establishment of the co-operative common-wealth, to beg the question for a few minutes, is one of the provisos for the men being good enough.

Well, can we do anything to fulfil our condition, so far as the vicious circle is concerned—for this alone can be in point, the other difficulties being, for the most part, a matter of unalter-able history? To ask that is to ask a far larger question, namely: how are we to deal with the vicious circle more generally, and not merely in respect of the condition we are at the moment discussing?

The answer, in so far as any verbal answer is possible, arises, almost indefinably, out of what I have already written and shall later be writing on a dozen different topics: out of the whole

of this letter, which itself is not so much a writing as a kind
of living. The answer to every question posed by human existence—the answer, as might better be said, to the question
of human existence itself—must be, in the modern jargon, an
existential one. Anybody who, for whatever reason, can do
so—why can some and not others? or can everybody?—must
leap in at every possible point: in the smallest things and the
biggest: in thinking, feeling, acting: in politics, economics, religious communion, personal relations—must leap in, always and
everywhere, with what, at the infinitesimal second which is also
eternity, is his whole being. To vary the metaphor, we must
gain a bit of ground here and a bit of ground there: to vary it
again, we must combine a number of public with a number of
private techniques. In the public sphere we must see to it, as I
suggested before, that as we get power and opportunity to introduce each new bit of machinery, we foster the spirit this
machinery is intended to serve and not its opposite; and, apart
from machinery, we must try, as every question arises, national
or international—I am going to say something that isn't usually
said, but why be shamefaced about it?—we must try to be good:
try when there's famine in India, try when the Germans are
beaten and require our aid, try when Mr Stalin provokes us.
This applies equally to leaders, and to ordinary men and
women who can influence them. In the private sphere, and
this again applies to both, we must go out from our selves into
the ineffable whole of which each of us is so trivial and yet so
crucial a part; and we must love God by loving our neighbour.
But with the right kind of love: with a love not so much expressing itself through works as identical with them, a love felt and
lived in the spirit of the Blake affirmation which it is now such
a pleasure to write out in full:

"He who would do good to another, must do it in minute
   particulars.
General good is the plea of the scoundrel, hypocrite, and
   flatterer."

These public and private techniques can be broadly classified
as the political and religious. But they are in fact one, and must
become one, for everything, as Péguy says, begins in mysticism
and ends in politics.

I said that people must leap in. No, *do* leap in: and the

amendment will make clear to you why, in spite of all the cautious formulations which have preceded this bit about the vicious circle, I believe that in due time, as the result of a vast act of existential co-operation, not only will our condition be fulfilled, but every possible good will be fulfilled also. As to whether men leap in of their own initiative or by the grace of God, and as to whether, or in what degree, these are two different ways of saying the same thing—I shall come to that presently.

Given, then, the fulfilment of our condition—given a co-operative commonwealth—will the atmosphere of such a commonwealth positively promote human virtue by encouraging other-regarding impulses over the whole field? Will it help men and women to be more gentle, more tolerant, more kindly, more loving? To be less jealous, less envious, less malicious, less aggressive? To be more pitiful and sympathetic, less censorious and self-righteous? To rejoice in another's joy and to sorrow in another's sorrow? To show mercy, to eschew retribution and punishment? Will it help them, in the old phrase that cannot be repeated too often, to save their life by losing it?

I claim that it will. But many, I ought to warn you, think otherwise: aggressiveness, they believe, is so fundamental that if you dam it up in one direction it will break out all the more fiercely in another. You cannot really argue about the nature of aggressiveness: you either hold this or that view or you don't. I think for my own part, with Ian Suttie, that hate is merely the frustration-form of love itself, distorted as protest, reproach, and an aggressiveness originally intended to compel attention: and that the varied forms of human emotion are interconvertible aspects of the same social feeling. And I think, with Erich Fromm, that the amount of destructiveness to be found in individuals is proportionate to the extent to which expansiveness of life is curtailed in them: the reference being, not to individual frustration of this or that instinctive desire, but to the thwarting of the whole of life, the blockage of spontaneity in the growth and expression of man's sensuous, emotional, and intellectual capacities. "Life has an inner dynamism of its own; it tends to grow, to be expressed, to be lived." If this tendency is thwarted the energy directed towards life undergoes a process of decomposition and changes into energies directed towards destruction; and the more life is realised, the less is the strength of destructiveness. "Destructiveness is the outcome of unlived life."

Now I believe that, once he has been given the opportunity, a man will find greater satisfaction for his life's "inner dynamism" —will find his life growing better, expressing itself better, being lived better—if he is quietly co-operating with his fellow human beings for the economic well-being of all, than if he is feverishly struggling either to "make money" or to save himself from destitution; and that his dynamism being thus better satisfied by virtue of his co-operation in the workaday sphere, there will be *pro tanto* less aggressiveness for erupting in other relations. Moreover, in more or less normal human beings the personality tends to develop as all more or less of a piece: a settled way of looking at things, of feeling about things, in one relation has a powerful effect on the way of looking at them and feeling about them in another. So, apart from reducing the available stock of aggressiveness in the individual concerned, his habit of co-operation over one field will facilitate a habit of co-operating over all the others; and because economic grab and greed have become unnatural to him, other forms of grab and greed—jealousy, envy, malice, self-righteousness, rejoicing in another's misfortune— will tend to be unnatural too. My repeated "more or less" and "tend" should be noted, because no more must be claimed than the following: that if a society is characterised by a well-established system of co-operative production and distribution, then the members of that society are likely on the whole, and positively by reason of the system being there as well as negatively by reason of its alternative, the competitive one, being absent—they are likely to be gentler, more tolerant, less envious and so on, than they would have been if the atmosphere had been different. (Other things being equal, including the degree of people's freedom from pathological twists resulting from environment in childhood: but this environment will itself be affected by the general environment.)

The matter, to borrow a term from anthropology, is one of social conditioning: a term I should prefer not to use, because it suggests an ironing out of differences, a stereotyping of personality, a suppression of deviants, which is repulsive to me. I like deviants, even "bad" ones. (But there is nothing wrong, there is everything right, about the best kind of social conditioning, which is conditioning for spontaneity.) At the moment, however, my point is simply this: that (a) people's characters are powerfully affected by the pattern of culture characteristic of their society, and (b) no element in the life of a society can do more to fix the pattern of its culture than its economic system—save only its religion: which in turn, if it is real religion, will involve an economic system compatible with it.


Patterns of culture are fascinating things. How many people, I wonder, have read Margaret Mead's "Sex and Temperament in Three Primitive Societies"? Presumably very few, unless it got into the Penguins. This is a pity, for to read it is to learn a great deal about the topic under discussion.

Dr Mead spent two years, 1931 to 1933, on the island of New Guinea, living with three separate peoples and investigating their patterns of culture. She visited first the Arapesh and then the Mundugumor. It is important to notice that, while her first choice was deliberate, her second was a matter of chance: she was not looking for a startling contrast, she accidentally found one. These peoples, moreover, live only about a hundred miles from one another, and there is nothing in the food they eat, or in their physical environment, to explain their differences. All apparently we can say is that for an unknown reason, and whether consciously or unconsciously, certain characteristics of human nature were selected at some period for social approval, and have since become more or less standardised.

I am going to reproduce something of what Dr Mead tells us about the Mundugumor, and a good deal more of what she found among the Arapesh. I shouldn't dare to do so, at the length I intend, in any piece of writing more formal than a letter: sense of proportion would forbid: but I am anxious that you should really get the feel of Arapesh society, and nothing shorter or less detailed, even if some of the details may at first seem irrelevant, would suffice for this purpose. So proportion must go hang, as the purpose is crucial; for in the Arapesh way of living, side by side with the Mundugumor, you have an incomparable illustration of my point, which is central for this essay, that different patterns of culture, however they may have arisen, condition people—I must use the disagreeable word again—to differences in feeling, thought and action so startling that some change in basic human nature might appear, though erroneously, to be in question. So fix in your mind where we've got to in the argument about socialism and goodness, with a view to picking it up in due course; and settle down in the meantime to an experience of the Arapesh which will surely be as refreshing to you in the hearing as to me in the telling.

## § 4. ARAPESH INTERLUDE

"The astonishing way," writes Dr Mead,* "in which the emphasis of Mundugumor culture contradicts and contrasts with the emphasis of Arapesh culture [which she had studied first] will be bound to strike the reader at once. During our first weeks among the Mundugumor there was much that was startling, much that was incomprehensible. The violence, the strangeness of the motivations that controlled these gay, hard, arrogant people, came to us abruptly, without warning, as we studied their customs and watched their lives." The Mundugumor, we learn, live among themselves in a state of mutual distrust and uncomfortableness: hostility exists between all the males of a household, between father and son as well as between brothers: life is riddled with suspicion and distrust. It is not unusual for a brother to go armed against a brother; a man hears of a relative's visit to his compound with apprehension or anger; and the sounds of angry voices are frequent in the by-paths and clearings and on the edge of the river.

It is important to realise that such viciousness is not accidental: it is deliberately induced and maintained. Mundugumor social organisation "is based upon a *theory* of a natural hostility that exists between all members of the same sex." Children are *trained* to feel uncomfortable in the presence of most of their relatives. Brothers, from early adolescence, "are *forced* to treat each other with excessive formality, avoid each other whenever possible, and abstain from all light or casual conversation. Fathers and sons are separated by early developed and *socially maintained* hostility. The small boy is *expected*, in certain circumstances, to defy and abuse his father. Every growing boy has *dinned into his ears* by an anxious mother the possibility that his father will rob him of his sister, and so of his future wife."

---

* I reproduce in the main Dr Mead's exact words, but do not always use quotation marks.

Everything that we call evil, rightly—for you mustn't be seduced by what you're reading, Timothy, into imagining the good to be just another name for the customary—is not merely socially sanctioned but socially respected, in so far as, among such a people, respect is not outlawed as such: doing a man down, for instance, and treachery, and lying, and boasting, and power-mongering, and a violent acquisitiveness: the latter, for the most part, in respect of women, for the Mundugumor are rich in material wealth, with a superabundance of land, much fish, and plentiful coconut trees, areca palms, sago palms, and tobacco plants. There is no passage more illuminating in the whole of Dr Mead's account than the following:

"There are also exchanges of food made between a pair of big men, and there are the victory-feasts that follow a successful head-hunting raid. The leaders in all of these undertakings are known to the community as 'really bad men', men who are aggressive, gluttons for power and prestige; men who have taken far more than their share of the women of the community, and who have also acquired, by purchase or theft, women from the neighbouring tribes; men who fear no one and are arrogant and secure enough to betray whom they like with impunity. *These are the men for whom a whole community will mourn when they die*; their arrogance, their lust for power, is the thread upon which the important moments of social life are strung. These men are the fixed points in the social system. Less important men shift their allegiance from one of the established big men to another, or begin to work with a man who, though still young and possessed of only three or four wives, is rising rapidly to a position of power. In this atmosphere of shifting loyalties, conspiracies and treachery, head-hunting raids are planned, and the whole male community is temporarily united in the raid and the victory-feasts that conclude them. At these feasts a frank and boisterous cannibalism is practised, each man rejoicing at having a piece of the hated enemy between his teeth."

The most horrible chapter in Dr Mead's book is the one in which she describes the development of the individual Mundugumor. "The Mundugumor man-child is born into a hostile world, a world in which most of the members of his own sex will be his enemies, in which his major equipment for success must be a capacity for violence, for seeing and avenging insult, for holding his own safety very lightly and the lives of others even more lightly. From his birth, the stage is set to produce in him this kind of behaviour." Even before the child's birth the husband has been furious with the wife for becoming pregnant at all: and the wife has associated her pregnancy with sexual deprivation, her husband's anger and repudiation, and the continual risk that he will take another wife and temporarily desert her altogether. "This attitude towards children is congruent with the ruthless individualism, the aggressive specific sexuality, the intra-sex hostility, of the Mundugumor. A man has no heirs, only sons who are hostile rivals by definition, and daughters who, defend them as he will, will eventually be torn from him. A man's only hope of power and prestige lies in the number of his wives, who will work for him and give him the means to buy power, and in the occurrence of some mild characters among his brothers. The phrase 'a man who has brothers' occurs every now and again in their remarks, and this means a man who, by a stroke of luck, has some weak-willed, docile brothers who will follow his lead, and instead of disputing his progress will form a more or less permanent constellation about him in his middle age. Allies whom he can coerce and bully in the days of his strength, not sons who will come after him and by their strength mock his old age, these are his desire. A wife who becomes pregnant has therefore hurt a man at his most vulnerable spot; she has taken the first step towards his downfall by possibly conceiving a son. And for herself, she has shifted her husband's active sexual interest into angry frustrated resentment—for what? Possibly to bear a daughter, who will be her husband's, not hers."

If the child is not killed straight away, then "almost from birth its preparation for an unloved life is begun. Very little babies are kept in a carrying-basket, a closely woven, rough-plaited basket, harsh and stiff and opaque. The child's body must accommodate itself to the rigid lines of the basket, lying almost prone with its arms practically pinioned to its sides. The basket is too thick to permit any warmth from the mother's body to permeate it; the child sees nothing but the narrow slits of light at both ends. When a baby cries it is not fed at once; instead, without looking at the child, without touching its body, the mother or other woman or girl who is caring for it begins to scratch with her finger-nails on the outside of the basket, making a harsh grating sound. Children are trained to respond to this sound; it seems as if their cries, originally motivated by a desire for warmth, water, or food, were conditioned to accepting often this meagre remote response in their stead. If the crying does not stop, the child is eventually suckled.

"Mundugumor women suckle their children standing up, supporting the child with one hand in a position that strains the mother's arm and pinions the arms of the child. The minute the child stops suckling for a moment he is returned to his prison. Children therefore develop a very definite purposive fighting attitude, holding on firmly to the nipple and sucking milk as rapidly and vigorously as possible. They frequently choke from swallowing too fast; the choking angers the mother and infuriates the child, thus further turning the suckling situation into one characterised by anger and struggle rather than by affection and reassurance."

Weaning is of a piece with suckling: "the whole weaning process is accompanied by blows and cross words, which further accentuate the picture of a hostile world that is presented to the child"; and the process of corruption continues uninterruptedly till adolescence. "By every turn and twist the rules of kinship are used among pre-adolescents to give licence, licence to tease small children, licence to insult one's father or mother, and licence to humiliate older people. Long before a boy is adolescent he understands the behaviour required of him. His world is divided into people about each of whom there is a series of prohibitions, cautions, restrictions. He thinks of his kinship to others in terms of the things that are forbidden to him in relation to them, and in terms of hostile attitudes he may take up: the houses that he may not enter, the boys whom he may not tease or punch because they are his 'brothers-in-law', and the little girls whose hair he may pull, the boys whom he may bully, the men from whose baskets he may purloin areca-nut or tobacco. He knows that one way or another he will have to fight over his wife, either fight his father who will wish to take his sister, or his brother who will wish to take his sister, or some prospective brother-in-law who will steal his sister, or if he has no sister, or loses her, he will have to steal a wife and fight her brothers. The little girl knows that she will be the centre of such conflicts, that the males of her family are already considering her with an eye to their matrimonial plans, that if she is exchanged as a young pre-adolescent girl she will enter a household where the quarrel will merely be shifted—instead of her father and brothers quarrelling as to which one is to exchange her, her husband and his father and brothers will fight over which one is to have her. As a result of all this Spartan training, pre-adolescent Mundugumor children have an appearance of harsh maturity and, except for sex-experience, are virtually assimilated to the individualistic patterns of their society by the time they are twelve or thirteen." As for copulation and marriage, these are characterised by jealousy, possessiveness, sadism, anger and an absence of tenderness and romance.

Dr Mead sums up what she calls the Mundugumor "ideal of character" as follows: "Both men and women are expected to be violent, competitive, aggressively sexed, jealous and ready to see and avenge insult, delighting in display, in action, in fighting. The Mundugumor have selected as their ideal the very types of men and women which the Arapesh consider to be so incomprehensible that they hardly allow for their occurrence."

The Arapesh! On Sunday night I was rereading Dr Mead's chapters on the Mundugumor for the purpose of this description, when I remembered that the Choral Symphony was being broadcast from Bayreuth to mark the first Wagner Festival since the end of the war. I tried the obvious European stations without success, until eventually, fiddling about with the knobs, I hit upon something that was certainly orchestral music but was otherwise unrecognisable. Then the wheezings and whistlings abated, and a phrase came through: it was the soaring melody of the third movement: and suddenly Heaven was in that room. Just so is one refreshed as one turns from the Mundugumor to the Arapesh; or as when, after the chorus of Furies in Gluck's *Orfeo*, one sees the Blessed Spirits in the Elysian Fields, and watches them dance, and hears them sing.

The mountain-dwelling Arapesh—there are Arapesh also of the beach and the plains—are as poor in natural resources as the Mundugumor are rich in them. The land is barren, the sago rare, the pigs skinny, the streams almost without fish. But "they do not feel themselves as trapped and persecuted, victims of a bad position and a poor environment. Instead, they see all life as an adventure in growing things, growing children, growing pigs, growing yams and taros and coconuts and sago, faithfully, carefully, observing all of the rules that make things grow. They retire happily in middle age after years well spent in bringing up children and planting enough palm-trees to equip those children for life. The duty of every child is to grow, the duty of every man and woman is to observe the rules so that the children and the food upon which the children depend will grow. Men are as wholly committed to this cherishing adventure as are women. It may be said that the role of men, like the role of women, is maternal.''

I have read few things more fascinating than the central chapter, entitled ''A Co-operative Society'', in which Dr Mead describes the Arapesh way of life—a way of life ''oriented away from the self towards the needs of the next generation. It is a culture in which men and women do different things for the same reasons, in which men are not expected to respond to one set of motivations and women to another, in which if men are given more authority it is because authority is a necessary evil that someone, and that one the freer partner, must carry. It is a society where a man conceives responsibility, leadership, public appearance, and the assumption of arrogance as onerous duties that are forced upon him, and from which he is only too glad to escape as soon as his eldest child attains puberty.'' After this introduction, Dr Mead goes on to explain certain details of Arapesh organisation which help us to understand ''a social order that substitutes responsiveness to the concerns of others, and attentiveness to the needs of others, for aggressiveness—the familiar motivations upon which our culture depends.'' The details given by Dr Mead are of the highest interest.

Clusters of villages are grouped into localities, which however have no political organisation. Each village belongs theoretically to one family line or small localised clan, which again, theoretically, possesses the hunting or gardening land; but in practice ''the Arapesh do not conceive of themselves as owning these ancestral lands, but rather as belonging to the lands; in their attitude there is none of the proud possessiveness of the landowner who vigorously defends his rights against all comers. The land itself, the game animals, the timber trees, the

M

sago, and especially the bread-fruit trees—these all belong to
the ghosts": namely the ghosts of the clan dead, who live on
the estate and are collectively represented by a sort of *genius
loci*. No one is particular about where he lives: as often as not
members of a clan live elsewhere than in their ancestral hamlet.

The same lack of individualistic possessiveness comes out in
the Arapesh attitude to their taro-gardens, banana-gardens
and yam-gardens, which are of crucial economic importance
to them. "Food is scarce and poor and it would seem likely that
under these conditions of hardship and poverty people would
be very possessive of and attentive to their own gardens.
Instead, the Arapesh have evolved a different and most
extraordinary system, expensive in time and human effort, but
conducive to the warm co-operation and sociability that they
consider to be much more important. Each man plants not one
garden, but several, each one in co-operation with a different
group of relatives. In one of these gardens he is host, in the
others he is guest. In each of these gardens three to six men, with
one or two wives each, and sometimes a grown daughter or so,
work together, fence together, clear together, weed together,
harvest together, and while engaged in any large piece of work,
sleep together, crowded up in the little inadequate shelter,
with the rain dripping down the necks of more than half of the
sleepers. This method of gardening is not based upon the slightest physical need for co-operative labour. But the preference is
strong for working in small happy groups in which one man is
host and may feast his guest workers with a little meat—if he
finds it. And so the people go up and down the mountain sides,
from one plot to another, weeding here, staking vines there,
harvesting in another spot, called hither and thither by the
demands of gardens in different states of maturity."

In similar fashion a man plants coconut-trees for his sons,
not on his own land, but all over the place, walking miles with
a sprouting coconut to do so; and although "the houses are
so small that they actually require very little communal
labour, no man, except one who has failed to help with the
house-building of others, builds alone. A man announces his
intention of building a house, and perhaps makes a small
feast for raising the ridge-pole. Then his brothers and his
cousins and his uncles, as they go about the bush upon their
several errands, bear his partly completed house in mind, and

stop to gather a bundle of creeper to bind the roof, or a bunch of sago-leaves for the thatching. These contributions they bring to the new house when they pass that way, and gradually, casually, a little at a time, the house is built, out of the un-counted labour of many."

In this way the men spend over nine tenths of their time responding to other people's plans, digging in other people's gardens, going on hunting-parties initiated by others. "Where all are trained to a quick responsiveness to any plan, and mild ostracism is sufficient to prod the laggard into co-operation, leadership presents a different problem from that in a society where each man pits his own aggressiveness against that of another. If there is a weighty matter to be decided, then the decision is arrived at in a quiet, roundabout and wholly charac-teristic fashion." The method is that of progressive consultation: one of the oldest and most respected men in the community may be eventually called in, and his verdict is quietly accepted.

As for warfare, it is "practically unknown among the Arapesh. There is no feeling that to be brave or manly one must kill. Indeed, those who have killed are looked upon with a certain amount of discomfort, as men slightly apart. The feeling towards a murderer and that towards a man who kills in battle are not essentially different. There are no insignia of any sort for the brave. But although actual warfare—organised expeditions to plunder, conquer, kill, or attain glory—is absent, brawls and clashes between villages do occur, mainly over women. The marriage system is such that even the most bare-faced elopement of a betrothed or married woman must be phrased as an abduction and, since an abduction is an unfriendly act on the part of another group, must be avenged."

Such clashes, however, are for the most part mock affairs. They frequently end in a few harsh words: otherwise, there is "a serial and carefully recorded exchange of spears in which the aim is to wound lightly, not to kill", and this goes on "until someone is rather badly wounded, when the members of the attacking party immediately take to their heels. Later, peace is made by an interchange of rings, each man giving a ring to the man whom he has wounded. If, as occasionally happens, someone is killed in one of these clashes, every attempt is made to disavow any intention to kill: the killer's hand slipped; it was because of the sorcery of the Plainsmen."

As might be expected in such a society, it is on the injured rather than the injurer that attention is concentrated. "The general policy of the Arapesh is to punish those who are indiscreet enough to get involved in any kind of violent or disreputable scene. In this society unaccustomed to violence, which assumes that all men are mild and co-operative and is always surprised by individuals who fail to be so, there are no sanctions to deal with the violent man. But it is felt that those who stupidly and carelessly provoke violence can be kept in order." The punishment, however, is not very drastic. "If the man has been steadily falling in the esteem of the community, if he has been unco-operative, they may take up his fireplace and dump it out, which is practically equivalent to saying that they can dispense with his presence—for a month at least. The victim, deeply shamed by this procedure, flees to distant relatives and does not return until he has obtained a pig with which to feast the community, and so wipe out his offence. But against the really violent man the community has no redress. Such men fill their fellows with a kind of amazed awe; if crossed they threaten to burn down their own houses, break all their pots and rings, and leave that part of the country for ever. Their relatives and neighbours, aghast at the prospect of being deserted in this way, beseech the violent man not to leave them, not to desert them, not to destroy his own property, and placate him by giving him what he wishes. It is only because the whole education of the Arapesh tends to minimise violence and confuse the motivations of the violent that the society is able to operate by disciplining those who provoke and suffer from violence rather than those who actually perpetrate it."

Food and property are in effect socialised—that is the word used by Dr Mead herself. The people "disguise all their trading as voluntary and casual gift-giving" and "any rigid accounting is uncongenial. As with trading from village to village, so it is in all exchange between relatives. The ideal distribution of food is for each person to eat food grown by another. The lowest man in the community, the man who is believed to be so far outside the moral pale that there is no use reasoning with him, is the man who eats his own kill, even though that kill be a tiny bird. There is no encouragement given to any individual to build up a surplus of yams, the strong reliable crop that can be stored and the increase of which depends upon the conservation of seed. Anyone whose yam crop is conspicuously larger than his neighbour's is graciously permitted to give a special feast at which all of his yams are given away for seed. His relatives and neighbours come bringing a return gift of their own selection, and carry away a bag of seed. Of this seed he may never eat; even when it has multiplied in the fourth or fifth generation, a careful record is kept. In this way, the good luck or the better gardening of one man does not redound to his personal gain, but is socialised, and the store of seed-yams of the entire community is increased."

A remarkable system is in vogue for producing leadership, which is required, however, only for the purpose of large-scale ceremonial operations. "The problem of social engineering is conceived by the Arapesh not as the need to limit aggression and curb acquisitiveness, but as the need to force a few of the more capable and gifted men into taking, against their will, enough responsibility and leadership so that occasionally, every three or four years or at even rarer intervals, a really exciting ceremonial may be organised. No one, it is assumed, really wants to be a leader, a 'big man'. 'Big men' have to plan, have to initiate exchanges, have to strut and swagger and talk in loud voices, have to boast of what they have done in the past and are going to do in the future. All of this the Arapesh regard as most uncongenial, difficult behaviour, the kind of behaviour in which no normal man would indulge if he could possibly avoid it. It is a role that the society forces upon a few men in certain recognised ways."

What happens is this. If a boy in his early teens seems to be potentially a "big man", he is assigned a comrade, a *buanyin*, whose job is deliberately to develop the other's aggressiveness and to foster a competitive spirit. *Buanyins* go out of their way to insult each other, in the hope of encouraging, exceptionally, the "toughness" characteristic of our own society. Everything typical of the Arapesh as a whole is reversed in this *buanyin* relationship. "A *buanyin* raises pigs or hunts game in order to give it publicly and ostentatiously to his *buanyin*, accompanied by a few well chosen insults as to his *buanyin's* inability to repay the gift. Careful accounting is kept of every piece of pig or haunch of kangaroo, and a bundle of coconut-leaf rib is used to denote these in the public altercation during which *buanyins*

dun each other. The young men on their way to become big
men suffer continual pressure from their elders, as well as from
their *buanyins*. They are urged to assume the responsibility of
organising the preliminary feasts that will finally culminate in
a big initiation ceremony or the purchase of a new dance-
complex from the beach. And a few of them yield to all this
pressure, learn to stamp their feet and count their pigs, to
plant special gardens and organise hunting-parties, and to
maintain the long-time planning over several years that is
necessary in order to give a ceremony which lasts no longer
than a day or so. But when his eldest child reaches puberty, the
big man can retire; he need no longer stamp and shout, he need
no longer go about to feasts looking for opportunities to insult
his *buanyin*; he can stay quietly at home, guiding and educating
his children, gardening, and arranging his children's marriages.
He can retire from the active competitive life that his society
assumes, usually correctly, to be eminently uncongenial and
distasteful to him."

Gentleness and a desire to co-operate are fostered in an
Arapesh not only from the day of his birth but before it. The
woman who wishes to conceive must be as passive as possible;
and after conception the man and woman work together
sexually until the mother's breasts show the characteristic swelling, and the child is said to be finished—a perfect egg, it will
now rest in the mother's womb. Up to that point—during the
first few weeks after menstruation has ceased—the father's task
is as important as the mother's: he must give his semen to feed
and shape the child, give it strenuously and actively, just as the
mother must give her blood. The Arapesh have no idea that
after the initial act the father can go away and return nine
months later to find his wife safely delivered. Such a form of
parenthood they would consider impossible, and also repellent.
But when the egg is perfect, a change is demanded; all intercourse is now forbidden, for the child must sleep undisturbed,
placidly absorbing food that is good for it. It is significant of
this whole process that the verb "to bear a child" should be
used indiscriminately of man or woman. And co-operation continues after delivery; the man lies down by his wife's side and
is now "in bed having a baby", and actively shares hence-
forward in the baby's nurture.

The course of this nurture is described in a chapter I must

quote from at length, such pleasure does it give me to cele-
brate in this way human goodness and sanity. "How," asks Dr.
Mead, "is the Arapesh baby moulded and shaped into the easy,
gentle, receptive personality that is the Arapesh adult? What are
the determinative factors in the early training of the child which
assure that it will be placid and contented, unaggressive and
non-initiatory, non-competitive and responsive, warm, docile
and trusting? It is true that in any simple and homogeneous
society the children will as adults show the same general
personality-traits that their parents have shown before them.
But this is not a matter of simple imitation. A more delicate and
precise relationship obtains between the way in which the child
is fed, put to sleep, disciplined, taught self-control, petted, punished, and encouraged, and the final adult adjustment. Further-
more, the way in which men and women treat their children is
one of the most significant things about the adult personality of
any people. We can only understand the Arapesh, and the warm
and maternal temperament of both men and women, if we
understand their childhood experience and the experience to
which they in turn subject their children.

"During its first months the child is never far from someone's
arms. When the mother walks about she carries the baby sus-
pended from her forehead in its special small net bag, or sus-
pended under one breast in a bark-cloth sling. If the child is
fretful or irritable it is carried in the sling, where it can be
given the comforting breast as swiftly as possible. A child's crying is a tragedy to be avoided at any cost. Suckled whenever
they cry, never left far distant from some woman who can give
them the breast if necessary, sleeping usually in close contact
with the mother's body, either hung in a thin net bag against
her back, crooked in her arm, or curled on her lap as she sits
cooking or plaiting, the child has a continuous warm sensation
of security. It is never left alone; comforting human skin and
comforting human voices are always beside it. Both little boys
and little girls are enthusiastic about babies—there is always
someone to hold the child.

"When the child begins to walk, the mother leaves it in the
village with the father, or with some other relative, while she
goes to the garden or for firewood. She returns often enough to
a crying and disgruntled baby. Repentant, desirous of making
restitution, she sits down and suckles the child for an hour. This

rhythm, which begins as an hour's absence and an hour's compulsory suckling, develops into longer and longer periods, until
by the time the child is three or so it is often being given a day's
abstinence—supplemented, of course, by other food—followed
by a day's nursing, in which the mother sits all day, holding the
child on her lap, letting it suckle as it wishes, play about, suckle
again, play with her breasts, gradually regain its sense of
security. This is an experience that the mother enjoys as much
as the child. From the time the little child is old enough to play
with her breasts, the mother takes an active part in the suckling
process. She holds her breast in her hand and gently vibrates
the nipple inside the child's lips. She blows in the child's ear, or
tickles its ears, or playfully slaps its genitals, or tickles its toes.
The child in turn plays little tattoos on its mother's body and
its own, plays with one breast while sucking the other, teases the
breast with its hands, plays with its own genitals, laughs and
coos and makes a long, easy game of the suckling. Thus the
whole matter of nourishment is made into an occasion of high
affectivity and becomes a means by which the child develops
and maintains a sensitivity to caresses in every part of its body.
Nursing is, for mother and child, one long delightful and highly
charged game, in which the easy warm affectivity of a lifetime
is set up." Meanwhile the child is learning, as a substitute for
the delight of its mother's breasts, lip-play in a hundred stylised
forms—bubbling its lips into the palm of its hand, tickling the
inside of its lower lip with its tongue, and so on; and this lip-play
"is the thread of behaviour which binds together the child's
emotional life, which ties the happy security it felt in its yielding
mother's arms to placid enjoyment of the long evenings by the
fireside among its elders, and finally to a contented, unspecific
sexual life."

While the small child lies on its mother's lap she builds up in
it a trust of the world, a receptive and welcoming attitude
towards food, towards dogs and pigs, towards persons. She holds
a piece of taro in her hand, and as she suckles the child remarks
in a soft singsong voice, 'Good taro, good taro, would you eat,
would you eat, would you eat, a little taro, a little taro, a little
taro', and when the child releases the breast for a moment a bit
of taro is stuffed into its mouth. The dog or the little tame pig
that thrusts an inquisitive nose under the mother's arm is held
there, and the child's skin and the dog's rubbed together, the

mother gently rocking them both, and murmuring, 'Good dog, good child, good dog, good, good, good.' *Mutatis mutandis*, the same technique is adopted to produce in the child an affectionate and trustful attitude towards all its relatives—which means, in effect, everyone whom it encounters, for there is no one whom it does not call uncle, or brother, or cousin, or the comparable names for women. And, because these terms are used with wide extensions, even the gradations of age implied in them are blurred. The child in arms is already accustomed to being chucked under the chin and called playfully 'my little grandfather' or 'my little fat uncle'. So a mild and always affectionate respect for age is combined with a blurring of clear relationship distinctions, which are lost in a sense of community; and so are distinctions of sex. The child does not learn that people to whom sex-relations are forbidden had better not be left alone together. This is a point so foreign to the Arapesh that it never enters their heads. Emphasis is always on the positive, not the negative; an Arapesh boy is taught by his parents: 'When you travel, in any house where there is a mother's sister, or a father's sister, or a female cousin, or a niece, or a sister-in-law, or a daughter-in-law, or a niece-in-law, there you may sleep in safety.'

Neither little girls nor little boys wear any clothes until they are four or five: they roll and tumble on the floor together without anyone worrying as to how much bodily contact results: they see women sleeping naked and men wearing their loin-cloths carelessly. "Thus there develops in the children an easy, happy-go-lucky familiarity with the bodies of both sexes, a familiarity uncomplicated by shame, coupled with a premium upon warm, all-over physical contact."

Children are not encouraged to grow up rapidly, or to acquire special skills or proficiencies: nor are they trained to be careful of their safety. They may do anything they like, however dangerous. A baby tries to climb one of the notched logs that serve as house-ladders; overcome with fright, it screams. Someone immediately rushes forward to catch it. A child stumbles; it is picked up and cuddled. The result is that the child grows up with a sense of emotional security in the care of others, not in its own control over the environment. This is a cold, wet world, full of pitfalls, hidden roots in the path, stones over which small feet stumble. But there is always a kind hand, a gentle voice, to rescue one. Trust in those about one is all that is required. What one does oneself matters very little.

As one reads Dr Mead's paragraphs about anger in little Arapesh children and its expression, one is reminded again and again of Ian Suttie's description of hatred and evil as frustration-forms of love. "Temper tantrums are almost always motivated by some insecurity or rejection point: these tantrums over rejection serve to channel anger as response to a hostile act on the part of another, and the definite training against aggressiveness towards other children completes this pattern." An angry child is allowed to kick and scream, to roll in the mud, to throw stones or firewood about on the ground, but he is not allowed to touch another child with whom he is quarrelling. This habit of venting one's rage at others upon one's own surroundings persists into adult life. An angry man will spend an hour banging on a slit gong, or hacking with an axe at one of his own palm-trees. The whole training of little children is not to teach them to control emotion, but to see that its expression harms no one but themselves. Mothers make their girls pretty grass dresses that will be ruined by a tumble tantrum in the mud, and place on their heads net bags the contents of which it would be a pity to spill.

Parental disapproval of fighting among children is always reinforced by rebukes couched in terms of relationship, such as 'Would you, his father's son, hit your mother's brother's son?'; and the fear of any rift between associates is carried into adult life. Where such rifts occur, the culture provides two methods of dealing with them. The first is a symbolic one. "So between relatives who are really angry at each other, the more enraged fastens a mnemonic knot of croton-leaf and hangs it up in his own doorway, which means that he will never eat with his annoying relatives again. To remove this formal sign of breach, a pig must be killed by the person who originally fastened the knot. But all of these highly stylised methods of breaking off a relationship are rare; a man thinks a long time before taking such a drastic step and establishing a position that will be very uncomfortable to maintain and very expensive to withdraw from."

The second method is of great psychological interest, and I want to quote Dr Mead's paragraphs about it almost in full. "The fear and discomfort resulting from any expression of anger is further worked into the pattern of sorcery. An angry person may not hit another, he may not resort to any thorough-going abuse of another. But one may, in retaliation, take on for a moment the behaviour that is appropriate not to a relative and a member of the same locality, but to a Plainsman, a stranger and an enemy. Arapesh children grow up dividing the world into two great divisions: *relatives*, which division includes some three to four hundred people, all the members of their own locality, and those of villages in other localities which are connected with them or their relatives by marriage, and the long lines of the wives and children of their father's hereditary trade-friends; and *strangers* and *enemies*, usually formalised as Plainsmen, literally 'men from the river-lands'. These Plainsmen play in the children's lives the dual role of the bogy man to be feared, and the enemy to be hated, mocked, outwitted, upon whom all the hostility that is disallowed in the group is actively displaced."

It is taken for granted among the Arapesh that all misfortunes, including untimely death, are the work of Plainsmen, who "sorcerise" a man by manipulating any of those exuviae—his food leavings, half-smoked cigarettes, perspiration, semen, and so on —which are collectively known as "dirt"; and little children are given baskets and bags in which to carry about their food-leavings so that they may not fall into the hands of strangers. "Fear of illness, of death, of misfortune is dramatised in this insistence upon care about one's dirt. The child is led to believe that hostility, itself a feeling that exists only between strangers (normally), regularly expresses itself in the theft and secreting of a bit of dirt. This conception which links fear and anger with a definite behaviour-pattern is compulsive in the adult life of the Arapesh. Suppose that a brother injures a man, or a cousin uses him hardly, not as a relative would normally act but becoming for the moment the 'enemy', the 'stranger'. The injured man has no sense of gradation to fall back upon; he has not been reared to a small circle of very friendly close relatives and a slightly less friendly circle of less close relatives. He knows only two categories of behaviour, that of a member of one's own wide and trusted group, and that of the enemy. The brother with whom he is angry enters for the moment the category of enemy, and he purloins his brother's dirt and gives it to the Plainsmen. But when a man dies, the death is not laid at the door of the man who stole the dirt. It is attributed instead to the sorcerer, whose behaviour the angry man originally imitated, compulsively, during his rage at his friend." Such a theft of dirt is disowned by the Arapesh themselves as invalid and intrusive, as the unexplained madness of a moment. But since an Arapesh is particularly vulnerable when he meets with the slightest expression of anger—for small boys are as carefully protected from aggression and struggle as the most tenderly reared little girls—fear and panic result, and the compulsive theft of dirt is very likely to follow. "When a man relates such an act, he does it without affectation, as he might describe an involuntary move-ment of his eyes in the presence of a bright light: 'He opposed me. He took sides against me. He helped the people who carried off my mother. I was staying with him in the house of my mother's brother. He ate a piece of kangaroo meat. He laid down the bone. He forgot it. He stood up and went outside the house. My eyes saw that no one was looking. My hand reached out and took the bone. I hid it quickly in my basket. The next day I met on the road a man from Dunigi whom I called grand-father. I gave it to him.' Such an account as this is given in a low, emotionless voice, without either pride or remorse, without any admission of genuine complicity. The pattern learned in early childhood has simply asserted itself as a whole."

As children grow older they begin to play games, but these are never such as to encourage aggressiveness or competition. There are no races, no games with two sides. Instead they play at being opossums or kangaroos, or one is a sleeping cassowary that the others startle. But games of any kind play a very small part in the children's life: more often the times when they are together in large enough groups to make a game worth while are the occasions of a feast, there is dancing and adult cere-monial, and they find the role of spectatorship far more engross-ing. All this early experience accustoms them to be part of the whole picture, to prefer to any active child-life of their own a passive part that is integrated with the life of the community.

The training that children receive about property "is one which encourages a respect for the property of others and a sense of easy security in the property of one's own family group, rather than any stronger sense of possessiveness. Children are rebuked if they injure the property of other people, and a gentle reiteration 'That is grandfather's, don't break it' will accom-pany a child's exploration on the premises of others. But the counter-remark, 'That is not yours', is not made. The distinction between 'mine' and 'thine' is not the point emphasised, but rather the need to be careful of other people's things. The family possessions are treated very differently. The child is given anything it cries for, which often results in its breaking its mother's ear-rings or unstringing her necklace of bandicoot-teeth. The house in which a child lives is not a forbidden world filled with treasures that he is constantly being bidden to let alone, until they come to assume enormous importance in his eyes. If the parents have something that they feel the child will injure, they hide it securely away so that the child will never come to desire it.

"As the child grows older, he is told that the carved wooden plate that is only used for feasts, or the bird-of-paradise head-dress that his father wears when he dances, is his—the child's. But his parents continue to use these things. His father takes him into the bush and shows him clumps of young sago and, teaching him the names of the clumps, he explains that these also are his. 'Own property' comes to mean things that belong to the future, something that is used by others now, or is not yet his own. When he grows up, he will similarly designate all of his belongings as his children's. In such a system no one becomes aggressively possessive about his own, and theft, locked doors, and the primitive equivalent of locks—black magic placed on property—are virtually unknown."

This is how Dr Mead sums up the characteristics of a typical Arapesh child by the time it is seven or eight years old: "Both boys and girls have learned a happy, trustful, confident attitude towards life. They have learned to include in the circle of their affection everyone with whom they are connected in any way whatsoever, and to respond to any relationship term with an active expression of warmth. They have been discouraged from any habits of aggressiveness towards others; they have learned to treat with respect and consideration the property, the sleep, and the feelings of other people. They definitely associate the giving of food with warmth, approval, acceptance, and security, and take any withholding of food as a sign of hostility and rejection. They have learned to be passive participators in the activities of their elders, but they have had very little experience of playing games on their own or organising their own lives. They have become accustomed to respond when others give the signal, to follow where others lead, to be enthusiastic and uncritical about new things that are presented to them. When they are cold, or bored, or lonely, they bubble their lips in a hundred patterned ways. They have learned to fear the stranger, the Plainsman, the man who walks among them with eyes alert for a bit of dirt that will be their undoing. And they have been taught to guard every chance piece of unfinished food or old clothing, to keep a sharp watch over these recently separated sections of their personalities when they meet a stranger. They have been permitted no expressions of hostility or aggressiveness towards any one of their hundred relatives, all of whom must be loved and cherished; but they have been allowed to join in their parents' sulky hatred of the sorcerers, and even to hurl a few small spears down a path that a departing group of Plainsmen have taken. So the basic pattern has been laid that in later life will make them identify anyone who hurts them as a stranger, and thus invoke the old sorcery-pattern of purloining the stranger's dirt."

When the first signs of puberty appear, a boy is made culturally self-conscious, for the first time, of the psychology of sex. Before this what masturbation there has been—and it has been slight because of the greater emphasis upon the socially acceptable pleasure of lip-bubbling—has been disregarded as children's play. But when a young boy begins to keep the tabus of his pubic hair, he is cautioned against further careless handling of his genitals. He becomes the responsible custodian of his own growth; and the sanctions are all in terms of that growth. If he breaks the rules, no one will punish him; no one but himself will suffer. He will simply not grow to be a tall strong man, a man worthy to be the father of children.

A boy's childhood is ended by the initiation ceremony. "From one who has been grown by the daily carefulness and hard work of others, he now passes into the class of those whose care is for others' growth. During his pubescence his care was for his own growth, for the observances of the tabu would ensure to him muscle and bone, height and breadth, and strength to beget and rear children. Now this care is shifted and he has instead new responsibilities towards those who after years devoted to his growth are now growing old themselves, and towards his younger brothers and sisters, and his young betrothed wife. There is no feeling here that he is subservient towards those older than himself, that he chafes beneath the power of those stronger than himself. Instead, the oldest and the youngest, the ageing parent and the little child, are placed together in Arapesh feeling, in contrast to those who from puberty to middle age are specially concerned with sex and child-rearing. From puberty to middle age one occupies a special position with responsibilities towards the old and towards the young. Half of the food in the world is set apart for the elders and the children, certain kinds of yams, certain kinds of taro, certain kinds of birds and fish and meat—these are for those who are not yet concerned with sex, or whose concern with it is over. There is no feeling here that the powerful and the strong appropriate the best foods, but rather there is a symbolic division into two equal parts from which all are fed."

There is no rivalry between men and their children. To grow his son, to find him the food from which he must himself abstain, has been the father's great delight during his son's childhood. Piece by piece he has built up his son's body. The Arapesh father does not say to his son: 'I am your father, I begot you, therefore you must obey me.' He would regard such a claim as presumptuous nonsense. Instead he says: 'I grew you. I grew the yams, I worked the sago, I hunted the meat, I laboured for the food that made your body. Therefore I have the right to speak like this to you.' And this relationship between father and son, a relationship based on food given and food gratefully received, is shared in smaller measure by all the old and young of a community. Every man has contributed to the growth of every child reared within the circle of mountains that forms his world. If a young man should so far forget himself as to speak rudely or hastily to an old man, the old man may answer, sadly, reproachfully: 'And think how many pigs I have fattened from which you took your growth.'

As the young grow strong, the old retire more and more. When the father retires finally, all that he does is done in his son's name; but the son must bear in mind his father's increasing age by little ritual acts of carefulness. "Thus at the end of his adolescence the Arapesh boy is placed in his society, he is initiated, he has manifold duties to perform, unaggressively, co-operatively, assisting his father and his uncles; guarding his father in his old age and his young brother in his childhood; and growing his small, pre-adolescent wife."

For an Arapesh boy does "grow" his wife. Betrothal and marriage among these people take their natural place in the general pattern of mutual aid. The father, seeking a wife for his boy, has in mind the kind of woman who will grace a man's house by her deft and happy responsiveness to everyone—to himself, to his guests, and to their children. A little girl who already at six or seven "can take her mother's place" has proclaimed herself as a desirable wife. Additionally, she should be sweet-tempered, but this is regarded as almost a corollary, for bad temper among the Arapesh expresses itself in "not giving things to people". The Arapesh regard marriage as primarily an opportunity to increase the warm family circle within which one's descendants may then live even more safely than one has lived oneself. It is for this reason that they regard incest "not with horror and repulsion towards a temptation that they feel their flesh is heir to, but as a stupid negation of the joys of increasing, through marriage, the number of people whom one can love and trust." Or, to put it in another way, incest is selfish: just as a man may not eat his own surplus yam-crop, so to appropriate for one's own purposes one's mother or sister would be of the nature of antisocial and repellent hoarding.

After the little girl of six or seven has been betrothed to a boy about six years her senior, she goes to live in the home of her future husband. Here the father-in-law, the husband, and all his brothers combine to grow the bride. Upon the young adolescent husband particularly falls the onus of growing yams, working sago, hunting for meat, with which to feed his wife. So the husband and wife live together like brother and sister, and when these many years of waiting are taken into account "one of the determining factors of Arapesh attitudes towards sex is intelligible. Actual sex-intercourse does not spring from a different order of feeling from the affection that one has for one's daughter or one's sister. It is simply a more final and complete expression of the same kind of feeling. And it is not regarded as a spontaneous response of the human being to an internal sexual stimulus. The Arapesh have no fear that children left to themselves will copulate, or that young people going about in adolescent groups will experiment with sex. The only young people who are believed likely to indulge in any overt sex-expression are 'husband and wife', the betrothed pair who have been reared in the knowledge that they are to be mates." As the little girl approaches puberty, her parents-in-law increase their supervision of her, both for her own sake and for the sake of her husband; for it is believed that premature intercourse will impede the bride's growth.

After the first menstruation ceremony consummation is near. But the betrothed girl's life goes on, for a time, as before. "The parents-in-law will continue their slight, unobtrusive chaperonage. She still sleeps in their hut, and if one of the daughters of the house is at home, the young sisters-in-law may sleep together. Just below the surface of articulate recognition by the community is the knowledge that sometime soon, in a few months, in a year, this marriage will be consummated." And now, just as the sun comes out after a morning of drizzle, and lights up the wheat, almost ready for harvesting, beyond my garden lawn, I think again of Gluck's Elysian Fields while poised at my desk to copy out, for your pleasure as well as for mine, little Timothy, the following passage; and I think, also, of a morning thirty-two years ago, when I wandered out with your grandmother from the cottage at Hurley to ask her, knowing that she was ready, whether she would marry me: "Meanwhile, the girl makes herself a lovely grass skirt; with young wives a little older than she is, she spends many hours plaiting the sago-shoot shreds that she has wheedled some old woman into dyeing a beautiful red. She keeps her skin bathed and shining, and wears her necklace of opossum-teeth or dog's teeth every day. No one is fairer or gayer in the whole of Arapesh than these young girls waiting, in lovely attire, for life at last to catch up with them. No definite day is set; as the months pass, the parents relax their chaperonage more and more. The girl is fully matured now. The boy is tall and well developed. Some day the two, who are now allowed to go about alone together in the bush, will consummate their marriage, without haste, without a due date to harry them with its inevitableness, with no one to know or to comment, in response to a situation in which they have lived comfortably for years in the knowledge that they belong to each other."

An Arapesh marriage is usually successful, but by no means always so; and I shall leave these delightful people with this

picture in your mind, for I think I have said enough to prove
my point. It is crucial, however, that you should understand
clearly what the point is, and what it isn't. Let me first give, in
a shortened form, Dr Mead's own summing-up of the matter
at the end of her book:

"When we consider the behaviour of the typical Arapesh
man or woman as contrasted with the behaviour of the typical
Mundugumor man or woman, the evidence is overwhelmingly
in favour of the strength of social conditioning. In no other
way can we account for the almost complete uniformity with
which Arapesh children develop into contented, passive,
secure persons, while Mundugumor children develop as
characteristically into violent, aggressive, insecure persons.
Only to the impact of the whole of the integrated culture upon
the growing child can we lay the formation of the contrasting
types. There is no other explanation of race, or diet, or selection
that can be adduced to explain them. We are forced to conclude that human nature is almost unbelievably malleable,
responding accurately and contrastingly to contrasting cultural
conditions. The differences between individuals who are
members of different cultures, like the differences between
individuals within a culture, are almost entirely to be laid to
differences in conditioning, especially during early childhood,
and the form of this conditioning is culturally determined.
There remains, however, the problem of the origin of these
socially standardised differences. Cultures are man-made, they
are built of human materials; they are diverse but comparable
structures within which human beings can attain full human
stature. Upon what have they built their diversities? Have such
traits as aggressiveness or passivity any basis in temperament at
all? Are they potentialities of all human temperaments that can
be developed by different kinds of social conditioning and which
will not appear if the necessary conditioning is absent?

"When we ask this question we shift our emphasis. Our
attention has been on the differences between Arapesh men
and women as a group and Mundugumor men and women
as a group. It is as if we had represented the Arapesh personality by a soft yellow, the Mundugumor by a deep red.
But if we now ask whence came the original direction in each
culture, so that one now shows yellow, another red, then we

must peer more closely. And leaning closer to the picture, it is as if behind the bright consistent yellow of the Arapesh, and the deep equally consistent red of the Mundugumor, we found in each case the delicate, just discernible outlines of the whole spectrum, differently overlaid in each case by the monotone which covers it. This spectrum is the range of individual differences which lie behind the so much more conspicuous cultural emphases, and it is to this that we must turn to find the explanation of cultural inspiration, of the source from which each culture has drawn.

"There appears to be about the same range of basic temperamental variation among the Arapesh and among the Mundugumor, although the violent man is a misfit in the first society and a leader in the second. If human nature were completely homogeneous raw material, lacking specific drives and characterised by no important constitutional differences between individuals, then individuals who display personality traits so antithetical to the social pressure should not reappear in societies of such differing emphases. If the variations between individuals were to be set down to accidents in the genetic process, the same accidents should not be repeated with similar frequency in strikingly different cultures, with strongly contrasting methods of education.

"But because this same relative distribution of individual differences does appear in culture after culture, in spite of the divergence between the cultures, it seems pertinent to offer a hypothesis to explain upon what basis the personalities of men and women have been differently standardised so often in the history of the human race. Let us assume that there are definite temperamental differences between human beings which if not entirely hereditary at least are established on a hereditary base very soon after birth. These differences finally embodied in the character structure of adults, then, are the clues from which culture works, selecting one temperament, or a combination of related and congruent types, as desirable, and embodying this choice in every thread of the social fabric.

"Some primitive societies have had the time and the robustness to reshape all their institutions to fit one extreme type, and to develop educational techniques which will ensure that the majority of each generation will show a personality congruent with this extreme emphasis. Other societies have pursued a less

definitive course, selecting their models not from the most
extreme, most highly differentiated individuals, but from the
less marked types. Alternatively, a culture may take its clues not
from one temperament, but from several temperaments. But instead of mixing together into an inconsistent hotchpotch the
choices and emphases of different temperaments, or blending
them together into a smooth but not particularly distinguished
whole, it may isolate each type by making it the basis for the
approved social personality for an age-group, a sex-group, a
caste-group, or an occupational group. In this way society becomes not a monotone with a few discrepant patches of an
intrusive colour, but a mosaic, with different groups displaying
different personality traits. Thus the physician learns the bed-
side manner, which is the natural behaviour of some temperaments and the standard behaviour of the general practitioner in
the medical profession; the Quaker learns at least the outward
behaviour and the rudiments of meditation, the capacity for
which is not necessarily an innate characteristic of many of the
members of the Society of Friends."

And this is the conclusion of the matter:

"Neither among Arapesh children nor among Arapesh
adults has one a sense of encountering a dead level of temperament. Individual differences in violence, in aggressiveness, in
acquisitiveness, are as marked as they are among a group of
American children, but the gamut is different. The most
active Arapesh child, schooled to a passivity, a mildness,
unknown to us, will be far less aggressive than a normally
active American child. But the difference between the most
active and the least active is not thereby reduced, although it
is expressed in so much milder terms. That is, although the
range in actual temperamental differences among the children
born into any society may be approximately the same, that
society may and will alter the interrelations between these
differences in several different ways. *It may mute expression all
along the line or stimulate expression all along the line.*"

## § 5. SOCIALISM AND GOODNESS (CONCLUDED)

You will remember how I came to describe for you these
startlingly different characteristics of Arapesh and Mundugumor

society. I had claimed for the machinery of socialism that just as it could assist negatively in the struggle between the self-regarding and the other-regarding elements in human nature by superseding a capitalism that encourages self-seeking, so, given the fulfilment of our one condition, it could assist positively too, by producing an atmosphere congenial to the development of other-regarding tendencies. My reason was that few things are more important for determining a pattern of culture than the economic system in vogue; and that patterns of culture affect very powerfully the way human beings think and feel. It is the truth of this latter contention that I have been trying to prove by the examples of the Arapesh and the Mundugumor; and I hope you will agree that, with Margaret Mead as spokesman, I have succeeded.

Or, to put it in another way, and to repeat, for the last time, a now familiar phrase, I have been calling in anthropology to support my contention that public ownership *can*, and if it issues in the co-operative commonwealth (defined, as I have defined it, in the minimum, economic sense) *will*, make it *easier* for men to be good. I have never gone farther than that, nor would wish to do so. I have never claimed, and do not believe, that any economic system, or any pattern of culture, can of itself *cause* goodness in a human soul. The goodness can be *caused* only by something that happens inside. It is what happens in the seed that is crucial—what happens in it, not what is there, for the apparently different elements are in sum always there, though with greatly varying strengths and in greatly varying proportions, and except, it may be, when there is a definitely pathological condition: yes, what happens in the seed, this is crucial: and yet the qualities of the soil and the air, of the general environment, are also potent, whether to help or to hinder. The analogy may be untenable, for I know nothing of botany or chemistry, but I think you will understand what I mean. For the human case, environment in childhood, the way children are brought up, is, in the present context, by far the most important constituent of the general environment, being largely the producer as well as the product of it; yet even this can do no more than help or hinder.

But what do I mean by goodness? I mean a going out of the self into a union which realises selfhood. I mean the goodness of Schweitzer, the goodness of St. Francis, the goodness of Christ.

In an earlier part of this chapter I dwelt on self-expression and self-development: the emphasis is now on their goal and their home—on that communion and community in which the circle is perfect, with alpha become omega and omega alpha. The emphasis is now on love.

No one could doubt, I think, that it is easier for an Arapesh to be good than for a Mundugumor. Yet, for all my delight in these people and my talk of the Elysian Fields, I would have you note several things about them. Note first the paragraph with which the last section ended: "Individual differences in violence, in aggressiveness, in acquisitiveness, are as marked among Arapesh children as they are among a group of American children, but the gamut is different. The most active Arapesh child, schooled to a passivity, a mildness, unknown to us, will be far less aggressive than a normally active American child. But the difference between the most active and the least active is not thereby reduced, although it is expressed in so much milder terms. Society may mute expression all along the line or stimulate expression all along the line." Note, secondly, that violence, fear, panic, those expressions of preoccupation with a self not yet lost in community, are always just a little below the surface —always ready to leap out when the pattern of security, the routine, one might almost say, of mutual aid, is for some reason broken. "This is the texture," says Dr Mead, speaking of Arapesh marriage, "this is the texture, the pattern, of Arapesh life, quiet, uneventful co-operation, singing in the cold dawn, and singing and laughter in the evening, men who sit happily playing to themselves on hand-drums, women holding suckling children to their breasts, young girls walking easily down the centre of the village, with the walk of those who are cherished by all about them." But when things go wrong, "when there is a quarrel, an accusation of sorcery, it breaks through this texture with a horrid dissonance that is all the sharper because the people are unaccustomed to anger, and meet hostility with fear and panic rather than with a fighting *élan*. In their panic and fright, people seize fire-sticks and hurl them at each other, break pots, cast about for any weapon that comes casually to hand. And this is specially true because Arapesh marriage has no formal pattern that takes account of anger and hurt." Or again: "They rely upon the creation of an emotional state of such beatitude and such tenuousness that accidents continually threaten its existence. And if this threat on occasion materialises, they manifest the fright and rage of those who have always been protected from hurt or unhappiness."

Note, thirdly, that retaliation—though with a minimum of violence, as we saw in the case of mock combats—is not merely sanctioned but demanded by the culture: "This feeling for righting the balance, for paying back evil for evil, not in greater measure, but in exact measure, is very strong among the Arapesh." Practically all the 'dirt' of mountain people that finds its way into the little caches of the Plains sorcerers, Dr Mead tells us, "is stolen not by these sorcerers, but by the mountain people themselves, by angry brothers and cousins and wives." And no remorse follows such thefts: remorse, the first step to repentance, a stirring towards the goal of a uniting, a life-fostering, a genuine as opposed to a formalised reconciliation.

Note, fourthly, that even in the normal life of the normal Arapesh the tendency to hate has been neither subdued nor sublimated; most of the latently available hatred has simply been rolled up into a ball, and directed, with a relative harmlessness, against the outsider. This is a small people living in a fastness of New Guinea, and not much "practical" evil results; but the end of that process, in a larger setting, is the civilised world of today, with its competitive manufacture of atomic and hydrogen bombs, and everything, spiritual and physical, that this implies.

Note, fifthly, that there are deviants in Arapesh society: violent, jealous, acquisitive men and women, who can find no happy place in that society, yet in another society might have developed, not into what they are, but into artists or seekers after truth or leaders of the better sort or even pioneering humanitarians. (Similarly there are deviants, gentle and co-operative people, among the Mundugumor; and you might bear in mind, if you're still inclined to wonder whether right and wrong are not mere matters of social convention, that while among the Arapesh it is the violent who upset life, among the Mundugumor it is the co-operative who make it possible. The Arapesh could get along without their deviants; the Mundugumor, as Dr Mead clearly shows, would disintegrate without theirs.)

Note, sixthly and finally—and this is most important of all—everything implied by the expression "social conditioning", or the even more hideous one "social engineering". I said earlier that there was everything right about one form of social conditioning, namely social conditioning for spontaneity: meaning by it such influence from the environment as would help every individual to realise his unique potentialities in a natural harmony with those of all the rest. But social conditioning as ordinarily understood—and social engineering, above all, as it has developed in the Soviet Union—is of a very different kind: it irons out differences, it produces a standardised type with a number of disenfranchised deviants. And, apart altogether from the question of deviants, "typical" goodness tends to be a rather superficial kind of goodness: for the deeper kind of goodness is something that not only happens in the depths of an individual, or, what comes to the same thing, in his meeting with the whole, but happens for him, in each case, uniquely; and spontaneity is of its essence.

I am not going back on my assertion, not for a moment, that it is easier for an Arapesh to be good than for a Mundugumor: nor on the more general one that a pattern of culture can make it easier for men to be good. If people are to be conditioned at all to develop in a given direction—if, as might be said, they are to be compelled, so far as they *can* be compelled, to become this or that—then it is clearly better that they should be compelled to become co-operative than that they should be compelled to become competitive, that they should be compelled to become gentle than that they should be compelled to become violent; for, general amenities apart, the habit of gentleness and co-operation will be helpful to the process, the essential process, in the depths. But not in the case of everyone; and not to the degree, in the case of anyone, to which another pattern of culture would be helpful. For the really valuable pattern of culture is one which, while naturally encouraging co-operation by reason of its economic system and other institutions, but never compelling it—always leaving the utmost scope for self-expression, in interstices of the system, by temperaments to which co-operation in its more obvious forms is antipathetic—is helpful in the case of everyone: and most helpful of all, directly helpful this time whereas the other kind of help is indirect, if an element is present in the culture which has not yet been mentioned. This is, in the broadest sense, a religious tradition: by tradition being meant, not something more or less external merely retained from the past, but something genuinely and continuously living and lived.

But if no economic system, no pattern of culture, can of itself cause goodness in a human soul, what can and does cause it? How does goodness happen? For it is with an attempt, in fear and trembling, to answer that question, which is the most important question of all, that I must now bring this chapter to a close.

*Brimpton, August 3rd*

*I have woken up, oddly, with a sense of great happiness and peace. Oddly, because I wasn't at all happy when I went to bed, and feared I shouldn't sleep at all. I had been listening to a broadcast of Berlioz' Symphonie Fantastique, which I greatly love: the waltz in the second movement is even more bitter-sweet to me than "Tales from the Vienna Woods". But the last two movements—the walk to the gallows, the Dies Irae, the tolling bell, the execution—affected me horribly. Always, before, I had enjoyed them as music; but now I heard nothing—could only see and feel: see and feel a man walking, walking—a man who lived and breathed—in an obscene ceremonial procession that had been rehearsed as for a play, and would end with his being deliberately killed. Ah, Christ! This was a murderer, yes: but he was also the Christ who is all men, stumbling on the road to Calvary. A week before, heaven had been in that same little room as the Choral Symphony came through from Bayreuth: now, instead of beautiful life, there was naked sado-masochism. The awful shame one feels, for the cold execution even more than for the murder it revenges: as for all unimaginative cruelties, and particularly those of the law! I recently heard a man being sentenced to five years' imprisonment, after pleading for mercy. How can I convey to you a sense of the wickedness that grimaced in the court at that moment? It was not so much a question of the sentence itself, which may have been necessitated, in the Judge's opinion, by the duties of his office: it was his demeanour—the contempt in his voice, the taking for granted of his own integrity and the other's worthlessness, the externality, the lack of fellow-feeling, the relation as between machines and not persons, the accent he gave the word "punishment", the nod of curt dismissal with which he finished and passed on—it was this that seemed to put out the sun and freeze the world into starkness. Don't think all this far-fetched and emotional, I beg of you, Timothy: the fact that a judge "judges" is the ruin of the world. A few weeks earlier the Lord Chief Justice, Lord Goddard, had spoken about juvenile crime at a conference of probation officers. "There is a craze," he was reported to have said, "for sending children to psychiatrists. I think it is wrong." If boys stole cigarettes he thought it was because they wanted to smoke, but when a psychiatrist answered the question for him he had brought in symbols of love and evil. The Government had passed laws which made it impossible to give any punishment to these young scamps. "I wish you could give some of them a jolly good hiding. Is it right that you should be called a sadist for advocating some form of punishment?" The question was rhetorical.*

*Children are being murdered at the moment by sex-maniacs. Ruth said to me last night, on our way from the station, "Why doesn't Scotland Yard make a broadcast appeal to these men, something like this: 'You are sick. If you give yourselves up we won't kill you or otherwise punish you, but will try to cure you'?" She's quite capable of making such a remark at Lord Goddard's dinner-table —not from moral courage, but from a naïf inability to understand that what is obviously right may sound fantastic, and that to say it in her forthright way may embarrass everybody, including me. The awful thing is that it s h o u l d sound fantastic.*

*     *     *     *     **

*But how plagued I still am by the demon of self-righteousness! Rereading the above yesterday evening—a couple of evenings later— I realised with the old familiar stab, the mixture of sadness and agony and fear, how infinitesimally I had cured myself, after all these years, of that boyhood evil. (But now, in the light of the morning, a wet-and-shiny morning, I can say "Ah but, Victor, a little! You weren't aware of it then: you're aware of it now.") It is easy enough to love criminals, and anyone who's sick or weak or maimed in mind or spirit: this comes naturally: the difficulty is to love the judges who condemn them. But "if ye salute your brethren only, what do ye more than others? do not even the publicans so?" Until one can feel about the Lord Goddards, whose weaknesses are merely of another kind, as one feels about criminals, one has advanced hardly a millimetre to the Kingdom of Heaven.*

*It is true that Christ, according to the Gospels, expressed himself with singular violence about Pharisees and "hypocrites". But to begin with, we are not Christ; Christ, if one may put it so, was in a special position. And whatever the historic Christ may or may not have said, and for whatever reason, the Christ in our hearts can have nothing but charity for anyone.*

    \*       \*       \*       \*       \*

*I must add a footnote to this a week later. A man has been charged at Bath with the murder of one of these little girls. He seems to have given himself up. During the two or three minutes that the proceedings lasted "he looked down at the floor". He is twenty. A big crowd gathered outside, and booed; the man had to be smuggled away by an underground passage. When I read of the booing, I was reminded of somebody's conviction, about twenty years ago, for the debauching of young girls. A newspaper commented, with obvious approval: "When he heard the crushing sentence he looked round the court as if asking for sympathy. But not a single man or woman looked back at him with anything but loathing and contempt." I thought of compiling for publication a book of press-cuttings, starting with that one, to be called "Christian England", but the project came to nothing. Christian England, that boos a man sick unto death! And yet behind the boos is an obscure sort of fumbling after goodness. These people act so vilely because the only kind of vileness they can understand is abhorrent to them. They have not yet tumbled to the fact that unimaginative lack of charity is the greatest vileness of all.*

What makes goodness happen? How, fundamentally, does a man realise, so far as he may, his innate potentiality for goodness?

The first thing to say is that I don't know. How can anyone know? One of the widest of the gulfs that divide human beings is between the people who know about such things and the people who don't. Some of the people who know never cease to amaze me. Not the ones who by no fault of their own are deficient in a sense of enquiry, or incapable of examining themselves, or unable to think clearly, or careless about truth. These are quite intelligible: and so are those who have fled, consciously or otherwise, from the torturings of doubt (whereas a man should accept, even rejoice in, his doubts as he does in his certainties—not that I can always do so) into a bogus kind of certainty which enables them to give up the struggle and be at peace. But there are other large categories of people, good people, honest people, spiritually-minded people, brilliant people, sophisticated people, even specially Socratic people, or people with all these qualities combined, who, so far as I can make out, really *know* about ultimate mysteries in a way that is unintelligible to me. They call their knowledge faith. (I am not jeering.) So a man with at least as good a brain as my own and at least as much honesty will tell me that he *knows* what occurred at the tomb of Christ: it was empty on the third day, and empty because the physical Body had miraculously gone from it. If you succeed in driving him back a stage, he will tell you he knows this because he knows something else; he knows that the teaching of the Church is the repository of truth. And so on. I do not understand him.

Now it may seem paradoxical that I should be talking in such a way, seeing that this letter overflows with expressions of opinion—of opinion about ultimate mysteries—set down with the conviction, and you may think with the dogmatism, appropriate to such statements as that the rain is coming down in torrents or that this is August Bank Holiday. The paradox is partly to be explained by the fact that you cannot be forever qualifying your remarks with an identical *caveat*: you cannot be forever interposing "I believe this to be true, believe it passion-ately, believe it with ninety-nine per cent of my being: my belief is so passionate that not to rule my life by it would be, according to my present way of thinking, unthinkable: yet there in the background, hardly ever interfering but always held in reserve, is one per cent of me that says 'Even in this I may be wholly wrong'." (I wonder whether the people I've been describing as unintelligible make a similarly tacit reser-vation—in which case they become intelligible to me immedi-ately?) I have always been convinced, as you may deduce from this letter, that what I believe to be true *is* true, not only fiercely but often, they tell me, intolerably so: and yet there has always been a residue—in respect of the very thing I have been convinced about—of sceptical agnosticism. And I cannot understand how, in a man capable of examining himself, this scepticism can ever be absent. Does it point to some defect in my temperament, this inability to understand the type of knowledge in question? Or to a saving humility, *malgré tout*? I don't know, but I frankly think the latter.

And now I must immediately qualify the last paragraph.

For you will remind me of a previous passage about γνῶσις and δόξα: about things that are a matter of immediate knowledge, as contrasted with things that are a matter of no more than, though perhaps the strongest possible, opinion. And here I am suddenly up against it. For I must confess that there are moments *in* which, rather than *about* which, there is utter, final, unquestioning knowledge, without the smallest possible residue of scepticism, however distantly held in reserve. These are moments of personal meeting. We all know such moments in the meeting with another human being, called love; many know them in the meeting, experienced as a meeting between persons, with nature, or with poetry, or with music; some know them in the meeting, through any of these or through the self, with God. Afterwards, when it is no longer a question of *in* or *with* but of *about*, scepticism may enter: but the recollection of what happened *in* or *with* is relevant, and may be decisive, for the choice of how one responds to that scepticism. This is why a man can know, as I well understand, that God exists and is loving; but how can he know anything other about God than he has experienced in meeting him: how can he know, for instance, that the tomb was empty, and that it was empty for the reason given?

But "ah" you will say "you have used γνῶσις, or implied that you were using it, about moments of another kind: about the moment, for instance, in the dining-room of the House of Commons, when Gilbert McAllister told of the District Commissioner who went unarmed to his death rather than kill, and you *knew*—you spoke of a flash of lightning that illumined everything, you spoke of hearing, almost physically, the voice of Christ—you *knew* that he had been right, and that the other, who had preferred to shoot, had been wrong. What have you got to say to that? You can't fall back on your subsequent doubt because that is not, just now, the point. What have you got to say about your conviction in the moment itself?" I should have to reply that this was a moment of meeting with God. I should have to amend my "Some know them in the meeting with God through any of these or the self" by adding "or through the words or behaviour of others". And then, if you are a good dialectician, you will take me a stage further. "But do you not *know*," you will ask, "without a suspicion of your implied *caveat*—haven't you made it clear, times out of number, in the course of this letter—that love is good and hate is evil, that forgiving is good and revenge is evil, that evil, nevertheless, has no real existence, that nothing can be "wrong" with the totality of things—and so on with a number of propositions, which are really variations of a single proposition? Don't you know such things as these invariably? Isn't the moment perpetual? Aren't you *in* the moment always? Don't you rule out, therefore, the possibility of any subsequent agnosticism *about* it since no question of "subsequent" can arise? And isn't this what lies behind your insistence on absolutes?" Ah, my dear Timothy, you are driving me very hard; I am driving myself very hard: the Hound of Heaven, I suppose, is after me: for I must give you, of course, the affirmative answer you desire, and say that, at certain points where the veil is rent or the barrier broken down, there can be a perpetual meeting, a meeting in the time that has then become eternity, with God. And the veil *could* be, not merely rent at certain points but completely rent: the barrier *could* be completely broken down. That is the meaning of the life and death of Christ, considered whether as history or as myth: Christ, the new Adam, and therefore the old Adam too; Christ, all humanity; Christ, the Son of God; Christ, who could say, with simple affirmation, "I and my Father are one"; and so Christ the Son eternally with God the Father—in an eternity of the Holy Spirit, their meeting and their love.

But I shall repeat, all the more defiantly for having been driven so far, that certainty about anything except what happens in moments of personal meeting, or in an eternal moment of personal meeting, is unintelligible to me; and, sympathising with all scepticism, I shall take the opportunity of proclaiming my profound respect for anyone who may be as sceptical about my own certainties as I am sceptical about his. It is also conceivable, but improbable, that in future I shall feel less than my now customary irritation at what strikes me as unjustifiable dogmatism.

The fact is that I don't understand "faith", as meaning to take the actuality of something on trust when you haven't experienced the actuality of it yourself: the something in question being, *bien entendu*, a matter of reasonable doubt. That is why all creeds, beginning with such words as "I believe with a perfect faith", and continuing with a series of propositions some of which are obviously debatable and unlikely to be self-evident to at any rate a number of the people reciting them, seem so—mysterious to me. I understand immediate knowledge, γνῶσις: I understand opinion, which may be of such a character, so powerful and convincing, that a man must rule his life by it: but not faith, in the sense just described. I also understand mood, by which I mean a settled way of looking at things and feeling about them, based on γνῶσις and opinion: a way of looking at things which may be, and in my own case is, so very much a part of one that again one must rule one's life by it. It was in this sense that I used the word mood in the subtitle of *A Year of Grace*—"passages chosen and arranged to express a mood about God and man": adding in a foreword that this mood had been dominantly but not invariably mine ever since, as a very small boy, I had sniffed the air in a London garden. Some reviewers seemed to imagine that by "mood" I meant "whim": it was an odd misconception.

So when I come to ask myself "How does goodness happen? How, fundamentally, does a man realise, so far as he may, his innate potentiality for goodness?", the answer is that I don't know, but have a mood about it.

The question, you will remember, is about something positive and stark, something that happens in the depths, and something that happens in the depths of a *person*. Social conditioning of any kind, as we have seen, including the presence or absence of certain situations in early childhood, can do no more than assist or impede this happening. The same must be said about psychiatry, and the condition of one's body, and the action of drugs, and so on. If the needs of a man's body have been satisfied, the need for food and sexual intercourse and rest: if a drug, on occasion, has given him a good night's sleep, and so quietened his nerves—then goodness may have been made easier for him; but "easier" expresses the limit. The satisfaction of these needs, except perhaps of that for sleep, may also, though far less commonly, have made goodness more difficult; and pain and grief may have made it, according to temperament and circumstances, either easier or more difficult. Drugs, it is true, can not only make goodness easier or more difficult, they can make it impossible; for they can destroy personality altogether, they can make a man into an automaton, and goodness, by definition, can only happen in a person. Personality can be destroyed, too, by certain morbid states, and by extremities of hunger and pain.

But now the form of the question must be slightly altered —from "how does goodness happen?" or "what makes it happen?" to "*who* makes it happen?" For it is only in personal terms, at the end, that I could ever conceive myself as asking it. Is it the man himself, or God, or both?

This is how I look at the matter; this is my mood:

Men have two experiences—the experience of personal responsibility, and the experience of original sin.

The experience of responsibility is an experience of real responsibility. Men know themselves not merely as desiring goodness—desiring it with a love which is also, simultaneously, a sense of free obligation—but as being able to achieve it by some effort of their own. Without this ability the responsibility would not be real; and the whole of our life—our spiritual life no less than our life in society—is based on an assurance that the ability is there. If in fact we *cannot* relinquish selfishness and greed, then a resolution to do so is wholly meaningless; yet we continue to resolve in spite of a million failures, and shall never cease to do so.

But the experience of original sin is no less poignant. The words of St. Paul come inevitably again to one's lips: "For the good that I would I do not: but the evil that I would not, that I do. Now if I do that I would not, it is no more I that do it, but sin that dwelleth in me. I find then a law, that, when I would do good, evil is present with me. For I delight in the law of God after the inward man; but I see another law in my members, warring against the law of my mind, and bringing me with captivity to the law of sin which is in my members. O wretched man that I am! who shall deliver me from the body of this death?" Can there be a single spiritually adult person who has not risen from his bed times out of number to echo St. Paul's words with no less than St. Paul's agony?

Now men may be capable of goodness, or they may be "sold under sin". But they cannot, in any sense that the human mind can understand, simultaneously be both; and nothing could be more blasphemous than to force a reconciliation by means of metaphysical or theological constructions that are repugnant to reason, for reason is sacred. And the case is even worse when we assume, by way of explanation, a divine morality less exalted than man's.

What it comes to is this. Both experiences are real; and neither can they be reconciled by reason nor may they be reconciled against reason. But if both are real, both must be aspects of one indivisible reality. So we must dutifully and peacefully accept both, and accept them as reconciled in that reality: a reality we apprehend, not by "faith" but by a living contact with it, to be existent and utterly "right", while having, in our human nature, no more than intimations of its nature: a reality beyond our freedom and unfreedom as it is beyond our good and evil, but a reality, none the less, that makes our freedom and unfreedom, our good and evil, terribly real distinctions for human existence, and distinctions to be disregarded only at the utmost peril. We have intimations of its nature, I said: for do we not live now and again in a fleeting realisation—without either ability or desire to explain—that compulsion to sin, and power not to sin, are somehow inextricably united?

The experience of personal responsibility, I would add, cannot be invalidated on its own ground by any theory of determinism, even by one that the experiencer himself may hold. If his reason finds, to its complete satisfaction, that his every act, thought and emotion are inexorably determined by a chain of causation, then of course he must accept its finding; but how possibly could his experience of freedom, which is an immediate experience, be thereby affected? He may not reject the finding, and cannot reject the experience: so he must accept both, falling back, once again, on their reconciliation in ultimate reality. The temptation is to reject the finding, as being far less vivid, far more easily played the fool with, than the experience; but it is a temptation that any honest man will resist.

The paradox of personal responsibility and original sin is repeated in the paradox of grace. We experience ourselves as capable of doing good by our own effort; but when we do anything good we experience ourselves as doing it by reason of grace. "Nevertheless I live; yet not I, but Christ liveth in me." The very prayer for grace to do good is itself experienced, with ineffable immediacy, as at once a free and responsible act, and put into our hearts by the selfsame grace we pray for. "Prayer," said John Saltmarsh, who was a chaplain in Sir

N

Thomas Fairfax's army, "is no other but the revelation of the will or mind of God"; and "The people think," said Rabbi Pinhas of Koretz in eighteenth-century Poland, "that they pray before God. But it is not so. For the prayer itself is the essence of the Godhead."

This, then, is the mood with which I answer the question, "How does goodness happen?" I do not know whether I have been at all successful in explaining it. Probably not. Perhaps it cannot be explained: perhaps others, whom I have never read or have forgotten, explain it better. Martin Buber comes nearer than anyone else I know to expressing what I feel, though there is quite a lot, even in so short a passage, from which I would dare to dissent:

"It is senseless to ask how far my action reaches, and where God's grace begins; there is no common border-line; what concerns me alone, before I bring something about, is my action, and what concerns me alone, when the action is successfully done, is God's grace. The one is no less real than the other, and neither is a part-cause. God and man do not divide the government of the world between them; man's action is enclosed in God's action, but it is still real action."

My own commonest prayer, when, amid the fever and fret, I remember to pray, is that I should be made like a sheet of glass through which good may come into the world, and like a sheet of iron which may shut out evil. (The words came instinctively to me, I remember, in another connection, at an earlier stage of this letter.) I know that I pray by grace and yet I know that I am responsible for my prayer: I know that I am responsible for my conduct, and yet my prayer is for permission, not to do anything good myself, but to be a channel through which goodness may enter. But not for my own sake, I add, again when I remember to: not for the sake of being good (which is the great temptation): but for the sake of goodness.

There is something further to be said, Timothy, before we finish with this topic. We ought to differentiate, when reflecting about it, between ourselves and our neighbour. It is the responsibility, the ability to be and do good, that we must stress in our

own case, albeit with great humility and with a proper for-
bearance when we fail. But in the case of our neighbour the
emphasis must be different; here it is original sin, or heredity,
or adverse circumstances, or the force of environment, that we
must keep ever in our minds, while striving none the less to
inspire him, in Spinoza's words, with a sense of "man's virtue
and power". And the more we are aware of the compulsion to
sin in ourselves, the more compassionately we shall sympathise
with this compulsion in others.

My strange Chinese box of a chapter, my discourse on
socialism with all its inner parts, is now finished, and we are
ready to pass on. I said when beginning this third and last big
section of it that the theme was "still freedom—the ultimate
freedom". Having come to the end you will understand why.
The ultimate freedom is freedom from egoism and greed:
freedom to live in community: freedom to love others—and no
less, with a true love, oneself. Can socialism be a midwife—*a*,
not *the*, midwife—of this freedom? Can it help men, more effectively than any other system of economic organisation—of mere
economic organisation, let me say—to be gentle and kind,
tolerant and forgiving? That is the only question, finally, worth
asking about it. And my own answer is that it can, provided
that it is the right kind of socialism.

A socialist must have his nose in blue books. His brain
must be wrestling with economic theory. But his heart must
be longing for the City of God.

And now let us return to Oxford, to consider my religious
development there.

# CHAPTER XXI

## OXFORD—II

IF THERE HAD BEEN no war, it is possible that I should have been baptised while at Oxford. Arrangements for the ceremony had been made some time during the summer of 1914. But I am almost certain that, war or no war, I should have called it off. And how glad I am that I did! Apart from anything else, your grandmother, when the time came, would never have married a *meshúmad*.*

All my thoughts and emotions about religion, in the narrower sense, were centred at Oxford on Christianity. It is true that I went one Friday evening, probably during my first term, to the cold little orthodox synagogue, which I visualise, though possibly by false association, as somewhere in the suburbs near Worcester; but the visit was not repeated. I dallied a little longer with liberal Judaism, which I felt to be genuinely religious and, what was much the same thing, to demand my support as revolting from orthodoxy; I still feel very similarly about it. A few liberal Jews were grouped round Basil Henriques, who was afterwards to found the St. George's Jewish Settlement in the East End of London and to become famous as a children's magistrate; and I occasionally went to his rooms, though some mixture of gravity, heartiness and evangelism in the atmosphere rather embarrassed me. I remember very well one difficult evening when Claude Montefiore was present. I don't know whether his name will survive into your day: it was famous in mine. He was a big ugly man, even stubblier and blacker in the face than the Forest of Dean (whom you must be getting quite curious about): but with eyes of such beauty, so large and deep and brooding, that you lowered your own as you looked at him. He was also exceedingly rich: and with a reputation, which I believe was well merited, for exceptional spirituality. You will judge from this description, correctly, that I found him unsympathetic; but this was probably due to some defect in myself, for he was widely and genuinely loved. He had founded

* Apostate.

the Liberal Jewish Synagogue in Hill Street, and had written a work on the Synoptic Gospels of which, or so many Jews believed, many Christian theologians thought highly. He was no more a Christianiser than St. Paul was a Judaiser—my father would have called him, in spite of his unorthodoxy, "a thoroughly staunch Jew": but being liberal of heart and mind he saw a great deal of good in Christianity, and Jews with such an attitude were far rarer then than they are now.

On the evening in question Montefiore had used the expression "my experience of God." Now this was something which for a long time had profoundly interested while simultaneously puzzling me. I was a curious mixture at this period, a sort of perpetual battleground between a dislike of precise formulations and a passion for them. Reality, I already felt, could be apprehended only in an immediate meeting with it, and then that was that: the world of this apprehension had no common border-line, for temporal consciousness, with the other world of logical statement, though all worlds were ultimately the same world: and there was nothing you could do with your apprehension, if there was any point in doing anything at all with it—with something that just *was*—but imitate it by means of poetry or painting or music: which might themselves have occasioned it, though a treatise on logic might have occasioned it too. On the other hand, something very strong in me detested irrationality, and therefore craved for precise formulations. In this latter respect I was rather like Sir Bernard Travers in *Shadows of Ecstasy*, a novel by Charles Williams that I very much hope you will read. I might have said, to use his words, that the intellect and logical reason is the last stability of man: and that though it can never *be* the truth it always approaches, for nothing can be truth till it has become one with its object, and such union it is not given to the intellect to achieve without losing its own nature, yet in its divine and abstract reflection of the world, its passionless mirror of the holy law that governs the world, the supreme perfection of mortality moves. "If A is the same as B and B is the same as C, then A is the same as C. Other things may be true; for all I know, they may be different at the same time; but this at least is true."

And yet I am wrong in saying that I was a battleground for two elements: they existed in me side by side, with no feeling of conflict between them.

So when Montefiore used that expression I felt at once that my opportunity had come. The analysing, Socratic part of me could at last get enlightenment; I could at last clear up a difficulty that had puzzled me so long. What exactly *was* this experience? Was it anything *more* than the joy and praise I had felt ever since I had been a small boy? Was it anything more *definite* than that? I was really dying to know. So "What precisely do you *mean* by your experience of God?" I asked Montefiore. "Please describe it to me."

Montefiore seemed very much annoyed. He may have thought I was "ragging" him, which was not the case. Anyhow, he snubbed me. He said, in effect, that this was a private matter which one didn't discuss with other people. Part of me—really the strongest part of me—ought to have sympathised, but didn't. And something in the atmosphere told me that everybody agreed with Montefiore. I had obviously dropped a brick. I went away, I am afraid, feeling—I believe now quite wrongly—that there had been a great deal of pious humbug about the whole business.

*Brimpton, Saturday, August 18th*

*I must comment, at the risk of holding you up, on the paragraphs just above. I cannot avoid doing so. For in the hope that you may profit by my example in some respects and be warned by it in others more numerous, I am trying to describe for you a whole personality, a whole way of looking at things; and the personality didn't suddenly stop dead at this point or that—in 1906, or 1914, or 1939, or, for the matter of that, on August 17th 1951. An expert technician could perhaps so order an unbroken narrative that, when the last word had been written, the writer would stand exposed in a light which had been growing brighter and brighter and was now capable of revealing everything: but I doubt it: for, the last word having been written, surely he would then have to write a whole second book, and publish it simultaneously with the first, explaining what he had become as a result of his writing? And so on, and so on. Not to add this gloss, anyhow, would be to falsify, as I see it, the whole enterprise.*

*So I want to tell you what I have been thinking about that Montefiore bit since writing it last week. I'm afraid that what I'm going to say will sound heavy and mealy-mouthed, but I can't*

*help that; for the point involved is not a trivial one—it's as import-*
*ant as atom-bombing, with which it's intimately connected: and you*
*can't play the fool with that sort of issue, however disagreeable*
*the effect you may produce. Very well, then, here is what I want to*
*say: I have been wondering at odd moments during the week whether*
*in writing as I did about Claude Montefiore I was sinning the*
*unforgivable sin, sinning against the Holy Ghost. For I wrote very*
*nastily about him, and the sly innuendos were made very much worse*
*by a parade of deliberate self-accusation—by carefully inserted*
*remarks about the defect being in me, and so on, which were meant*
*to look well.*

*The key passage about this sin, to which I have previously given*
*a different but equally valid interpretation (though really, at*
*bottom, the same interpretation) is St. Mark, Chapter 3, verses 22,*
*28–30: "And the scribes which came down from Jerusalem said,*
*'He hath Beelzebub, and by the prince of the devils casteth he out*
*devils'. And he called them unto him, and said . . . Verily I say*
*unto you, All sins shall be forgiven unto the sons of men, and*
*blasphemies wherewith soever they shall blaspheme: but he that shall*
*blaspheme against the Holy Ghost hath never forgiveness, but is in*
*danger of eternal damnation:* Because they said, He hath an
unclean spirit." *The words emphasised have a kind of special*
*explicitness, as if the commentator were saying "Don't let there*
*be any mistake about what Christ meant: this is what he meant."*
*It is clear, too, that the blasphemy in question is not blasphemy*
*against Christ as such; for we read in St. Luke, Chapter 12, verse 10*
*(and similarly in St. Matthew) "And whosoever shall speak a*
*word against the Son of man, it shall be forgiven him; but unto*
*him that blasphemeth against the Holy Ghost it shall not be*
*forgiven."*

*There is a fine passage in Ouspensky's A New Model of the*
*Universe dealing with this question. "The Holy Ghost" he writes*
*"is that which is g o o d in everything. In every object, in every man,*
*in every event, there is something good, not in a philosophical and*
*not in a mystical sense, but in the simplest, psychological and*
*everyday sense. If a man does not see this good, if he condemns*
*everything irrevocably, if he seeks and sees only the bad, if he is*
*incapable of seeing the good in things and people—then this is the*
*blasphemy against the Holy Ghost. There are different types of*
*men. Some are capable of seeing the good even where there is very*
*little of it. They are sometimes even inclined to exaggerate it to*

*themselves. Others, on the contrary, are inclined to see everything worse than it is in reality, are incapable of seeing anything good. First of all, always and in everything, they find something bad, always begin with suspicion, with accusation, with calumny. This is the blasphemy against the Holy Ghost. This blasphemy is not forgiven; that means that it leaves a very deep trace on the inner nature of the man himself.*

*"Usually in life people take slander too lightly, excuse it too easily in themselves and in others. Slander constitutes half their lives, fills half their interests. People slander without noticing themselves what they are doing and automatically they expect nothing but slander from others. They answer the slander of others with slander and strive only to forestall them. A particularly noticeable tendency to slander is called either a critical mind or wit. Men do not understand that even the usual everyday slander is the beginning of the blasphemy against the Holy Ghost. It is not for nothing that the Devil means slanderer. The passage in the Gospel, that they shall give account even of every idle word in the day of judgement, sounds so strange and incomprehensible to men because they do not understand that even a small slander is the beginning of the blasphemy against the Holy Ghost. They do not understand that even every idle word remains . . .*

*"The parable of the unjust steward refers to the creation of the other, of the contrary, tendency, that is to say, the tendency to see the Holy Ghost or the 'good' even where there is very little of it, and in this way to increase the good in oneself and liberate oneself from sins, that is from 'evil'.*

*"Man finds what he looks for. Who looks for the evil finds the evil; who looks for the good, finds the good."*

*You might think it a good idea, my dear Timothy, to get that passage typed out and pasted up above your bed (as I used to paste up photographs of Destinn above mine) side by side with the mezzuza we gave you when you came to see us at Easter. For slanderous gossip, imputation of bad motives, witty or sarcastic innuendos are common form with nearly everyone: certainly, to take my own case, hardly a midnight passes without a stabbing recollection (when I bother to think back on things at all) of some idle word that a few hours before I have spoken so lightly, or of someone else's idle word that I have so lightly acquiesced in. "But I say unto you, That every idle word that men shall speak, they shall give account thereof in the day of judgement." For I wasn't exaggerating when I said that the point involved was as important as atom-bombing. He who would do good to another must do it in minute particulars; failure to do good to another, whether he be near or far, whether you know him or not, ends in the destruction of humanity. And to calumniate is not to do good, but to murder.*

*I should be misrepresenting Ouspensky, however, if I failed to add his qualification. "At the same time," he continues, "nothing is more dangerous than to understand this idea of Christ's in a literal or sentimental sense, and to begin to see the 'good' where it does not exist at all.*

*"The idea that in every object, in every man and in every event there is something good is right only in relation to normal and natural manifestations. This idea cannot be equally right in relation to abnormal and unnatural manifestations. There can be no Holy Ghost in the blasphemy against the Holy Ghost; and there are things, people and events that are by their very nature the blasphemy against the Holy Ghost. Justification of them is the blasphemy against the Holy Ghost.*

*"A great amount of evil in life occurs just because people, afraid of committing a sin or afraid of appearing not sufficiently charitable or not sufficiently broad-minded, justify what does not deserve justification. Christ was not sentimental, he was never afraid to tell an unpleasant truth, and he was not afraid to act. The expulsion of the money-changers from the temple is a most remarkable allegory, showing Christ's attitude towards 'life', which tries to turn even the temple to its own ends."*

*I disagree with a great deal of this: the passage, taken as a whole, presupposes, or seems to presuppose, a fundamental dichotomy which I do not recognise, and to say that there are "people" (as well as "things" and "events") who "are by their very nature the blasphemy against the Holy Ghost" is the blasphemy against the Holy Ghost. Moreover, while we dare not justify, in our earthly dimension, what does not appear, in our earthly dimension, to deserve justification, and Ouspensky is right in insisting on this: yet to condemn without charity to the offender is to become as sounding brass or a tinkling cymbal. And note "in our earthly dimension". Nothing, nothing whatever, is ultimately to be condemned. We must say with Spinoza that whatever is, is in God, and nothing can exist or be conceived without God; and with Léon Bloy that all that happens is divine. Perhaps Ouspensky himself, whose system, I am told by those more familiar with him than I am, rests on a clearly stated principle of unity in diversity, might have emphasised, in another context, that the anathema implied in the passage just quoted is to be understood only within the framework of human relativities. But even so I should still disagree with a good deal of what he says in this passage.*

\*            \*            \*            \*            \*

*Suddenly—a rowan-tree round the corner of the coppice, with wheat stooks and pale autumn blue behind its berries and leaves. That was after breakfast this morning, as I was wandering about the garden to find a place for my deckchair and stool. And later, as I lay in the hedge with high summer now back again, a single black-berry leaf, transparent, was swaying, but hardly (was it swaying? was it still?), between my eyes and the sun—its drawing even freer, but more careful too, than Leonardo's. "And all a wonder and a—" not a wild but a breathless desire.*

As I sit here and reflect about my brief dalliance (it cannot have lasted more than a term or so) with liberal Judaism, there comes into my mind an image of almost complete dissociation: between me as the one party and liberal Judaism as the other. Nothing really passed between us. I was looking at it, the whole time, quite from the outside: I was in no way engaged. And it wasn't engaged with me, either. I approved of it intellectually, even judged it, in my hatred of orthodoxy, admirable; and, staying there, it was willing, on its side, for me to go to it if I wished. But we felt no love for one another: we failed to make even the first tentative gesture that leads to a handshake.

Oh, let me cut through everything I was going to say after that—all about the coldness and flatness of liberal Judaism, its impersonal ethicism and moralism, my conviction, which was a passionately moral conviction, that I dare not, in loyalty to spirit and truth, but keep it at arm's length as something par-ticularist, alien, hedging off, ununiversal—let me cut through all this and get straight to the heart of the matter, which is this: that I was on my way to the adoration of Christ.

Long since, as you will realise, I had given a wholehearted assent, both intellectual and emotional, to the ethics of Christi-anity: by which I had meant, not every rule of conduct enjoined in the New Testament, or even, according to the Gospels, by Christ himself, but, more generally, the whole way of thinking, feeling and living expressed in Christ's words as recorded. "Resist not evil": "Let him have thy cloke also": "Love your enemies": "Lay not up for yourselves treasures upon earth": "Take no thought for the morrow": "Judge not": "God is a spirit; and they that worship him must worship him in spirit and in truth"—it had been, when I had first read these phrases, as if I had had no need to read them, as if they were expressions of a self-evident reality (the only reality) which I knew eternally and was now remembering, and as if any doubt on the part of others about the absolute truth they revealed could be due only to some humanly inexplicable but finally irrelevant misunderstanding. You must not infer, however, that my assent had been exclusively intellectual, if indeed any total assent can ever be such. In and by the very act, rather, of judging "This is sanity, this is self-evident truth", I had also been adoring reality, I had also been delighted by the beauty inseparable from it. Or, to make another attempt to express what is in my mind, I had been profoundly moved, not so much by the beauty and lovableness of the Sermon, the Parables, and the expressions of forgiveness and pity ("Neither do I condemn thee"), as by the way in which, lighting up the landscape of reality, they eternally witnessed that beauty and the real are one, and that this one is lovable.

So if, during my first term at Oxford, someone had said to me "Are you a Christian?", I should have replied "Ethically, yes, in the sense that I 'believe in' Christian ethics. In any other sense, no." As to Christ, I thought of him, at this time, as a Hebrew prophet—by far the greatest of Hebrew prophets, it is true, but still "just" a prophet. I loved him and reverenced him as I loved and reverenced Socrates, that other beautiful hero of the search after truth—more intensely, but in much the same way. It would not have occurred to me, at any time before 1912, to describe what I felt for him as adoration.

But before passing on to that, I must qualify what I said just now about having been ethically a Christian. You must not understand by this that my actions, thoughts, words and feelings were unusually or even averagely consistent with Christian teaching. On the contrary, I was selfish, self-righteous, envious, jealous: spiritually, though not I think physically, greedy; capable of great anger: careless, often, of other people's happiness, and given to judging them. I was marked by these uglinesses hardly, if at all, less disfiguringly than in the old Elgin

Avenue days. I knew them to be wrong, for I wanted to be loving and generous; with part of me I *was* loving and generous —not merely because I wanted to be, but spontaneously: and frequently I felt great remorse. But I was spiritually lazy, so far as my own person was concerned (the qualification is important), as well as spiritually greedy: or—perhaps this is a better way of putting it—I had failed to realise either that to be good oneself is one's best contribution to goodness, or that the price of being good is eternal vigilance in a million minute particulars. I was not to understand these realities until some twenty years later, when Hitler came to power in Germany; and I was not to understand them fully until, just before Munich, world war seemed inevitable. Then at last I knew that whatever I might do publicly and politically in face of all this hatred and evil, yet to try, every minute of the time, to be good and loving oneself was the final answer. And from that time I did, very consciously, try —not wholly without success (mock modesty is a vice, for to depreciate oneself is as blasphemous as to depreciate others), but with frequent forgetfulness and appalling setbacks. And it was not till much later still—not, I think, till after my experience of hell in 1943—that I fully realised something else: namely, that while conscious vigilance about minute particulars is immensely important, even more so is such a change in one's being as will make goodness natural to one: that to win such a change one must quietly put oneself in a posture for the receipt of grace: and that conscious vigilance about minute particulars is chiefly valuable as a preparation for this posture. I have talked a great deal in this letter about minute particulars, just as I have talked a great deal about losing one's life to save it: that is because, taken together, they are the secret of living.

When I said that, at Oxford, I was spiritually lazy, I asked you to take note of the qualification "so far as my own person was concerned". For just as you must not infer that I was an even averagely good ethical Christian in my own conduct, so equally you must not infer that I was anything but passionately eager to see Jews, Englishmen and the whole world become ethically Christian in theirs. A curious paradox, perhaps, but one that you may understand. And when I say ethically Christian, I mean ethically Christian: in politics, in economics, in personal relations, in everything. Here I was very far from being spiritually lazy: I burnt with the fiercest conversionist fire, I would happily have worn myself out (and later on, temporarily, did wear myself out) to make the whole world good—poor sinner that I was!

And now I must return to the Person of Christ. I find myself at once in the greatest difficulty; for after sitting a long day before my library fire and brooding over the past, I am no nearer disentangling what I felt at Oxford—about the Incarnation: it is of this that I must speak—from what I felt subsequently and what I feel today. All I can do, I think, is to tell you what I have gradually come to feel about it; and I ought to wait a bit, perhaps a week or so, before making the attempt, because although my emotion is very precise I do not at the moment see how I can formulate it.

A way to do so came to me on Monday night, about twenty-four hours after I had written the preceding paragraph, as I stood for a few minutes by the open window at Ladbroke Grove just before going to bed. I had switched off the light, and as I put my head out over the Square and smelled the leaves and the earth and the soft warm rain that was falling, I was moved once again, moved it may be for the millionth time, by an ineffable emotion of worship and gratitude. And as I lay in bed afterwards this is what I thought:

(1) I have always felt a vast, single, living bliss *behind* everything. I have always been certain it is *there*.

(2) I have always felt a life and a bliss *in* everything—I mean in every particular, in stones and chairs and mantelpieces and paper as well as in what is ordinarily called life: and it is through my meeting with these particulars, living and what are usually thought of as other than living, that I establish communion, feel myself mingled, with the bliss beyond.

(3) There is in me an imperative need, not only to establish communion, not only to merge myself, but also to worship. Or perhaps I should not speak of an imperative need, but should simply say that I *have* always worshipped—my life has been filled with a sense of worship, my being has been worshipful about the sum of things. I have worshipped the vast, single, living bliss beyond—that has been the central fact of my life;

and I have worshipped it at once in and through the whole body of particulars, and in and through such single particulars— every single such single particular—as good deeds on the one hand and stocks and stones on the other.

(4) In religious language, I come to God through the world: in Platonic language I come to the Idea through the particulars. I don't mean that I deduce the Idea from the particulars: I mean that it is in the particulars that I feel and love the Idea. And Christ (whether the historic Christ or the Christ in our hearts—I shall soon deal with that) is the Supreme Particular.

(5) I worship the beyond in and through the particulars, but do not worship the particulars themselves. Not the "ordinary" particulars. I *do* worship the Supreme Particular, as I worship the beyond. I worship Him as very close, very friendly, very accessible: I worship Him in the way Blake tells of, the way common, I suppose, to all Christians:

"Then I see the Saviour over me,
Spreading his beams of love, and dictating the words of this
    mild song . . .
I am not a God afar off, I am a brother and a friend;
Within your bosoms I reside, and you reside in me;
Lo! we are One; forgiving all Evil; Not seeking recompense . . ."

(6) Christ, the Supreme Particular, is, for me, a concrete individual, one Person, with a man's nature: but typical of men as no other man is typical. His nature is essentially ours—ours, not merely a model for ours (though it is that as well): which is another way of saying that our nature is essentially His—that this is what we really are, the rest being error and misunderstanding. To the extent to which we realise this—to the extent to which we "believe in" Him, we are in Him. He is each one of us—every man—all but completely released from bondage to error and unreality; to the error and unreality of self-centredness as opposed to communion, of what Blake calls "selfhood":

"O Saviour, pour upon me thy Spirit of meekness and love,
  Annihilate the Selfhood in me, be thou all my life,
  Guide thou my hand which trembles exceedingly upon the
    rock of ages."

"Be thou all my life"—that is the crux.

Most men, in this sense, do die in Adam, and those of them who "believe in" Christ do live again in Him.

And all this being so, worship by a man of Christ 'as the Supreme Particular is worship both of God and of humanity.


This treatment of the Incarnation is of course completely subjective, and will be criticised accordingly. You must decide for yourself whether the criticism is valid. What I have been saying, you may think, amounts to no more than this: that I have need of a Supreme Particular, and that when I call Christ that Particular all I mean is that Particular for *me*. Very well; I shall not demur. And if you go on to ask "But why Christ? Why not Krishna, or some other Avatar?", the answer is simple: on the boy born in Elgin Avenue to his own special heritage, and developing as he has slowly developed through a variety of specific experiences, Christ's teaching has made an impact as of the *utterly* true, Christ's personality has made an impact as of the *utterly* adorable, Christ's living and dying has made an impact as of the *utterly* good. I tremble as I add, but in honesty I must, that when I say utterly good I mean utterly good within human possibilities. (This is not such bad theology, either.) I do not regard Him as finally flawless. And even as I tremble I know that Christ will forgive me, for He would wish me to be divinely critical even about, perhaps specially about, Himself. But then again, I wonder: is it perhaps my own imperfection, my human imperfection, that allows me to see imperfection where nothing but perfection exists?

So my Christ, my Supreme Particular, could be no other, if I was to have one, than Christ. If I had been an Indian, Sri Krishna might have made the same impact on me. For I think that there are several Christs, but only one for each person. There are Christs, perhaps, not our Christ and yet our Christ, on earths and in dimensions of which we know nothing:

> "With this ambiguous earth
> His dealings have been told us. These abide:
> The signal to a maid, the human birth,
> The lesson, and the young Man crucified.

> "But not a star of all
> The innumerable host of stars has heard
> How He administered this terrestrial ball.
> Our race have kept their Lord's entrusted Word.
>
> "Of His earth-visiting feet
> None knows the secret, cherished, perilous,
> The terrible, shamefast, frightened, whispered, sweet,
> Heart-shattering secret of His way with us.
>
> "No planet knows that this
> Our wayside planet, carrying land and wave,
> Love and life multiplied, and pain and bliss,
> Bears, as chief treasure, one forsaken grave.
>
> "Nor, in our little day,
> May His devices with the heavens be guessed,
> His pilgrimage to thread the Milky Way,
> Or His bestowals there be manifest.
>
> "But, in the eternities,
> Doubtless we shall compare together, hear
> A million alien Gospels, in what guise
> He trod the Pleiades, the Lyre, the Bear.
>
> "O be prepared, my soul!
> To read the inconceivable, to scan
> The million forms of God those stars unroll
> When, in our turn, we show to them a Man."

What a God it is who has given us, not only the "ordinary" particulars, but a Supreme Particular! And what a universe it is that can boast, not of one Supreme Particular, but of many!

Being the sort of person I am, if Christ had not existed I might almost have been tempted to invent Him. It may even be (though I don't believe it, Toynbee's great excursus notwithstanding) that, in one sense, men *have* invented Him: it may be, I mean, that the Gospel story is a mere amalgam of various happenings that have occurred, or have been imagined to occur, in many different places at many different times. Well, what of it? Then God, we should have to say, has put a Person, a Life and a Death into human consciousness, as a paradigm of the Way. On the one reading (to express it in its orthodox form) God was born, by God's grace, very man in a manger: on the other, God is born, by God's grace, very man in men's hearts: and I cannot for the life of me see why the one Christ should be any less "real", any less to be worshipped, than the other.

Or we should have to say, looking at it now from a slightly different angle, that out of the depths of its consciousness— out of the love and understanding in its heart—humanity has bodied forth a myth that incarnates the ultimate truth. Christ would then exist—would always have existed, would forever exist ("Before Abraham was, I am") as essential, as Divine, Humanity. Is that non-existence?

Beethoven "invented" the Quartet in C Sharp Minor, opus 131: that is to say, God put it into Beethoven's consciousness, with Beethoven's co-operation. Doesn't it then exist? Isn't it "real"? Listen to it, my dear Timothy, next time you have the chance (for you are certain to love music) and answer me.

I was delighted, the other day, to come across this passage in a book by Sri Aurobindo, the Hindu philosopher and saint who recently died:

"Such controversies as the one that has raged in Europe over the historicity of Christ would seem to a spiritually-minded Indian largely a waste of time; he would concede to it a considerable historical, but hardly any religious importance; for what does it matter in the end whether a Jesus son of the carpenter Joseph was actually born in Nazareth or Bethlehem, lived and taught and was done to death on a real or trumped-up charge of sedition, so long as we can know by spiritual experience the inner Christ, live uplifted in the light of His teaching and escape from the yoke of the natural Law by that atonement of man with God of which the crucifixion is the symbol? If the Christ, God made man, lives within our spiritual being, it would seem to matter little whether or not a son of Mary physically lived and suffered and died in Judea."

No, it would matter a great deal, because we are flesh and blood, and to part with a Christ of our own flesh and blood would be grievous. And yet in another sense I would go even a little further than Aurobindo. Whether or not the Incarnation—unique or otherwise—is, in the popular sense, a fact,

scepticism about it would appear to be more reasonable if
Christ is "historical", as you know I believe Him to be, than
if He is not. If He is "historical", there is nothing far-fetched in
the idea that people have drawn false deductions from a
remarkable life and death. But if the Gospel narrative is a
myth, it is difficult to understand how it can have come into
being except by way of explaining what would then be, so to
speak, a fact in its own right: the incarnation of God—his
incarnation, unique or otherwise, as Christ—in innumerable
men's hearts. Roughly by the same token, various parallelisms
—and in particular the recurrent "dying God" beliefs—would
appear to confirm Christianity, at least in one interpretation of
it, rather than the reverse.

Such, then, is what I feel about the Incarnation: a matter
partly of knowledge—of immediate experience—and partly of
mood, and not at all one of "faith" or dogmatic precision. And
it's no good people telling me that it's all very vague
(simpletons!) and that I *ought* to have dogmas. I am merely
describing. It is not a question of what ought to be, but of what
is. The reality, for me, is that I adore Christ. Whatever may
be the truth about the Gospel story, whatever may be the
metaphysics of the matter, He lives and reigns for me eternally; and whether or not I should hesitate to call Him Lord,
I can assuredly call Him Master.

If my view of the Incarnation, when at Oxford, is inseparable,
as I think back, from later views, I can remember quite clearly
what I felt there about the Resurrection, the Atonement, and
the doctrine of the Trinity.

In the physical Resurrection I was interested hardly at all.
I doubt whether I ruled it out intellectually, as an event that
couldn't possibly have occurred: but my mood, to bring mood
into it again, very definitely was that it hadn't. I feel much the
same today, if a little more strongly in both respects: I am even
readier to admit its possibility, but inclined still more empha-
tically to deny its occurrence: indeed I am of the opinion, which
I hope I shan't be thought offensive for expressing, that no
educated man genuinely "believes in" it now—believes in it

(without mental reservations, interpretational gymnastics, or half-conscious self-deception) in the way in which he believes, say, that cruelty is vile. Interest in the matter at all, other than a generalised interest in anything miraculous, derives, it seems to me, from an undutiful repudiation of death—part and parcel, surely, of that very self-centredness Christ forever rebukes us for: as well as from an overestimation of the body not a bit less lamentable than that underestimation of it so prominent in a lot of Christian sermonising. But the spiritual Resurrection is another matter: this is an undeniable fact, and of supreme importance. The spiritual *Resurrection*. It is not merely that Christ lives eternally—whether the Christ of Judaea or the Christ in our hearts: the Christ Who lives eternally—this is the pith and core of the matter—is the same Christ Who physically dies. He lives, you might almost say, *because* He dies: the death, that particular death, guaranteeing the eternal life. You might almost say it, but not quite: for there is no question of condition—the death and the life are facets of one crystal, expressions, inextricably united, of one reality. And men who identify themselves with that death, however infinitesimally, by sympathetic insight and in humble imitation, are thereby helped, not to "win" eternal life—for themselves (no idea could be more meaningless, no wish more unChristlike), but to increase its variety and richness. Christ, in this sense, has truly conquered death.

As to the doctrine of the Trinity, my interest in it was genuine but superficial: I approached it as if the meaning of existence were a problem to be solved intellectually, and this might be the missing clue. The approach was through Platonism. Although I began to read "Greats" officially—in so far as at any time I read anything prescribed—only during my last term at Oxford, I had long since been steeped in Plato: I loved him and knew a good deal about him, though in a rather amateurish sort of way. (I have always been an amateur in the bad sense —or perhaps amateurishness isn't bad, but merely has defects that are inseparable from its qualities. I have genuinely given myself to a number of interests, and to some of them simultaneously, at different periods of my life: have been passionate about them, lived for them, worked day and night at and for them: and over a long period of years my devotion to one or two of them—politics, for instance, and teaching in some form or another—has never varied. But I have been expert at almost nothing, or perhaps at nothing at all. I doubt whether I am even an expert publisher, although I have been, on the whole, a successful one. To give a trivial example, I know nothing about paper sizes: after a quarter of a century in publishing I haven't the faintest idea of what "quad demy" means. Passionate about politics—lively, day by day politics as well as political theory—I have never even attempted to get into the House of Commons. Devoted to music, I can play no instrument, however badly. There are several reasons, I think, for this curious state of affairs, which fascinates me. I am interested in too many things—not in too many things absolutely (such an idea would be grotesque, with the world so full of wonders), but in too many things for expertise in any one of them to be probable, given my deficiencies: I am impatient, always want to press on, can't be bothered with any detail that seems unnecessarily, at the moment, to be holding me up, however important in reality it may be: and I've nothing of the mental facility, the power to grasp everything in a flash, that makes a great barrister. I'm the worst puzzle-solver in the world—how I envy puzzle-solvers!—and though I like setting quiz papers I hate answering them.)

Plato, as I was saying just now, had for a long time enthralled me: I found in him, rather confusedly and perhaps with some misunderstanding, an intellectual confirmation of my instinctive pansacramentalism. But I was puzzled at first by the problem of connection: how—by what process or through what instrumentality—did the particulars come to "partake of" the Idea, did the sensible come to "partake of" Form? What bridged the hiatus? I leaped at Plato's answer in the later Dialogues: "his last word," says A. E. Taylor, "on the problem how the sensible comes to 'partake' of Form is that it does so through the agency of divine goodness and wisdom." Ah, I said, but this is trinitarianism: divine goodness and wisdom is the Holy Ghost linking God the Father, unmanifest, with God the Son, our universe of manifestation: the three being one. But, I went on to say, isn't Christian trinitarianism superior to Platonic trinitarianism? Doesn't it explain what Plato can never explain? For isn't it something actually *happening*, a living, concrete, flesh-and-blood *occurrence*, whereas the other is a cold theoretical construction? Perhaps I obscurely felt what

I was afterwards to read in a sermon by John Smith, the Christian Platonist:

"God made the universe and all the creatures contained therein as so many glasses wherein He might reflect His own glory. He hath copied forth Himself in the creation; and in this outward world we may read the lovely characters of the Divine goodness, power, and wisdom. But how to find God here and feelingly to converse with him, and being affected with the sense of the Divine glory shining out upon the creation, how to pass out of the sensible world into the intellectual, is not so effectually taught by that philosophy which professed it most, as by true religion. That which knits and unites God and the soul together can best teach it how to ascend and descend upon those golden links that unite, as it were, the world to God. That Divine Wisdom, that contrived and beautified this glorious structure, can best explain her own art, and carry up the soul back again in these reflected beams to Him who is the Fountain of them." To quote so far is sufficient for my purpose, but the sermon as a whole is so beautiful that I cannot refrain from copying out a little more: "Thus may a man walk up and down the world as in a garden of spices, and suck a Divine sweetness out of every flower. There is a twofold meaning in every creature, a literal and a mystical, and the one is but the ground of the other; and as the Jews say of their law, so a good man says of everything that his senses offer to him— it speaks to his lower part, but it points out something above to his mind and spirit. True religion never finds itself out of the infinite sphere of the Divinity; it beholds itself everywhere in the midst of that glorious unbounded Being who is indivisibly everywhere. A good man finds every place he treads upon holy ground; to him the world is God's temple; he is ready to say with Jacob, "How dreadful is this place! this is none other than the house of God, this is the gate of heaven."

But there was a good deal of intellectual play-acting in my approach to Trinitarianism: I was not, or at any rate not deeply, engaged. Very different was my reaction to the Atonement. That Christ atoned or atones, this spoke intimately to me: I responded to its beauty, and, not at all understanding what it meant, yet felt it to be true and important. So I began to study the literature, and was revolted. At the back of almost everything I read was some variant of the idea that humanity by its sinfulness had outraged God, or God's honour, or the law of righteousness: that this outrage must be made good: that nothing but condign punishment would suffice: and that Christ, by his suffering on the Cross, had given due satisfaction on behalf of humanity, or on behalf of such men and women as might identify themselves with Him by faith. Apart from the question of whether, on the theory of original sin, men were themselves responsible for their sinfulness, what wickedness and irrationality were here! This tyrant who exacted punishment—and for an outrage against himself or his honour—was he really the God of Christianity? And how conceivably could it be either just or loving that innocence should be punished "on behalf of" guilt? Little stomach though I had for a God who dealt in punishment at all, I much preferred Exodus:

"And Moses returned unto the Lord, and said, Oh, this people have sinned a great sin, and have made them gods of gold.

"Yet now, if thou wilt forgive their sin—; and, if not, blot me, I pray thee, out of thy book which thou hast written.

"And the Lord said unto Moses, Whosoever hath sinned against me, him will I blot out of my book."

Or Ezekiel:

"The son shall not bear the iniquity of the father, neither shall the father bear the iniquity of the son: the righteousness of the righteous shall be upon him, and the wickedness of the wicked shall be upon him."

If forgiveness was to be ruled out, let there at least be justice.

That innocence should be *willing* to bear the punishment of guilt—should offer itself as a substitute—no love could be greater than this: but what sort of God would accept such a substitute? Not a God, certainly, whom men ought to worship. A God worthy of respect, to say nothing of worship, would surely feel like this: "I have learned from the innocent what love really means: I too will show love, and forgive"? Mere men had felt as much, I reflected, and had acted accordingly.

Nor could I see that matters were in any way improved if one dwelt on the Divinity rather than on the Manhood of Christ.

And then there was the theory that Christ, by His death, paid a ransom to Satan, the *quid pro quo* being that men should be released from his power: but Christ, being God, was exempt from death: so Satan—and God knew it in advance—would be cheated of his bargain . . .

And yet—I felt again and again that the Atonement was a fact: that Christ, by His death on the Cross, did eternally atone for human wickedness; and that not only through the ethics He taught, but also by His life and crucifixion, He was a Way—or a very special Way? or the only Way?—to universal salvation. Intellectually arrogant, I did not go on to ask myself then what I should ask myself now (though I am still intellectually arrogant, they tell me): namely, whether Anselm and the rest, experiencing in their lives something infinitely precious, were not merely attempting to explain it in those penal or legalistic terms which even saints had not then—and have not now, for the matter of that—yet expelled from their thinking.

While reflecting on these matters—in the presence of a beauty and truth behind a veil I could not draw aside—I got to know Hastings Rashdall. This was a stocky little man, oddly dark, and rather like Socrates, but uglier: he was known as the Rasher, and taught theology at New College. I reverence his memory, as much for his opposition to befuddlements, an opposition of the sort people nowadays call woolly, as for his habit of unsparing consideration. He taught me what is indifferently known as the Origenistic, Abelardian, or Moral doctrine of the Atonement; and at once the veil had vanished, and I understood why, not knowing what the Atonement was, I had yet known it to be a fact. I always speak of the doctrine as Abelardian, rather than by another of its titles; for to do so is to pay a tribute of reverence to one of the great tragic figures of our history, one, I cannot help thinking, whom Christ would specially have loved. He had that passion for the critical intelligence which is deeply religious: he understood that intention is the secret of morals: and he was a great lover. At a time marked by cynicism on the one hand and neoism on the other, he, like Hastings Rashdall, is doubtless out of fashion: but this will pass, along with the contemporary mania for honouring, particularly in writers, contempt for humanity and the spirit that denies.

The Abelardian doctrine is most succinctly expressed, not in anything the master wrote himself, but in a sentence of Peter the Lombard, his disciple: "The death of Christ justifies us [or makes us just or good by making it easier for us not to sin], inasmuch as through it charity is excited in our hearts." But I think I had better give rather fully, though in an abbreviated form, Rashdall's own account of the matter in "The Idea of Atonement in Christian Theology". I shall not use quotation marks, because, with a few modifications that you can supply for yourself, he speaks for me as surely today as when he taught me at Oxford:

Christ's death, then, was an incident in a real human life. The particular mode of death was the outcome and culmination of the mode of life which He had chosen. The death came to Him as the direct and necessary consequence of His faithfulness to His Messianic calling, of a life devoted to the doing of God's will and the service of His fellow-men. His death has been more to Christendom than other martyr-deaths, just because He was so much more than other martyrs, because His life was more than other lives; because His Messianic calling was a unique calling; because, in fact, of all that has led Christendom to see in that life the fullest revelation or incarnation of God. There is nothing in the fact that the necessity for the death did not arise from any objective demand for expiation which can diminish the gratitude and the love which such a death, taken in connexion with such a life, was calculated to awaken towards the Sufferer. And if the character which is revealed by that Sufferer be the character of God himself, then the love that is awakened towards Christ will also be love of the Father whom in a supreme and unique way Christ reveals. And that love will express itself in repentance and regeneration of life. When the efficacy of Christ's death is attributed to the moral effects which it produces, that does nothing to diminish the love which the contemplation of such a death is calculated to awaken in the mind of him who believes that the whole life and death of Christ was one of love for His fellows, and that in Him who so lived and died the love of God was uniquely and supremely manifested. Such a view of the matter does tend, no doubt, to attribute the saving efficacy of Christ's work not *merely* to the death, but to the teaching, the character, the life of Him Who died. It tends, in short, to represent Christ's death as only a part, though a necessary part, of that whole incarnation or self-revelation of God, the object of which was to make known God's nature and His will, to instruct men in the way of salvation, and to excite in them that love which would inspire sorrow for past sin and give the power to avoid sin in the future.

If we can say that in humanity generally there is *some* revelation of God—a growing, developing, progressive revelation, and a higher degree of such revelation in the heroes, the saints, the prophets, the founders and reformers of great religions—then the idea of an incarnation becomes possible. If we can say that God is to some extent revealed in all men, then it becomes possible to think of him as making a supreme, culminating, unique revelation of himself in one human character and life.

It is only through human love at its highest that we can understand the divine love. Gratitude for ordinary human love —love pushed to the point of self-sacrifice—is the strongest power that exists in this world for attracting to that goodness of which love is the supreme element the soul that has it not, and for producing repentance for that lack of love in which sin essentially consists. In proportion as it is felt that human love reveals the love of God, the answering love which the self-sacrifice awakens will be love to God as well as love to man. The love shown by Christ will have this regenerating effect in a supreme degree in proportion as it is felt that the love of Christ supremely reveals the character of God.

Christ's whole life was a sacrifice which takes away sin in the only way in which sin can really be taken away, and that is by making the sinner actually better. The insistence of popular religious teaching upon the atoning efficacy of Christ's death loses all ethical value in proportion as it isolates and disconnects the atoning efficacy of that death from the saving influence of Christ's life, His teaching, His character.

And here it is necessary to insist upon the importance in this connexion of Christ's *teaching*—that is to say, of the moral ideal which it represents and the corresponding belief as to the character of the God whose nature is revealed by that moral ideal. For many of the earlier fathers, it is not too much to say, it was *primarily* by His teaching that Christ became the Saviour of the world. It was upon the appeal which this teaching made to the reason, the heart, the conscience of mankind that they based their conviction that in Him the Logos was supremely revealed: it was precisely in and through His teaching that His "Divinity" was manifested. The recognition of the supreme importance of Christ's teaching about God and human life, and a profound veneration for the character which that teaching exhibits, are an absolutely essential condition of our being able to discover any permanent meaning in the traditional doctrines of the atonement and the incarnation. It is upon the appeal which that ideal, embodied in the teaching and character of Christ, has made and still makes to the conscience of mankind that any intelligible modern interpretation of the Catholic doctrine of His divinity must depend.

Unless the teaching of Christ does present itself to us as containing the eternally true pith and marrow of the moral ideal, and a true representation of the essential character of God, we have no basis for any theory of Christ's divinity, or even for exalting Him to that central and supreme position among the prophets which would be assigned to Him by most Unitarians. Reverence for Christ as a teacher must be the foundation of any Christology which can find a meaning for the idea of a divine incarnation in Jesus. And it may, with equal truth, be said that it is only in the light of Christ's teaching that we can find any present meaning in a theology which makes much of His death: for it is only in the light of His teaching about the love of God and the supreme place of love in the ethical ideal for man that the cross can be given its true meaning as the symbol of self-sacrifice—not of mere negative self-renunciation or self-denial for self-denial's sake, but of self-sacrifice inspired and directed by love of that moral ideal which is fully realised in God, and by love of the men who are made in the image of God. It is because it is the typical expression of that spirit of self-sacrifice which dominated His life that the death of Christ has played, and will continue to play, a large part in its saving efficacy. When most of the theories about Christ's death have become obsolete and unintelligible the cross will still be the symbol, known and understood by all, of this central feature in Christ's character and in the ideal for which He lived and died.

More and more the great spiritual dividing line between men will be the line between those who really accept Christ's ideal of life and those who do not. Those who heartily believe in that ideal will probably in most cases find it possible to accept also Christ's outlook upon the universe as a universe guided and controlled by a conscious Will the nature and purposes of which may best be understood in the light of that same ideal. Those who believe that love is the thing of highest value in human life will generally believe also that "God is love indeed, and love Creation's highest law." But even if through intellectual perplexity they fail to do so, such persons may be placed among those of whom Christ said, "He that is not against us is for us", though they follow not with the great army of Christ's professed disciples. Many, doubtless, are being saved by this ideal who do not call themselves by Christ's name or formally associate themselves with those who do. . . .

That is all I want to quote from Rashdall. I would only add a passage from Hebrews that has meant a great deal in my life and can mean a great deal in yours: "For in that he himself hath suffered being tempted, he is able to succour them that are tempted."

A day arrived in 1914 when I reached the conclusion, or perhaps only pretended to reach it, that I was sufficiently a Christian to "become" one; and the Rasher made arrangements to baptise me during the autumn in a Cathedral—I think Durham or Carlisle—of which he was shortly to become Dean. But I was uneasy from the start, and think, as I said at the beginning of this chapter, that I should in any event have "cried off".

There was a great deal to make me uneasy. In the first place, I doubted my motives. Passionately convinced that the ethics of Christianity were the key to universal salvation (I had the grace not to be much interested in my own salvation—for it is a grace: one should be interested in one's own salvation only because one also is a person, and only to the extent to which one is interested in the salvation of others): already on the road that was to lead to adoration of Christ: not at any rate intellectually dissenting from the trinitarian doctrine: wholeheartedly accepting the atonement in its Abelardian interpretation—was I justified, I wondered, on the basis of this and no more, in burning my

spiritual boats and joining the Church? I could not help suspecting that behind my decision there must be something more than
this—especially as there was so much about the Church that
I profoundly disliked.

Trying to remember what this "so much" was, I find myself
in a now familiar difficulty: one applying to my early thought
about Christianity alone, and not at all, for instance, to my
thought at the same period about Judaism or politics. The difficulty is this, that I cannot disentangle my earlier from my later
thought. I remember with precision only one strange example
of my pernicketiness: I disliked, for some obscure reason, the
choirboys' surplices, especially, for a still obscurer reason, when
they were starched. I have sometimes thought since then that
suppressed homosexuality was at the bottom of this idiosyncrasy,
though I can find no reference to anything of the kind in Freud,
and cannot see the connection.

So I shall use the past tense in referring to my dislikes about
the Church, but shall ask you to remember that I may be
speaking anachronistically.

I disliked, then, its dualistic otherworldliness: I disliked its
carrots and sticks, its punishments and rewards in the hereafter:
I disliked a great deal of its record in public and international
affairs: I disliked its dogmatism: I disliked its corporate, institutional self-righteousness and arrogance: I disliked—how I disliked!—its notion of hell: I disliked, above all, its recurrent
crucifixion of Christ. Wanting fellowship with Christians, wanting publicly, by some definite avowal, to stand forward as the
Christian I half believed myself to be, I was continually troubled
by the clashing of this desire with my distrust of institutions as
such. Should I not be landing myself, I wondered, if not into the
fire, then at least into the identical frying-pan I'd got out of
by my revolt from institutional Judaism? Was not a horror of
institutionalism, with its outrage to freedom and spirit, the
very thing that had led me to Christ?

(And though I am a little more willing now than I was then
to be charitable about the sinfulness of institutions, which is the
sinfulness, like my own sinfulness, of the human beings who
make them up: and though I cannot know, while suspecting
and even observing in the lives of others, what membership of a
Church may mean by way of communion with and in Christ,
and what a compensation this may be: nevertheless my view of

institutions is substantially unchanged. Membership of an institution places too great a strain on average human nature; and while the creation and development of institutions are part of the divine plan, their chief value, in terms of the final result, is that they are there to be perpetually fought against.

I do not believe that the Church—any Church—will ever really be the Body of Christ. The Body of Christ is the fellowship, free and almost casual, of all who love Him, and try to follow Him, and would pity and forgive, in His spirit, their fellow human beings: whether Churchmen or not, whether dogmatically Christians or not: including those rationalists and atheists, as they imagine themselves to be, who, in Hastings Rashdall's words, "do not call themselves by Christ's name or formally associate themselves with those who do", but yet "accept His ideal of life.")

All this and much more being so, why, I again asked myself, had I made my decision? Was the really decisive factor—and now I am remembering very vividly indeed—not so much a positive desire to join the Church, as something very much more negative, maybe something unworthy? If I took this last step I should be leaving, once and for all, everything stuffy and outlandish in my Jewish background: I should be gone from the Jewish backwater, I should be swimming down the sunlit waters of the main European stream. So was this my fundamental motive? Well, why not? What was wrong about it? I *was* European and contemporary: I *did* feel a moral passion to be done with particularism. But why, to be European, must I join the Church? Many people left it with that very motive. Shouldn't I, by joining the Church, be protesting too much? Then whom did I want to protest to, myself or others? And was I quite certain that nothing social or "worldly" was mixed up with all this? No, I wasn't at all certain.

My uneasiness was increased by two other considerations. I loathed antisemitism then as I loathe it now: my attitude to Judaism could no more make me an antisemite than my attitude to caste could make me anti-Hindu. At the period of which I am speaking, Cecil Chesterton and I were both present one night at a meeting of the Fabian Society, which was private—he as the guest of the evening, I an outsider smuggled in by a friend. He made a slimy, smeary, nudging, winking sort of antisemitic speech; and after waiting in vain for some protest I attacked

him myself. I was afterwards told that I had surpassed all limits
in offensiveness, and that my behaviour had been particularly
shocking in view of what was due to him as a guest and of my
own dubious status there. I mention the episode, not because I
am proud of it (though I really am, rather), but to prevent you
drawing false conclusions, in the matter of antisemitism, from
anything I may have written in this chapter.

Well, I was the sort of Jew, and remain one, who in the presence of antisemitism regards formal apostasy as disgusting; and
though I came across very little antisemitism during my two
years at Oxford, I came across just enough of it to make me
pause.

Finally, there was my father. He had been horribly wounded
by my sister's conversion: could I wound him again still more
horribly—for I was his son, not his daughter—without being
sure, at the very least without being sure, that my motives
were unmixed and that what I had contemplated was inexorably
demanded by conscience?

The decision was taken out of my hands. Whatever I might
have decided if the impulse had remained, it left me in the turmoil of war. It has never returned: though my love of Repton
chapel, and my joy in its services, were of such an intensity that
had I stayed there much longer anything might have happened.

§ 2

And now I have come to what I have so long been waiting for,
the summer term of 1914; and I tremble as I trembled at the
beginning of this Oxford record, when offering you my Silver
Rose. For even if I have spilled all the rest of the Persian attar,
I would wish to keep forever unspilled that most precious drop
of it that lingers at the heart of my flower.

What gave those summer months their breathless quality of
incommunicable magic? Was it the weather? Was it a prevision,
of the kind now being investigated by Rhine and others, by
which we saw, without knowing that we saw it, what was so
soon coming, and found doubly precious a security of mind, an
absence of menacing shadows, that must presently be gone? Or
do I imagine in the boy of those days an emotion I can feel only
now because of everything that has happened meanwhile, as a

man in his prison cell might muse about the sun and the flowers that once he had taken for granted? I do not know the answer. And yet I cannot help thinking that some special visitation of beauty blessed the place during those last few months of the old world, and that I was not then, and am not now, a victim of the pathetic fallacy.

I was lodging at the time in that quarter of the College, to the left as you enter from Holywell, called Pandy: but no one ever seemed to know why, for Pandy was short for Pandemonium, and if anything we were exceptionally quiet. Even during an Eights Week rag, when a wonderful bonfire was made with a whole row of lavatory doors, and the Dean (here at last he comes) was discovered on a lawn spreadeagled with croquet hoops, or so I heard—he was known as the Forest of Dean, so black was the stubble on his face within an hour of his morning shave—even then peace breathed o'er Pandy. Our excitements, if more *outré*, were gentler. A distinguished inhabitant of the quarter was Father ——, so known, I imagine, for exemplary devotion to the practice of his creed: a heavyish undergraduate with an oblong face and enormous moustaches: and when racing was on, which appeared to be always, a remarkable procession of small boys could be seen on their way to his rooms, with those little black pouches for telegrams attached to their middles. Still more distinguished, even then, was J. B. S. Haldane; and his sister Naomi, afterwards the wife of Dick Mitchison, and, though still a young schoolgirl at the time, already a capable eugenist, was delightful to look at as she made for his staircase nearby, with her arms full of field-mice and guinea-pigs. Jack Haldane, who brooded a good deal, was our only obstreperous element, being always at feud, in a friendly sort of way, with the slimmer and more gentle Paul Hobhouse. I was reminded of this the other day when I came upon a letter written by Bernard Strauss from the front. "My beloved Golgotha," he says—I like to remember his affection for me—"I have just received your two letters: as I read the first, I imagined for a moment that I was back in Oxford, listening to you declaiming in faultless English with your back to my mantelpiece, with Douglas Jerrold sprawling in an armchair, Agnew with his patient smile, and Jack Haldane and Hobhouse struggling by the window." Declaiming in faultless English: how I must have talked and talked! But you can easily imagine it from the length of this letter.

"He *talks* too much" was how my mother was fond of describing me.

✱

"Leaving our rooms, we often checked our way
    As on a sudden wonderingly we saw
The summer grass sweet-smelling, where it lay
    Through the stone archway of our corridor:
Like men that, gazing from some hidden place,
    Might catch a glimpse of Beauty unaware,
And hear her very tones, and see her face,
    And so in adoration linger there.
They are terrible now, those corridors. The hue
    Of midmost summer blazes on the Hill;
The Garden laughs to heaven; at the west side
    The Tree puts on its glory of strange blue:
But the corridors are grey and very still
    Like monasteries where all the monks have died."

So I wrote for Bernard, putting it into rhyme, when I went back
to Oxford one morning just before he was killed, many of my
other friends being already dead. This grass, which was greener
that summer of 1914 than any in Oxford, and its grass is the
greenest in the world, lay sunk like a garden a little below the
level of our rooms: and just beyond it, across a narrow path, a
bank of less *soigné* grass sloped gently upwards to the grey of the
old city wall. Night after night we "slept out" on this bank. The
bloods drank champagne, which I, of course, couldn't afford;
but as pearl changed to rose I would find myself looking at the
sky with that freshness of peace which you very rarely feel except
when waking in the open air—and then off to play tennis and
back to a breakfast in J.C.R. hardly less extravagant than the
bloods' champagne: porridge, sometimes, with a lot of brown
sugar and cream, followed by a steak and fried onions and
glasses of lemon squash. All this must sound awfully gross; but it
wasn't really, not in that mood and with that setting. Breakfast
was preceded by a steaming bath, with the bloods in adjoining
ones singing at the top of their voices. Their favourite ditty was
"Tickle up the baby's bottom", and Bolton the bath man, who
was teaching me to use a cut-throat at the time, always muttered
with a rather timid irritation when he heard them tuning up.

I have loved sleeping out ever since. I have slept out all over the world, if you will allow me a measure of exaggeration. On the balcony at Ladbroke Grove, before the big bow window was made: on another balcony, at Beauvallon in the South of France; and on the deck of a ramshackle cargo boat—that brought me home across the Indian Ocean, when the first world war was over, to marry Ruth.

On the opposite side of the wall was New College garden. There is a passage in Ansky's *The Dybbuk* which runs as follows: "In all the world the holiest land is the Land of Israel. In the Land of Israel the holiest city is Jerusalem; in Jerusalem the holiest place was the Holy Temple, and the holiest spot in the Temple was the Holy of Holies." Let me adapt this a little: "In all the world the holiest university is the University of Oxford: in the University of Oxford the holiest college is New College: and the holiest spot in New College is New College garden." There are other ruralities at Oxford: the lake at Worcester, for instance ("the *swans* are *reserved* for the *dons*"— now I wonder why that has come into my head, for it isn't about Worcester at all, it's about St. John's, Cambridge), and Addison's Walk at Magdalen; but New College garden—how shall I explain what its gentleness meant to me? The other day, when I mentioned to John Strachey my simile of the Silver Rose, and expressed my fear that I should ruin everything by my clumsy descriptions, he said "Try to do it indirectly." Well, I will try: I will put it like this. I had always loved London, as you know, but had loved it because I loved the world, and London was the world to me: I hadn't loved it, I mean, in any way as specifically English. But coming through the Pandy gate into New College garden that summer, I fell in love with England as England; and though nothing of a patriot, for all men are men to me, I have loved her as England ever since.

Or was it in a punt on the Cher that I really fell in love with her—moored to a shady bank, or feeling the punt-pole ripple as I hurried after a read and siesta to the Cherwell Hotel for tea? Or was it when cycling to Wallingford for market-day lunch, or, on late afternoons, down Cumnor hill? Or was it, to finish as I began, during talks through the "sacred" night—talks so often repeated that daytime, for all its beauty, seemed nothing but the pleasantest of interludes in a symposium indefinitely prolonged?

o

England! A few nights ago I was walking at half past one in the morning through Westminster Hall. Dick Acland was with me. We were leaving the House of Commons, where we had been attending a late committee-meeting of the Association for World Peace; and as I looked up at the hammer-beam roof in the dim light, I made some trite remark about this being the greatest piece of architecture in the world. (The roof dates, you know, from early in the fourteenth century, but had been blitzed during the second world war and was reconstructed a few years ago.) Whereupon Dick told me the following story. The original beams had been cut from the oaks on some estate —I forget the name of its owner—where they happened to be exceptionally fine. The same estate was chosen when the new beams were wanted. After marking various trees, the surveyors, or whoever they were, came suddenly upon a colossal trunk, almost leafless but still alive. "That's the best of all," they said eagerly. "We must have that one." "Ah, no," said the present inheritor. "We refused you that one the first time."


The golden term ended, and I came down to London for the vac. Harold Rubinstein and I were in the gallery at Covent Garden for the last performance of the season. The Destinn was singing Aïda. We would not let her go: twenty-two times— I counted them—she returned to acknowledge our shouts. Then I took up my stand in Floral Street to see her leave, and she gave me a rose. War was declared five days later.

# INTERLUDE BETWEEN PARTS II AND III

Brimpton, October 14th, 1951

We have been in America, Ruth and I, since I finished Part II, on our annual trip to find American books for publication in England; and that's important nowadays, when the supply of English manuscripts isn't as big as it was. We got back a fortnight ago. The break from the old life, in which I could get on with this letter, was complete: I work in America sometimes twenty-two hours out of the twenty-four, getting up at five to write my notes home to London, dealing with New York correspondence from eight to ten, visiting publishers and agents till one, lunching with a publisher or agent, visiting publishers or agents till six, dining with friends, and reading—books, manuscripts, galleyproofs—till two or three o'clock in the morning. One enjoys it after a fashion: every morning, as one sets out, there's the hope of discovering treasure, and what a joy it is when, after tossing a dozen things aside with only the opening paragraph read, one's mind is suddenly held by a sentence, and one exclaims to oneself "Ah, here may be something"! But it isn't all enjoyment, by any means. Every year I have the same experience. It is not merely that the chase obsesses me in what you might call a normal sort of way: I am held again by another kind of obsession—by the old boyhood obsession of "extra work", by the feeling that if, when I've done what I ought to do, I don't go on and do what I needn't do, somehow I'm letting everything down. If I don't get good books, I think, and a lot of them, I shall go broke; and *now* is the opportunity for getting them—an opportunity that will never recur. So I have to go on, even though I'm dropping with fatigue and must wash my face to keep my eyes open. This is absurd, Victor, I tell myself: what does it matter if you *do* go broke?—you know perfectly well that going broke is irrelevant. (And so I do; I am certain that, if I really went broke, the minute after I shouldn't care a damn.) But my arguments cut no ice with me: I am driven by something that can't be modified by argument.

So, in those intense three weeks of absorption in momentary affairs—which is something very different from giving oneself to a moment of living, or, to put it in another way, from losing oneself in eternity—the impulse to go on with this letter, which had carried me forward, almost day by day, since the middle of January, left me utterly; and I have been afraid, ever since I got home, that it would never come back. But it has come back today; and what has brought it back has been my need to give thanks.

How can I be silent on this Sunday afternoon of our Indian summer? I have praised my garden at every season of the year, save only autumn; and as I love autumn best of all—that half-closed look about her eyes when hot sun has cleared away the mists—I should feel myself a disloyal ingrate if I failed to paint her picture for you. I am sitting again in the sunk garden, but now everything that's level with me is going to seed: only cosmea and coreopsis still straggle high, with, closer to earth, a few remnants of petunia and snapdragon. But on the parapets above— what a glory of dahlias! Little singles in front, of a colour like the colour of my rose-quartz crystal: great yellow ones behind, with their petals packed to bursting round a darker heart—and those claret-coloured pom-poms which, *simplices munditiis*, have the air of rebuking such vulgar exuberance. The sun is like June's: the greenness of the trees seems dark and deep with essential greenness: and a hush is over everything. But no—some birds are singing: I had not noticed them, for indeed they make the day more breathless.

There are other things I want to praise. I want to praise England, as I praised it just before going away. The office had hired a car to bring us up to London on our arrival from the States, and the sun was shining mildly as we drove out of Southampton towards Winchester. How small, gentle, strong and old our regained England looked! There were little gardens everywhere, and little pubs; and, perhaps best of all, there were people—in the country round New York you never seem to see anyone walking. I looked at the meadows and hillocks with half-closed eyes, and dozed, and looked again: they were still there, they would still be there for ever.

But there is great beauty in New York too, and, sitting here in the train on my way to Paddington, I find that already, after no more than three weeks, I want to see it again very soon. We had a little apartment on the nineteenth floor of the Beverly Hotel, which is where 50th Street meets Lexington: and every morning, if I was not up too early and if it was fine—as it usually was, for often I might have been back in the bamboo

lanes near Singapore, so blessedly tropical was the weather—
I would stand at our bedroom window, which looked east, or
rather a little north-east, straight down Lexington, and would
watch the sun come up on my right. The Lexington lights
would still be on, stretching almost endlessly to the horizon:
and one suddenly saw oneself, back in the middle thirties,
motoring, one might have imagined for ever, down a Roman
road in France—but thought, with a pang, not how like the
two roads were, but how different in their likeness. And yet—in
what, I ask myself, does the painful difference consist? Not,
certainly, in the leafiness of the one and the stoniness of the
other: for if you go to Rome, and, standing for a moment on
the Spanish steps, look down the Via Condotti; or, again, if
you go to Paris, and, emerging from the Place de la Concorde,
look by night down the long lighted vista of the Rue de Rivoli;
you are aware of no alloy in the gold. Is it simply, perhaps,
that some quality of peace, some sense of mellow wisdom won
by a long patient sharing in the miseries and nobilities of the
human race, seems to bless all old things, and even the newest
things in old cities: and that New York—physical New York—
has not yet had the time to grow spiritual? Every morning, as
I looked at the lights down Lexington, I said to myself "How
beautiful!" And then I said "Yes, but what is wrong? Why
isn't the unity complete? Why, somehow, isn't my standing
here an act of worship?" And yet, if I hadn't returned next
morning to look again, I should have felt myself guilty of some
faithlessness: so perhaps I was worshipping after all.

But beautiful, anyhow, the vista was; and what was to
follow was more beautiful still—especially when the autumn
mists were so heavy that my lights down Lexington should
have been obscured. (Why weren't they? Was it something to
do with the height of the buildings and the level of the mist?
Or _were_ they obscured, sometimes, and am I confusing two
kinds of morning?) Gradually, as the sun rose, a broad and
massive battlement, softened and mysterious, would appear in
the sky to the right of Lexington; for the impression there was
not of individual buildings—though an airy garage would
always catch my eye—but of a rolling, curving mountain
mass. Meanwhile, on the other side of Lexington, two or three
dim pinnacles would be rising, with a beautifully strong grace,
out of the sea of mist that bathed their lower parts; and then

something ancient would revive in me, and for a moment I would be back—I had the same vivid fantasy morning after morning—amid the bastions and palaces, the hanging gardens and ziggurats, of a romanticised Babylon.

When the sun was up I would go into the sitting-room, and look for a moment, from the northern window, at Rockefeller Centre; and here I was back in another experience—a real experience this time, though perhaps, during the Captivity, Babylon had been real to me too—for I might once more have been watching, with everything on an immensely greater scale and again, ah, with all that spiritual difference, as I had been used, so long before, to watch through Tuscan daybreaks by the Giotto Tower. And, apart from the Tower then and the Centre now, there was a reminder—how shall I put it?—as if specially for me. You will remember that when I had at last left the Tower and returned to the hotel, I would find those low houses that faced me on the Arno all flushed terra-cotta with the unseen sun. Well, just across the chasm of Lexington, and far on our side of the Centre, a hideous red-brown building, a sort of American Prudential, faced our windows; and as I brought my eyes back to it from the beauty beyond, the whole vast surface, stretching down those nineteen floors and up to the heavens, would be glowing—obliquely glowing—with the old radiant earthiness.

These were our American daybreaks. And the sunsets! Whenever we could, we would hurry back home before daylight had gone: and would sit for some moments facing northward, as the green lights came out in the slim skyey columns against a background of fading rose. This was fairyland; and often, at moments such as these, the heartache as for something absent was stilled. A young American, sitting with us one evening, said "It's corny, of course, but it's beautiful." Beautiful, certainly: corny, not in itself, but only, by a sort of transference, when people who have seen it so often come to praise it by rote.

(This living in the whole of my life as I write this letter, Timothy, has the effect, sometimes, of appearing to abolish time. I have just paused a minute to light my pipe, after finishing the last of my American cigars: and for the first time, I swear, since about nineteen eight, I was smelling, not the tobacco I smoke today nor my seasoned old pipe, but a mixture of two other far more poignant smells: ancient, atavistic, eternal smells: the smell of my first ounce of tobacco, and the smell of the first raw briar my mother gave me—she was determined, in her romanticism, that I should grow up masculine. I was very sick after that early try-out: I was queasy, with the identical queasiness, a minute or so ago.)

Babylon! Always, in New York, the word comes into my mind; but not always with the significance that I gave it just now. There are times, as I walk down those great streets, when I am suddenly terrified cosmically: for I feel myself caught up into the presence, not of anything human or personal, but of that Moloch so destructive for all its unreality, impersonal power. Do not misunderstand me for a moment, my dear Timothy. I am far from thinking that New Yorkers, in the mass, are either less human or less humane than the inhabitants of any other great city: indeed, if you are going to draw distinctions at all, which is a silly thing to do, and if you are considering, not potentialities, but a realised development, then they are clearly much gentler than many. I am far from thinking, either, that any serious body of opinion in America would apply its resources, consciously and maliciously, to the hurt of others: Americans, on the contrary, are remarkable, by and large, for their love of peace, are generous as few others are generous, and are passionate, within their historically conditioned understanding of the word freedom, about freedom for everyone. But—New York is too rich, too mighty, too splendid: the wealth, the might, the splendour seem to have acquired, not so much a life, as a force, of their own: and you have the impression of a dazzling great machine that must forever go grinding relentlessly on. There is nothing, nothing at all, you think—no "standard of living", no material prosperity —that is impossible of achievement in this Babylonian climate; and, at the present stage of human development, when we are all still, spiritually, infants, there is something frighteningly impious about such measureless capacity. It was for an impiety such as this, they say, that Atlantis was submerged; but Atlantis was only an island, whereas America is a heart-land that gives life to half the world. And what is happening in America is merely, writ much larger, what is happening almost everywhere else. The "writ larger", however, is important. Sometimes when I look up in my New York walks at a great towering block, so beautiful after its fashion as it glistens in the sun, I seem to hear, not very far away, the low baying of the Eumenides.

And then, talking to American after American, and finding almost complete unanimity between us, I tell myself that I am a man of little faith: that the whole long history of scientific and technical advance has for origin, far in the background, an urge to co-operate with God—an urge to know, to reach out, to actualise potentialities: and that the machine, being thus, ultimately, itself a product of spirit, will someday merge again with the spirit from which it came.

§ 2

I am going to write a few paragraphs about how we lived in America, Ruth and I—not so much about the things we did, which were humdrum enough, in themselves, by almost anybody's reckoning, but rather about how, doing those things, we "got on" with one another. I think of these paragraphs (before writing them) as a kind of prelude to the essay on marriage which I have it in mind to compose when I come to 1919: or not really a prelude, but the desultory tuning up of a few important instruments. I shall say one or two things in that essay which may conceivably shock you even when the world has moved on another dozen years or so—though I doubt it: things, for instance, about so-called "sexual fidelity": so perhaps it's a good idea that, in the meantime, you should read something quite unexceptionable. Not that this is my motive in writing what I'm just going to write: I am writing it, as I wrote about my dahlias and the New York sunsets, out of a desire to praise.

And of course, when it comes to it, I can't say anything adequate. If you were here with me by my open window, on this gently shining morning of October the twenty-first, I should point to everything outside, and say "*that* is what it was like"—very bright, very peaceful, very deep. Or if I were a composer, I could imitate it in music. But you're not here, and I'm not a composer; so I shall give what can only be a hint or two in words.

We have been married for more than thirty-two years:

we are both nearly sixty: my behaviour, with her knowledge and consent, has not invariably been such as to commend it to strict monogamists: I am, in many ways, an impossible man to live with: and she has one or two characteristics which, when I am at my most intolerant, I find intensely and recurrently irritating. But—though "but" is not at all the right word—we know consciously on our honeymoons, what we have known less consciously every minute of our lives since a month before our wedding, that our marriage has been essentially—it is a very large claim, and you must note the word "essentially"—perfect: and that a marriage which is perfect, even if only essentially, would be sufficient justification, in the absence of all other justifications, for the sum of things. "Blessed art thou, O Lord, who makest the bridegroom to rejoice with the bride."

I mean by a honeymoon a time of some length when we are always together. From the middle twenties till about 1937 we were constantly having honeymoons: I have told you something already of our holidays in Italy and France, I have still much to tell you about Salzburg, and often, in addition, we would get off for a long week-end at Easter or Whitsun—to Paris or Venice or Rome. The world, at such times, was no longer with us: we were with one another in the world. There have been many other times, of course, every week since we married, when our lives have had the same sort of feel: Friday evenings at Brimpton, motoring to the Cotswolds, and those lunches or dinners, by ourselves, at a London restaurant, when affairs have dropped momentarily away from us and, both a little tight, we have been wholly together. But these are not real honeymoons; they are too short, too quickly over; intimations of a honeymoon, you might say, rather than the thing itself.

After the late thirties our honeymoons had been getting rarer and rarer. First there was the pressure of my anti-Nazi campaign; then the war: next, my "Save Europe Now" work: and, when that was over, an anxious concentration on the reviving of V. G. Ltd. We were ready for a renewal; and when, in the Spring of 1948, we went to America for the first time, it was something more compulsive than book-hunting that took us there.

Of all our New York honeymoons, this last one—perhaps

because every year now one learns a little better how to live—
has been the best. I told you, at the beginning of this interlude,
about my twenty-two hour days—and Ruth's were only a few
hours shorter: but the fever and strain were enclosed, as perhaps never before, in the peace of our togetherness.

When I attempt to particularise, I find myself thinking, very
oddly, first about food. Or perhaps it isn't odd. Love-feasts are
to be found, after all, in the ritual of more than one religion:
and everyone understands that the breaking of bread is a sacrament, if at least two are present. Why this is so I cannot tell.
Perhaps we feel very obscurely that at a common meal the
unity of men with one another, and of humanity with earth, is
realised.

Our love-feasts were the meals Ruth prepared in our diminutive kitchen, and that we eat at a little glass-topped table, sitting
side by side on a sofa: breakfast in particular, quiet and slow,
with its sense of a recurrent expectancy and a recurrent fulfilment. Even the happiest meals with others were not love-feasts.
We had to be alone.

We breakfasted, usually, about seven; but an hour before
that, which was also an hour after I'd got up, Ruth would have
brought me my early morning tea. If our ancestors had
invented a special benediction for early morning tea—early
morning tea shared by husband and wife—I should have said
it every day in New York: anyhow I thought it. A lot of people,
I suppose, will wonder if I'm cracked, with the fuss that I'm
making about something so ordinary; but

"They have not known; they are not in the stream."

They'll think, too, that *I* ought to have got it for *her*.
Why? Why I for her rather than she for me? And you will
have realised long ago that I have never learned not to be
helpless.

After breakfast we bathed and dressed; and then, while I
did my paper-work, Ruth did the phoning. By a quarter to
eleven we were ready for our visits to publishers. We walked
down the corridor and waited a few moments for the lift. These
moments of waiting together before the day's adventure were,
I think, the best moments of all. We were not of course naked;
but otherwise, perhaps, we were a little like William and
Catherine in the garden at Felpham.

## § 3

As you will see from the heading, this bit about America was to have been an interlude between Parts II and III. But it has suddenly become, for the time being, a sort of epilogue; for a week or so ago (it is now mid-November) I decided to go back on my previous intention and to publish Parts I and II by themselves. The Labour Party had been defeated at the polls—this was my reason: for I wanted what I had written about socialism to be read pretty soon—during the next few months rather than the next few years—by socialists and antisocialists alike.

This letter has grown in a curious and undisciplined way. When it started in the library last January, it was to be a modest little affair of well under a hundred thousand words: or say, in lay language, of two or three hundred small pages. Then it looked like developing into a large fat volume, of the kind that our booksellers love: one at first of some three times the originally contemplated length, and then, by April, of anything up to seven or eight hundred large pages. But I was determined either not to publish it at all, leaving it, instead, for you to read, when the time came, in manuscript, or to publish it as a whole in one volume; for the value it would have, should it have any value, would reside, not in isolated sections or parts, but in the complete *ensemble*. I wanted everything to be read in the light of everything else; and that is rarely possible when a work in several parts comes into the shops at yearly or perhaps two yearly intervals. I doubt whether even an autobiographical masterpiece, such as *A La Recherche du Temps Perdu*, can make more than a fraction of its proper impact unless read pretty continuously: but works like that survive, and generations can read them as a whole: whereas I can have very little hope that this letter will prove anything but ephemeral. Indeed, a feeling that this is so—that the whole thing is not very important anyhow—makes me a little less regretful than I should otherwise have been at isolating these Parts from the rest.

I must place them, nevertheless, in their setting: I must guide you through the maze. I must relate what has been written in these Parts to what will presently be written in the Parts to come.

Sitting at my fireside last January and looking round the room, I was quickly led back to the second of my *anni mirabiles*: to my joy nearly ten years ago, in 1942. Thence I jumped backwards again, to the earlier of my *anni mirabiles*: to my joy when I was teaching at Repton during the first world war. I described, you will remember, how I made two discoveries there: that the boys were good, and that their goodness was blocked in the civic and international spheres by their prejudice and ignorance. To explain the effect this discovery had on me—what I did about it at Repton, and how it determined my whole future life—I had to explain what sort of person I was: so I went back to 1899, and then worked forward to Oxford. Thus:

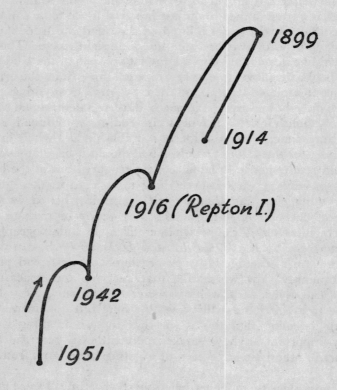

1899

1914

1916 (Repton I.)

1942

1951

And here is the rest of the diagram:

1914

(Repton II)
1916

1919 (Marriage)

(Establishment
of V.G. Ltd.)
1928

1933 (Hitler)

1936 (Left Book Club)

1938 (Munich)
1939 (Nazi-Soviet Pact)

1943 (Hell, II)

1945 (Save Europe Now)

1951

I shall begin Part III with some account of my reactions to war in the autumn of 1914, saying as little as possible about my inglorious pseudo-military career. Then will come the second Repton chapter, which, with 1933, 1938, and 1943, is central to the whole design. I shall describe in some detail the experiment in political education which David Somervell and I carried out there, and how in that dawn the place blossomed like a rose, and David and I blossomed with it: and how it became inevitable from this time that, as I could no longer teach, I should become a publisher. Then, when I get to 1919, I shall take the opportunity of writing a full-length disquisition about marriage and parenthood: I am greatly looking forward to this. My fumbling approach to publishing will follow, with a few remarks, perhaps, about my early Zionism: and these may possibly develop into a chapter, which, if it happens, I shall try to keep down to a minimum, on "the Jewish question" and antisemitism. From 1928, when my business was established, to 1933, there will be three main themes: publishing, music, and a world that was too much with me; and here, apart from the element of autobiography, there will be a chapter on publishing and bookselling as such, which I shall expand to the maximum. I shall try to explain in it why I consider the whole foundation of the book business in this country to be thoroughly rotten: why, in my view, the position has long been deteriorating and must continue to deteriorate unless drastic measures are taken to set it right: and what these measures should be. There will be a tribute to Penguin Books in this chapter, and also much libellous matter.

Hitler's accession to power is the next landmark; and I shall tell of the change it produced in my life—my inner life rather than my outer life—and of the far deeper change that took place in me at the moment, just before Munich, when war seemed inevitable. There will be a lot, in this portion, about the Left Book Club, and why I founded it; and, more generally, about the political element in my publishing that had steadily been increasing since 1928. I plan to include here, also, what I hope will be a delightful interlude at Salzburg.

Somewhere about this time there will be an essay on marxist communism. I shall treat of it, not as Antichrist (this seems fashionable nowadays, particularly among ex-communists) but as a Christian heresy: as moved in its origins by a Christian

impulse to seek the goal, which is a Christian goal, of in-
dividuality-in-community, but seeking it through a monolithic
institutionalism that must render its object forever unattainable: as an instrument of the divine purpose, in spite of everything, like the systems and ways of thought it opposes: as
distorted by error and issuing (the Inquisition!) in atrociously
unchristian behaviour, but not to be totally disavowed without a blasphemous Manicheism: and as something we must
combat, not in the spirit, itself largely Stalinist, of a hate-
mongering anticommunism, but with a righteousness that
surpasses the righteousness of the communist pharisees—we
must not only loathe what is loathsome in it, but must also
loathe loathing it. I shall have something to say, in this connection, about ends and means, or may merely quote Aldous
Huxley, who has done the job admirably. The section will finish
with a midnight in Paris, when I read the last paragraphs of
a report, more than a thousand pages long, of a Soviet trial, and
saw the world, for some terrible hours, as an executioner's
puppet-show; and with the morning, not much later, when
news of the Nazi-Soviet pact came up with the morning tea—
and there, across the newspaper, were swastikas flying in the
Moscow airport and everyone smiling.

I shall speak, in the earlier part of the war, about the
National Committee for Rescue from Nazi Terror, which did
its infinitesimally little to save Jews from the incinerators; and
shall link it up with the "Save Europe Now" of 1946 and after,
which did its infinitesimally little to save Germans from
starvation. Meanwhile, with a glance again at 1942, I shall
describe how, in a way familiar to psychologists, neurologists,
and writers about religion, my joy of that year toppled over
into the hell of 1943: how, after many months, the voice at the
inland cliff, which was also my own voice, spoke to me and
said "A humble and a contrite heart he will not despise": how,
at that moment, the long and painful process of recovery
began: and why I am more grateful for that year than for anything else in my life. Then there will be a final word, or more
probably a long chapter, about Christianity, and the world's
desperate need of it: about how (and it is this to which everything will be seen to have tended) we must fulfil our own
natures, and help God, by healing the breach between religion
and politics, between the sacred and profane—thus realising

the intention of Judaism: and about how, when it comes to it, we cannot help doing so. At the end of everything will be a sermon for you in the manner of Father Zossima, telling you how you may live far more decently than I have.

And now I must say good-bye to you, Timothy, so far as this letter, or this instalment of it, is concerned; and it really is a letter as well as a convenient device for enabling me to say all the things I've long wanted to say, in the sense that it is very specially addressed to you. I hope the good-bye is only temporary, but things may turn out otherwise; for I may die, or fall ill, or wish to write no more.

There has been a lot about Judaism, Jewishness and the Jews in this letter; and because, in spite of a good deal I have written, I am something, I suppose, of what is called a "Jew at heart", I shall give myself the pleasure of ending with a Benediction which, with curious misinformation, many Gentiles imagine to be of Christian origin: so I raise my hands above your head, and say, May the Lord bless you and keep you; may the Lord make his face to shine upon you, and be merciful unto you; may the Lord lift up the light of his countenance upon you, and give you peace. Amen.

Bad I am, but yet thy child.
Father, be thou reconciled,
Spare thou me, since I see
With thy might that thou art mild.

I have life before me still
And thy purpose to fulfil;
Yea a debt to pay thee yet:
Help me, sir, and so I will.

GERARD MANLEY HOPKINS

# THANKS

THERE ARE SEVERAL people I wish to thank for helping me with this book.

First, my wife.

Sheila Hodges has had many parts of it rehearsed to her as I wrote them, and has read the proofs three times. Her spiritual and literary taste is as sure as her patience and sympathy are unfailing; and I should be making a fuss about my debt to her, were I not aware that she dislikes counting-house talk as much as I do.

Elizabeth Booth, who was my secretary at the time, helped me throughout by the freshness of her goodwill—and also by the charm of her presence: if there were several of her set at different angles up a stalk, she would look like a lily of the valley.

I would thank my nephew Hilary Rubinstein for a specially gracious courtesy.

Others who have been extremely kind, and have made valuable suggestions, are Stephen Appleby-Smythe, John Collins, Charles Raven, Harold Rubinstein, and John Strachey. Harold Wilson and Professor Ian Bowen of Hull were good enough to read the section on the conquest of world hunger.

I am very grateful, also, for the encouragement given to me by my American publishers: Dick Simon, so direct and loyal, and Max Schuster, in whom warm-heartedness and wit are so delightfully mingled.


# A NOTE ON MEMORY

A GOOD DEAL OF this book is a record of things remembered. To that extent, memory rather than accuracy is the main point of it. On the whole, therefore, I have not thought fit to check up on my memory, which may occasionally, though I think rarely, have been at fault. I will give two trivial examples. The name of the bearded giant at the South Kensington Museum may not have been exactly Sherborne Smith, though that was the general contour and sound of it. And it is just possible that the Sunday afternoon concerts at the Albert

Hall were not held in summer, and that I have telescoped two experiences (the concerts and the park) not actually coincident in season. Such errors could have no significance: and if I had accidentally found any I should have been reluctant to correct them, for to have done so would have been, in all but the most obvious sense, to falsify.

But I have made a big exception. Where a mistake might mislead in a matter of real importance I have checked with care. For instance, the chapters descriptive of orthodox Judaism have been thoroughly "vetted".

Gilbert Murray, by the way, who took me for Greek verse at Oxford, and one of the few really great men I've known, tells me, as I pass these pages for press, that σύννομα μᾶλα (see p. 267) *can* mean "clustering apples", but almost certainly *does* mean "sheep feeding together". He advises me to leave the passage as written. I have done so, as μᾶλα will always be apples for me.

In spite of what I thought to be most careful proof reading by myself and others, I have discovered two aberrations since the body of the book was printed. In the last line but one of page 16 "the first subject" should read "the second subject"; and in line 14 of page 18 "Governor" should, of course, read "Minister". There are, no doubt, other similar aberrations. I would ask to be forgiven for them.

## SOURCES AND ACKNOWLEDGEMENTS

THE TRAHERNE (page 26) is from *Centuries of Meditation*, published by P. J. and A. E. Dobell; and the Dionysius (page 31) from *The Divine Names*, translated by C. E. Rolt and published by the S.P.C.K. *The Life of Blessed Henry Suso by Himself* (page 52) is published by Methuen in a translation by T. F. Knox. George Meredith's *Love in the Valley* (page 103) and *The Ordeal of Richard Feverel* (page 266) are published by Constable. The Martin Buber extract (page 119) is from his *Hasidism*, published by the Philosophical Library, New York. The Walter Scott editions of Ibsen (pages 139 and 140) are now published by Heinemann. The extract on page 155 is from Wordsworth's *The Prelude*. The passage by Bertrand Russell (page 248) is from *A Free Man's Worship* in *Mysticism and Logic*, published by Allen & Unwin. G. Lowes Dickinson's *A Modern Symposium* (pages 248 and 300) is published by Allen & Unwin. The Coventry Patmore extract (page 282) is from *The Rod, the Root and the Flower*, published by The Greywalls Press. The St. Francis de Sales (page 328) is from *Introduction to the Devout Life*, published by Methuen in a translation by the Rev. Thomas Barns. The poem by Walter de la Mare (page 332) is from his *Collected Poems*, published by Faber and Faber. I have to thank Dr. Margaret Mead warmly for permission to quote so extensively from her *Sex and Temperament in Three Primitive Societies* (pp. 348 sqq.); the book is published by Routledge. Ouspensky's *A New Model of the Universe* (page 391) is published by Kegan Paul. The poem on page 399 is by Alice Meynell and is reproduced by kind permission of Sir Francis Meynell. The Aurobindo extract (page 401) is from *The Synthesis of Yoga*, published by The Sri Aurobindo Library, Inc., New York. Hastings Rashdall's *The Idea of Atonement in Christian Theology* (page 408) is published by Macmillan, and I am grateful to the executors as well as to Messrs. Macmillan for permission to reproduce so lengthy a passage.

# PUBLISHER'S ANNOUNCEMENT

WE HOPE TO HAVE ready for publication in the autumn of 1953 the second instalment of this letter. It will be called "AND ALSO MUCH CATTLE"

*Printed in Great Britain by*
*The Camelot Press Ltd., London and Southampton*